# CHASING SHOOTING STARS

## A SOUTH AMERICAN
## PAPER TRAIL INTO THE PAST

*For Tom and Kara,
friends forever!*

*[signature] x.*

ANGELA JEFFS

**FRONT COVER:** main image, my grandfather's attache/suit case, then photos from left to right, my father aged 14 in Liverpool in 1924; Sam in Buenos Aires in the 1940s; Sam and his sisters and brother-in-law in Hoylake, 1940s; my father, mother, Bridget and me on holiday in Brixham, 1950.

**BACK COVER:** mi familia in Santiago, Chile, 1999

FOR LEE AND BUFFY
AND ALL WHO FOLLOW ON (ESPECIALLY MAX)

# CONTENTS

*My sister Bea is sending Angela my silver cup, or tank, which was a*
*birthday or christening present to me from someone, and I hope*
*she will take care of it, as an ornament, and remembrance of*
*Grandaddysammy when he is chasing shooting stars.*

**SAMUEL CHARLES EDWARD LOADER**
Cumberland Hotel, Marble Arch, London
*21 September, 1951*

# FROM THE PAST TO LATE 1999
## Canada → Argentina

*Above:* Samuel Charles Edward Loader and his father Samuel Turner Loader, Consul for Uruguay and Vice-Consul for Argentina, Buenos Aires, 1898

*Above right:* Samuel Turner's brother William in his garden in Liverpool, with wife Sarah (Sara)

*Right:* Last chance to relax – Lake Muskoka, Ontario, Canada

*Left:* Dr Julio Bustamante at home in Caseros, Buenos Aires

*Below:* His wife Maria-Elena Bustamante Loader, a new-found cousin born in Chile

*Left:* Family maid Marta, whose Paraguayan smile also helped me keep going

# Argentina

**Left:** *My grandfather en route to South America (date unknown)*

**Below:** *His home from home for many years*

**Below:** *Handwritten postcard dated 1929, with an X marking the location of the company office*

*Buenos Aires, a city of magnificent colonial architecture (above, Teatro Colon) and uniquely developed local talent (right, tango street musicians in El Centro)*

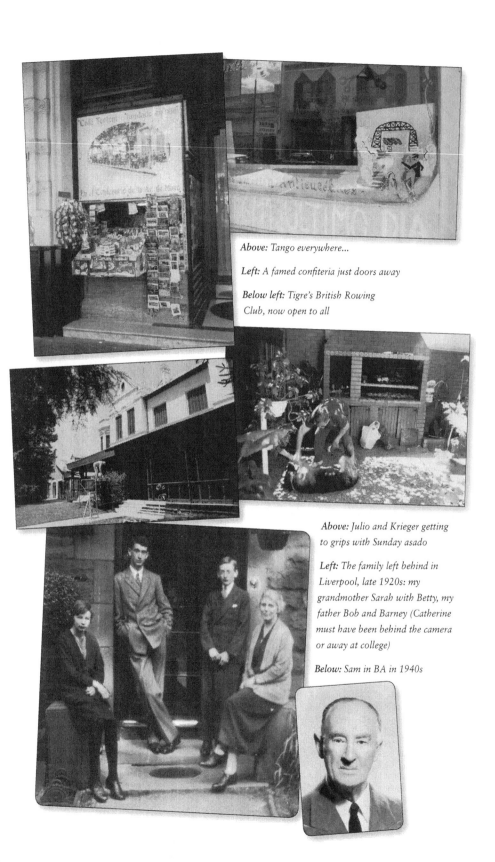

*Above:* Tango everywhere...

*Left:* A famed confiteria just doors away

*Below left:* Tigre's British Rowing
Club, now open to all

*Above:* Julio and Krieger getting
to grips with Sunday asado

*Left:* The family left behind in
Liverpool, late 1920s: my
grandmother Sarah with Betty, my
father Bob and Barney (Catherine
must have been behind the camera
or away at college)

*Below:* Sam in BA in 1940s

*Left: Being christened at Sunfield, 1941: left to right. Nurse Skinner, Albert Price, my mother (holding Angela Deirdre), father and Aunt Jo*

*Below: Sam's cousin Charles and his wife Mercedes in Santiago, 1940s*

# Argentina → Chile

*Left: Santiago de Chile's foundation stone: Santa Lucia Hill*

*Below: A niche never visited... did I wake him up?*

IN LOVING MEMORY
OF
CHARLES JOSEPH LOAD
WHO DIED ON 30th JANUARY 1954
AGED 74 YEARS
AT REST

*Left: First gathering of the clan: Back row, left to right: Daniel, Pepe (Joseph), Guillermo (William); front row (ditto): Olga, Silvia, Angela, Maria-Elena, Luis with daughters Javiera (sleeping) and Camila*

*Right:* Second gathering, with four of Charles' children attending: Guillermo (standing), Josefina Leticia (centre back), Alejando (Alexander) and Eric Walter (both sitting lower right)

*Below:* Claudio in the garden of the house poet Pablo Neruda built, La Chascona

*Above:* Josie's wedding in Coventry, 1951: Back row, L-R: my aunt Kathleen, uncle Eric, father, mother and Uncle Arcos (Albert Price). Front row: Alison, Angela, Bridget

*Right:* Third gathering (remains of the evening): Ricardo (lower left, sitting) with his mother's arm on his shoulder and daughter Carole behind, Silvia Rosa with brothers Guillermo (his arm around her) and Pepe (with cousin Betty inbetween) and sister Josefina. Jose is centre back, with the beard!

# Chile → Argentina → Uruguay → Argentina → Japan

**Above:** Crossing the Andes: connecting countries, connecting families

**Left:** Sam in Piriapolis, 1952. Handwritten on the back: "In the shade but still going strong."

**Above:** The hotel in Piriapolis where Sam stayed so often, and where he died

**Above right:** Montevideo: postcard dated 10/1/51. Message to my father typed on the back, including, "I wish Josie all the best of luck"; signed Grandaddysammy/SCE Loader/Father

**Right:** His unmarked grave in Montevideo. (But far far far from the end of the story...)

# AUTHOR'S NOTE

Early in the twenty-first century, the South American nation of Argentina began an unprecedented psychological and economic meltdown. Around the same time, I entered into a not-unconnected unravelling of my own.

In late 1999 I made a journey to not only Argentina, but also Chile and Uruguay. I was the fourth generation to go to South America and, as far as I know, the first woman to travel alone. My great-great grandfather, great-grandfather, grandfather and father – bearing the surname Loader – all tried their luck there – with varying degrees of success.

I went because for years it had been a dream, and then one day it seemed like a good idea. I was spurred not only by the romanticism of wanderlust spiked with plain old curiosity, but – a more recent desire – the need to make reparation, mend old wounds. I saw the trip as a chance to somehow draw the living and the deceased of my family together again.

When I returned to Japan, where I am currently living, I thought I had failed in just about every respect – a belief that once again drove me half crazed with despair. Recognising a pattern of old, I sought help, to alter my personal programming and so remember who I really am.

Listening today to tapes made on that month-long trip at the end of the last millennium, I marvel at the woman I was at that time: good-humoured, determined and even admirable in one sentence; sniping at family members and wallowing in self-pity in the next.

My intention in telling on myself in this way – which some who know me have found raw to an extreme – is to help me better understand myself, and by association help my children better understand why their mother behaved and reacted in the ways she did during their childhood. My hope is that this enables them to forgive my transgressions and the undoubted effect these have had on their own lives.

However, what I perceived then concerning what I thought were abortive travels is not what I perceive now, near a decade on. My reality at that time is not my reality today.

Now I see more clearly how trauma can be passed down through generations; in my family what happened nearly two centuries ago continues to reverberate. Having found a resting place of my own, my hope is that others – future generations especially – can find their own sense of understanding, acceptance and peace.

Oh yes, and in answer as to why a woman called Jeffs is writing about a family called Loader... I kept my married name as a connection with my children, and also because by the time of my divorce in the 1970s, this was how I was known, both personally and professionally. In this timeline, historically and legally, I suppose I am Angela Deirdre Loader-Jeffs-Ueda. But let's keep things simple:

ANGELA JEFFS
Zushi, 2010

# PART 1

# EARLY DAYS

*The gladdest moments of a human's life, methinks,*
*is the departure upon a distant journey to unknown lands.*

**SIR RICHARD BURTON**

(journal entry dated December 2, 1856)

*The woods are lovely, dark and deep,*
*But I have promises to keep,*
*And miles to go before I sleep,*
*And miles to go before I sleep.*

**ROBERT FROST**

(Stopping by Woods on a Snowy Evening ,1922)

**SUNDAY APRIL 4**

*My father sent a telegram to the war office. He wants to take part*
*in the war with Argentina… At teatime I was looking at our world map,*
*I couldn't find the Falkland Islands. My mother found them.*
*They were under a crumb of fruitcake.*

**SUE TOWNSEND**

(The Growing Pains of Adrian Mole, 1984)

# FALSE STARTS

COVENTRY, NOVEMBER 14, 1940

*As the first sirens commence their whining ascent into a full-scale crescendo of warning, a young married couple of less than six months runs out of the house where they are lodging in Radford, an area to the north of Coventry in the English Midlands. As the first wave of bombers drones overhead and buildings begin to explode and ignite all around, turning the sky from red to a crimson-black inferno of flame and smoke, they kneel in the middle of the street, their arms around one another...*

*Such perfect timing – the night above well starred, clear and frosty: ideal conditions for Nazi high command to test a new bombing technique from a base in France. Code name: Moonlight Sonata.*

*Over a period of eleven hours, some 1,200 high explosives, 50 parachute mines and 30,000 incendiaries turn the medieval gem of a city centre into an inferno. Seventy-five factories are destroyed. Two thousand homes reduced to rubble, with thousands more damaged, more often than not beyond repair. Five hundred and thirty-six people are killed, followed by 19 deaths in hospital; over a thousand are injured. And yet, despite 6,000 to 9,000 rounds (history disagrees on this point) being fired by static and roaming anti-aircraft defences, not a single enemy aircraft is reported as brought down.*

*Back in Radford, the woman kneeling in the middle of the road weeps, fearful that the nine week-old foetus in her womb is picking up on her terror; she imagines alarm bells ringing throughout its nervous system, creating havoc.* Oh God, *she wails,* What kind of a world is this to bring a child into?

*Her husband hugs her even harder, for he – a man of few words at the best of times – is trembling too much to speak. There is no reply from any source, corporeal or spiritual, only what appears to be and feels like the end of the world.*

*Already I am pig-in-the-middle. Already there is a smudge of shadow on the horizon of my emotional wellbeing. Could this have been the time – indeed the reason – I start biting my nails?*

## 40 RANULF CROFT, COVENTRY, 1946

Open the curtains, *my mother instructs, which is strange because she has only just closed them.*

*I pull them back... and scream at the face that terrifies through the glass: as fine an interpretation of the Wizard of Oz's Wicked Witch of the North as anyone is likely to see during a postwar British Halloween. The face is green (poster paint), straggling white hair (the kitchen mop) surmounted by the ubiquitous pointy witch's hat (waste cardboard and paper). A long thin crooked nose taps on the glass; fingernails tipped in silver paper (saved from cigarette packets) beat an unmusical accompaniment.*

*I scream and scream and scream, despite the fact that my mother is laughing, saying* No, no, it's Daddy, don't you see it's Daddy, pretending...

*But maybe it wasn't me screaming. Maybe it was my sister who, being three years younger and of unusually placid temperament, was the real baby. It's hard to know for sure after so many years. Especially since I – allegedly – was always the brave one, protecting, rationalising, trying to make things right for everyone else.*

*Maybe I was simply screaming inside. Certainly without much conscious effort I have held Halloween in fear and loathing ever since. Which is why it came as a bit of surprise to my own daughter when she moved to Canada in 1990 to get married, for there the custom (adopted from the USA, adopted from Europe) is BIG. Although observed in her childhood at her primary school in north west London, in her own home just down the road in Kilburn it was hardly noted in passing.*

3

## CRACKLEY WOODS, KENILWORTH, 1949

*I am hanging upside down from a tree, stupid skirt stuffed into stupid knickers, the ground below a sea of eye-spiking misty blue, stretching into woodland on every side. My family is wandering here and there, pulling greedily at the flowers in what can only be described as a blind rhapsody. Yet for me, the sight of the white stems, ripped from the bulbs that nurtured them deep in the earth below, and the smell of their sweet sour sappy discharge, disturbs.*

*We come here to celebrate my birthday if the weather is fine, which doesn't happen very often, but often enough, seemingly, still to create a deep impression in me. We travel by bus from Coventry, with a picnic to spread out on a blanket and casually crush the flowers below – the first broken heads of the day, the first whiffs of that strange familiar scent! Despite the destruction, I am overwhelmed to be the recipient of such generosity of beauty on my special day. I feel it is all for me, and have never since been able to see a bluebell wood – or indeed a simple scattering of blooms, for they are now an endangered species – without feeling that pain in my heart that otherwise only ever comes with unrequited and lost love.*

## COVENTRY–FORNETH, 1951

*My aunt – my mother's younger sister Jo (Josephine) – marries a Scottish landowner at St James, Styvechale parish church in Coventry. Being the oldest, I am Chief Bridesmaid in pink and mauve net and, while liking the idea of being pretty, feel a bit of a prat. I have just woken to the fact that the headlines in my father's newspaper –* The Daily Telegraph *– do not seem to say the same thing as headlines on the same topic on the front pages of other newspapers. This differential fascinates; the reason seems more important than frocks, but, being a dressmaker and quite the fashionista, my mother does not agree.*

*At my new uncle's house on Forneth Estate in Perthshire we eat in a dining room with faux marble pillars but lots of silver and family portraits that are the real thing, waited on by a manservant of some kind. Again the romance of such a sudden change in our fortunes charms, but also I am acutely embarrassed that an adult should have to serve a child. I feel worried for those who live and work downstairs and decide (if not during that summer holiday, then well within the next couple of years) to become a Socialist. Helping Kiki (Mrs McColl, the cook) pluck a grouse hung so long in the dairy that the feathers pull away to reveal a heaving mass of maggots, turns me into an instant vegetarian.*

*Several years later, the film On the Beach (1959) finally awakens me big-time to the insanity of nuclear war and the proliferation of nuclear weapons among so-called developed nations.*

*I can quite see why I gave my parents a lot of trouble.*

**40 RANULF CROFT, COVENTRY 1953**
*My father has gone to his Conservative Club; my mother is out teaching. Where is my sister? No idea. I know only that I'm alone in the house for my favourite new BBC radio serial, Journey Into Space. As with books, the radio is a constant source of solace... an escape yes, but also a defence. I can go into books, but voices carry me away on a very personal level and provide an immediate and very present bulwark against reality. I sit with my back to the wall in a corner of the dining room, where the radio sits on top of my father's oak bureau, which came from Dove Cottage and belonged originally to my maternal grandfather. I face the fully open door, through which I can see the hall and the front door – a well-mapped escape route from danger. Because Journey Into Space is the most terrifying drama imaginable, with a spooky theme tune and a disembodied voice that begins "A journey into space. What is space? It is nothing; yet it exists everywhere. Space – the limitless, infinite, awful, lonely, utter blackness to be found beyond the universe... But the imaginative human mind is a fast traveller, so let's move in and take a look..."*

**THE KING'S HIGH SCHOOL FOR GIRLS, WARWICK, 1954**
Every poem, essay and letter you write must have a clear beginning, middle and end, *Miss Wilson would say, beaming – more often-than-not at me – over the metal rim of her glasses, pulling her cardie over her ample bosom, tugging at her tweed skirt. Small, rotund, in love with language, she is*

5

remembered as my first champion beyond the limits of immediate family: the first person to offer genuine unconditional approval.

You show a spark of talent, *she would observe, handing back a piece of work covered in red ink;* One day you may even be able to write.

*One day...*

*The day perhaps I realised that life was not as simple as beginning, middle and end, and tried to explain as much in words: that there are no finites, only an ongoing stream of reinventions that link the phases of our lives.*

*I see my own existence as a river that will continue to run long after my physical body has been returned to the particles of stardust from whence they originated. A body of water – sometimes as reduced as a trickle and at other times as wide and deep as the ocean – that began in the well-spring of my mother, continues as my own, and flows on through my own children and beyond...*

*I am a roller-coaster succession of highs and lows that sometimes falls off the edge... More often I dapple the shallows, float in a daze of conformity midstream, or thrash against the hard knocks of submerged rocks. I know the temporary calm of lapping sandbanks; the exhilaration of slap-happy white water; the terror of the sudden plunge over an unforeseen drop.*

*And while I never know true peace, here's the beauty: the water, though constant, is always in transition, always changing.*

**COVENTRY, NEW YEAR, 1954**

*My father receives a telegram from Liverpool, addressed to:*

    *LOADER 40 RANULF CROFT STYVECHALL (sic) COVENTRY*

*The message is equally short and to the point, as telegrams were in those days, with no postcodes to complicate matters and help push up the cost:*

    *THE SUIT CASE DESPATCHED TODAY BY PASSENGER TRAIN STOP*
    *PLEASE ARRANGE TO MEET SAME AT COVENTRY = AYRTON AND*
    *ALDERSON SMITH +*

*My father goes to the station, meets the train and takes possession of the case, banded in copper wire by Mr Alderson Smith himself, since found to be unlocked after being cleared by Customs.*

*Do I see it? Does my father show me what is inside? (What remained inside, that is, after Senor or Mr Unknown had enjoyed a good sniff around.) I don't think so. At age twelve, nearing on thirteen, I would remember, surely. But then maybe not, what with ambition and the goal of growing up as quickly as possible, set firmly in my sights. (With youth culture in its infancy, I wanted only to be seen and regarded as "Adult".) But I like to think I would remember. Except (even after the most serious reflection, casting repeatedly into the darkest depths of memory) I still don't.*

*On January 7, a letter arrives. Attached is a list:*

*ONE SUITCASE CONTAINING PERSONAL EFFECTS*

*OF SAMUEL C.E. LOADER, DECEASED*

*Contents:*

*1. Portable typewriter*

*2. Small attache case containing the following:-*

　*1) Various coins including 5 halfcrowns, and three shillings.*

　*2) Small electric iron.*

　*3) Personal papers.*

　*4) 3 shirt studs in small case.*

　*5) 1 cigarette holder (amber).*

　*6) 1 wrist watch (Ostara).*

　*7) 1 watch (Longines) with chain.*

　*8) 1 watch (Herbert Wolf) with chain and key.*

　*9) 2 rings.*

　*10) Various studs, pins and spectacles.*

*3. Cancelled British passport C.209817 issued at Buenos Aires on 28th November 1945.*

*4. One length of cloth.*

*5. One alarm clock. (This latter entry hand-written as if added as a second thought)*

*The official stamp at the bottom, from the British Embassy – Consular Section – Montevideo, signifies closure: THE END.*

*Little did they know.*

## CHAPTER 1

# READY, STEADY, LET'S GO

**OCTOBER 31, 1999**

Remind me, says son-in-law Ross, hoisting my bag into the back of the car for the drive to the airport. Just how did all this begin?

Beginnings are the least of my worries, I reply. Here I am, about to fly in the face of malevolent spirits, and no-one seems to care one jot except me.

My daughter, Buffy, turns in the front passenger seat and gives me a look. It's one I know oh-so-well: *My mother – much as I love her – has said something silly again.*

I'd brought her up not to be superstitious, she accuses.

Okay, you go instead, I suggest. You fly 10,000 miles into the unknown on Halloween. See how you like it.

But then why should she. This is my journey, and mine alone.

The car's engine starts first time despite the cold and we're off. Off my bloody head, I suspect, as my stomach begins to churn and the cowardly twin of my Gemini self whimpers inside my head: *I want to go home.*

Was it only this Sunday morning we were on Taylor Island – one of hundreds of wooded outcrops dotting the waters of Lake Muskoka, north of Toronto. Buffy, Ross, their friend Mel and I had made our way there Friday evening to prepare and lock up the cottage – owned by my son-in-law's mother, Gloria – for the winter ahead. Many of the properties on the shore opposite and roundabout were already shuttered and closed. Hard to believe that in a month or so the lake would be frozen; the only way across to trek over ice – apparently a far safer endeavour than it sounds.

After retired neighbours packed up their boat and headed back to the city Saturday afternoon, we had lit the wood-burning stove and battened down the hatches. Then, foolishly perhaps, we'd reinforced our sense of isolation with a rental video from Parkdale's Blockbuster store – *The Blair Witch Project*. As the tale of superstition and witchery (and that most dreadful of infections: plain, unadulterated fear) began to unravel our psyches, bottles of wine passed with increasing speed along the sofa.

Today, after lunch, I climbed the hill behind the cottage as Ross struggled to drain tanks and turn off the water. Buffy and Mel were busy scattering cloves over the draped furnishings (Gloria's anti-mice device). Nellie – a winning candidate for the Millennium White Boxer Calendar – pounded the wooden deck of the dock, sensing it was almost time to head back home.

Surrounded by scrub and woodland not unlike that filmed in Connecticut, I tried to summon a sense of losing my bearings to the point that terror might take over from rational judgement. Yet in the golden beauty of that near-perfect autumnal day, with reflections off the lake teasing my eyes amid a landscape stippled with colour and light, it was near impossible.

Here a tree still fully clothed, ablaze with colour. There, a single leaf hung with strength and delicacy from an otherwise bare branch: pure ikebana. The gentle rustling at my feet turned out to be nothing more or less than a small vole, snuffling for food and quite oblivious of the monster rearing overhead. Somewhere, birds called. From down the hill, on the lakeside: laughter.

*This is the reality,* I remember consoling myself: comfortable familiarity, with nothing and no-one – real or imaginary – to fear.

Now, however, making our way through the streets of Parkdale on All Hallow's Eve, rationale is once again under attack. Peering out into the gloom on this, the most mysterious and feared night of the pagan-turned-Christian calendar, I see that the streets have a life of their own.

Warm light from open doors, in which adults are outlined bearing plates, bowls and buckets, spills out into moonless gardens and the darkness beyond. As flitting figures manifest, emerging from the shadows to criss-cross in front of the car, we drive with studied care on this night of nights: the ancient Celtic festival of Samhain which marked the arrival of winter, first transformed in medieval England into a Christian festival preceding All Saints Day on November 1st and then, centuries later, transported overseas and made North Americas' own.

Witches, goblins and ghosts in miniature cruise the streets in search of sugar and saccharin, as scared of their own reflections as they are in delighted thrall to fear. Skeletons of polystyrene and white-painted card dance from balconies; trees festooned with cotton wool, toilet paper and Christmas angel-hair appear ethereal; pumpkins glow terror in part-ironical, part-jocular spirit from steps and along garden walls. Welcome, they grin, glare, sneer: Trick or Treat?

You okay back there? Ross asks, reaching me through the fog of my musings – most probably because I have as yet failed to answer his original question: How did all this begin?

Fine, I reply, still avoiding the subject; How are we doing for time?

Since most Torontonians are either dishing out goodies, stuffing themselves, or sensibly keeping well out of the way, the motorway is near-empty and we arrive at the airport with time to spare. Walking anywhere with Nellie is a delight. She is so friendly (overly needy some might say) and funky-looking, being more pink than white with frilly (and frothy) bits around her chops, that people are inevitably drawn to her. So that's how we pass the first fifteen minutes; standing in Departures like proud parents as Nellie meets the public. Imagine, I joke, this may be the closest I ever get to being a grandmother!

Look, it's late, I say, after checking in. It's already 10.30 p.m. with the flight on schedule but still not boarding.

Why not go home; you're both working tomorrow. I hate goodbyes anyway. The longer we hang around, the worse I'll feel. I'll give you forty-five minutes, then ring to check you got back okay.

The pain of parting is always tortuous. When people ask these days where home is, after living so many years in Japan, the necessity to reply always gives me grief: if I am to believe the old adage that home is where the heart is, my own is surely split asunder.

My son Lee is in London, Buffy's made her life in Canada, my mother and her sister (my godmother Aunt Jo) both live in Scotland. My sister, Bridget, remains in Coventry, within striking distance of the house where she was born. My mother and Jo's sole remaining first cousin and family member of their generation, Eric, living with daughter Alison since his wife, Kathleen died, is also in England, near Rickmansworth. And my second husband, Akii, being Japanese, is at this very moment (according to the time difference) locked onto his computer screen in Tokyo.

Home, I always say as firmly as I feel at any one particular moment, is wherever I am and whosoever I am with that I care for at any one time.

There seem to be few people waiting for my flight. This is good: I can stretch out, sleep. Heartened, I buy postcards and scribble messages to most of those mentioned above. The girl at the kiosk is so accommodating I could kiss her; another Laotian refugee. The first, working in the flower shop in Toronto's Hudson Bay Company Store on Yonge Street, has promised not to forget Buffy's birthday next month – dusky pink roses will be delivered. It's interesting that I trust her so implicitly, something to do with living in Asia and being comfortable around Asian people in general, perhaps.

I ring Buffy and all is well, they're off to bed.

Lucky you, I hear myself saying with deep feeling. Look, I don't want to do this, I don't want to go; I must be insane to go to a country without knowing a word of the language.

Don' be silly, Mum, she laughs. You went to Japan and survived. I know you, you'll have a ball. Cheer up. Have a drink. Get a grip is what she seems to be saying. Get a life, more like!

I ring Kevin – recently returned to Toronto from Japan – and spill the beans: I'm terrified. What if, what if, what if... Being a drama queen himself, he commiserates quite beautifully and I am immensely cheered – at least for the first five minutes after putting down the phone.

Realising we are being summoned to board, I panic and end up sticking all the stamps on the cards upside down and have to tease them off and start again. What a mess. A child begins to cry. I empathise deeply while at the same time praying she is sitting absolutely nowhere near me on the flight. I need my own space for my own tears, real and imagined fears; Kevin would understand.

I wish I could ring Alan. But Al has chosen to move on in his life without taking me along. I knew him in London, after which he moved first to Japan, stayed three months with us and, after moving to Tokyo (three years in total), moved on to Vancouver, and then drove east to Toronto. If he continued in the same direction much longer, I had noted maybe rather too dryly in an e-mail, he would soon be back where he started. I never heard back after that, and the Japanese-sounding girl at his address in Toronto last week said he had just moved to Washington with her brother. Well, at least he's turned south.

Now I am heading south too, but going rather further. Washington DC is a stone's throw away, a mere spit in North America's eye.

I'm going to Argentina.

I have an aisle seat in the centre block. Economy class, of course. Booked through H.I.S. in Tokyo, where 153,000 yen bought me a ticket from Narita International Airport to Buenos Aires via Toronto (with one stopover en route, already accomplished) and Brazil's Sao Paulo. Considering the miles to be racked up, and that the aircraft was more than half empty on the first leg between Japan and Canada, with sleeping room all the way, I consider this the most amazing value. Am I the lucky one or not?

You can tell I'm feeling better already.

The plane – incredibly – is nearly full. Where did all these people come from at the last minute? I am arranged, strapped in, ready to go. The man sitting alongside me, in his mid-forties maybe, is well muscled, has a shaved head and sports a gold earring. His young companion – dark, slender, more Latino-looking than Caucasian – may be a son, but could be a lover. Having just talked with Kevin and pondered upon Alan's desertion, I am inclined to the latter. Equally, I am open to being proven completely wrong.

The small navy and black backpack wedged between my feet is rather the worse for wear. It has seen me through more than a few adventures, but not recently. In those first years in Japan, when the economy was booming, I was out of there on a regular basis every three months to renew my tourist visa: to Indonesia, Malaysia, Singapore, Hong Kong, Macau, the Philippines, Taiwan, South Korea, China... But recently dwindling resources (in large part connected to Japan's recession) have carried me back and forth to the UK only: family problems, one after another, inevitable in most cases but not always.

Most of my clothes are in a black canvas holdall in the cargo bay. Hold all: now what brilliant mind conjured up this perfect product description? The bag at my feet on the floor contains valuables and immediates: camera, Filofax, guidebooks, purse, make-up, toothbrush and towel. (I am already using the tape recorder, making notes in as unobtrusive whispers as possible.) I give the fabric a gentle nudge with my toe and feel the firm reassuring comfort of an A4 ring file.

This is my bible for the trip: it's raison d'être. In one sense, the collection of papers it contains answers Ross's original question concerning how the project started. As the plane rises into the phantasmagorical night, I pray that the spirits are kindly rather than angry and spiteful (I know for sure they are with me). Already, Ross – together with Buffy, Mel, Nellie (the dog) and Alice (the cat), Taylor Island and Toronto, Kevin and absent Al – feel, just as the Argentine scribbler W.H. Hudson once wrote, Far away and oh so long ago.[1]

In the summer of 1989, I was spending a limited but precious amount of time with my mother in Perthshire. She hangs out in a converted croft-cum-cowshed (a very nice cowshed it should be said) just 300 metres along the road from her also widowed sister, who nowadays lives in three old servants' cottages knocked into one – a very much grander affair. Forneth, the village outside which they both reside – a small hamlet really, since there is not even a shop – is about halfway between Blairgowrie and Dunkeld. Yes, the same Dunkeld and Birnam of *Macbeth's* location, though I have yet to see the walking woods of Dunsinane, even at my most inebriated.

My mother had been pottering in her bedroom – preparing for "popping off", as she calls it. (In solicitor's speak: *getting her affairs in order.*) I was in the living room, gazing out over the landscape to the hills beyond; the loveliest of gentle rolling views with roses and purple buddleia in close-up in between. Back then, at age seventy-nine, she was still an active gardener.

Tell me what to do with these, she said, appearing suddenly in the doorway. Usually I hear her shuffling along the corridor (her feet are a pain these days – the bunions I fear she has passed on to me), but not this time: I was probably too entranced, astonished that the raspberry field across the burn had turned wild in so short a time. (Blairgowrie is still a major centre for soft fruit growing, though sadly every year there appear to be fewer acres under cultivation. An illusion, I hope.)

She was holding in her hands a pile of letters in their envelopes, tied around with string.

Do you want them? she asked. They're from your grandfather to your father. Bob (my father) kept them in his bureau, and I'm clearing it out.

She must have misinterpreted the look on my face because she withdrew the bundle, saying never mind, she would throw them away.

I was across the room in a flash. No way, I said; I'd love to have them, read them. Maybe, I joked, I might even learn something to my advantage.

Your grandfather through and through, my mother observed tartly.

Now there was a man on the make who knew how to look after himself, she continued in similar vein. Always had to have the best; never satisfied with staying put and accepting his responsibilities and limitations. It was his ruin, and everyone suffered as a result.

This was the family lore of old. A man I can have met only two or three times on his rare visits to the British Isles from across the Atlantic, and yet my memory of him – however much romanticised – is strong and clear: tall and well built, with sandy hair and a moustache. A cream suit...or some other pale colour. Panama hat. And a silver, or maybe even a gold-topped cane – though I'm not so sure about that!

Once a birthday bike arrived, *With love from Granddaddysammy* (the name he gave himself in later years) – a sparkling brand-new black, red and chrome Hopper that gave me my first real taste of daredevil, independent travel. (The scars on my knees are living proof.)

Another time there was a watch, a thin square Omega that in this case was most definitely gold, but which soon after disappeared. For years my mother told me that because I had scratched my initials on the back, she had commandeered it for safekeeping because I obviously could not be trusted with something so valuable. (When she did finally relinquish it in 1995 after years of nagging, there were no initials, no deliberate scratch marks at all; yet in such appalling condition after forty years of someone else's irresponsible wear and tear that it was irreparable.)

What I largely remember of my grandfather is this idealised figure who lived "Abroad" (an exotic enough word in itself) and who sent us food parcels during the postwar period. I like to think I can see my mother now, scrabbling through the tins of tropical fruit and – in my wild imagination – stuffed tongues of humming birds. (Where did such a notion come from?)

Why can't he send us good red meat, she would cry, hurling a jar of guava jelly across the room; I mean what is Argentina if not corned beef!

That was where the parcels came from: Argentina. Also the pile of letters my father had accumulated, I quickly surmised from stamps and postmarks. But the first to find its way into my father's possession, dated 1936, was posted from Liverpool; the last from Uruguay, in 1954. Even as I took in these two pieces of information, my mother was back again, bearing the small leather suitcase in which the correspondence had been stored, and which now rattled with... what?

I was fascinated. Hooked to such an extent that when I returned to Japan the following month, I took the case and its contents with me. Trips back to the UK being as they are – mad dashes to see friends and family and to get my house straight in (at that time) less-than-salubrious Walthamstow – there had been no chance to investigate or read beyond the first letter or so. Back in our tiny shack of a teahouse in Kamakura's Ogigayatsu (Valley of the Fan), where we were living at that time, I would have all the time in the world.

All the time in the world to laugh and cry as I pieced together a story that would turn my own madcap adventuring upside down as well as inside out, leading me in directions I could never have imagined in a thousand years. But none of it could have been accomplished without Andy, to whom I had written soon after my return to Japan, asking for help.

I had first met Andy Melia in 1983, at a production of Yackety-Yak, a new musical based on the songs of Lieber & Stoller, directed by Rob Walker at the Astoria Theatre in London's Charing Cross Road. Seated next to one another, we quickly discovered we had things in common: a love of theatre, The Beatles (Andy firmly believed he was a reincarnation of John Lennon) and by association at least, Liverpool. A Liverpudlian born and bred, he was there as a friend of the famed local McGann brothers, four of whom – Joe, Paul, Mark and Steve – were appearing in the show.

Won over by his flattery (or possibly acute discernment: You're the first person to stimulate my grey matter since I moved to London!), Andy and I became friends. And stayed friends. (He and his wife Joan even came to stay with us in Japan in the summer of 1998.) In 1985 I visited him in

Liverpool – my first ever contact with the city of my father's birth. Andy showed me around, pointing out over the Mersey and recalling how as a boy he used to watch the most beautiful white cruise ships streaming by, heading for port or seawards to begin the Atlantic crossing.[2]

I have a vivid memory of staying at his parents' house at Crosby. (Andy told me the name was Viking in origin: "by" refers to a settlement or town, thus Crosby means the Place of the Crosses, which is interesting enough in itself.) But back to his home, Sandiacre, described by Andy as a suburban myth; while neighbours and such-like assumed the house had been named after the sand dunes nearby, it was apparently named after a horse that his father won an arm and a leg on – or so the family had been led to believe.

Welcomed in the manner of Honoured Guest, I was seated at the dining table with Andy, his brother and father, being served by mum, who then retired to eat in the kitchen. When I expressed a furiously embarrassed concern on her behalf, Andy's eyebrows shot into his hairline. My father's Italian, he shrugged later, as if that explained everything.

In fact Andy Melia Sr was not necessarily Italian. On the few occasions I had recalled the incident over the years, Andy Jr let it go as Angela being oversensitive Angela. Yet his father was born in Liverpool, in 1911, the same year as my own, but on what Andy terms, "the other side of the track". This affectionate nod acknowledges both his father's socially impoverished background, and his reputation as the leading local bookie in the Liverpool area from the 1960s onwards.

Melia is a Mediterranean name, perhaps from Sicily but also quite possibly Spain.[3] Andy believed his patriarchal family connection could go back to the sixteenth century, when Spain was trading with Catholic Ireland: maybe a Spanish sailor who married an Irish girl, whose descendants moved to Liverpool during the potato famine. The blight that began in 1845 killed over a million people and resulted in mass emigration from Ireland to the Americas. Such a paradox: the introduction of a root vegetable by Sir Walter Raleigh from the New World to his estates in Ireland via England, helped provide the United States of today with much of its original European stock. How the world goes round.

Andy's mother Noreen Melia (nee Sheahan) had been born in Fulham in 1914. Her family moved to Port Sunlight when she was four, to work for Lever Bros, the soap manufacturer. Her own mother, Honore, was an Irish farm girl who went to London believing all the kerbstones to be made from solid gold. She worked as a maid for the Labour politician Sir Stafford Cripps and used to go ahead to the family house in Cannes to prepare for summer vacations.

As to Noreen hanging out in the kitchen while family and guests ate in the dining room, Andy's wife Joan says her own mum did the same; it was customary. Maybe, we agreed, a cultural trait of northern working-class origin – the only way a woman could find a bit of peace and quiet and time to herself after the daily grind, rather than the Slave-in-Kitchen scenario that (Angela being Angela) I had originally assumed.

Now a successful freelance copywriter based in Formby, Andy was a bit lost in the early days of our friendship. The UK was in a terrible mess: Margaret Thatcher's Tory government dismantling unions and the mining industry by what I felt were the most cruel and devious means imaginable; unemployment rife; homelessness on the increase; the gap between rich and poor ever-widening.

Active for a while on Liverpool's fringe theatre scene, he directed and produced a play there. *The Need For Heroes: The Greatest Story Never Told* – based on the story of one-time Mersey beat stalwart Rory Storm, who after reverting to introverted stuttering Alan Caldwell (his original name) committed suicide with his mother in 1971 – played at The Neptune Theatre for two weeks in June, 1987. (Sadly we have both lost touch with his co-author, Shirley, a talented young local actress at the time.)

But mostly Andy had time to spare. When he'd returned to Liverpool from London for good, I'd mentioned casually that though my father had grown up there I knew little to nothing about my patriarchal family connections to the city. As Samuel Robert Loader was also born in 1911.

Andy thought it interesting. I'll look into it, he said. And six months later mailed me the rough outline of a family tree together with eleven pages of the most irreverent notes covering the skeleton of a family history as can be imagined.

*It's been a LOADER hassle but very intriguing and enjoyable,* he scribbled in a covering letter, with attached photos of a tombstone in Anfield Cemetery. One page of his researches began: *Other Family Members – tales of MURDER! SUSPENSE! HOMOSEXUALITY! PIETY! BATCHELORDOM AND SPINSTERHOOD.* I mean, who would not be amused, caught up, entranced and overwhelmed with curiosity?

So here I am. Dinner over. Lights dimmed, passengers settling down. Any ghosts and spirits keeping pace in the first hours have long begun to trail as the time frame begins to slip. Yet still I cannot rest.

Instead I open the bag, and first turn over lovingly in my hands, an original copy of *The South American Handbook 1937*. Found in a second hand bookshop just off the Charing Cross Road on my last trip back to London, and costing 45 pounds sterling (a small fortune more than the two shillings and six pence it was priced at brand new), I could hardly believe my luck: another pointer.

Next I retrieve the file (wrapped in the towel) and begin to wade through the mass of papers that precede the letters themselves: newspaper clippings collected over the last decade and memorabilia that, together with information gleaned in Liverpool, tell me something of my grandfather's early years.

But there is too much and I am more tired than I think. So I turn to those eleven pages scribbled from Liverpool, and go back to the beginning according to the Gospel of St Andrew.

# CHAPTER 2

# THE GOSPEL ACCORDING TO ST ANDREW

**OCTOBER 31, 1999 CONTINUED**

He had backtracked three generations – an outstanding accomplishment it seemed at the time. Yet as he reminded in a later fax, it was far easier to trace people in the nineteenth century than, say, in the 1950s. All he had to do was go roll the census records, held in Liverpool Library.

The first UK census was taken in 1801, which is why – information prior to this date regarding the general populace being difficult to obtain – my own research is currently, well, stuck. (The first census to survive in Japan was conducted over ten centuries before, in 721, by Emperor Tenchi, from his seat of power in Nara. An even earlier count was allegedly lost.)

The first four British demographic counts were just that: head counts only. But in 1841, the returns began to give details on individuals. Census counts are now conducted every ten years, with results not made public until 100 years later to protect the confidentiality of the information.

The Family Records Centre in London holds the returns for England and Wales for 1841, 1861, 1881 and 1891. (It is also the central registry of all Births, Marriages and Deaths.) The 1901 census will be made public in January 2002 and – naturally enough these days – will be available online.

But in 1989, when Andy first began his investigations, we are talking migraine-inducing microfiche. (Arriving in Japan three years before then, I was using a typewriter and carbons! The domestic fax was still a fantasy; the PC even more of a dream. The internet? Unheard of.)

My direct line began, as far as Andy could establish within such constraints, with my great-great grandfather, John Loader. Born in or around 1816 in Shrewsbury, in the county of Shropshire, he arrived in Liverpool in 1843, accompanied by his wife Susan (one year younger and from Welshpool, some 30 miles away just over the border into Wales). Nor were they alone, but with a two year-old son, bearing the given names Samuel Turner.

Why did John Loader make such a move, as momentous an enterprise in those days as traveling to the moon today? Let us assume that age-old reason migration: to better his economic circumstances and that of his family. It is doubtful there was money for any easy mode of travel. Most likely he and Susan walked, sharing the load of little Sam and any possessions, perhaps cadging the occasional lift on a passing farm cart, and sleeping where they could, in fields and ditches. Nor would they have been solitary seekers of a better life, for this was the period in Liverpool's history when it was a mecca for the poor and dispossessed.

The city had not always been as prosperous. Like Buenos Aires, it began as an artificially contrived settlement on a river opening onto the Atlantic Ocean, but here any similarity ends – for now at least. As a waterway the Mersey was neither long nor large, but sprang in the Pennines, a range of hills to the north that received above average rainfall, so creating a powerful force. Nearing the coast, the banks suddenly opened out to nearly three miles wide, as if to embrace the freedom of the open sea, but then almost as quickly narrowed again, creating a unique tidal basin. This was known roundabout (using the vernacular of today) as the Liver, or Lever Pool, perhaps because of the seaweed that flourished in the sluggish water along the banks. (Older pronunciations and spellings include Lyrepole and Lyverpoole.)

In 1206, King John was seeking a supplementary route to Chester across to Ireland. Scouts soon came across the Liver Pool, at that time located in the Parish of Walton and containing the villages of Aigburgh, Toxteth, Kirkdale and Crosby. Inland, the royal surveyors mapped Croxteth, Roby, West Derby (with its old Norman castle) and the parish church of Walton-on-the Hill, a local landmark even then.

The following year, King John granted Liverpool a royal charter, with freemen, trading rights and other privileges. Streets quickly developed, laid out along the lines of a letter H, so providing possibilities for seven names. All these thoroughfares exist today, but with only Castle Street, Chapel Street and Dale Street retaining their original appellations.

History could be said to be on the city's side. Many early travel writers were concerned with its escalating good fortune, including Daniel Defoe (c. 1660–1731) who not only found the time to conjure up *The Life and Strange Surprising Adventures of Robinson Crusoe*, but always took note of new developments on his visits to Liverpool. Growth as a busy market town and port was steady until the first recorded slave ship took leave in 1700. The added influence of the industrial revolution (which between 1750 and 1850 changed first the face of northern England and then progressively – or ruinously, depending on your point of view – the rest of the world) caused a huge leap in the city's fortunes.

Creating a triangular route of operation, slavery provided local merchants and ship owners with riches beyond their wildest dreams. Vessels would be loaded with manufactured items – alcohol, textiles (clothes and woollens made in Yorkshire and Lancashire), pots and pans and pottery (Staffordshire), metal bars, gunpowder and weapons (Birmingham in the Midlands) – to be exchanged for slaves at ports along the African west coast. In 1781 alone, fifty-three ships – which were powered by wind and sail well into the 1860s – transported 28,200 men, women and children into hell.

The abductees were stowed in close confinement and darkness to suffer the fifty to sixty day journey eastwards across the Atlantic. If they survived (for while it was in the owners' interests that they be kept alive, those paid a pittance to look after them were not so scrupulous) they were put ashore either in the West Indies or the southern colonies of America, to be sold as indentured workers on plantations. The vessels would then be reloaded with sugar, rum, mahogany, or tobacco, for the run back to Liverpool.

There were profits to be made on every leg of the journey, and the financial benefits were much enjoyed by the upper middle-classes. Soon Liverpool was larger than Bristol (having left poor Chester behind long ago) and second only to London as Britain's major port.

By the time John Loader set out to better himself, slavery had been abolished (though not until after a fierce reactionary battle, especially in Liverpool which in commercial terms had most to lose). There was a rail service between Liverpool and Manchester and the first steam ship had made the Atlantic crossing to New York; emigration was in full swing. In the forty years between 1810 and 1859, some five million people sailed for the New World (America having achieved independence from Britain in 1783), and half a million to Canada, with two thirds leaving from Liverpool. They came not only from England, Wales, Scotland and Ireland, but the furthest reaches of Europe, with the stream of human traffic peaking in 1840–1850.[4]

It makes sense, therefore, to suppose that my great-great grandfather had been thinking to try his luck abroad. Maybe he had planned to emigrate, but somehow landed on his feet in the port, and with some basic security, decided to stay put. At age twenty-seven or thereabouts he would appear to have been bright, ambitious and determined, firstly in making the move at all, but the subsequent attempts he made to lift his family up the rungs of the social ladder. He had a succession of jobs, each improving on the last: beer house worker, mayor's messenger, bookseller, stationer... As he began to earn more money, a servant was hired. Susan especially must have felt a great sense of relief; she was by this time a mother to eight. After Samuel had come Susan (born in 1845 and named after her mother in the manner of the times). Followed by William,

Charles, Gertrude, Sarah and Hannah (the first time I realised there were twins in the genetic pool) and Harriet in1858. Yet of these eight children born to John and Susan, only two appear to have married and procreated to carry on the line: Samuel and his brother William.

In 1873, with John Loader in his late-fifties – and elder son Samuel Turner aged thirty-two – the strangest thing: my ancestral Shropshire Lad disappeared from the records. Dead, Andy assumed. But no. In 1881, aged sixty-five, great-great grandpa popped up again, his occupation newly classified as Gentleman. He settled in Tuebrook, formerly a gentrified part of Liverpool, and was last heard of in 1890, when he died at the extremely ripe old age (for those days) of eighty-one.

So where did he go to for those missing eight years? (His disappearance, wrote Andy, Makes me suspect that he went abroad and coined it, possibly with some of his children and possibly – knowing something of subsequent events – to South America.)

Did his son and heir go with him? My great-grandfather first appeared in Liverpool directory records described as a Merchant's Clerk, aged eighteen. (This long before his father dropped out of sight.) But then an even more remarkable thing... By 1884, aged fifty-three, Samuel Turner's business address had gone so up-market that it was on the historic map: Consulate of the Oriental Republic of Uruguay, The Temple, Dale Street, bang in the city centre within spitting distance of the Town Hall, and still a prestigious address today. He was described also as Merchant for L. Johnson & Co.

Two years later he was still at the same address in Dale Street, but reclassified as Vice-Consul, Argentine Republic. In 1887 he was listed in a trade directory as, Samuel T. Loader, Commission and Forwarding Agent. (Business cards among the memorabilia in my grandfather's attaché case provide confirmation: he was trading with South America, more specifically Argentina and Uruguay.)

He died, ironically, on a Good Friday, aged just fifty-seven. His passing over – a curious phrase this, linking this world with the next – and subsequent interment in Anfield Cemetery was considered noteworthy enough to warrant a mention in the local paper. (By this time Andy had extended his researches to include cemetery records, Gore's Directory, records of wills and testate, obituaries of Liverpool businessmen and – the best news of all – personal interviews)

Running the headline *Death of the Argentine Vice-Consul* in its obituary column, The Liverpool Courier of March 31, 1899 observed that many citizens would hear the news with surprise as well as regret:

*Mr Samuel Thomas* (an editorial slip here?) *Loader... had been Vice-consul for the Argentine republic since 1886, six years before Mr Hansen was appointed to the consulate... he only took ill on Wednesday last week, being attacked with pleurisy, from which he died yesterday.*

Five days later the newspaper reported the funeral of *THE ARGENTINE VICE-CONSUL*, but without actually mentioning the day it took place. This detail apart, it gave his address as Fair View, Belmont Drive, Newsham Park, named the minister who conducted the burial service as Reverend William Hodgson, M.A., and listed the chief mourners: *Mr C.E Loader, Mr W.H.Loader, Mr C.W Loader, Mr C.E Newbould, Mr W.R. Lloyd, Mr R. Holding, Mr W. Rees, Mr H.W. Loader, Mr A.J. Macay, and Mr Henry Crawford.*

There was more: *The general company at the graveside included J.C Pereira Pinto (Brazilian Consul).* As Andy observed, obviously he (Samuel Turner/Thomas?) must have been an important and well-respected man in his day.

In the manner of the times, the women in his life are conspicuous by their "absence" at the leave-taking. There is no mention of his widow, my great-grandmother Martha Jane. Likewise any female children he may have fathered – presumed by Andy at this stage to number just one: Gertrude Mary who is interred with her parents in Anfield Cemetery. Very much in the Victorian tradition, it was a formal send-off and then quickly back to business.

Martha – a tough cookie by the sound of it – lived another sixteen years, dying across the River Mersey on the Wirral in 1915. She can hardly have been much of a spendthrift, bequeathing 764 pounds sterling (a lot of money in those days and presumably what remained of the 2271 pounds left to her by her husband) to Florence Susan Loader. Flo, Andy surmised, must have been a sister-in-law. In fact, she was Samuel and Martha's eldest child, born like my grandfather in Uruguay. Another daughter, Beatrice, came later.[5]

Most of this information came as a complete surprise. The facts were clear enough, but the how, whys and wherefores began to stir a thousand question marks in an already fomenting mental brew. Why had I never met Florence, or indeed heard a whisper of her very existence? Similarly, why had I never known before investigating the contents of that attaché case that my grandfather had dual nationality? Certainly I had no knowledge of any such high-flying connections in the diplomatic service.

Also, who were all those Loaders at the graveside? My grandfather, obviously, as number one son (the C.E.). The bare bones of the family tree Andy had composed explained the rest: W. H. would have to be Great-Uncle William; C.W., Great-Uncle Charles; but who was H.W.? The only Hs listed of that particular generation are women: Hannah and Harriet. Could H have been Herbert, one of William's sons and so my grandfather's first cousin? Possible, but never proven.

Another name that puzzled was that of Newbould.

The attaché case had yielded four means of official identification, three in my grandfather's name and one in my father's. The oldest – or what certainly appears to be the oldest being on yellowing paper and more than a little worn – is a *Cedula de Identitidad* (Certificate of Identification), issued to Samuel Charles Eduardo Loader in Buenos Aires in the name of Republica Argentina. Unfortunately the date is illegible, but his fingerprint is clear, and his date of birth in the Cieudad (city) of Montevideo given as January 26, 1881.

However, a subsequent ID, issued November 14, 1951 in Montevideo by the Republica O Del Uruguay, gives his name as Samuel Charles Eduardo Loader Nowbould. This I now know to be in the Spanish tradition: the father's family name being secondary to that of the mother. So, my great-grandmother was a Nowbould, or a Newbould. The spelling may be different, but the similarity could not be ignored. Martha, being of British stock and Victorian upbringing and so a woman with her own particular place in his-story, was doubtless regarded as best represented at her husband's graveside by a male relative.

On his earliest ID card, my grandfather's occupation was listed as Exporter. His last passport – one of those nice weighty navy-blue leather bound jobs made defunct by progress – was issued in Buenos Aires on November 28, 1945. Valid for ten years – his death made doubly sure by stamping *CANCELLED* across every page – he is described as a British Manufacturing Representative. To make this paragraph even more colourful, his height is given as 6 feet, 2 1/2 inches, eyes brown, and hair auburn.

**NOVEMBER 1, 1999**

I am woken early morning by a hand gently shaking my shoulder – my papers, having slipped sideways, lie strewn on the cabin floor. It is the same steward who handed over an un-requested double gin and tonic with a conspiratorial wink before dinner. But that was over New York, and now, he whispers, We're over the Atlantic Ocean, adjacent to Central America, close by the Dominican Republic.

He's nice, very likeable, with a florid complexion (those small broken veins that suggest rather than prove a life of dissipation), an exceptionally world-weary expression, and tired feet. Wait[er]ing around at 30,000 feet must be a hell of a job after age forty.

We commune in whispers so as not to wake those dead to the world as we know it. Our lips move synchronously in murmuring shadow, as we talk of our work as a journalist and an airline employee respectively, and the differing pressures they bring to bear. I tell him that I was previously a freelancer in London, an editor who in 1986, after moving to Japan, transformed herself into a scribbler to be edited.

He says he has only ever worked for Canadian Airlines, with no idea of long the security of this particular status quo is assured. He finds a copy of *On Course*, an in-craft publication which contains a message from President and CEO Kevin Benson, explaining the company's response to Onex's offer: to fix Canada's broken airline industry by merging the country's two major carriers into a strong and profitable international flag carrier.

Admittedly I know very little about Onex Corporation, as founded by Winnipeg-born Gerry Swartz. But during my stay in Toronto, I had gone to offer moral support to Buffy (working part-time to help fund her studies in graphic design) at Indigo, a bookstore so recently opened in the Eaton Centre that the smell of fresh paint was over-powering and staff still finding their feet.

Buffy had reservations, fearing she was selling out: big box stores like Indigo and Chapters (its American rival) have been destroying small shops throughout Canada.

I'm really scared, she confided, That they'll be the end of all my favourite small bookshops in the city... my only way of rationalising the job? At least it's Canadian. (The American movie *You've Got Mail* (1998), starring Tom Hanks and Meg Ryan, depicts the phenomenon but cops out of the main political issue in favour of romance.)

Indigo is one of those new-style literary comfort zones, where you can take a book to the coffee shop, or curl up in a soft squidgy sofa, to while away an illicit afternoon or rest up weary feet after a spot of hardcore retail therapy. It also just happens to be the brainchild of Swartz's wife, Heather Riesman – a pretty ambitious woman in her own right.[6]

The day I chose to play the supportive parental in-store spy was especially busy, and the reason quickly became apparent. The charismatic Mr Swartz was holding a press conference to back up his offer to save Canada's carriers from being swallowed up by a monopolistic American whale. Dapper in a dark blue suit and pale blue shirt, with curly black hair and impassioned eyes, he was holding forth, no holds barred. The crowd gave him a hard time, with representative pilots and crewmembers ranked along the walls like heroically-inspired pillars of wisdom. But he held his ground.

Since 1990, Canadian Airlines and Air Canada had lost a combined total of nearly two million Canadian dollars. Contributing to these losses was the fact that more than 80 per cent of tickets sold by the combined carriers are heavily discounted. (I think of my bargain ticket in the light of this revelation and feel almost guilty; might the nice decent guy with whom I am now discussing the issue lose his job in small part because of a cheap deal obtained in Tokyo?)

Swartz reckoned his mini-empire to be in a good position to merge the two airlines and so maintain his country's independence. As he explained: As of June 1999, Onex had consolidated revenues of over $14 billion, assets of $11 billion, and employed 58,000 people, making it one of the largest companies in Canada. A monopolistic Jonah in the making, desperate to be heard and most importantly, to be believed: *Trust me.*

Do you trust him? I ask the steward, lifting the window to see the faintest of smeared lines of light dividing the darkness from left to right.

I don't know, he shrugs; who could tell? Swartz seems nice enough, but really, can anyone in big business be trusted? Of course in terms of national pride it would be sad to see this part of Canadian business go the American way, but maybe it might pan out better in the long run?

There are arguments for and against, racketing to and fro, but largely they are making him feel very, very tired. The unions? Well, they do their best, but the bottom line is he believes people like himself are powerless. He's trying not to worry because what's the point? His fate is in the hands of others.

Fate, I ponder after the steward drags away despondently to help quiet another fretful child. I recall my extreme irritation with my Japanese husband's most commonly applied expression to any problem or obstacle: *Shikata ga nai*, It can't be helped! At moments like these, as Beethoven once said, I want to seize fate by the throat!

Why, even that most rational of men, Abraham Lincoln, could feel overwhelmed at times of crisis: I claim not to have controlled events, but confess plainly that events have controlled me.

After fifteen years in Asia, my own life stands revealed as a continuing battle for control. Even in full recognition of this fact, still I struggle... against the elemental forces of nature, against the manmade forces of greed and indifference, against the genetic and behavioural constraints of family.

*See how far I've run, See how far I've run,* I hum, to the tune of Three Blind Mice. I'm no different to Alan really, I realise, which suggests such an unsettling jolt of self-revelation that I back off hastily into sleep again.

Or doze rather. I wake again at daybreak proper to look out over an ocean of green as far as the eye can see in any direction. Amazonia, I breathe, grinning from ear to ear at the very thought.

I was always like this, from my earliest childhood. Brimming with curiosity, yet astounded to find myself realizing so many dreams: traveling by jeepney across the mountains of northern Luzon in the Philippines; standing on the Great Wall of China; exploring the backstreets of Gion in Kyoto; seeing the sun rise above Alishan, Taiwan's most sacred mountain; descending from the border with Myanmar on a bus in northwestern Thailand with children of the Hmong tribe asleep in my lap and slumped against my shoulder, their clothing decorated with intricate embroidery, the most exquisite silver ornaments...

The next time I open my eyes we are descending into Sao Paulo. There is the glitter of commercial skyscrapers and luxury high-rises, then a seemingly endless panorama of cityscape giving way to urban sprawl giving way to shanty town *favelas* giving way to... Jungle! It reminds me of walking in the old Australian silver mining town of Broken Hill, seeing the road beneath my feet mist with red dust and then dissolve into the gum trees, kangaroo tracks and billabongs of bush country. Here, blood-orange fingers trickle and tail off between shacks of tin and cardboard into a groundcover of luxuriant verdure.

With an hour to wait in transit, I am made to feel quite extraordinarily small and insignificant, especially when compared to living in Japan where a) as a westerner I am highly visible, and b) women are mostly bust-less, bum-less and astoundingly slim and firm-fleshed, even in old age.

Here I am surrounded by what I consider to be tall, shapely and extremely well-heeled Brazilians, all brimming with confidence and energy and, in the case of the men, extraordinary machismo. But then I realise they are not as I had assumed, but Argentines. Well, of course! We are about to board the connecting flight to Buenos Aires. And soon enough, we do. The noise is terrific, everyone in full throttle, Portuguese giving way to Spanish: my first experience of South American culture shock.

It is on this last leg of the flight that the enormity of what I am doing strikes full force, and I begin to shake. There is only one thing to do, I decide: hold my right knee and hope for the best.

Just the week before, interviewing a friend of a friend in Tokyo, I had admitted my worst fear: that having arrived in Buenos Aires and booked into some small hotel, I would lose all sense of purpose. That my intentions, vague and disparate as I know them to be, would escape – drift away, like that Australian sand drizzling between fingers and toes.

Brian was very good. A British-born New Zealander based in Albany, near Auckland, his company IAS Learning Group (as founded in 1989) stands committed to raising the self-esteem of not only those employees of companies worldwide willing to spend the money, but also local youth. As he told me: We're looking for leaders in the twenty-first century. We tell kids that in the metaphorical sense they can do anything, even fly like eagles, and believe me, they do.

He had a good trick, he told me. When I began to lose myself –

meaning my sense of self – I should grasp my right knee. This would not only provide a distraction from the self-destructive path of thought onto which I had allowed myself to step, but act as a reminder: I was about to re-run old patterns of behaviour and thinking that would not be helpful to the task ahead.

To stop myself feeling too ridiculous - flying ever southwards at 30,000 feet, clutching my right knee, as lunch is served - I re-order Andy's notes and find myself once more enthralled. The fun starts, he had scribbled (on page 5), With your great-great aunts and uncles...

Great-great Aunt Susan had died a spinster in 1926, leaving 132 pounds sterling to her brother William (last heard of at his father's funeral). As for twin sisters Sarah and Hannah, they were still unmarried and living at home at ages thirty-six and twenty-six respectively.[7]

Charles – a devout and godly soul who acted as sexton at the family's local church in Anfield – worked as a cotton broker, ending up as Secretary to British Empire Life Assurance. He died unmarried and early, in 1904, aged fifty-three, leaving over a thousand pounds to sister Sarah. (And so the family money went round and round...)

William was another pious do-gooder, keeping himself to the fore of the congregation at St Margaret's. But Bill (as I am sure he would have hated to be called) displayed a strong entrepreneurial streak, starting up a printing and bookselling business. Later this developed into a stationery and allied post office concern. Siring half a dozen offspring by one Sarah Price, he appears to have lived a long and self-righteous life.

Andy agrees: Dying in 1929 aged eighty-one, he went straight to heaven after leaving the business in the capable hands of youngest daughter Alice.

Regarding these six Great-cousins (as they would be described in genealogical terms), this is where the fun *really* starts: Walter (outed on his wedding night); Alice (obviously the blue-eyed girl of the bunch); Arthur (a book-keeper and staunch family man, so the soundest-sounding of the lot according to the social mores of the times); Annie (also unmarried);

Herbert (ditto); and another Charles (a bit of a black sheep apparently, which in my book makes him especially interesting).

In no time at all, or so it seems, we are descending into Buenos Aires. Below, the sea is the strangest ever experienced. Not blue or jade or slate-grey, but a soupy, reddish-brown. Silt, I quickly surmise, carried nearly 2,000 miles (1,826 to be exact) from its source in the central highlands of Brazil – the deepest interior of the South American continent. We are no longer above the ocean but approaching over an estuary that stretches a metric 220 kilometres at its widest point between Argentina and Uruguay: the Rio de la Plata.

There is a port. A city. Suburbs. Then just as swiftly, flat farmland – the first sighting of Argentina's famed *pampa*, stopped only in its relentless fertile stretch westwards by South America's backbone: the mountainous range of the Cordillera de los Andes.

Warned of turbulence, the pilot begins a rapid descent of 10,000 feet. Snatched up and tossed around on rising thermals, I clutch everything within reach – knees, armrests, even the spirited muscled arms of my companion alongside. But sadly he is long gone; a Uruguayan, working in Canada (another Canadian Airlines employee) and returning with his son to visit friends in Montevideo, he'd changed planes in Sao Paolo.

The plane threatens to shake itself to bits, swings violently from side to side before landing with a fierce bump amid what can only be described as a building site. Ezeiza International Airport is either being developed or demolished, with thick terracotta-coloured mud and mud-covered construction equipment on every side.

I am shaking too... take-offs and landings have never appealed except in principle, or dreams. The memory of an emergency landing in Manila (lights failing to indicate whether the wheels were properly locked) has not faded one jot in over a decade: the American in the seat in front remarking in tart disbelief that he couldn't believe he had survived Vietnam to die in the Philippines in peacetime; the pilot squeaking with fright as he instructed us to adopt crash positions...

Waiting for my bag to carousel through, fear and dismay gives way to cool detachment. Alongside, an Argentine in his late fifties, elegantly groomed and be-suited, is welcoming a far younger couple – most probably Jewish, quite possibly doctors – to his city.

Tomorrow, he intones in fluent but sexily accented English, We will begin work. In the evening, cocktails, a concert, later dinner. Over the weekend we have arranged a trip upcountry, to an *estancia*, for riding and *asado*, our Argentine barbecue.

Now that's the way to do it, I think – or least one way to do it. Me? I have little planned beyond emerging into Arrivals. The vagueness of this adventure has done nothing but turn my stomach for hours; yet now I feel a great calm – that state-of-otherness that descends (on me at least) when the possibility of death is transformed into the miraculous relief of survival. From previous experience I know exactly what to do: find a map, take a shuttle bus into the city and drift, allowing fate, glorious fate, to have its way with me and the ensuing proceedings gather their own momentum.

My passport is stamped. I have nothing to declare (apart from Total Insanity, and such a term appears for some quite incomprehensible reason not to warrant space in my Spanish phrase book). I am ready for anything.

Except this: a young man at the barrier holding up a misspelled card: ANGELA JEFF. And a short prettily plump woman with blonde-streaked hair gathered into a casual chignon and eyes as brown as my own, bouncing up and down with excitement, calling Hola! Anhela, hola!

I don't know why I should feel so stunned. Yet still I can hardly believe my eyes. It's Maria-Elena.

CHAPTER 3

# MARIA-ELENA

**NOVEMBER 1, 1999 CONTINUED**

Outside the sky is grey with drizzle. Very English, I remark, and two heads turn inquisitively. (I realise I can say this in Japanese, but not Spanish, so hardly useful. Inglese, I say hopefully, pointing upwards, to which Maria-Elena and the young man who is driving look puzzled, shrug, and share a moment of tolerant amusement.)

The landscape is another matter: intensely green – that young spring green that so dazzles it hurts the eyes. We are on a motorway into the city, with meadows of lush grass divided by white-painted fencing and gates on either side. Very Kentucky, I imagine, never having travelled America beyond Manhattan. Something to do, I surmise, with there being so many splendid horses on view through the rain-spattered glass – thoroughbreds from tail to Maine.

I feel both at home and completely lost. Rugby posts are familiar, but all the road signs are in Spanish and much of the exotic vegetation unknown. Wonderful to see trees reaching to their natural height, the tips of branches dipped in limey brilliance – even some with pale mauve flowers that are reminiscent of China, without quite knowing why.

Of course, it's Spring. I have moved from one season to another, cleverly missing out winter altogether.

Casa, casa, announces my companion, waving her arm towards a roundabout, upon which people appear to be living in tumbledown litter-strewn confusion. God, I think: I do hope not.

Si, si, confirms Pablo, but semi-circling this Third-World to take a side road. Not to be confused with Pablo No. 1, he is sweetly shy and neatly packed in pressed shirt and trousers. My first thought on seeing him holding up that hysterical sign at the airport was that Maria-Elena's son, of the same name (and roughly the same age, build and colouring) had returned miraculously from Madrid. But no, Pablo No. 2 works as a personal driver; my cousin, however many times removed, has her own chauffeur.

In February 1993, I heard of an Irish acquaintance in Tokyo about to head off to The Americas in search of a permanent home. While waiting to hear whether his application for a Green Card had been approved, Jerry decided to make friends with San Francisco, where he hoped to settle. Just in case, however, he was planning also to check out both Buenos Aires and Rio (de Janerio).

Little imagining that he would have the time or inclination to remember, I asked a favour: if he found himself anywhere near a local telephone directory in Buenos Aires's central district (El Centro), would he take a peep and see whether by some remote chance the name Loader was listed?

The idea that there might be family in the city had crept up on me so slowly and insidiously that it was a surprise to hear myself voicing such a request. My grandfather had never re-married; indeed he died (as far as I know) still married to my grandmother. But the possibility niggled: might there not have been a second family, a common-law family that no-one in England knew about? Twenty years is a long time to remain alone, unattached, far from home.

Still I was more than a little surprised when Jerry returned and faxed me a page of telephone numbers. I exaggerate, of course. There were just five – different addresses, but all preceded by the same name: Maria-Elena Bustamante Loader.

Having this information to hand, it took a year to get my act together. Looking back, asking myself why, I have no reasonable answer. True, life was busy. But *that* busy?

It took a piece of luggage to get me off my backside. Taking out the rubbish one first Monday of the month (Big Garbage Day), I had found – amongst the still extravagant throwaways of Japan's post-economic Bubble era – an ancient cabin trunk: green, with leather-bound corners and trim and metal clasps, covered in South American shipping stickers. Inside, the maker's label: *Madera y Papal Industria Argentina – Antiqua Bauleria del Porvenir – Vallerinos Hnos. Casa Fundada en 1880. Requonista 516-Buenos Aires.*

The likelihood of finding a piece of luggage of this type in Japan at such a point in my life was just too extraordinary to be ignored. I dragged it back to our two-floor shack of wood, paper and tatami matting in Hayama, to where we had moved from Kamakura in 1991; I have it still. Assuming such treasure to be a direct message from the gods, I immediately put pen to paper to write to this unknown woman bearing my surname.

Drafting a letter led naturally enough to the problem of translation. At that time, I had no connection with Spain, nor indeed knew any native Spanish speakers. The only possibility, I decided, was Luis.

Luis was a neighbour – an English-speaking Hispanic-American engineer working on the Yokosuka Naval Base across the other side of the Miura-peninsula, south of Yokohama and Tokyo. Some ten thousand US citizens live and work here, with the more independent-minded personnel choosing to live off base rather than on. As a civilian, with a Japanese wife and baby daughter, he was holed up in a small apartment block, named inappropriately (as ever in this country) Sun City, on the fume-ridden main road between Hayama-machi, the small coastal sprawl where we lived at that time, and Zushi-shi (which, being larger, hosts our nearest railway station).

Since he was always happy to stop and chat, the next time we met I asked for help.

Well, Luis replied frankly, My Spanish isn't as good as it was in the Philippines, but I'll ask a friend and we'll do our best.

Several weeks later I posted off five letters dated June 30, each containing a brief account of my family's Argentine connection, and wondering whether by some remote possibility we might be related.

It was not until mid-August that I received a reply, by which time I had given up hope. Even without Spanish I could work out that the news was positive. Since Luis was not around, I sought long-distance assistance (via a new and completely different route) from Isabel, a Spanish woman married to a Japanese, with two children, living in Tama New Town in the western suburbs of Tokyo. I posted her the letter; Isabel posted back a translation. Though killing, the suspense proved well worth the wait.

It seems that Maria-Elena had received my letter with what she termed *great emotion*. She felt that even if we turned out not to be related, we should be! (I liked that.) She had always experienced a strong desire to find her roots in England, a trait she had passed on to her younger son. Just six months previously she had asked a friend traveling through London to look in a telephone directory, with an aim similar to my own.

She confirmed that her grandfather was my grandfather's first cousin Charles Joseph Loader Price (remember the alleged black sheep of that branch of the family?) Just to refresh your memory (and my own) he was the son of Great-Uncle William Loader and Sarah Leticia Price, who ran the Liverpool post office where two of Charles' sisters – Alice Mary and Anne Louise – also worked. There were other siblings, but Maria-Elena could only remember Fedric (Frederick) Walter and Eribert (Herbert), whose names in English she was unsure how to spell.

Maria-Elena's grandfather used to tell her mother that when rumours began to spread of impending war, he and an unknown cousin boarded a ship to avoid the draft. During the voyage, there was an epidemic of yellow fever, and no one was allowed off the ship until it reached South America. News that the 1914 war had started caused his cousin to disembark in Uruguay. (Who could this have been, I wonder?).

Charles stayed aboard and kept right on going, thinking to return to England. On reaching Chile, however, the news from home was so bad that he decided to stay put. Fate then grabbed him by the balls: he married, had children, put down roots. Like my grandfather, he died in 1954. Another coincidence.

Maria-Elena was envious of my sentimental remembrances of Sam. Her own memories, she confided, were far from happy; Charles was not a nice man; a conflicted despot who alienated much of his family. (What is it with Loader men, that they estrange themselves by one means or another from those to whom they should be closest?) So it was that my cousin found herself in Argentina at age sixteen, brought to Buenos Aires by her mother, trying to find her own place in the world.

Thinking to make contact with her grandfather's cousin, she found the name Samuel Loader in the telephone book.

I rang and rang, Maria-Elena wrote; When someone finally answered they said he had died the year before and his family had changed address. (His family? This is something I observed with more than a little interest!)

Year after year she had checked the directory in case another Loader came to light, but nothing, no one. The only entry was Maria-Elena's own, listed five times because she and her husband – a doctor – owned various properties in her name. She and Julio Cesar Bustamanate had two sons, Julio Jr then twenty-four and a lawyer, and Pablo, a student of political science, described as being very, very proud of his British ancestry.

In 1986 (the year I left for Japan) Maria-Elena had visited England, returning with a handful of earth from that green and pleasant (but deeply unhappy) land as a treasured memento. Unfortunately, her lack of English had precluded any attempt to try and make contact with anyone, a situation with which I now fully empathise.

Anyway she concluded, I was only in London, and I knew my grandfather came from Liverpool.

So did mine. And here I am now, checking him out. Checking out the likelihood of a second family now made more than a fanciful possibility by Maria-Elena's letter.

The routes we pass along into the city of Buenos Aires are a succession of snapshots in sharp relief, yet as soon as I try to convey such images to memory, they instantly dissolve one into another. The main impression concentrates into a single long main thoroughfare, with sporadic bursts of life and colour as we pass through shopping areas, but off which at some final point we turn and turn and turn again, with streets and sidewalks displaying ever-increasing urban poverty.

It is something of a relief when we draw up in front of a house and there is something concrete, solid and in good repair to look at. Maria-Elena bustles out and rings the bell in a white-painted wall marked 3472 beside a pale-blue painted door with decorative Art Deco echoes in the narrow vertical glass panel. But this is not the door that opens: it belongs to the house next door.

Her own home is fronted by a head-high fence, but designed for security rather than decoration. Painted white, the gate is simply an extension of the same design, with a brass handle and lock. Behind, to the left, vegetation runs rampant – palm trees, and bougainvillea ready to spring into flower; to the right, a path that runs along the side of a single floor, to the door into the two-storey house and a garage at the back.

Along this path now hurries a man in (I guess) his early sixties, of average height with greying hair, a pleasant worried face and glasses, carrying a little too much weight for the best of health, and wearing a white doctor's coat. Also an Indian-looking woman with jet black hair caught back in a bun, wearing a turquoise nylon overall, and a smile that makes up for the lack of sunshine. Jangling an impressive-looking bunch of keys she shoos away a girl hanging around with no obvious intent, good, bad or otherwise, opens the gate, and there are Holas all round. Julio Sr kisses me shyly on both cheeks and intimates welcome. Marta, introduced as The Maid, clasps my hands in her own small brown palms, and then whips away my exceedingly heavy holdall from Pablo No. 2 with a strength and speed that astonishes for someone so diminutive.

The house is as low, dim and cool inside as it is alive (with greenery), bright (with white paint), and warm (red brickwork) without. It is Dr Bustamante's clinic or surgery that juts out at the front; it has its own entrance, nearer the gate. The ground floor is otherwise L-shaped and open-plan, with a huge TV and sofas around a coffee table in one corner, a dining area close to the back window (the table with a pile of English-Spanish dictionaries at the ready), and a separate kitchen area. There are nets at the windows and heavy vertically slatted blinds in dark wood. In one corner, near the front door, a staircase angles up and around. Like the floor it is tiled in marble.

Upstairs I am shown the bathroom, with the master bedroom alongside at the back. Across the landing, which has a heavy-framed metal door out onto a tiled verandah on top of the surgery, are two more bedrooms. The one at the back is used as an office, with bookshelves, and Pablo's computer.

The other, overlooking the verandah at the front, was Pablo's own (before he went to Madrid) and before that, his grandmother's. The bed is a semi-double, with the largest rosary – golf-ball sized wooden beads and a cross of equally generous proportions – ever seen by this non-Catholic, hanging above the bed head. There are sliding windows (which I am advised in sign language to keep locked at night), more nets, more heavy-duty blinds. A large wardrobe. And along the back wall, a shelf with books and CDs... I dissolve into mild hysterics when I see who is grinning a Welsh welcome from the top of the pile: Tom Jones.

So here I am, I dictate into my tape machine, which because I am recording over old music, has the disconcerting habit of lapsing into John Lennon's *Imagine*. Here I am, and I have a base. God bless Maria-Elena. God bless Julio Sr. God bless Marta. And God bless Pablo – all three of him (since I am now seeing double with exhaustion and culture shock): a holy trinity if ever there was one.

I received Pablo's first communication in mid-summer 1995. He was answering my letter of one year before, worried to have never received an answer to his mother's reply to my initial enquiry.

42

Quite rightly so too. As I wrote back on August first, my neglect of her was unforgivable. My excuse was that I had written to Andy, asking him to check out the story she had provided about her grandfather, because it did not tally with what I had been told. There was also the recurrence in London of my son Lee's heart problems after twenty years of good health and fitness. But in fact, I was fudging; and I could make no sense of my withdrawal at a point at which I should have been beside myself with excitement and planning to get on the next plane. As to leaving Maria-Elena dangling in suspense for a year, there could be no absolution.

And yet here I lie on Pablo's grandmother's bed, in Maria-Elena's home, forgiven if not shriven. I had not expected such unconditional generosity. I am filled with shame – and puzzlement.

Thanks to Pablo's perseverance four years previously, I had learned that he was twenty-two, with the middle name Ruy. His maternal grandmother, Ana Luisa Loader Cruzat (who had brought Maria-Elena from her native Chile) lived with the family.

My mother answered you by airmail, he wrote, But we never got an answer, so we imagined (it) never reached you. That wouldn't be surprising with our mail system. Now I'll tell you what I know of my family history...

According to Pablo's version of family lore, his great-grandfather Charles was born August 14, 1879. He had ten brothers and sisters – *ten?* And was a soldier in some African colony. After he left the army, he took a trip around the world and reached Chile in 1906. He went on traveling, returning to settle in around 1915 with a contract to work at the embassy (British, presumably). Also he had a cousin in Buenos Aires with whom later he used to correspond: my grandfather, Sam.

Charles married in Chile, had twelve children – *twelve!* – five boys and seven girls, and died at age seventy-five. As well as keeping in touch with two of his sisters back in England, Anne and Alice, there was also a cousin on his mother's side, one Vincent Price. It was some time after

Maria-Elena and her mother moved to Argentina that they learned Sam had gone to Uruguay, where he had died aged seventy-four.

It turned out to be a minor miracle that Maria-Elena had received one of my letters, picked up by the concierge of one of the properties owned jointly with her husband. (The others disappeared without a trace.)

With that profoundly apologetic letter of August 1995 I sent photocopies of all the relevant photos and documents I could find, coming up to date with my own family.

This bundle was received with great pleasure, read a postcard from Pablo showing the city at night from the sea front and dated July 1996: My family and I enjoyed it a lot!

Having replied, it seemed safe to assume that correspondence was properly underway. But no. Another year elapsed, and now it was Maria Elena's turn to apologise.

Awful things had happened (she wrote), which only increased my indolence. It seemed that she and her husband had been through some terrible crisis, as yet unresolved. She was trying to start again, standing by his side, and just hoping it would be worthwhile: Only time will tell.

Pablo had intimated at trouble earlier in the year on the back of a postcard of the Rio de la Plata, taken with an infra-red camera, the developed areas of Montevideo and Buenos Aires to each side of the river clearly visible, and numerous tributaries feeding the main flow from the south.

Family troubles are better here, he scribed in small careful capital letters: My brother Julio is getting married on 6 July. Try to understand this house is in shock and revolution. But we never forget you. Will you come here some day? It would be wonderful.

In the same envelope was another card, this time a wedding invitation. Crafted from white plastic, with seed pearls and a gold cord, it was cut and the edges teased to resemble cutwork embroidery. A beautiful piece of work made all the more precious on hearing that Maria-Elena's mother had made it by hand – a Spanish tradition.

The request inside – *Participan a Uds. El enlace de sus hijos Paula and Julio* – provided the perfect opportunity to visit. But the timing was bad: my son was ill again with heart trouble; the cutting-edge high-tech procedure of the previous year had backfired. So it was back again to London that summer, for the surgeon to try again.

Perhaps everyone in Buenos Aires gave up on me for a few months after my failure to show at such an auspicious occasion; most probably they were just too busy. But with Lee recovered and seemingly stable, touch wood, there was yet another minor miracle: thrown onto the garbage tip in Hayama that following spring, a plate (only slightly chipped) depicting a cruise liner in picture-perfect weather. On the back: O.S.K Line, ARGENTINA MARU – BRASIL MARU and, underneath the maker's mark, the name Noritake (a famed producer of fine porcelain) and the registration Nippon Toki Kaisha (Japan Ceramics Company) 1939.[8]

I was being nudged again.

I am reading all this family correspondence under one of those ceiling fans found in tropical climes that whip the air in circles: *whap, whap, whap.* My first impression of the interior of the house was less than positive, but already I can see the error of my ways; it's just that I'm not used to such heavy furniture and dark furnishings, nor living with guns and knives as practical decoration. (They are on the walls, everywhere.) True, my uncle had a gun room in Forneth House, in Scotland, but those weapons were intended for shooting game, which is bad enough, but most certainly not people.

There are other things. But they must wait, because I can hardly keep my eyes open…

Very sensibly, Maria-Elena awakens me two hours later. She wants to run me up to Caseros (not Casa, Casa, as misheard) to show me the station, and introduce me to the place where I can send e-mails and make international phone calls. (Pablo's computer is ancient and if Maria-Elena thinks it unreliable, who am I to argue.) So we sally forth onto Lisandro de la Torre, named after a Socialist senator who shot himself in the head in Congress over a corruption scandal, and almost immediately I fall into a pothole crossing the road.

Despite signs of grinding poverty, I like Caseros. With nearly half a million inhabitants, it heads the district of Tres de Febrero, named after its important place in Argentine history. The Battle of Caseros was fought here on February 3, 1852, forcing Buenos Aires to join the provincial confederation. General Justo Jose de Urquiza gave General Juan Manuel de Rosas a severe drumming, so bringing the nation of Argentina together for the first time under one system of legalisation.

Today Caseros is a volatile mix of fading middle class and unemployed, with many trapped in the mindless criminality that accompanies ignorance, impoverishment and lack of hope. But this is not clear as such as we make our through a maze of small side-streets to the main road of San Martin (named after Argentina's topper-most hero of all times, of whom more later) and speed towards what appears to be the city centre. Yet there are no superstores here, only small local shops and cafes, clustered this side of the railway line and a station that bears a startling similarity to Walthamstow Central, my local in northeast London. I feel remarkably at home, enjoying a store stocked with buttons and ribbons, lining up a camera shop for film processing, and planning where to eat breakfast tomorrow.

The Telefonica place is run by a woman who tells customers which booth to use for calls, and orders malingerers off the computers. A very beautiful native man with long dark hair turns every so often to acknowledge my presence but seems unwilling to budge. When in his own time he does finally relinquish his seat, it is to inform me gravely that he has good friends in Islington, North London. Three youths giggle hearing us speak English. One points to his chest and taking a deep breath proclaims proudly, We hooligans! At which everyone erupts into laughter.

I get the message. The atmosphere, while not unfriendly, puts me in my place. Well, that's fine by me. I e-mail my husband (Akii) and Buffy, then phone my mother who has recently reached microwave stage in her own technical proficiency. Walking back (it's a good fifteen minute hike along a dusty, noisy thoroughfare) I realise Caseros is nothing like Walthamstow (how could it be?) but reminds me more of Manila, where in 1988 large parts of the Philippine capital resembled a rubble and litter-bestrewn war zone. There is the same sense of incompleteness, as if things have begun to deteriorate even before being properly completed. (A signature of the Marco reign; Imelda was squandering all the loot assigned for social development on designer shoes).

Across the road from her home, Maria Elena waves me into a small hardware store and introduces me to the blond woman behind the counter who, I am told, teaches English. I am unable to grasp how much English Rosita can actually speak and I never get to see her again anyway, except to wave to her in the early morning when she waters and sweeps the broken pavement in front of her shop with a kind of gritty pride. But it is clear what my cousin is up to: she is showing me off and at the same time trying to make me feel at home.

The smartly dressed young man hanging around outside 3472 turns out to be a smaller, nattier version of Pablo; his older brother, Julio (nicknamed Julito to distinguish him from his father). He tells me in excellent English thank goodness that he works in the legal department of a bank in the centre of the city, and that together with his wife Paula (who speaks only Spanish) and one year-old son Santiago (who says nothing at all but can still make his demands clearly known) has come to say hello.

We all sit down to dinner, which consists of two types of pizza brought in from outside. One is so thick and soft it is surely made with polenta, but proves to be cheese and onions baked on top of bread. This and a more regular type with tomato sauce we wash down with a sweet red wine brought in (oddly, I think) from Julio Sr's surgery.

It's only 9 p.m. but I'm in bed, physically exhausted but my brain racing.

Searching for something to read to take my mind off the immediate future, the only title in English I can find on Pablo's shelves is a thick paperback: Austrian journalist Gitta Sereny's investigation into the mindset of Albert Speer, who as Hitler's right-hand man denied to the end any direct responsibility for Germany's Final Solution. Hardly the stuff of light holiday reading, but maybe providing some insights – regarding the nature of blindsiding – into a country that provided a safe haven to both Jews and Nazis during and after 1945.

Just as the world pictures Japan as a conflicted culture of geisha, Mt Fuji, raw fish, cherry blossom, rice wine and robots, run by an army of grey-suited salary men, so too there are stereotypical images of Argentina: *pampa*, *gaucho*, tango, beef and Nazis. Maybe Ms Sereny and her epic investigation, *Albert Speer: His Battle With Truth*, will help me get to grips with the historical reality that is Argentina: a country that a century ago was the sixth richest in the world, but in 1999 is among the poorest, struggling to come to terms with some of the dirtiest wars dished out against any form of opposition by oligarchic opportunists and military juntas in-between.

Also there is the matter of distance. Argentina is a long way from anywhere – even other parts of Argentina. And I recall the first four references to the country that caught my eye in 1991, clipped at random from newspapers and magazines: the rise of the country's first allegedly democratically-elected president, Carlos Saul Menem; a crusade by the Christian evangelist Billy Graham due to be broadcast to twenty countries in Latin America and the Carribean; an ink pact between Argentina and Brazil to prohibit the non-peaceful use of nuclear technology; and a short item from the December issue of the *Guardian Weekly* concerning the family of the deceased British publisher Robert Maxwell: it seems that the oldest of his seven surviving children, Philip, a physicist living in north London, made an early decision not to work for Dad. After a bitter argument, he left for Argentina, *To get as far away from my father as possible*.

Is this why I am here, still trying to escape my own demons? Is this why my grandfather came here, to escape his own? It's time I started finding out, in this city's El Centro.

# CHAPTER 4

# EL CENTRO

**NOVEMBER 2, 1999**

I'm on the train, and what a train! Built like a tank and having seen infinitely better days, it trundles, clanks and shudders towards the city centre with as many passengers hanging off the outside as inside. It's only 8 a.m. and I'm on my way, my stomach lined with tea (boiled with milk), cream crackers and a mozzarella-style cheese sliced from a lump the size of my head. Maria-Elena, it appears, is on a diet!

People are very quiet; many appear semi-conscious, as if drugged. But that's not why. Nor is it like the amazing ability of the Japanese to catnap on demand. No, this locked down state appears to be lodged in some deep depression, relieved only by the stream of hawkers that peddle wares from carriage to carriage – a relief to me at least, because no one else takes a blind bit of notice.

The first time it occurs I sit to attention, unable to believe the quiet dignity and poise of the middle-aged man who on entering the carriage dips his head courteously and launches into a seriously impassioned spiel to sell a set of cheap plastic pens, five for less than one peso, as pegged to the dollar in 1981. He selects, at random, several passengers to inspect the products in close up, and when no one bites, thanks us stoically for our time and attention and moves on. No sooner is the door closed behind him than he is replaced by another vendor at the other end of the coach – what turns out to be an endless procession, systematically working the train with each salesperson giving their compatriots just enough space and time to make a decent sales pitch.

Batteries, chocolate bars, religious pictures, lottery tickets, puzzle books, tissues, and all manner of junk items beg our indulgence and custom throughout the forty minute journey, as our train runs parallel to (but inland from) the Rio de la Plata, heading for the city centre. In Japan such things are given away as promotional freebies; here they are the stuff of basic survival, which makes me think.

Did my grandfather ever have to live such a hand-to-mouth existence? With such a privileged, nay exalted background, I doubt it. Little is known of his earliest days – at what age he returned to Liverpool from Montevideo, and where he spent his formative years. Or indeed when he first spent any length of time in Argentina. All I know is gleaned from letters and paper memorabilia, and additional information – such as my grandparents' wedding certificate – dug up by Andy four years ago from Liverpool's well-ordered archives.

On 17 April 1909, in St James''s Parish Church, West Derby (the County of Lancaster as it was then) and described as a General Merchant, aged twenty-eight, of 137 Moscow Drive, Samuel married Sarah Stroyan, twenty-six, said to be of No Profession. She was given away – like a promotional freebie – by her father, Gilbert Stroyan, a draper, living at 19 Rocky Lane. Witnesses included two of Sam's sisters, Florence and Beatrice, and Sarah's brother, Alexander.

There followed, to my mind, a period of great confusion. Number 136 Moscow Drive was both home and a company address until 1917 or so, when an office was opened at 44 Dale Street. Mrs Sarah Loader (my grandmother) was registered nearby at 19 Craigburn Road, Old Swan; but in 1926 Arthur Ernest Loader (one of William's sons; the earnest book-keeper, remember him?) moved in. Within three years the house was in the name of his widow, Margaret.

Since there is no mention of my grandmother between 1926 to 1934, it can be safely assumed Sarah was moved to Las Piedras (*piedra* is Spanish for stone, or jewel), with her good fortune: Catherine Mary (born 1910); my father, Samuel Robert, the year after, then Edward (Barney) and finally Elizabeth (Betty).

Las Piedras was a large detached property in Thomas Lane, Broad Green (a largely leafy undeveloped area in those days, so accurately named). It lay just around the corner from Knotty Ash (made both famous and infamous by the comedian Ken Dodd who was done over by the taxman in the early 1990s for hiding the golden eggs of his earnings under the bed, but luckily managed to save his bacon). Here the Loaders lived in considerable comfort, with my father and his siblings much enjoying the steam trains that ran along the bottom of the garden – Railway Children indeed. Yet their father is noticeably absent from the few family pictures of that period; where was he?

For clues I have only to turn to the contents of his attaché case. In 1914, for instance, he was home and, in the impending shadow of the Great War, had joined the Corps of Special Constables in the city. In a letter dated May 24 of that year from Liverpool's Central Police Office, he was appointed Chief Inspector: in charge of G Division, having the supervision of 5 Inspectors, 25 Sergeants, 214 Patrol Constables and 186 Reservists. An official photograph shows him seated in the centre as the most top-ranking of this gallant band; his straight back, lean confidence, moustache and jug-handle ears make him easily distinguishable.

Yet what is this? A document dated 1916, with the address San Martin 254, and the phone number Florida 269-273, listing 5 *Toros Shorthorn bulls, Importados a n/Consignacion por Los Senores, Samuel T. Loader & Co.* (The first ever shorthorn to be imported into the country to improve cattle stocks had arrived sixty-eight years previously.) But Samuel Turner had died in Liverpool in 1899. Who was running the company in Buenos Aires?

Not my grandfather, it would appear, because in August 1919, following the end of the First World War, Special Chief Inspector Loader was given permission by the Honourable Superintendent of Special Constables, Hatton Garden, for a six month absence of leave, with all good wishes for a speedy and prosperous trip. Speedy indeed, because two photographs dated October show him relaxed in a Mango Grove in Rio. But which *rio*, where? In Spanish the word simply means river; no more, no less. Or is there some connection here with those Loaders found in consular records in London, born in Brazil, also in the late 1800s?

In 1925 (my father would have been fourteen, suggesting he spent most of his early childhood in Old Swan), Sam resigned from the special force once and for all. The next we hear, he's back in South America, addressing postcards to his children at Las Piedras. *Dear little girl,* he writes to Catherine (she would have been fifteen, and since she grew to near six foot, was surely a late developer): *I am staying in a hotel at the end of this bridge. Hope you are all well, love Father.* Not exactly lavish in description but as always, it's the thought that counts.

There are other photos: an ostrich (of all the funny-looking things, but interesting as a metaphor); a rooftop view of Curacao (an island off Venezuela) built in Dutch style; oil refineries; a favourite bathing place; oil palm plantations. Also postcards, some unused: a native man hanging out in a hammock; a robed priest holding up a cross and pontificating before a crowd of indigenous people (shades of the film *The Mission*); the Kongingin Emma pontoon bridge in Curacao; and an oil well on fire at La Nova, Maracaibo, the second largest city in Venezuela after Caracas.

*I am fit but rather sad at the prospect of being away from you all,* he wrote to Catherine on March 3, 1927. While again absent from Liverpool, the Trade review of the Liverpool Chamber of Commerce returns a poem submitted for possible publication on the subject of failure. Was it fear that pushed him to clip it out of some magazine? Some sense of foreboding? Did he simply regard it as encouragement to himself as much as others? Or maybe he simply regarded the author, Edmund Vance Cook (1866–1932) as a Jolly Good Poet. (I do hope not.)

*Failure*

*What is failure? It's only a spur*
*To a man who received it right,*
*And makes the spirit within him stir*
*To go in once more and fight.*
*If you have never failed, it's an even guess*
*You never have won a high success.*
*What is a miss? It's a practice shot*
*Which we often must make to enter*
*The list of those who can hit the spot*
*Of the bull's eye in the centre.*
*If you have never sent your bullet wide,*
*You have never put a mark inside.*
*What is a knock-down? A count of ten,*
*Which a man may take for a rest;*
*It will give him the chance to come up again,*
*And do his particular best.*
*If you've never been bumped in rattling go,*
*You never have come to the scratch, I know.*

February the following year, still in (or back in) Venezuela, he sends a card to his wife (nicknamed Sal) showing a projected view of Maracaibo, addressing her as *Dear old girl* and saying he's awaiting orders to sail. (Home, presumably.) Barney gets a picture of a main street devastated by a fire, signed *Daddy*. Catherine is told he's off to Colombia very soon. Baby Betty gets – rather unsuitably some might think – a photo of an oil gusher, called La Rosa. Did she cry a lot, perhaps?

From April through to October though, he is in Colombia, either working for or having close links with the Tropical Oil Company. Photos show a small dapper dark-haired and moustachioed chap identified on the back as Mr Price seated, standing, and on horseback. Could this be the Vincent Price that Charles Loader used to write to? Was he another member of my grandmother's family? Or could the name be purely coincidental? So many puzzlements one could go crazy...

There are more postcards, showing local views of Barranca Bermeja in northeastern Colombia, a South American cowboy town if ever there was one, ruled over by the Planta Electrica y de Hiuelo, the Tropical Oil Company's electric and ice-making plant – shades of Paul Theroux's novel community in *The Mosquito Coast*. (In those days it would have taken a good week to travel upriver from Barranquilla, located on the delta of the La Magdelena river on the Carribean coast, with many a detour by road and even rail.) Most touching of all, there are exterior and interior shots of the Foreign Bachelor's House #675, El Centro. Sam's room. Sam's chair. His hat hanging on a peg. The family photo gallery on the wall beside his bed.

In October, Louise Paterson, Secretary to the Ladies Auxiliary, was writing to thank him for all his hard work as President of the International Club: *We will miss it very much... Hoping you have a pleasant journey.* To which the new President and Committee contributed their own flowery tribute: *Your splendid cooperation, always graciously given, has been of the greatest assistance.*

Whatever he had been doing there, Sam was going home. After which there is no first-hand information to be had on any other long-distance expat adventuring (since everyone involved is now dead) until the mid-1930s, when something happens.

I am standing under trees in the Plaza de St Martin, listening to a tiny bird streaming such an unexpected powerhouse of song that I am thrilled to the marrow and tears fill my eyes. Sadder still that this strange blend of joy and sorrow must be tempered by commercial cynicism: the broad flight of steps to my right (the top half of the park being on a distinct slope – a rarity in this part of the city) is marked as being not unconditionally funded by American Express.

At the top of the stairway, twenty-five stone plaques are arranged in a semi-circle, flanked by flags and each bearing twenty-five names. The first to be so commemorated is Juan Raul Serradori; the last, Cristobal Lopez. Two of six hundred and twenty-five mostly young Argentines who were sacrificed in April 1982 to the personal ambitions of two political leaders desperate to maintain power: President Leopoldo Galiteria (a lieutenant general who had led a successful junta the previous December) and British Prime Minister Margaret Thatcher. *A los Caidos...* (To the Fallen) reads the official stone, as unveiled by Presidente Menem on December 24, 1990.

I feel a tremendous surge of shame. Shame because the first thing that comes to mind as I stand before the memorial and bow my head, is that the so-called Falklands war was a travesty. A despicable charade, that in combination with the miner's strike of the winter of 1984, made good enough reason in itself to take a break from British politics and try life elsewhere. Argentina has been calling the islands Malvinas since 1698, when they were so-named by French sailors. Heavens, I wise up; I must remember not to refer to them by that other F appellation if the subject ever comes up, otherwise I might find myself in hot water.

I'm standing above the monument on a terrace designed (if I understand the sign correctly) to offer a representational view of the Theatre of Operations in the South Atlantic. The park slopes away through a delicate mist of spring green towards the British Tower and Retiro Station, built in the heady years between 1890-1930 – Argentina's economic heyday – to (respectively) chime out time in the style of London's Big Ben, and connect Buenos Aires with the furthest reaches of the country to the north and west.

Turning to see a fountain splashing a little way uphill, I head over to where a historical plaque depicts a large mansion, captioned as *Regimento Banaderos a Caballo, March 16, 1812.* A statue of General Jose St Martin, Argentina's Maximum Hero (such quaint wording) seated astride a horse and waving a sabre, offers a quote from the man himself. As I leaf haplessly through my phrasebook for a close approximation to a translation, a newly emergent sun scatters a fine spray of rainbows at my feet, and a posh dog parades past wearing a nappy.

The whole area is fascinating, providing an excellent introduction to the city's early fits and starts.

When the first known European explorers tried to come ashore, they found the coast inhospitable and the indigenous population unfriendly. Juan Diaz de Solis (who with such a name can only have been Spanish) found landing anywhere along the marshy shoreline a terrible trial, and then got eaten by cannibals for his trouble. That was in 1515. Five years later, the Portuguese navigator Ferdinand Magellan nosed his fleet of five vessels around the estuary; soon enough, unimpressed, he set his bearings southwards to find the strait that would bear his name

Settlement was attempted in 1526 by the Venetian explorer, Sebastien Cabot. It was he, in the service of Spain, who named the delta (larger than the combined land masses of Holland and Belgium) Rio de la Plata, after imagined silver deposits. As soon as it was confirmed that there were no known ancient civilizations to loot, as in central America, largely because the land was not lode-rich in precious ores – the only commodities understood by the Spanish court – the trial community fell apart.

In 1535, Pedro de Mendoza landed to reconnoitre the site, naming it Puerto del Santa Maria de los Buenos Aires. Again there was a strong local resistance and by 1541, the invaders were forced into retreat. But instead of heading out to sea, Mendoza took the remnants of his party upriver, sneaking past hostiles to where the delta forked to become the Parana and the Paraguay rivers. Choosing the former, he sailed right up to the Paraguayan border of today (an extraordinary journey in itself), stopping at a range of small hills and naming the new colony Asuncion. Although conquistadors began penetrating the south over the Andes from Peru in 1543, Asuncion was the first permanent colony in the east of what is now Argentina, and remained so for the next twenty years.

From this time on, the region was mired in bloody struggles between the Spanish and indigenous population. It was not until 1580 that under the leadership of Juan de Garay, settlers felt secure enough to start putting down roots in Santa Maria, which quickly dropped the saintly title it didn't deserve and settled for having Good Air (Buenos Aires). Thereafter it sank into a languorously corrupt state until the late eighteenth century, serving as a seaport for the illicit trading of African slaves and Peruvian silver with Brazil by Portuguese merchants.

From its earliest period of development San Martin and its environs was a residential area with strong commercial overtones. Some four centuries later it would link Plaza Mayor to Retiro Station through Barrio Recio. In the meantime, towards the end of the seventeenth century, a Governor Robles built the pictured country house on this very spot, naming it El Retiro. Prior to being demolished in 1818, it was rented by the Royal Company of Guinea for housing slaves.

This is an important piece of information, because an African-American friend in Japan has asked me to keep a sharp look out for black faces. It is thought that nearly one million slaves passed through Buenos Aires between 1563 and 1776. Where are their ancestors now, George wants to know. Here is my first clue.

From 1744, the area was known as San Jose and in the nineteenth century earned the nickname Stone Pavement City. It was completely covered in stone flagging, most probably to assist those flocking to see the bullfights in the Plaza de Toros in Barrio Retiro. (I look about, trying to imagine the roar of the crowd, the stench of fear, blood, sweat and excitement – the hustle and bustle and click-clacking of hooves and feet on the paving, the clink-clank of shackles and the weeping and wailing of Africans snatched from far-distant homes, weak with exhaustion and terror.)

During British invasions of 1806 and 1807, this gentle slope and its environs witnessed fierce struggles towards conquering and defending the city. In honour of those actions, it was named Campo de la Gloria. It was renamed Campo de la Marte after military activities carried out during the creation of the Regimiento de Granaderos da Caballos in 1812, as led by General St Martin. Going down in history as the liberator of Argentina, Chile and Peru from Spanish rule, the plaza was named in his honour in 1878, the centennial of his birth.

On the far side of the park is the immediately recognisable Kavanagh Building, built in 1936. Art Deco in style and 199 metres high, it was in its time the tallest building in the world constructed from reinforced concrete. I love it; still soaring above surrounding buildings with a certain constructivist grandeur, it looks not dissimilar to an up-sized pile of gigantic white plastic Lego.

The Palacio San Martin on this side of the park is something else. A private residence until 1936, my grandfather may well have caught the end of the family's removals and even witnessed the Foreign Ministry making it ready for ceremonial occasions. Designed by Alejandro Kristopherson for Mercedes Castellanos de Anchorena and her children (I want her exotic name as well as her extraordinary home), it consisted of three separate residences connected to a central hall – unusual enough in itself but also an eclectic blend of French Academia and Bourbon style.

Wow, I breathe into my tape recorder, if this is in any way typical of the range of architecture this city has to offer, I love it already. At which point a professional dog walker passes by with seven superb pedigree specimens on a tangle of leads, all trying to cock a leg or poo at the same time; ranging in size from a miniature dachshund to an Afghan hound, the sight is pretty comical. Still laughing, I bend down to study – in utter astonishment, I have to say – the most extraordinary botanical droppings ever seen. They are all around and under my feet, ranging from a foot long to over a metre, twisting naturally and covered in spines.[9] But the tree from which they have fallen is lost in the spreading branches of those all around. A decision is made and I stuff three specimens into my backpack. These are coming back for identification, whatever the rules of quarantine.

Already it is after lunch, and I am expensively fed and watered: *noquis fiorenti* (6.50 pesos), followed by a *cafe doble* (3.40), courtesy of Cafe Plaza on Avenide Santa Fe. (Spanish, I have decided – at this level at least – is a doddle.) Also I have maps and a wodge of literature, courtesy of Informacion Turistica, which as in Japan (and maybe everywhere else in the developed world these days, since standardisation seems the convenient but dumbing rule) is indicated with a small *i*. It took ages to find (largely because I was being a dimwit and too easily distracted) so the seating was welcome, as was advice with regards traveling to Chile, the Iguaz Falls, Asuncion, Corrientes and Rosario. All are possible, I am told; I just need time and money. Time is an especially precious commodity because this country is huge. On a map, traveling from Buenos Aires to Rosario may look as short a run as say, London to Oxford, but believe me it's most definitely not.

I wander, working my way back towards Retiro. Already I understand how the main thoroughfares are laid out, like the spines of a fan, radiating from the port area and shoreline and shooting straight as an arrow out into the *pampa*. Could the route San Martin that passes through Caseros start here in El Centro? It certainly makes sense.

Quite by accident I find myself in the British Arts Centre at 1334 Suipacha, Capital Federale. Is this anything to do with the British Council, I wonder, remembering what author Miranda France had to say about this particular institution in her book, *Bad Times in Buenos Aires*. She found the staff snooty to the point of rudeness, and said so. Which cannot be said of the British Council in Tokyo, in which I have – and have had – some extremely warm and helpful friends. Ian, Jenny and Emma in particular, take a bow.

In the foyer, two young men with their feet up on the information desk smile and nod, and almost immediately I feel I have fallen into a time warp. Peter Sellers is showing at the Cine La Mascara until December. Quality English drama is being advertised by the Actor's Repertory Theatre: *The Fall of the House of Usher*, by Edgar Allen Poe, commemorating the 150th anniversary of the writer's death on October 7, 1849. The poster offers a quotation designed to raise goose pimples: *Through the pale door, a hideous throng rush out forever and laugh... but smile no more!*

Also the equally spell-binding sell: discover Poe's grotesque and spine-chilling world of symbolic and spine-chilling madness.

To bring visitors back into the real world, there's an ad for Thames Valley University – study for a Master of Arts in English Language Teaching; English at the Cambridge Centre; also Professional English Business courses: then the enlightenment that this place is called AACI (Association Argentina del Cultura Inglese) and nothing to do with the British Council at all. It is 4 p.m., Argentine time, and four hours ahead a TV is showing the weather in Europe. It is a dark, wintry evening in London. There are floods in France.

Very happy to be here and not there, and in search of a particular museum, I begin – despite the fact that my feet are already beginning to hurt – what I assume will be a relaxing stroll up Avenida Libertador. (This wide thoroughfare – an illusion heightened by vistas of flat open parkland to the right and a conspicuous lack of people and traffic – runs the El Centro side of Retiro, following the coastline and the rail tracks and then heading off at a tangent who knows where.

My idea is to walk to Palermo, the next station on the line back to Caseros, because as I could see earlier from the train, it has an especially pretty park, and (as I learn later) more practicing psychiatrists to the square kilometre than any other part of the city. But as rain begins to fall, I wonder if it's such a good idea. I'm tired, overwhelmed by size, space and under-population. Yet the inducements to continue are strong – amazing monuments, colossal buildings, gigantic trees of ancient lineage, at this point connected by paths scattered with shards of broken pottery that paint dazzlingly impressionistic colour combinations: green and blue ceramics on red earth littered with mauve and yellow flowers, for example.

I pass unseen somewhere to my left, the Cemeterio de Recoleta, where Maria Eva Duarte de Peron is enshrined if not entombed. At the Biblioteca Nationale, a retrospective commemorating one of Argentina's most controversial literary icons, the magical realist Jorge Luis Borges (born 1899 and only recently deceased) entices. A little further on a monument is being raised to Evita.[10] It doesn't say when it will be finished, and peering in between the plastic walls erected all around I see only some kind of high-ranking cleric moulded in concrete offering a blessing. Whatever the grand design, it's most certainly happening; the noise is incredible. If you need a landmark, the memorial is right alongside An Olde English red telephone box. (On the other side of the road, the National Museum de Belles Artes is showing exhibitions of Paul Klee, European architecture, and pre-Columbian artefacts.)

At Libertador 1850, in front of the National Automobile Club of Argentina, two guys are wrestling with a wheel. At the Museo National de Artes Orientale, there is a show of African art. I cross a road called after Sanchez de Bustamante, once the president of Mexico, I believe; also a family name well known in downtown Caseros! The very next street is Billinghurst, which is somehow just so redolent of fishy Middle England that I laugh out loud. This provokes a girl approaching to ask me for a light to change her mind.

Libertador has changed personality once again, flanked by the beauty that comes only with the extreme affluence of old money – ornately decorative private houses and apartment blocks wrapped around by sweeping ornamental balconies and carefully orchestrated swathes of flowering vines. Next to the Volvo showroom, an elderly man is being lifted into an ambulance. Lucky him, I think in a moment of unsympathetic weakness; I'd do almost anything to be carried the rest of the way.

The address I am looking for – the Jose Hernandez Museum of Popular Argentinean Motifs at 2373 – is next to the Korean Embassy, spelled Corea. Yet despite my guidebook stating that it is open Monday through Friday, it's closed. Disbelieving and furious – I am now very damp and have walked an extraordinarily long way – I stomp back across the road and seek solace in the *Confiteria Dandy*, where I am given Perrier water as a service; in Japan I pay 600 yen for a small bottle. The tea bag is labelled Green Hills, and there is a biscuity thing with the caramel spread Dulche du Leche on the top.[11] As if this is not blissful enough, the waiters wear matching waistcoats and bow ties in a tartan check of beige, blue and a paler shade of the same, with a neatly folded towel laid across the shoulder, just so.

Determined now to see Argentina's idea of a Japanese garden, I march on, rejuvenated. But I'm once again distracted, this time by a statue of a generously endowed Greek god in close proximity to an even more massive sculpture: a bull with nuts the size of footballs. Ahead I can see a huge square, another grandiose fountain dead centre. Overhead seagulls are wheeling and calling, reminding that I am near the sea. And it's raining – warm rain and not unpleasant, but insistent. (Every time I go into a tea or coffee shop – *confiteria* – it stops; every time I come out, it starts again.) The Japanese garden? I'm too late: closed.

At Libertador 3300, I turn left along Avenida Sarmiento, past the zoological gardens. Steely skies now bucketing down, I give up at any attempt to stay dry. A hamburger joint called Titanicale titillates – well, semi-amuses. I note also that the construction industry builds with wooden scaffolding, in the same way that Hong Kong uses bamboo; there really is nothing quite like it, seeing a high rise going up without its usual protective metal jacket.

On Plaza Italia I pause and take breath, huddling under the roof of a bus stop. I'm trembling, breathing really hard. Time to call it a day, I decide, and turn right towards Palermo Station, just in time to catch the rush hour. The park is sodden, and I haven't seen a single sign for a psychiatrist, despite the area's nickname: Villa Freud.[12] Nor have I caught any glimpse of my grandfather, in body or spirit; indeed I haven't had much time to think about him even. But I have paved the way to tracking him down, and that after all is the purpose of the exercise.

I get all the way back to Caseros and manage to remember the route along St Martin to within a few blocks of Maria-Elena's home. It is at this point that I realise I'm lost, unable to recall which street to turn down and where to go from here. Nor can I remember her address or phone number, and my address book is on the bedside table; being a Filofax it's heavy and I didn't want to risk losing it.

Shit, I think. Help.

CHAPTER 5

# HELP

NOVEMBER 2, 1999 CONTINUED

The staff in the pizzeria, adjoining the garage on the corner are very sweet. They sit me down with a coffee, try unsuccessfully to find a *medico* Bustamante in the local telephone book and then, seeing the look on my face, scurry off to make a second cup. While they are busy percolating (and presumably wondering what the hell to do with me next) I turn out my pockets and bag and, among the accumulated clutter find Julito's portable phone number scribbled on a bill for a double Queen-sized duvet and cover, as purchased in Toronto and by now on the high seas bound for Japan.

While waiting for him to come and pick me up (his muffled hoots of laughter down the line making me feel unbelievably stupid), I sort through the debris: receipts, notes of currency exchange, ticket stubs, a scribbled note from Buffy telling me how to take the streetcar to University, and other bits and pieces relating to Canada go into one pile; three booklets in another – *The Bulletin (Le Boletin), Naturalement Argentina* (a tourist guide and map in Spanish only) and *Buenos Aires Day & Night – The Most Complete BA Guide, With Everything a Tourist Needs in Order to Enjoy the City.* Also paper napkins from *confiterias* and restaurants (because they always give the name and address in full), and a bunch of business cards picked up at random: Bansai – a leather factory (but sounding vaguely Japanese); sushi bar Morizone (which could be Italian) and Restaurant Japones Kitayama (no room for misunderstanding here). Also Aldo

Sessa, specialising in art books; Eguiguren, in Arte de Hispanoamerica (including silver *gaucho* gear and colonial artefacts); and several ads for tango shows and studios.

With time to spare, I begin re-reading my copy of the *Buenos Aires Herald*, which originally – like *The Japan Times* (for which I write) – was designed to meet the needs of the far from home English-speaking ex-pat community. The front page leader (with only a slightly bigger space than *Bloody Hostage Drama*) reads *Uruguayan Elections – Runoff Race Begins*. It seems the political map of Uruguay may be changing dramatically after one hundred and sixty years of shared power between the Colorado and Blanco Parties. Inside the paper on page 9, a Bloomberg Market Report advises that Argentine shares closed slightly higher yesterday, as the market awaits news of the budget and take-up under the new government of President-elect Fernando de la Rua.

I'm delighted to learn of such auspicious timing. Feeling as if I am on the brink of something new in national politics, I hope very much to be around for the safe delivery of a new era – on both sides of the Rio de la Plata!

I'm equally delighted – if rather more sheepishly so – to see Julito. Santiago, however, is less than happy. At that fractious age when toddlers are just beginning to feel suspicious of the wider world around, he had kicked me on first meeting in a very unchristian manner (and this despite being named after an apostle: Santiago is Spanish for St James), and now does so again, seeing me as a threat to his security. But that's okay I smile through my teeth, determined to show tolerance. All children go through phases, and this is one of them. Adults too.

We drive back to their apartment (small, neat, and one of those five addresses in Maria-Elena's name to which I wrote) to wait for Paula to come home; milkmaid pretty, with pale freckled skin and reddish-blonde hair, she's a qualified audiologist working part-time. In ringing his parents to explain my whereabouts, I can tell from her husband's style of delivery that he is enormously amused by my embarrassment.

But I also recognise there's no intended hurt in his teasing; Pablo banters in the same way, calling me Funny when he means he doesn't really understand the cultural context of a word or action, forever battling to gain the upper hand in any discussion in order to keep face. It's a form of machismo that is played as a game rather than to offend. Except, of course, by the very nature of its existence, it does.

Dropping me off at the house, Julito and Paula are very sweet, kissing me goodbye and saying, Well done! Wracked with conflicting emotions, I hear Maria-Elena talking on the phone, telling someone how Anhela Fantastico (Fantastic Angela!) found her way into the city and back, only to get lost six blocks from home. Ah well, I sigh, now they know not only how deeply intrepid I am, but also how deeply flawed. Going upstairs to fetch some dirty washing, I find it has disappeared. This serves to disturb further, because I don't want anyone doing it for me.

Supper is pizza again. Just as I'm wondering if Maria-Elena ever cooks (and also whether it be would construed as rude to head for bed so early – or rather to my room, to do more reading and plan the next day), visitors arrive. He is tall, well built, bearded; she glamorously well rounded, in a black sweater and slacks, her ears, neck and wrists agleam with gold. They both advance towards me, arms and cheeks extended. Fortunately I remember to move forward rather than back; in Japan no one touches, let alone embraces and kisses on first meeting. (Nor in Middle England, when I think about it.) But when you have been living away from such easy intimacy, the slightest gesture towards close physical contact with strangers can initially at least be very daunting.

We sit down. A bottle of wine is opened. And there is talk – conversation for nearly one hour about escalating crime. (I remember the headline in the newspaper, reporting on the escape of four prisoners and the ensuing mayhem caused in the Greater Buenos Aires town of Ville Galicia.)

Buenos Aires is becoming so dangerous, says Eva. I should never –

ever – come back on the train and then walk through Caseros after dark, she warns. Everyone agrees, shaking his or her head, looking mournful and disgusted.

Well-built-and-Bearded (I never do learn his name) picks up on his wife: The economy is dreadful, with no jobs, only more and more violence. Where will it end? At which point Eva brings out a small roll of fabric and with a professional flick of her wrist unrolls a display of necklaces, bracelets and rings across the surface of the dining room table.

She is jewellery designer, Maria-Elena announces proudly.

Oh dear. Those items I find remotely acceptable turn out to be Italian-made; her own designs leave me cold – an embarrassment in itself. Also I have to sidestep the fact, without causing even more offence, that gold is not really my bag. Old gold can be lovely, true. But new? Not in my book. (Tacky, vulgar, trashy, you name it.) Spreading my fingers, adorned with just three simple silver bands, I demonstrate that I am hardly into acquisition let alone investment. And then it hits me. I am being hit upon: Eva has come – been invited? – in the hope of making a sale. In my reluctance to buy, however, I place Maria-Elena in a quandary; in order to save face, she asks me to choose something as a present from her and Julio. Deeply furious to be put into such a position, I pick out a slender chain hung with tiny hearts (one of the cheapest items on view) and say it will make a perfect present for Buffy, whose birthday it is very soon.

From us, says Maria-Elena, beaming with relief; Tell her it's from her family in Argentina.

Escaped upstairs, cataloguing my day's work, another business card comes to light. Katmandu it reads, and then goes on to explain (confusingly) that it offers *The Best Indian Cuisine in Town*. Which reminds me – by an association that will eventually become clear – that I never did finish explaining how I came to be here in Caseros.

It was in February 1997 that Pablo wrote to say that he had spent his summer vacation at the family's apartment in Miramar (not far from

Mar del Plata, the most visited resort on the Argentine coast), and was studying hard for his final exam at university. He had an e-mail address. Also his brother-in-law – Paula's brother – was traveling around England, and planned to visit Liverpool.

Pablo wanted my husband to know that his best friend in Buenos Aires was 75 per cent Japanese and descended from the Onoda family, with a famous uncle now living in Brazil – the same individual who had been discovered in 1973 on a remote island in the Philippines, apparently unaware that the Pacific conflict had ended nearly three decades before. (Infamous more like, was Akii's comment: Old soldiers like Onoda were crazy; he most probably killed a lot of locals over the years, eluding imagined enemy.)

In December 1997 news came that Pablo's grandmother – Maria-Elena's mother – had died. Having been diagnosed with cancer, she succumbed to a heart attack three months later.

My mother is very shocked though time makes things easier, he wrote: But we're still sad, especially when the year is finishing and she is not at the table with us.

As so often is the way, bad news was softened by good: brother Julio would be a father in four months time. And Pablo was finished with university and working temporarily for local government. Again he pressed me to visit; again I realised I had missed the boat, left things too late. With Ana Luisa gone, I would now never have the chance to personally thank her for that beautifully crafted wedding invitation, or question her closely about the family.

By March the following year – 1998 – Maria-Elena was still grieving, visiting the grave weekly, crying a lot. Ana, Pablo informed me, was born on August 24, 1920 and died October 8, 1997. Continuing: My mother's father (Great-Uncle Charles) died two years ago. I met him on my first trip to Chile in 1993, but he never acknowledged his daughter and never gave her money.

Pablo then referred to a trip I had made to the Embassy of Chile in

Tokyo earlier that year. Waiting to interview Jaime Lagos, the Chilean Ambassador to Japan, an aide had found me a telephone directory to Santiago and its environs. He kindly made a photocopy of the Loaders listed, and excitedly I had written to Pablo, asking who they were.

All relatives, he informed me: And there are more! – I told you my grandmother (Ana) had eleven brothers and sisters, and one of these sisters, Adela, had eleven children of her own.

Crikey, I had thought. What have I started? Even more interestingly, where will it end? I had always wanted a large extended family, but so prolific, so extensive?

It was in this letter also that Pablo began to reveal his own passion for history, but it was not especially good news: I am fanatic, he wrote, Especially about the Second World War. I like bayonets, also helmets; I have ten now. I have several combat knives too, preferring the ones with a curved blade. Also I like to write poetry.

Ah the romanticism of death, I remember thinking; very Japanese. Indeed, in the next paragraph Pablo was waxing lyrical about Nippon: I would kill a person to get samurai armour.

Then just as passionately, a swift reversion to sentimentality: My girlfriend Maria Fernanda has a Japanese nickname, Kioka, which means nice perfume.

Moving on equally fast, a list of statistics: Argentina covered 2,776,889 square kilometres. Since Japan only covered 377,750 square kilometres, it would fit seven and a half times into Argentina. And since Japan is one third larger than the UK, well, work it out for yourself; maths never was my strong point! With over 126 million people squeezed into predominantly coastal areas, Japan had an average density of three hundred and thirty people per square kilometre. In Argentina, where one third of the entire population lives in Buenos Aires and its immediate environs, that figure is only twelve.

Yes, Pablo continued, We are only thirty-four million people here, with all weathers. Big mountains (Ocancagua in the Andes, which peaking at 5,959 metres puts Japan's 3,776 metre-high Fuji-san rather in the shade) The widest river in the world (as already described). The Iguaz falls (which makes Canada's Niagara resemble the model for a far grander plan). Plus deserts. Snow. *Pampa* (grassland). And tropical forests.

Pablo's first nephew – a kick boxer in the making perhaps? – was due in May: We expect he will have red hair, like my brother's wife, and also my father, when he was younger.

My mother, Pablo added, Wants you to visit here; you have a room when you come.

A fetching postcard of Chile's capital city, Santiago, backed by the Andes, followed soon after: This is a lovely city; you can ski in the mountains and the same day go to the beach in Valparaiso or Vina del Mar.

Searching for a job, Pablo was also, Investigating the process of transition to democracy.

In August he pleaded with me not to travel to Argentina by sea. I had been checking out the possibility – a romantic notion sorely tested (as it turned out) by the cost. Even by cargo and container vessels (many of which take a small number of paying passengers these days) we were talking thousands of pounds rather than the hundreds optimistically envisaged.

We want you alive, Pablo urged; Anyway your money will be more useful spent here in Argentina.[13]

Then came the news that Pablo and Fer (as Maria Fernanda was known) were planning a trip to Europe. Commencing January 1, 1999, they would spend forty-five days making the classic Grand Tour: Spain, France, Italy, Germany, Belgium, Holland and England, where (he wrote): I want to go to London, Stonehenge, Bath, Birmingham, Shrewsbury and Liverpool. Please be my bridge to kindred.

Which is why in February earlier this year, I came to be standing at the top of the escalator at Walthamstow Central, waiting for two young Argentines with backpacks. And there they were, exhausted but smiling as broadly as in photographs received over the years. I had wanted to help organise their trip, but they'd arrived ahead of me, and sad to say had met no one, talked with no one and come away from Liverpool in particular feeling more than a little disappointed. In fact it was a miracle I was in England at all; my ex-mother-in-law had died in Shropshire and Akii and I were over for the funeral.

Pablo and Fer stayed in Walthamstow while we travelled to Shrewsbury (a remarkable irony this, being from where John Loader – my great-great-grandfather – had first set out to populate the world). The evening of our return, with the night train to catch to Scotland, we brought a huge take-out curry for supper. Arriving back from a day of sightseeing, Pablo and Fer's eyes stood out on stalks.

What was it, they asked, wrinkling their noses in disbelief.

Curry, we chorused, equally incredulous. Curry, it appeared, was not on the Argentine menu. (Except that now, from the name card in my hand, I learn that it is, but in Nepalese guise.)

We have no Indians (as meaning from the Indian continent), Pablo had explained with a dismissive wave across the kitchen table. With regards to the country's indigenous population, he was equally casual: We killed them all.

There was another point of contention: Pablo had been on a buying spree in Europe, and it was not stuff that I wanted in my home. I tried to explain that I was investigating the possibility that my grandmother Sarah was Jewish, and even if she was not, it was totally against the grain to collect or house Nazi memorabilia. A very unhealthy preoccupation, I thought. But Pablo only laughed; he couldn't/wouldn't take me seriously. I requested him to stow his purchases in a locker at the station, but I doubt he ever did. Fer stayed only one more week, while he set about finding a language school in the West End for a month-long intensive English course.

I left him with Lee, who was initially cautious, but with whom Pablo eventually formed a close bond. Playing football every Sunday,

Lee reported, it was a wonder Pablo didn't get his head kicked in on more than one occasion. His curious brand of politics, idiosyncratic English and naivety concerning the racial mix and mores of a truly cosmopolitan culture, got him into more trouble than he ever realised. But he had a great time, arriving back in Buenos Aires with blue hair.

The next thing I knew was that he and Fer (herself a lawyer) had decided to go try their luck in Madrid for a year and study for their Masters'. Pablo wanted me to change my plans, put off my proposed trip by a further twelve months, because for one thing his parents did not speak English well (if at all), and he personally wanted to show me around. But for some reason suddenly, I couldn't wait.

I had enjoyed no direct contact with Maria-Elena from that time on. Pablo and Fer had left for Spain, and though I let them know my date and time of arrival by e-mail, I had no way of knowing for sure what would happen next, if anything. I had prepared myself to be independent, which is the way I have largely travelled before. And yet I chose to wear a skirt on the final leg from Toronto, which is a first! So maybe a part of me was expecting to be met...

My thoughts and emotions are becoming ever more convoluted. I'm grateful for the welcome, the comfort, the unconditional generosity and warmth. Isn't this what I always yearned for in a family? Yet Caseros is so downtown it's out of town – and I do enough commuting already, in to Tokyo! Also I get the feeling that Maria-Elena thinks I'm on vacation; she is talking of shopping and long lunches, while I am set on museums and tramping the streets of central Buenos Aires in the hope of hearing the echo of a cane tip-tapping, or a glimpse of Sam's spirited shadow turning a corner.

As I reload my camera, I hear a series of sharp reports outside. An engine back firing, I think sleepily, yet for some reason break out in goose bumps, as if someone is walking over my grave.

## NOVEMBER 3, 1999

As I descend into the kitchen the next morning, Maria-Elena asks if I heard the gunshots last night.

See, she says, determined to prove the point, We told you it was dangerous!

With this, I have a sudden mental picture of Pablo rushing out of the house to seek revenge with a loaded Colt 45 – this following on from an incident during which his mother (who was climbing out her car after a trip to the bank) was attacked for her handbag by four men on two motorbikes. He had told me of this incident in London and I'd quite forgotten until now. Little wonder the gates at the front of the house are always locked, the outside walls topped with spikes. Fear breeds panic breeds neurosis.

I watch Marta busy with dishes, while Maria-Elena opens an outside door into a huge garage, with a large stone sink (good for washing undies, I make a mental note) and half a dozen cages of twittering songbirds, then another door onto the back patio. For the first time I notice that this exterior space is occupied by another massive bougainvillea, a loquat or biwa tree (a specimen of which I have in my own garden in Japan), the largest free-growing rubber plant ever seen, more twittering caged birds, and one very large German Shepherd.

Pablo had told me about his dog – Krieger, being German for warrior. But he had neglected to consider that in disappearing off to Madrid, Krieger would be on his own. The animal's persistent and often quite demented barking arises from being no longer walked on any regular basis, or groomed. You would think the neighbours would complain; I most certainly would – to the RSPCA, or its Argentine equivalent, assuming there is one – if only I knew how.

Marta fascinates. I want to know her background, her ancestry. So Maria-Elena makes enquiries on my behalf. Marta is Gurani Indian, her mother from Corrientes, south of Paraguay, and her father, Paraguayan. She still speaks her native language, Gurani, especially to her father.

Twenty years in Buenos Aires – and having dispensed with two husbands, the last of whom was much younger – she has spent the last five in service to the good doctor and his wife. Once she won the lottery, but feeling as if she had landed on cloud nine went through her winnings in no time at all (much to her employer's obvious disgust). Maria-Elena professes some astonishment in my interest. Which makes me feel equally astonished: that she is not.

Swinging my backpack onto my shoulder, Maria-Elena reaches for a jacket and her handbag. I come with you, she announces, and does just that.

It's a taxi to the station, of course, from the mini-cab service on the corner. The car is held together with string, as are the driver's trousers; as big as a sumo wrestler but far less than halfway to being as fit, he drives in his vest, sweaty flab a-rippling. Maria-Elena insists on paying, and while only a couple of pesos, this is not the point. Does she not realise I'm on a budget? May be not. The assumption by many when they hear I live in Japan is that I must be rich. In fact, being freelance, I am in a continual state of financial embarrassment, always juggling like crazy to stay one step ahead of disaster. Also my priorities are different; my only extravagance is traveling – keeping up with friends and family and seeing something of the world.

With my cousin all dressed up and me totally dressed down, we begin our day with a quick inspection of Estacion Retiro, a station that needs money spent on it big-time. It is not just grimy, but filthy with neglect, which best reflects its tragedy. Every part of this grand edifice (for no amount of soot, dirt and decay can hide its original glory) was transported from England by ship and assembled onsite. (The best view of its impressive French-style frontage is from the Torre de los Ingles or British Tower on the Fuerza Aerea Argentina – Argentine Air Force Square – a large flat open grassed space in front of the station.) Within fifty years of being named capital of the newly independent and unified Argentina in 1862, Buenos Aires had grown into a colossus. This was when the British invested in the country big-time, especially in building railroads.

Nowhere is this better exemplified than inside the museum alongside the station. (I spotted the sign yesterday.) Maria-Elena is surprised by its existence and while initially not showing much enthusiasm, quickly becomes engrossed. The two floors – one an interesting walkway which provides views of the lower level – are stuffed with, well, stuff: plans, models (one of Station Once, pronounced *on-chay*, built in 1907; another of the barque Don Benito, by the Short Brothers of England), maps, floor-to ceiling shelves of leather-bound books lettered in gold, telephones dating from 1895 (my ancestors may even have used them), and train fittings. A beautiful little Victorian-style ceramic toilet in decorative blue and white, *Made on Merseyside*, inspires a quick note: must tell Andy.

Most engrossing of all are the photographs. The earliest, dated 1857, records covered wagons crossing the *pampa* to lay rail tracks. A shot of Libertador (sadly not dated) shows a single track laid on earth and the station just a wooden shack. One huge engine is captioned as being made by the North British Locomotive Company in Glasgow. But the picture that most entrances is of the train El Libertador (1902) that travelled between Buenos Aires and Mendoza, just this side of the Andes. Everything about the interior is superbly crafted and impeccably furnished: marquetry that dazzles, with the design of veneered walls, tables and chairs echoed in the upholstery. Swagged velvet drapes, generously endowed tassels, exquisite lighting. As for the chairs, they are (progressively) on pivots, so that you could watch the world passing by or turn them inwards for a well-earned rest from that self-same pastime.

I had read in *Fodor's 92 South America* (which shows just how long I have been considering this trip) that it was still possible to make the journey. All the named trains, it reports – El Libertador to Mendoza, Rayo del Siol to Cordoba, and the Expreso Lagos des Sur to Bariloche – are diesel-drawn. Many carry uniformed hostesses, are laid with wall-to-wall carpeting, with a movie car in the back. A movie car? Could anything be more splendid, I remember thinking at the time, only to have learned at the Tourist Office yesterday that such luxuries are a thing of the past. Not only are there no more hostesses or on-board film shows but, saddest of all, there are hardly any trains.

It is, we agree with a couple of friendly visitors, a terrible shame. Balding, in a dark overcoat, Roberto teaches English. He says he'd be thrilled if I could find the time to call by and say hello to his students – it's not often they get the chance to meet someone from England, let alone an Englishwoman living in Japan! His friend Pedro is a psychiatrist, but so twitchy and lacking in confidence that he himself appears much in need of help. He too asks me to visit – his apartment! How kind, I say. Most definitely not, I think. But I will consider Roberto's invitation, taking down his phone number at Escuela Angel Gallardo on Ayacucho y Quintana; it might be fun.

I suggest we take a bus to the museum that proved closed the day before. But Maria-Elena has already hailed a cab. Over there, she points half way down Avenida Liberatador, hurtling along a lot faster than I was moving less than twenty-four hours earlier: Julio and Pablo's university, she informs with pride – such a vast institution for the teaching of law that I cannot understand how I missed it. We get as far as the front door of the Museo de Motivos Argentinos Jose Hernadez, and see through the glass a small army mopping the floor. Again, closed.

Being decanted by yet another taxi (I have given up the fight) into the heart of the business district on Avenida San Martin – I was right, the street begins here and for all I know ends in the Andes – is an exciting moment. Because this is where my grandfather set up shop when he arrived back in Buenos Aires in the 1930s.

To explain this event we must backtrack a little. But only as far as the first letter dated 1936 that Samuel Charles Edward sent my father in Birmingham. It may not have been the first, of course, but it is the first that has survived. It took some time to determine the address from which it had been mailed, Sam's writing being even more characterful than my own, but eventually I worked it out: Lee & Co, 44 The Temple, Dale Street, Liverpool.

*My dear Bob,* he scribes, *I was certainly pleased to get your letter, as I could not understand why you did not reply to the note I sent you through Betty. I have not had a reply from her. I have seen Mother three or four times & Catherine once accidentally, but they were not warm in their greeting. They apparently do not want me at 33, and that's that! Off down to London, it is in the lap of the gods whether I am to go out again at the end of next month.*

That was written on May 9. To recap, Bob was my father's nickname, derived from Robert; not wanting to be known as Samuel Jr, he left his first name to his father.

Two days later, from 61 Deane Road, Fairfield (an address quite unknown to me but according to Andy opposite Wavertree Park and but a stone's throw from the Anfield area much frequented by Loaders) he was asking my father to find him a B&B in Birmingham for 3/6d. *I might be able to go to Coventry from there to the Triumph Motor Cycle Company, who have given me their Agency for Uruguay and Argentina.* He signs off, *Cheerio, Father,* and then adds a PS: *I'm going to London on the overnight bus.*

By the end of the month, he was fixed to sail on June 20, planning to stay in Uruguay and Buenos Aires for a month, as he might be wanted back in Britain for September 22. (There are no indications as to why or by whom.) *I am going out on my own this time, owing to the uncertainly of trade, & I have been able to book a passage to investigate the opportunities of opening a business as their representative.* Sam wants to know how my father is fixed; *there will be plenty of work for <u>two</u>, but slender enumeration until I get established.* He also asks for a timetable for buses running to Coventry, and how much such a journey would cost.

There are numerous points here. He is living like a gypsy. He is frantically trying to re-establish himself in terms of creating business abroad. He is strapped for cash. And only my father is readily communicating with him. What on earth is going on?

A letter dated October 22 announces that having arrived back from South America on the third, he had just spent two weeks in Glasgow. (Staying with his older sister Florence, I can safely assume.) Planning to come to Coventry, he again asks my father to find him cheap lodgings, *no matter how lowly*. (I love that.)

Days later he is castigating my father for not replying quickly enough for now his plans are all changed. *Here's Your Indy Dog!* he scrawls as a postscript, perhaps not wanting to alienate the one member of the family still speaking to him. *He says prospects for you and me in B/A are good!* And *Spanish, keep good.* That my father spoke Spanish came as a surprise; where and when did he learn it? As for the Indy Dog, don't ask. Japan is so riddled in quaint and unfathomable superstitions that nothing surprises.

There is a second letter from The Temple in Liverpool dated October 31. It appears that having gone to his office (or rather that of Lee & Son) on Dale Street, ahead of leaving for South America, Sam had found a communication awaiting from the Director of the International Petroleum Company in Toronto, Canada, to whom he had written asking about possible placements for my father.

(Toronto, I think; where Buffy lives. Astonishing how the coincidences – the threads of an increasingly intricate web – are beginning to interweave. )

Sam reports that this head honcho (Myers by name) says, *As regards Bob, I regret that I have nothing to do with the placing of men in Venezuela – I hesitate to recommend anyone. However, if you care to do so, you might like to write to Mr Henry Linam, General Manager, The Creole Oil Company of Venezuela, Caripito, Monogas, giving my name as a reference.* Myers then instructs Sam to tell my father to send a letter immediately, via Trinidad.

My grandfather is gleeful: *The Dog's working already!* he chortles.

In a subsequent communication, apologising to my father that mail had not been passed on by Mr Lee, Sam drafts the letter he believes his son should write to this introduction in Eastern Venezuela.

It was more family lore that as a young man my father spent time in South America, but now I had some details. At age nineteen, he had spent sixteen months with the Tropical Oil Company, working in the accounting office and directly responsible for transport. Having signed a two-year contract, confirming his appointment as an Office Assistant for $150 (US currency) a month, dated April 24, 1930, he had sailed the middle of the following month, boarding in Liverpool and bound for Barranca–Bermeja in northeastern Columbia. (Founded in 1536, the city is today home to the largest petroleum refinery in the country, owned by the state company Ecopetrol.) Only one thing puzzled: he claimed he was very keen on mechanical engineering, which is not how I remembered him at all. Was this wishful thinking on Sam's part, or a tongue-in-cheek tweak to help him get the job?

Further proof of my father's adventuring was his new passport, valid until May 1, 1935. Also a 1931 membership card to the Tropical Golf Club, certifying S. R. Loader as A *Member of Good Standing*. Two photos, from what looks like an induction ceremony, show my father standing and sitting among a gathering of men who would not look out of place in the Nazi party. Short oiled hair with side partings and equally nasty little clipped moustaches seem to be the fashion, though I'm glad to say my father fails completely in this department. Instead he stands tall, spare and clean-shaven, his dark wavy hair refusing orders.

He was *let out* (meaning fired) in July 1931, due to a *general curtailment of staff*. As to his homecoming I have only my mother's story to fall back on: Your father had begun taking Articles to become a solicitor (with Lee & Son most like), but then That Man (grandpa, Sam) came and waved the prospect of South America under his nose again. He ruined Bob's life!

For a young man, the attraction was surely irresistible. But when my father returned to England, even after his first excursion, the chance of a decent profession was gone. The ongoing ramifications of America's Great Depression that had hit Wall Street in 1929 and the build up to a second world war in Europe made sure of that.

Even now, my mother is bitter. Which is thoughtless and a waste of energy, really, because without that sequence of events – indeed if he had done one small thing differently – she would never have met him, and my sister Bridget and I would never have been born.

By the end of 1936, the Old Man was still beetling about Britain, keeping busy. (My father never did send that letter to Henry Linam, choosing instead to move around the Midlands doing God knows what: selling ice-cream, working as a door-to-door salesman, living in cheap boarding houses, surviving as best he could, my mother says. I have no doubt that he stayed in the area to be near her. Still it must have been a horrible life.)

Sam in the meantime had been making contracts all over the place, with Singers in Coventry, the *Bicycle Boys* (Triumph?), Fieldings in Stoke-on-Trent, the Campbell Tile Company (where he signed as their Agency for white ceramic tiles) and others. Also he had the selling rights for Holford cycles in Brazil as well as Uruguay and Argentina: *they're selling a lot*. He sent my father 3/9d for Christmas, with an extra 1/6d for cigarettes. For his part: *I wrote to your Mother and she sent me a few shillings to help me along. I wish I could get together again. I wrote nice letters, hoping for approach, but she said little. However, it WILL all come right. Your loving Father.*

It was surely not a very happy Christmas. Nor indeed a happy New Year because my father is increasingly elusive and all-too-often my grandfather's letters are returned *Whereabouts Unknown*, as if X marks the spot.

CHAPTER 6

# X MARKS THE SPOT

**NOVEMBER 3,1999 CONTINUED**

All things considered, Maria Elena and I have a lovely day. San Martin is a hustle and bustle kind of place – London's City and New York's Wall Street in miniature. After a lot of asking around in commercial banks, all flummoxed by the sight of Japanese currency, we are eventually directed to Puente Hnos at Sarmiento 444. Here all the clerks are male, utterly charming in an aloof laid-back kind of way, and do not even blink when I push small fans of 10,000 yen bank notes across the counter to be changed into peso.

We meet Julito for lunch, who makes his way towards us through the midday crowds looking every inch the suave little legal beagle he undoubtedly is. Where shall we go, he wonders. He and his mother huddle, then agree: Madero... And hail a taxi. (What is it with this family. Does no one ever walk?) Just as the renovated Albert Dock in Liverpool is that city's new pride and joy, so it is with Puerto Madero for Buenos Aires. This has never been a coastal town as such – there are no beaches and the estuary is continually being dredged. It was once a flourishing port, of course, but as its importance diminished, docks along the front fell into disuse and dereliction. It was a similar story in Liverpool.[14]

However, on September 9, 1998, for the first time in twenty-six years, a new neighbourhood – the forty-seventh – was added to the map of Buenos Aires. It may have the fewest residents (just a few hundred) and the least number of streets, but the 170 hectares of prime real estate make it the most expensive area in the city, as well as (ostensibly) the safest. At its heart, block after block of renovated red-brick warehouses face water: imported from Manchester, lock, stock and barrel; first opened for business in 1899, closed ten years later, now recycled. It's the largest investment made in the city in the last five years, and while it can be easily argued that the money could have been far better spent elsewhere, Julito says there is a pride among *portenos* (as the inhabitants of Buenos Aires are called) that did not exist before.

We eat an Italian-style lunch in one of Port Madero's forty restaurants, and I am urged to marvel at the other multifarious delights of the development: a complex of eight cinemas, the Argentine Catholic University (UCA), a church, hundreds of offices and apartments, a yacht club – and the Frigate Sarmiento which, after being a school for naval officer cadets for thirty-seven years and making thirty-nine trips around the world, is now moored as a floating museum at Dock 7.

Julito – who tells me there are two hundred different commercial banks in Argentina, most with representation in the capital – shows little inclination to return to work; he's so laid back it's worrying. (The writer V.S. Naipaul once wrote that the failure of Argentina is one of the mysteries of our time. If Julito's work ethic is standard, maybe there is no mystery?) I fear a tussle when I pick up the bill, but after an initially polite No, no, he leans back with a broad grin and spreads his hands: Okay, you win.

I do like him. (Despite our differences!)

Eventually we manage to push and shove him back to his office... Passing by, it should be noted (I have a professional interest here) the home of Argentina's leading newspaper, *La Nacion*, which as the name jingoistically implies, leans to the right. From San Martin we walk (just a couple of blocks, each measuring exactly 128 metres square and numbered American-style) past the classically Greek-style facade of the Catedral Metropolitana into the very heart of the old city. Again I feel as if I am on hallowed ground. But this is not the occasion to stop in time;

Maria-Elena is keen for me to see the Cabildo, on the west flank of Plaza de Mayo.

Built in 1711 in Spanish style – thick stone walls, worn red tiled floors, ponderously beautiful shutters and doors – the building served as an early seat of government, used by councillors of the Viceroy. (When Sam arrived back in 1937, it was still being used as government offices.) Today it has a museum at its heart, filled with heavyweight Spanish antiques of wood and iron and equally impressive canvasses, both in terms of size and subject. Battle pictures predominate – smoke, flames, flags, uniforms, blood and guts. Here are soldiers of the English infantry (1807–08) – regiments of the Hussars and Grenadier Guards in uniforms of blue and red, all looking very gung-ho; another depicts the night of July 2, 1807, with defenders still manning the guns and serious discussions underway; a third shows the surrender, with residents out on their balconies wondering what comes next and the British flag looking very dejected indeed.

For two hundred years, from 1536 to 1776, Buenos Aires survived as a colony of Peru, as ruled over by Spain, and by smuggling, largely silver and slaves. The Argentines resented Peruvian domination, and a strong anti-Lima separatist and increasingly nationalist movement developed. Anxious to control the situation, Madrid liberated Argentina from Peru, and established it as a new vice-royalty. It was called the Vice-Royalty of the Rio de la Plata, and Argentina became known as the United Provinces of the River Plate.

This situation did not last long. Like every other part of South America, Argentina was desperate for independence. British invasions of both Buenos Aires and Montevideo in 1807 and 1808 tried to relieve Spain of a small corner of its empire, and it was the ethnically mixed-blood Creole militias, not the forces of the viceroy, that fought off attacks. This gave them a taste for power over their own affairs – a privilege denied by the Crown to the Spanish American elite since the Conquest. In 1816, after two nationalist revolutions against the Spanish, the viceroy was thrown out.

In 1826, Juan Manuel de Rosas, who owned vast tracts of land in the province, was given full dictatorial powers by the Federal party, and was soon running the entire province like one enormous *estancia*. Nowadays most Argentines regard him as a madman and a killer, but at the time he was venerated as a champion of the underdogs – the native population, blacks and dispossessed – and an enemy of the sophisticated (used here in its original meaning of corrupted) elite of Buenos Aires.

In his second term of office, from 1835–1852, Rosas gave full rein to spies, death squads, all the trappings of state terror. Yet despite (or maybe because of) his bloodthirsty tactics – his *gaucho* troops (the cowboys of the *pampas*) were ordered to slit the throats of the enemy without compunction – he paved the way for the eventual unification of the country. Remember the Battle of Monte Caseros?

What intrigues most in the Cabildo are the maps. The oldest, dated 1709, is a hand-tinted drawing of Plaza Ciudad, the city being little more than a tight-knit community grouped around a central square – the one I am looking into right now, out of the window: Plaza de Mayo. Situated amid marshland, the buildings are ordered into blocks, with only a few major constructions (a fort, a canal). Another sketch, dated 1713, is a little more detailed, but not much. This was a tiny remote stronghold a long way from anywhere. (What is now Tokyo – then Edo – began in much the same way a century before, but with Shinto shrines and Buddhist temples in place of Christian churches.)

Declared a historical monument in 1933, the Cabildo is a fine strong cool building, (I like the fact that kids are allowed to run about, their laughter echoing around the cavernous spaces to mix with the songs of birds in the trees outside and sounds of passing traffic.) Simple in design, a terrace runs around the back, where a courtyard offers more splendid trees – some throwing flames, their thorny branches ending in clusters of bright vermillion flowers. The scene is further enlivened by a small craft market – leather, silver, trinkets – with soldiers in traditional uniform at the gate, chatting up the girls.

Pablo told me about these uniforms in one of his mailed history lessons. He had begun by explaining that *gauchos* were once partially attired courtesy of British industry: The *gaucho's* working tool was his knife, called a *facon*, made of intricately worked silver with a Sheffield blade; as for his trousers – copied by European fashion designers in the 1970s as *gaucho* pants – one style was made from Irish linen.

During the Crimean war of the 1850s, Pablo wrote, when Turkey was allied with Britain, English entrepreneurs had the idea to reproduce the trousers worn by Turkish soldiers: roomy but gathered at the ankle. At that time British trousers were tight-fitting, which were hardly comfortable or practical in combat. Hence, the now ubiquitous combat trousers. Huge sales were made to Buenos Aires (mainly through dumping); being sold at guaranteed low prices they became especially popular among the poor.

The same thing happened with the top hat, continued Pablo. In England, top hats were worn by both the aristocracy and the aspiring, but over-production again encouraged export to Buenos Aires, and soon rich and poor alike (the latter often lacking shoes) could be seen sporting the headgear. So popular did the style become that it was adopted (with a few alterations) in 1806 for the city's first defensive force, the Patricias Regiment. And here it is below me, one hundred and ninety-three years later, worn with aplomb and though reduced in height and adorned with a wine-red plume, not that much changed.

No sooner have I put away my camera than I am being whisked away to another museum: the National Historical Museum in the district known as San Telmo. Housed in a stunning 1850s villa, guarded by stone lions and faced with groups of highly polished brass plates in memory of this event or that person, its thirty rooms recreate the colonial passage through time. Much to my joy the first exhibit recalls the fact that there were people in this land before Europeans made it their own. There is a map (drawn up as if in haste and tacked away almost out of sight behind a door, but still a map) that shows which tribes occupied which parts of the lands between here and the Andes. Realising my tape has run out,

I take out my notebook, only to realise that Maria-Elena is hovering. Never mind, I think, I'll come back.

The slave trade is similarly hinted at. Where there are pictures with Africans portrayed, they are either maids and menservants (as in many of the pictures in London's National Portrait gallery), or shown letting off steam in their own communities. Again I feel I need more time and so allow Maria-Elena to whisk me through room after room of tableaux depicting transported European lifestyles and ranked waxworks of famous generals. She points out Jose San Martin's uniform on show, and I dutifully pause... for a micro-second.

We amble back down into El Centro, along cobbled streets divided by tram lines, past lovely twin-towered Catholic churches, a plaza where we stop for a cold drink, and what Maria Elena tells me is one of the oldest (and most certainly the smallest) houses extant in the city. Squat, painted white with dark bottle green details, with just one tiny door and the merest gesture of a window in thick stone walls dating from 1786, it has been a national monument since the year I was born. It is also famed for being the one-time residence of Esteban De Luca, Poeta y Soldado – a poet and a soldier. Seems he wrote Argentina's first national anthem, the Marcha Patriotica, which adds up.

As we travel back to Caseros, I wonder again where all those black faces had gone. Long before George had tried to impress upon me the existence of an African presence in Ireland before the Celts – that the name Moore, and indeed the very word moor derives from the moorish culture of North Africa... that one sultan employed 20,000 European slaves in his stables alone... and that in the eighth century, the Islamic-Spanish city of Cordoba enjoyed several miles of street lights while most of Europe lay in the uncivilised filth and shadows of the Dark Ages – I had clipped an article from the Washington Post. In August 1993, journalist Don Podesta was asking much the same thing of South America at large: why in cities like Buenos Aires where once blacks made up to 40 per cent of the population had their presence all but disappeared?

In the Argentina of 1836 (when Sarmiento was at his most politically active) Podesta estimated that out of the total population of 63,000, 15,000 were black. Today, out of the population of thirty-four million, only 4,000 are counted as black immigrants – largely descendants of the impoverished island nation of San Verde off the West Coast of Senegal and mostly arrived this century. The disappearance of Argentina's black population, Podesta continues, is one of the great historical mysteries in this part of the world.[15] There are hypotheses, of course: that African men were recruited in large numbers for wars against Spain, Brazil, Paraguay and local tribes, and many died. Following on from which black women turned to white men and those of mixed blood, with their lighter-skinned children more easily assimilated into white society.

But who knows. It is all very odd. I have been in Argentina three days and have yet to see a black face. A very different experience to, say passing through Sao Paulo, where the airport presented a startling cross-section of the genetic melting pot that is now Brazil. Maybe a black population is more visible there because slave trading was not outlawed in Brazil until 1888. Argentina had called a halt seventy-five years before, in 1813. But just as Podesta had no real answers, as of this moment, neither do I.

## NOVEMBER 4, 1999

The day once more dawns warm and fair and I am up and out as soon as I can thank Marta for ironing my knickers (my clothes found neatly folded on my pillow last night on return). I have never had my underwear ironed before, and try to explain to Marta that a) it is unnecessary and b) not part of her job. She (not understanding a word) simply smiles and pats my arm. I must be careful she does not start ironing that too.

My mission today is clear: check out some of the early addresses that my grandfather used in the early days of his exile. But first I buy my daily paper, and then I pop into the cafe near the station for a *cafe doble*, here costing only 1.60 peso! The owner, who looks Italian, offers a courteous bow; his assistant, appearing to have stepped out of the Amazonian jungle and into European clothing, offers a smile of the sweetest gravity. I sit happily by the window, under a faded portrait of Eva Peron (once and for always Argentina's topmost heroine) and read more about junta indictments as reported yesterday. The Spanish judge behind the arrest of former Chilean dictator Augusto Pinochet is charging Argentina's former military rulers with atrocities during the country's Dirty War.

Judge Baltasar Garzon has issued international warrants of arrest for ninety-eight military and police officers – including a dozen junta members – on charges of genocide, torture and terrorism during the country's most recent dictatorship of 1976–1983. Today the government is lashing back, saying Spain has no right to interfere in domestic matters. Our sovereignty is at stake, storms outgoing president, Carlos Menem.

My goodness, I think, as I buy my ticket and – after crossing the bridge to the far platform – wait for the train to take the strain. What a confusing and turbulent country this is.

I am standing on San Martin, walking down to the Plaza de Mayo, looking for No. 132. This was the address my grandfather gave my father in a letter written from Liverpool on February 25, 1937, in which he describes himself as being full of pep and keen to start pulling his fortunes around. *I am off on Saturday on the PHIDIAS.[16] If I make good I will send for you. Well, Sunny Boy, keep going strongly. I know you will make good & have great faith in you. Hasta la mas.* He then adds on the back that the envelope in which he is posting the note is courtesy of his colleague, Horacia Cook: *We have just been appointed Representatives for Garratt Co. (Export) of Glasgow, who did a good trade in whisky with B/A a few years ago and wants to get going again.*

But where No. 132 should be standing is a concrete box – a minimalist-looking financial institution with a green sign reading X Ban (for Banque X?). The buildings to either side (also banks – Amerique du Sud, Galicia, Provincia, as well as Boston and Citibank) are intact in their original architectural splendour, but not the one I am seeking. Unsure if I am reading the address correctly, I cross over and check with various doormen in other institutions. I even enter X Ban itself – and am quickly shown the door by a smooth be-suited security guard with dark glasses and an insistently firm hand.

Well, never mind. Although I feel an initial pang of disappointment, Sam was not at this address for long. Indeed by February 1938 he was in a different part of town altogether, working out of the offices of Duranona & Cia., Representaciones de Importacion, at Victoria 673. From here he writes tersely that my father's letter received on the *23rd ulto* was the first in over a year. *I did not get a* (Christmas or birthday) *card from you, but anyway it is natural I should be pleased to receive news from anyone when it is sent in the right spirit.*

The hurt is obvious. So too is the pride.

*I am finished with the love of money business* (he continues) *and if things are to come right, I shall be required to be approached in the future on an entirely different basis, especially if the things which have been said were meant. If they were not they have to be withdrawn in the proper way.*

He notes that my father has *sacked Mr Slater,* his boss, which, while a joke, suggests my father is unemployed again. Sam warns his son that he is going to say exactly what he thinks, to leave no-one guessing: *therefore do not take offence if I say anything out of order.*

*As regards Betty and Catherine, I know they have been influenced against me wrongly, so there I have nothing against them, only ignorance of facts. As regards Barney, I note, and shall always note when the 17th of February comes along. The day he cowardly, in a fit of temper, hit me on the nose causing my glasses to break my nose. The day of remembrance is next Thursday.*

Despite the dramatic revelation of such an incident, he moves crisply on to say that he is glad my father went home for Christmas: *I can assure you I was thinking of you all, as I am much more sensitive than most people. I hope they all sung Goodwill, and All Peace on Earth, etc. They have shown precious little of it to me. My family has been taken from me and I feel pretty bad about it all.*

He notes that his birthday is on the 26th (of January), not the 24th as perhaps my father had imagined. *I stood myself a special dinner, at one of the best restaurants.*

And then begins to rail bitterly again. *I am not one to let anyone down, and therefore with the same spirit expected to be stood by, but all the faith was in fancy religions, and not in me. I had faith in myself, and was determined not to take a step down, as I was pressed to do, for the sake of degrading other branches of the family.*

The intimations of financial failure and a fall from grace are obvious.[17]

The reference to fancy religions had brought me up sharp. Sam was referring, I realise now, to my grandmother's keen interest in anthroposophy. Although she was described on her marriage certificate as having no profession, I had always understood her to be an occupational therapist at Liverpool's Walton Hospital. (Unfortunately this is difficult to verify, due to the hospital's tangled history.) If she had enjoyed such a job before her marriage, she must surely have been on the very cutting edge of early therapeutic practices; if she had become proficient after hitching her fortunes to Sam, it would explain perhaps how she kept the family's head above water after showing him the door.

A strong woman with high principles (which apparently did not include forgiveness of a partner's failings as a provider, though there may of course have been more to it), she was drawn to the teachings of Rudolf Steiner, the German mystic and social philosopher. As to the root of Steiner's doctrines - and by implication therefore also my grandmother's own – these lie in the metaphysical musings of Helena Petrova Blavansky, born in Russia and after many world travels, nicknamed the Sphinx of the Nineteenth Century.

In 1877 (having reached North America) she published *Isis Unveiled*, containing an outline of teachings concerning cosmic and human evolution. (Nowadays it is seen as a preparatory sketch for a new belief system, as described in W.Q. Judge's book, *Ocean of Theosophy*: That ocean of knowledge which spreads from shore to shore of sentient beings... Embracing both the scientific and the religious, it's a scientific religion and a religious science.)

Blavansky's motives were as determined as they were idealistic: solely to bring about a universal Brotherhood, based on the essential divinity of Man. To this end she had invited interested parties to her rooms in New York on September 17, 1875, for a lecture on Egyptian antiquities and the magical sciences of Egyptian priests. So impressed was her audience that within twenty-four hours an association was formed for the Study and Elucidation of Occultism: The Theosophical Society.

The first meeting of the British branch of the Society[18] was held in Great Russell Street in the summer of 1878. By this time Blavansky had hooked up with the Hindu reformer Swami Dyanand Sarasvati, thinking the alliance to theosophy's advantage. In time, she grew disillusioned with Sarasvati and links weakened.

Still theosophy blossomed. Which is where Rudolf Steiner (1861-1925) comes into the picture. Originally the General Secretary for the German branch of the Society, his views of occultism began to differ from those of the group's leader, and he left – forced out some say – in 1912. Being a handsome charismatic individual, many followed him, including the entire German membership. Developing his own doctrinal ideology as Anthroposophy, he attempted to explain the world in spiritual terms, on a level of thinking independent of the senses.

The Anthroposophical Society of Great Britain[19] has no record of a group in Liverpool at the beginning of the twentieth century. But there was a branch of the Theosophical Society in the city, headed in 1924 by a Dr Duborg, with the address Islington 120. It may have been therefore that my grandmother came to anthroposophy via theosophy. She is shown by records in London to have been a paid-up member of the Liverpool branch of the Anthroposophical Society as later founded, and most certainly what she took on board there from its teachings and values was to rule her life – and the lives of her children (and indeed grandchildren!) – more than anyone can ever have foreseen. Sam was openly sceptical, which may not have helped plead his case when the financial going got rough. Neither theosophy nor anthroposophy claim to be religious dogmas as such, but when belief systems other than your own are seen as a threat to your immediate world, it is easy to see how they might be regarded as false or *fancy religions.*

It is a pity though that he was not more open and curious for, put simply, anthroposophy is about being aware of our humanity. And who possibly could be threatened by that?

Already I have a clearer picture of Sam the Man: Sam the Survivor, Sam the Self Absorbed, Sam the Sceptic. (He treats himself well, but then since he is all alone why shouldn't he: *I have spent what surplus money I have had traveling, seeing the country.* Lord, I think, my mother was right; he *is* just like me.) *A month ago I went up to the (Gran) Chaco with two friends by car, a run of a thousand miles through a country covered with maize, sunflowers and cotton. I got as far as Resistencia, and Corrientes, and then back to Restistencia... taken by the richest man up there, Dr Quijano, with whom I stayed the night.*

As a businessman, he desperately wants to be seen in a good light, as having fallen on his feet: *Friday afternoon I went out to a dairy farm and stayed there the night. This is owned by the father of one of the partners of this firm. (Duranona & Cia.) I am partner of the British section, rank the same as the other partners, and treated just the same.*

He is quite the snob and by choice a bit of a loner: *I have not set out to cultivate friends, that kind of thing is foreign to me, so if any one gets to know me they have to come very close, and be something out of the ordinary.*

He is emotional, deeply hurt, and angry enough to cast himself as the innocent victim while blaming just about everyone else: *I know perfectly well that when people know I am well on my feet, they will want to come under my wing, but that I will not have on any account , until I am perfectly certain that tranquillity has been reached in all sections of the family. The whole thing is a mad romp, and how people can live with such weights on their minds I am hopelessly at sea to explain. I have been ignored and thrown out, so to get things straight, I am prepared to wait and wait and wait.*

I love the description of the scandal back home as a Mad Romp, and consider it the alternative title for this similarly inclined adventure.

I also love the idea of Sam the Intrepid Traveller. Where was it I read that the Chaco tribe of the *pampa* believed in a female god named Kasogonaga, who hung from the sky creating humans? Lovely that.

One year later, my grandfather has headed notepaper with the address Avenida de Mayo 841, about as prestigious a location as you can get even today. It is a lovely wide (well, relatively wide) tree-lined boulevard of hotels, restaurants and *confiterias*, and second-hand bookshops, and I wander in a dream, savouring the thrill of finally coming face-to-face with Sam's past. The hotel at 841 is still there, but oh no… I don't believe it… 840 across the road (his business address in later years) is no more. The buildings to either side stand proud, but in between? A building site. Again X marks the spot.

With the afternoon sunshine turning from clear light to gold, there is time to check out one more address. Feeling as if fate is throwing me more than a few demolished bricks, I make my way diagonally across Plaza de Mayo, laid out with fountains and benches and herbaceous borders of bright scarlet and yellow (again clashing violently with the colour of the earth). I falter in front of the Casa Rosada (Pink House). For one thing, it is here that that the Madres de la Plaza de Mayo gather every Thursday, both to mourn their missing children (among the 30,000 estimated to have disappeared between 1976 and 1982), and to remind those inside of injustices still be to rectified.[20] (The plaza is also used by demonstrating grandmothers, who since 1977 have sought the return of grandchildren, abducted by officials from imprisoned pregnant daughters and given away to high-ranking officials.) I am brought to a startled halt because Argentina's national seat of executive power is boarded up for repainting;

but so that tourists do not miss out, I am treated to a same-size photo-montage of the surreal thing. Cleverly distracting, that.

Standing on Avenida Leandro N. Alem, I study a copy of a black and white photo postcard dated August 11, 1939 (written just weeks before the start of war in Europe), which shows a certain building with a certain window on the fifth floor marked in ink with an X, and the handwritten message: *my office here.* Writing to my father on August 18 – the arrival of a letter from England after months of silence taking Sam quite by surprise – he notes that he's busy settling into an office at 471, the Calvet Building, on the main road out of the city to the North.

As Andrew Graham-Yool – journalist and editor of the illustrious *Buenos Aires Herald* – relates in *Goodbye Buenos Aires* (a book based on his father's life story), the Old Calvet, as it was known to the English-speaking community, stood on the corner opposite the central post office. Six stories high, with a leaded roof and Parisian-style mansards, it was said to be quite a landmark in those days, both for ships offshore and landlubbers seeking sea legs. The basement was used for storing wine and it was said you could get drunk on the fumes alone. In 1930 however, when Douglas Noel Graham-Yool moved in, the top floors were rented out as private apartments, with a heavy turnover of guests. Being nine years behind, and several generations apart, it is unlikely he and Sam crossed paths, but being both British and keen to better their fortunes, you never know.

Sam came to the Old Calvet almost by accident. During his absence the previous year, when he had made a trip back to England, Duranona y Cia had fixed up one of his representations with a man he knew to be unsound. Indeed, just the month before writing, the individual concerned had reported that he could not carry on, having no funds.

So, Sam to the rescue: *I took charge, paid the draft and customs duties, and am now the importer. I have 75 cases* (of whisky) *to take up and will be ordering another 50 next week, as moving it along. Have decided to take the plunge and have my own offices, and have myself... fitted the place out as a private office or exhibition room, and have an Irak (sic) carpet, two leather lounge chairs, a bookcase, two typewriters, and a depot where I can store as many cases as I like. I am preparing for a campaign... arranging propaganda of various sorts.*

He does not understand why my father had not written to him at the Gran Hotel Hispano, Avenida de Mayo 841. (This could be because it is the first time he has mentioned this address in full.) Yet he reckons to have written from his quarters in the hotel many times, with no correspondence from anyone in Liverpool. *I get roundabout news now and then but nothing of importance. I have asked time and time again for Betty's address, and also your own, but no notice has been taken of my letters. When I was in B'ham* (the previous year) *I hunted for you, went to Daisy Street, but could not find you, so suppose you had left. Or was it Henry Street?*

For some reason my father's letter has unsettled him: *I had nasty dreams last night, in connection with the trouble that has arisen. I don't know what is going to happen in the future, but I am not through entirely, until I get letters asking me to return, without being bought. I will not make any money matter a condition of my returning, they must accept me as they turned me out, otherwise it is useless considering anything. I have wanted very badly to help Betty, but that was denied. Now it is all off as far as I am concerned.*

Being late afternoon, this normally heavy-duty road is exceptionally busy, and it takes some time to get my bearings. When I finally line up the buildings with those pictured on the card, one is missing: the Calvet Building is no more: this time, X really does mark the spot.[21] While the disappointment and upset is extreme, with the feeling that there has been a concerted effort to wipe all trace of Sam off the map in advance of my arrival, it's easy to rationalise in one way at least: if this was Tokyo, one historic building in a block would be a rarity, rather than the other way around. Really Buenos Aires is surviving remarkably well. Come to think of it, so am I. And after all – to quote Scarlett O'Hara in *Gone with the Wind* – tomorrow is another day.

CHAPTER 7

# TOMORROW IS ANOTHER DAY

**NOVEMBER 5, 1999**

Following in Sam's footsteps, I decide to counteract any despondency by giving myself a treat. Which is why by 10 a.m. I am at the Teatro Colon buying a ticket for the opera. Amazingly, there are only three seats left: two in the stalls and one up in the Gods (the topmost balcony). I blanche at the idea of denting my budget with a seat upfront, so the gods have it. Not that I mind at all. Theatrical vertigo has never been a problem; most of my experience of drama and dance has been from the cheapest seats, either on the back rows, or standing.

With my ticket secreted away, I roam the exterior of the building. Opened in 1907, it is quite a pile – the size of a city block, and emphasised as such by being painted a rather unfortunate shade of vomit. Modelled on the Paris Opera but the interior even more lavishly decorated, the TC – I hesitate to call it simply the Colon – boasts a stage (the biggest and most elaborate in the world when first constructed) that holds six hundred, with its own orchestra, chorus and corp de ballet and – an exciting prospect – regular tours for theatre buffs and architectural and interior design specialists. Maria-Elena and Julio are dismissive, both of its architectural merit and cultural value. To them it is simply a playground for the rich and any repairs a complete waste of money. And in many respects they are right. (Similar arguments have raged in London about the voracious financial appetite of the Royal Opera House in Covent Garden.) Still it seems to me that I cannot stay in Buenos Aires without this singular experience.

Jerry, who had found Maria-Elena listed in a local phonebook back in 1996, felt much the same way. I had asked for his advice and impressions in a vague last-minute attempt at preparations for my trip, and this is the gist of what he mailed on October 21, just ahead of the first leg of my own journey. According to his passport he entered Argentina on March 16, 1993, and stayed two weeks, mostly in Buenos Aires but with a trip to the pampa thrown in. He still has the Lonely Planet Guide used on his visit and had, believe it or not, marked the post office where he looked up the name Loader; the Telefonica/ENCOTEL office on Avenida Corrientes, very close to the pedestrianised shopping street. He failed to recommend his hotel, there being no air conditioning to combat the humidity of late summer. But he did think the city very beautiful, and very European.

Me too. As the days pass Buenos Aires becomes increasingly seductive.

Jerry had found it a great place for walking, just as I am doing now. He always felt safe (never having strayed far from the centre and most certainly not into neighbourhoods like Caseros!) but did remember a highly visible police presence. People stayed out very late, with streets still lively at three in the morning. The areas of San Telmo and La Boca were full of charm. As for the *portenos*, he found them stylish, very groomed; the women (a bit of a generalisation here) blonde, heavily made-up and stretched-looking. He had heard on the grapevine that Buenos Aires was the world capital of plastic surgery, and now could quite well believe it.

You must definitely go check out the Teatro Colon, he urged, describing a dance performance caught there as *the* highlight of his trip. And I ought not worry about lack of Spanish; most people seemed to have a few words of English, and more than a few were fluent. I am finding this to be true, but only in the centre of the city; in terms of traveling further afield and contributing to Maria-Elena's noisy and highly animated dialogues with taxi drivers, I am stumped, kicking myself for not being better prepared. True I had done a short course at Tokyo's Temple University Japan, but all that had done was waken me to the fact that as the only westerner and beginner in the class (everyone else being Japanese and at intermediate level), I had one mean advantage: since the few European languages with which I am familiar share roots in Latin and Greek, I might not be able to say very much, or indeed keep up much a conversation on the state of the world, but with regards reading, I thought I might be able to puzzle out the gist of a written phrase and sentence with a fair degree of accuracy.

At the back of the theatre, near the subway Tribulanes and across the road from the Instituto Libre, groups of students are gathered under trees on Plaza General Lavalle, carrying wedges of strapped books and chattering like vivacious magpies. School's out, it appears, and I glance at my watch: midday.

The front of the theatre (or is it the back?) faces what is alleged to be the widest street in the world; the famed Avenida 9 de Julio. (This owes its breadth to a singular design: a busy central thoroughfare flanked by strips of green and secondary parallel roads.) To my right, halfway along, in the centre of the Plaza de la Republica, stands the Obelisk, built in 1936 to a height of 65 metres and the designated heart of Avenida 9 de Julio. Sam would have just missed its symbolic unveiling, or maybe not?

Having stocked up on film at the first Fuji photographic centre seen in the city, I eat (more pizza) on the corner of Avenida 9 de Julio and Avenida de Mayo and then retrace my steps of the day before. I have made a decision: remembering Eva the Jeweller's words about not returning after dark: I'm going to stay in the city tonight, and try for a room in the hotel where Sam hung out.

In tune with my recent run of ill fortune, the Gran Hotel Hispano – which announces itself brightly enough with two highly polished brass plaques, one to each side of the narrow doorway – is full. This where he had a front room, fixed up with carpets bought by himself: *I have a balcony where I can sit in my deck chair, and watch the terrific traffic, and thousands of people go by. If I want anything at all, it is within a hundred yards or less.* All the conveniences then, and yet I can't stop thinking about the Old Man, claiming on the surface to be perfectly happy while admitting that it's tough to get going again, and in looking into the future seeing only a business trip back every two years or so, *with nothing really to stay for, even if I could. I have asked for letters from each one, but nobody writes.*

Excepting his eldest son, that is, and then only intermittently. In March 1938 Sam is complaining that my father is slow in sending ideas for representations. Business in Buenos Aires is good, having sold 8,000 bicycles and he expects this figure to reach 15,000 in the coming season. But it could be better, he grumbles. His departure to England has been delayed; he imagines leaving in early June: *a nice time to enjoy the summer. I would stay until the middle to end of August, to get back in September sometime.*

He thinks himself lucky to have joined Duranona & Cia, as it has brought him into contact with, *some of the best families in Argentina.* (Such a snob!) He has been invited to share a house with a cotton expert working with a major Liverpool and American firm: *a beautifully furnished place with a housekeeper who is a very good cook.* (In the manner of many such fancies this failed – that word again – to pan out; he stayed put.)

Also he was recently out at Tigre, along the river: *to a birthday party of an Old gentleman who has taken a fancy to me. His wife's mother was related to the patriot and martyr General Lavalle, who gave Argentina its independence. We had lunch under great trees a hundred years old in the quinta* (colonial estate) *of the old general, and afterwards tea in the house. I was honoured and felt higher than I have ever been in my life.*

He was hoping to make the trip back again in 1939, but with this new business, was feeling more tied. *But I shall make the effort, as I have my ticket already.* In the meantime, he was finding pleasant enough diversions, being a member of the Chamber of Commerce, and having joined the Tigre Boating Club for the summer to give himself something to do.

I am also pleasantly diverted: by being offered a room at 951, the Novel Hotel (the name pronounced more like the Peace Prize than a storybook), just a few doors down from the Gran Hotel Hispano. In a way I'm more pleased because this was where Sam was to move in later years. I am given (by the very friendly pony-tailed young man on the tiny front desk who whoops enthusiasm when presented with my story in a nutshell) a view over the street on the first floor for 38 pesos. While it may not be the same room, there being no mention in his correspondence of which floor or a specific room number, the heavy key for No. 8 is original (I asked) and when I fling open the white-painted wooden shutters with brass handles and locks, I look straight out onto – or rather into! – a tree. Of course, it would have grown enormously since he was here. There is hardly room to swing a cat on the balcony, though I guess a small chair could be wedged in sideways. As for the interior of the room, only the ceiling light appears anyway near original. For the rest, the decor is utilitarian and very 1970s. Nevertheless I am utterly charmed, feeling a sudden flutter of what can only be described as Extreme Happiness.

I lie on the bed and as my eyes roam every nook and crevice of the high but tiny room, enter that curious state that lies somewhere between meditation and sleep. As a child, I would regularly disengage from the physical world, float up from my body and push off from the walls and ceilings, even fly out the window and over the city and the fields beyond – a state I can only describe as blissful. Sadly I lost the ability as I grew into my teens. Forty years on, here I am, once again coming close. How strange. How wonderful. How...

When I wake, it is nearly four. I head towards Corrientes, in the general direction of the theatre, with no concrete plan in mind other than to find an internet cafe and send some e-mail. I am open to further

101

distractions and soon enough one presents itself with a bow and a flourish: three elderly men – dressed in dark suits and homburg hats that have undoubtedly put in some service over the years – playing live tango music on the sidewalk. There is quite a crowd, and quickly I understand why: they are brilliant, and I am charmed all over again.

This has to be close to the real thing – whatever the real thing is these days. The two musicians are seated, one playing *bandoneon* (the small accordion of German origin that is unique to the tango genre), the other, guitar. Backed by their well-honed harmony, the vocalist – a charismatic performer with a great sense of humour – is the crowd stopper, his voice sweeping the scales with well-honed emotion. At the end of one song, a man hovering in the background takes his place – the Tom Jones of the tango, I decide, for women in the crowd are near wetting themselves. Catching the voices, the music, the applause on tape, I only wish I could play it to you now.

Off Lavalle, still smiling, still humming, I see a sign: *Wordnet Internet Cafe*. And on entering a tiny plaza selling punk records and studded leather clothing (three decades too late, but doing a roaring trade), climb a flight of steps to the first floor. The young man in charge, with short curly hair and a wide infectious grin, sets me down and connects me to hotmail. (Now that is service; in most places they just leave you alone to get on with it) Alongside, a Chinese youth wearing glasses and a baseball cap is actively surfing, never breaking his attention for one obsessive microsecond.

I open my mailbox and see four messages: from my editor James at *The Japan Times* in Tokyo, from Akii to say he had tried to phone but not made much headway with Marta, one message from Buffy and another from… my cousin Alison in England, passed on from Hayama. Since this last bodes badly, I open it first. Yes, my uncle is very ill with pneumonia and Alison fears the worst. Shaken – Eric is ninety-four, and as my mother's and Jo's first cousin and sole remaining family member of their generation, he has been the mainstay of my family for as long as I can remember – I turn to Buffy, and find her near hysterical with fright and fury.

She and Ross had been having trouble with their landlady ever since the woman – a graphic designer, in her thirties, with a penchant for the Gothic – had bought the house and moved in above them. It was obvious that she wanted them out, in order either to raise the rent or extend her own territory, but instead of making herself clear and maybe coming to some kind of acceptable compromise, had instead waged a vindictive war of active dislike. Before driving me to the airport on October 30, Ross had found the lock on the front door loose, and (very sensibly I thought) reported this to the owner. She had banged her door in his face (I heard it slam) and later left the house, stalking past us, just as we were loading up, without a word.

It seems that the trouble suddenly involves a court order to get tenants of ten years evicted within twenty days, citing leaving the front door in a dangerous state, a dog that barks night and day, and turning the garden into an open sewer. This after putting a lot of time, effort and money into creating a comfortable home, with all the accumulated junk (and pets) this implies. Having dinner with Kevin one evening, just around the corner from the flat he had reluctantly been forced to buy, we had already been given ample proof of how difficult it was finding rented accommodation in Toronto. Buffy was beside herself: What are we going to do?

My girl is in trouble, which means that I am in trouble too. Heading for a Telefonica (most likely the very one that Jerry used six years before but suddenly this seems of little importance), I ring Canada. Buffy is at work but I talk with Ross, who while angry and distressed is relatively calm. They have already been to a lawyer who describes the case as "laughable". Offering to sign an affidavit concerning the incidents described, I am ready to swear that Ross advised his landlady of the door's condition, and that during the week I stayed, I never heard Nellie bark once inside the house or indeed out (except when lunged at by a mad Bull Pit terrier in the local Dog Park, which reduced us all to raising our voices). As for the garden being used as a canine convenience, Buffy ought surely be awarded a medal for community pooper scooping.

When I ring Alison it is to be told that Eric had died in his sleep just hours before.

I thought it was odd, she said: He always says goodnight when I leave him (in the nursing home) but last night he said goodbye.

I stand on Avenida Lavalle trembling. What do I do now? There is nothing I can do in Toronto. There is nothing I can do in England. Alison has promised to let me have details of the funeral, which, in line with Eric's wishes as a professed atheist will be simple and his ashes scattered. Yet still I feel as if I should be heading straight for the airport. I most certainly should not be going to the opera. And yet this is exactly what I do. As deaf to the heady tuning of instruments as I am blind to the extravagant beauty of the theatre, I am aware only that the interior is very dark and gloomy with dusty plush and aged gilt, and the domed ceiling above painted with a heavenly scene of cherubs and angels.

My grief concerning my uncle is astonishing even to myself. He had been ready to move on ever since his wife of sixty-three years had died a few years before. Always finding time to visit on trips back, I would hold his hand and watch tears rolling down his cheeks; I just want to see Kathleen again, he would weep. Now that they are together again (if that is indeed what happens in the afterlife... that souls are somehow reunited before they reincarnate) I should be happy for them both. So why then do I feel such distress? Why do I suddenly feel so very alone?

The opera is an amazingly dark piece and feeds my mood with a kind of profoundly terrible beauty. Leading character John Sorel (sung by the Buenos Aires-born baritone Luis Gaeta) returns home after attending a clandestine political meeting, pursued by Secret Police. Realising that he must escape the country, his wife Magda (the American soprano Susan Bullock) goes to the Consulate to try for a visa. No-one can get to the Consul, she is told; she must fill in papers. There follows a tragic mime that depicts the appalling daily misery of those in a totalitarian state who wait without hope of ever breaking through the soul-destroying bind of bureaucratic red tape.

Magda is harassed by police desperate to find John, by now hiding in the hills. Their baby dies. Again she tries to see the Consul; again she is turned away. John, hearing of his child's death, creeps back to comfort his wife. After he is caught, a secretary promises to call Magda with the news. But it's too late. She has turned on the gas. As the phone rings, she stretches out her hand, only to expire. The phone rings on... and on... The curtain falls.

El Consul, written in 1950 by Italian opera composer Gian Carlo Menotti (born 1911, like my father! and Andy's!) was first performed in Montevideo in 1951, and premiered in Buenos Aires on October 20, 1953. It was voted Best Staged Musical of the year by Time Magazine, won a Pulitzer Prize, and has since been translated into fourteen languages. Striking out critically as it does at the injustices and weaknesses in any totalitarian system and repressive regime, I am helped along famously in understanding the subversive aspects of the piece in two ways: a part-bilingual programme, and the fact that the opera is sung in its original English.

Curiously, the effect is cathartic. Though what my neighbours must think does not bear thinking about; unstoppable tears course down my cheeks throughout the three acts and the two intervals, while loud sobs – escaping on occasion despite all attempt at restraint – further punctuate the drama. Certainly they appear to have some effect on the young woman to my right; she is on her feet every time the curtain falls, shouting Bravo! Bravo! in such deep rich tones she must surely be a student contralto. Or maybe she is simply reacting to my histrionics, assuming me moved by the drama onstage, and responding in kind.

Exhausted but unable to sleep, my feet sore and blistered, I limp past my hotel, past Sam's address of old, and turn into the Tortino. Still in a state of shock but empty of tears, there is a sense of feeling cleansed and immensely relieved and happy to be alive. Ordering a half bottle of wine and then a brandy I watch a beautiful child risk the danger of abuse, begging from table to table, his hair water-falling like a gleaming blue-black wave down his back. He is followed by a stunning young Creole of undoubted European and African ancestry (the first seen, I note) who enters like a god and swaggers his way to the back of the restaurant, showing off the very lovely blonde following on as if she were no more valuable than a Rolex watch.

As the alcohol begins to take effect, I see in detail for the first time the shutters in the ceiling above, painted with leaves and flowers and opening upwards. My waiter, Alberto, has a handlebar moustache. Only the constant use of portable phones distinguish the past from the present; in all other respects it's as if I have stepped back nearly a century. Does the sign *La Bogada*, I joke weakly, scrawling another note on the corner of my serviette, mean *The Bog*?

I feel a surprising sense of relief for Eric; he'd not really felt life worth living since Kathleen left him alone and had always said that up until that point, he had enjoyed a long and remarkably privileged life. I allow the vivacious atmosphere of this illustrious cafe to swirl around me, with first a piano tuning up, one note painstakingly repeated to achieve perfect pitch, and then tango music and voices and laughter acting as blotting paper to any remaining emotional force. Is this what Sam did, I wonder. Sitting here, night after night? Struggling to come to terms with the past through the more palpable realities of the present? He never mentions the Tortino by name, even though it was so close to where he lived and worked, but surely it is the kind of place he would have enjoyed, just as I am enjoying it now.

### NOVEMBER 5, 1999

As I tell Maria-Elena the next morning, after returning early to relay my sad and difficult news, I had woken calm and clear-headed, having slept like a log. No nightmares. No revelations. No visitations. True I have to look up each of these words in the dictionary for translation into Spanish, but we are getting on like a house on fire. I am glad to have had a break, but also feel happy to be back, ready for a day of mucking about on the river. Having made calls – updating Akii, asking Lee in London to organise flowers, and checking with my mother and Jo on their own handling of Eric's demise, I change tapes in my recorder and note the days covered, ending Friday. But hold on: today is Friday. Yet also apparently was yesterday. Yesterday WAS another day. To have two Fridays with the same date makes no sense at all, but I have no time to work out where the mistake has occurred, for an error of some kind it has to be; we are off to Le Tigre, the boating resort on the river where my grandfather used to roll up his sleeves and let off steam.

But wait. Another surprise. For here is Pablo No. 2, arriving at the front gate to gather us up, carry us away. My heart sinks; I'm being organised again. I know Maria-Elena is being kind and generous the only way she knows how, but I had imagined a different scenario, a different kind of experience. Is he going to take us the whole way, follow us as we stroll around, as if we are some kind of *grandes senoras*? Perish the thought.

I need not have worried (if worrying is what I am about, and certainly the probability of twin Fridays is not a likelihood to be taken lightly). It is a beautiful day to follow the coastline, windows open, a gentle salt breeze whipping off the sea, the sun on my face and arm (for a one-sided tan).

There, points Maria-Elena, towards a large blank-faced official-looking complex set back from the road to my right across sweeping lawns. In the sunlight it does not look unattractive, and yet...

Bad things happen, she says; Many people die.

My heart leaps. Could it be the infamous Naval Mechanics School, where thousands of men and women were taken for interrogation and torture in the bad old days of *la guerra sucia* (the Dirty War of the 1970s), during which some five thousand are believed to have died?[22] I find it difficult trying to imagine any form of barbarity taking place on a similarly lovely day twenty to thirty years ago. Especially any horrors affecting the young women, imprisoned in the school's hospital until their babies were born and claimed by junta officials as their own, then disappeared. And because of my failure to empathise in the sunshine of my Latin American vacation (as it might be described), I can only turn away in pained shame.

On the left, we pass the presidential private quarters, catching glimpses of red-pantiled roofs hidden away behind red-brick walls. It's all very Spanish! How extraordinary then to suddenly pass a house decorated with innumerable images of Father Christmas. (The festive season comes as early to this part of the world as any other, it seems.)

Maria-Elena has just said something most interesting: that whilst she had personally disliked former president Peron but approved of many of his policies and actions, she likes Menem, but does not like some of the things he has done. She confides also that she used to come here forty years ago to dance.

Many *confiterias*, where people came to tango, she recalls, smiling at the memory.

I'm still smiling at all those Santas, my scattered emotions still trying to make sense of scrambled days in confusion, the neat modest facade of the compound where Eva Peron used to have her ambitious way with all and sundry, and the horror of that innocent-looking establishment that witnessed so much torment.

Pablo drops us off at a station called Libertador (seemingly miles inland from the road of the same name I tramped that first day), at which point I realise that our destination – a popular beauty spot upriver – is still a way to go. And here comes our train, streamlined, clean and comfortable, with electric doors and plump unstained upholstery, bearing a closer comparison with Japanese trains than my local from Caseros. The passengers are different too; well heeled, and paler – meaning more Caucasian than dark-skinned. The urban landscape becomes progressively upmarket too, with private homes winking *Come Hither If You Can Afford Me* signs from stands of ancient trees and succulent banks of flowers and vines.

Tigre has a different feel – like a British resort off-season: superficially dead but behind the scenes busily revving up for the spring into summer. We leave the tiny station, thirty-five minutes and 18 miles inland from the city, and walk along the river's edge, where soon enough the Buenos Aires Rowing Club – founded in 1878 – comes into view. Swiftly I realise that there are rowing clubs all along the river, monumentally designed to resemble British university colleges (Oxford, Cambridge and so on), German castles, French chateaux… I have never seen anything quite like it, and can't stop taking photographs. The amount of money floating around at the end of the nineteenth century must have been phenomenal.

A man informs us that the Tigre Boat Club is across the river, so we saunter over the bridge in the sunshine. Below us, the pinkish-brown muddy water swirls in sinister fashion, decorated with islands of water hyacinth – some small, some vast, some bobbing and twisting with the current, others gliding with the unruffled dignity of swans.

Sometimes animals, Maria-Elena gestures mysteriously, at which point I see waterfowl nesting on one tangle of vegetation, and something brown and furry on another. (Best not to take this any further!) I tell her that I have some water hyacinth in a *hibachi* in our garden in Hayama, but in trying to explain quite why I would use a ceramic pot traditionally used for holding charcoal to warm hands in winter as a garden ornament, I trip over myself: even in English words fail me.

A lot of the clubs are being renovated; despite the extreme poverty that grips nearly half the population, there seems to be money enough floating around. The US Club Regatta (regattas are held here every November and March) is being done up too, alongside a small funfair for kids. We now come to a point where I realise that we are on an island, with other distant landmasses all around. There is water every which way I turn – an unimaginably large delta – and across from where the waters divide once again, one of the largest sports clubs ever seen, a vast detached wooden mansion of several floors, the upper half in mock Tudor style surmounted by a cupola, sitting grandly amid extensive grounds. My goodness, I think, is that it? But no, it's another establishment altogether, with its own landing stage for boats to cross over: Club de Regatas la Marina (1876–1996). Whatever next, I wonder.

The address I am looking for is to our left, past a very pretty restaurant, with red and white checked tablecloths, green and white parasols and shaded by palms. But for now it is the club that grabs attention. It is small and modest. There are roses behind the front wall. The front lawn is newly mowed, the scent of fresh-cut grass almost making me swoon with nostalgia. A man of native appearance wearing a straw hat sits casually aloft astride on a trestle, painting the eaves a dark glossy green. A woman is chatting to him from the doorway, but stops as we approach.

Is this the British rowing club? we enquire.

Used to be, she replies; Now it's mixed; anyone can be a member.

I'm pleased to hear this; progress, I believe. Maria-Elena is explaining that my grandfather used to be a member, and on the woman's invitation, I step forward to decipher the plaques that decorate the front of the two-storey building. *Founded July 17, 1878,* reads one worn but still vigorously polished brass plate.

Waved inside, I step into the cool interior and gasp, because while the space is empty, the walls are a sea of faces. As my eyes sweep the photographs – a century of coxes and crews – I look for Sam, keenly seeking his eyes to meet my own. Instead, a stream of ageless young men in whites, their faces inscrutably proud, are monochromatically recorded through the decades only to explode into colour in 1993, after which their features and the romance of their endeavours somehow seem to fade. The first club house here of any distinction was built in 1896, with three floors, a tower and wrought iron balconies. And very fine it was too. As for the photo of three guys on horses striking poses on the edge of the river, while crews get into their stride on the water: such style.

I note the rules and regulations, as posted for all to see: *The name of the club is the Tigre Boat Club and its object is to afford members the opportunity of accustoming themselves to the management of boats. The headquarters of the club is in the Municipality of Las Conchas, Province of Buenos Aires, with the power to establish branches outside the federal capital. The club colours shall be black and golden yellow.* (The same colours as my secondary school uniform, I note.)

*Members,* the edict continues, *Must be 18 years of age, they must be of British or North American descent, and be able to speak English.* The entrance fee for Ladies was 25 dollars, and an annual subscription of 10 dollars. Members paid 200 dollars. There were special rates for Cadets and Camp Followers. (I make a note to send a postcard to Kevin in Toronto, informing him of this.)

Lady members are allowed the privileges of ordinary members on weekdays and can take out boats and introduce visitors on these days. (Well thanks very much.) But they are not to retain boats or introduce visitors on Sundays or Feast Days. (Why not? Unfair, she cries.)

There are Rolls of Honour for members lost in the two great wars, including a Miss Thurn of the Nursing Services. Next in line, the commemoration of a presentation in 1936 to a William Herman Crabbe on completion of twenty years service as president to the club, catches my eye. This new official may well have known Sam, maybe enjoyed a drink with him, even shared a dipping of oars downriver. Who was he? I quickly forget this conundrum after finding a graph showing the confluence of the mighty waters outside; it's awesome.

I stand in the centre of the room, with its stone flagged floor, dark green shutters and long curtains. I turn again from wall to wall but no, he is not here. There are some beautiful boys, racing from Tigre to Rio Santiago in 1955. But they would not have known him; by this date he was dead. Moved by his absence, I find myself in tears again. (Eric is much on my mind. Indeed, I have a photo of him and Kathleen in my backpack, having brought them along for the ride. )

In the boathouse next door, the sculls are narrow and gleaming; it's hard to imagine how anyone of any age or size would fit. At the back, a swathe of green lawn, swings, a swimming pool (still empty – the season hardly begun), a badminton net (someone playing already), and an open barbecue area under a hacienda-style roof. Birds are singing in profusion; small white puffballs of clouds polka-dot the bright blue sky. All in all it's a pretty nice place, a pretty nice day.

Just the place, I visualise, to let off a few fireworks after dusk. November 5 is Bonfire Night in the UK, commemorating the failure of the Gunpowder Plot of 1605, when English Catholics tried to blow up King James I of England and VI of Scotland and his parliament. But never the best time of year for a outdoor party, huddled in the wintry cold. Here, now, in Spring, would be much more fun.[23]

By the garden gate, on a more public noticeboard, a truly antique regulatory gem: Tigre BC was founded on the banks of the River Lujan forty-seven years ago (my goodness, it has been pinned up a long time!) and has maintained forever since the essential Anglo-Saxon atmosphere which its founder strove to preserve.

In the 1990s, however, discrimination has been thrown to the wind, and a recruiting drive is underway: *Join us! Get your family to join! Do you know that a day on the river is the most economical form of enjoyment and exercise? The return fare from Retiro is only 1.50 pesos during the summer months. Picnic lunches are supplied by the club at reasonable rates, or you can economise (and bring your own). Relaxation from the city's turmoil is to be found at a spot like this.*

Also: *Young men! Wouldn't you like to row in a crew of eight good men and true? Your ambition will be fulfilled... by joining the Tigre Boat Club.*

Alongside, a photo bizarrely shows two security guards (the British Engardos de la Securidas), nicknamed Starsky and Hutch. What strange time warp is this, I ponder.

Spotting Maria-Elena still chatting with the housekeeper, I wander over to join them. It seems the woman was once married to an Englishman. She used to be a Senora Atkinson, but no longer: Senor Atkinson got the boot. She has a different name now, and seems a whole lot happier about it.

My cousin and I enjoy a late lunch in that charming little restaurant, and I am allowed to treat her again. But while I get my way here, I fail miserably when it comes to taking a boat from the quay on the way back to the station. I favour a lovely-looking historic tub; Maria Elena wants to go on a catamaran. We argue, until she catches on to the fact that if we go out now by any type of vessel, we may not be able to get back tonight. Boats are the one regular communication link for all the scattered communities in this delta region, so they stop at every island. I think this sounds fun, but she doesn't.[24] Very much in the Japanese wifely tradition, she has to get home to cook Julio's evening meal and that is that.

We saunter back through a district where furniture making is the speciality. Whole families are involved: women sanding, their husbands or partners polishing, the kids fetching and carrying. Outside one house, a huge pile of bamboo catches my eye. I take out my camera only to remember I finished the roll on the far side of the bridge, snapping a fading mural of a Gainsborough-style English lass painted with the river in the background and in eighteenth century costume – with bustle, gartered stockings, a straw hat tied beneath the chin: Damn.

Nearer the station, what I assume to be a huge amusement park under construction turns out to be a penny casino.

Everyone loves to gamble, says Maria-Elena. That's how Marta lost all her money. She is *estupido*. Stupid.

I say nothing.

Remembering that I have two Fridays to sort out – forty-eight hours of activity and remembrance in what should be only twenty-four – I am feeling more than a little stupid myself.

The journey back is a scattering of random notes: A rugby field at San Fernando… loveliest houses imaginable at Punta Chico – shades of Hampstead, Sevenoaks, but Spanish!… at Borges (yes, really) all the cafe tables on the platform have umbrellas reading *Aqua Minerale – Echo de los Andes*… willow trees edging the shore, sad looking palms, lots of crap… how come coastlines have to be defiled in this way? Lovers of the Day: facing the train on a grassy bank, young, beautiful, dressed in white, she lying on her back on top of him as if he is a life saver, or spoons meshing, eyes closed, he stroking her hair…

When we get back, Julio is slumped on the sofa, stripped down to his underwear, watching football on TV. Well of course. It's the weekend.

CHAPTER 8

# IT'S THE WEEKEND

**NOVEMBER 6, 1999**

Don't ask where the day goes. I sleep late – very late, dreaming ever more alarmingly of spells cast, Groundhog Days, empty skulls and lunatic asylums – then take the train into the city simply in order to spend an hour on the computer. It's an excuse, I guess – as much to myself as anyone else. I feel guilty to have lain abed so long and want to be seen to be active and productive to make up for it, please those in authority: in this case, Maria-Elena and Julio; I am under their roof after all. Where does this feeling come from? It's as old as I am, and that's the trouble.

I'm all over the place emotionally. The vendor with a tray of small plastic dogs with nodding wagging heads, hanging around the ticket office in Caseros, amuses so much I buy one for Santiago, even though the Karate Kid in the guise of sainthood still hates me. The next moment I am cursing like a trooper for missing the train – fuck, fuck fuck! – unable to gather the confidence (like the Angela of old) to make a flying leap for a handle or window frame, along with all the other passengers running late. Furious to find myself waging such a war with age I sit in frustrated wait, until I feel a warm tongue lick my ankle – a thin, scarred black and tan stray curled up under the bench, offering unconditional canine therapy.

By the time I'm settled on the next train that comes along, I am seething all over again. I've left Santiago's present on the seat above my new friend – a dog day indeed!

The exterior of my carriage is grey-to-rust covered with graffiti. Inside the

114

seats are blue – green for the incapacitated – and when we draw into a station the light changes and the whole interior is flooded peppermint green. A native child turns to his mother with a beatific smile and then smashes his fist against a fly on the window pane. Beyond the glass, two ponies are tethered; their owner, his own mane a stream of shining black hair, lies alongside, deep in flowers and wild grasses, chewing a long plumed stem. At the next stop, hanging out of the window, a huge ragged unwashed and uncombed family of multi-generational women and their children climb aboard. Maybe Peruvian, or from somewhere deep upriver, few have shoes, the faces of the little ones smeared with unhealthy-looking snot.[25]

In my compartment, LOTD (Lovers Of The Day) No. 7: a middle-aged couple, slumped forward, their arms supporting one another across the space, fast asleep.

Another rebalancing occurs: a women in her forties – one of the tucked and streamlined European-looking blondes that Jerry took as his model – moves distastefully in her seat, trying to avoid any direct contact with her neighbour: a young dark-skinned woman, baby at breast. The mother, instinctively aware of the hostility, flushes with anger. I feel uncomfortable, embarrassed. I have met discrimination before, but not this quietly seething offensiveness, this total lack of respect.

Waiting for stamps to send postcards tests my patience to the limit. It takes several minutes to assess that I need to take a ticket to get in line; as I take my place with No. 24 being served, I note that I am No. 54. Another good long ten minutes pass before No. 35 crosses the line. I wait another twenty before being waved to the counter. Service (when you get it) is efficient and polite, just painstakingly slow. There seems to be a lot of paper involved, and a great number of imposing stamps – the rubber kind! My receipt is impressive enough to deserve framing.

Messages of various kinds – electronic and snail mail – sent, received and understood, I am back in the Tortino sitting alongside a pastel drawing by Raquel Sciurano of... what? Some aspect or detail of the *confiteria* I suppose, though it's hard to find a bearing with such a treasure house of pillars, decorative glass and lamps. (Victoriana, Art Deco and Art Nouveau have always been a heady mix in my book.) There's another drawing by Julio Cesar Vergottini (which I note only because Maria-Elena's husband is also Julio Cesar). I compare the decor to the utilitarian decor – sickly pink carpet and revolting red and orange-striped bedspread – of my room in the Novel Hotel two nights before, and can only breathe a sigh of relief.

Welcome back to the oldest social gathering place of its kind in Argentina. Panelled in wood, with marble-topped tables and a long bar down one side, above which a notice reads *Los Amigios del Tortoni*, it has always been a haunt for many of the country's most distinguished creative names in the literary and musical world: Carlos Gardel, for example, hated by many for his outrageously camp behaviour but still regarded as the greatest tango singer of them all, and whose death in an air crash in 1935 brought the city to a standstill; Sicilian playwright Luigi Pirandello who in 1934, just two years before he died, won the Nobel Prize for Literature; Polish-American pianist Arturo – Arthur – Rubinstein (1897–1982); Spanish lyric dramatist Federico Garcia Lorca, who gave up the ghost at the tender age of thirty-four; and of course, Borges – he who asked the question the world continues to ponder: Where did the fault lie for Argentina being such a sad country?

What was it about that early part of the 1930s that remains so alluring? Because maybe, after the Great Depression, between two world wars, expectation allowed itself to flourish once again? Although past its peak of affluence – like Japan in the 1990s, its own economic bubble having burst in 1989 – Argentina was still basking in the glory of what had gone before, and creatively on a spin. Maybe Sam hoped to catch its tail wind, sailing into some new economically and socially upward spiral. He certainly began with great hopes, putting much energy into creating a strong aura of optimism.

Sam was a *chanta*, a much-esteemed word in Argentina, meaning someone who took chances, an opportunist, an entrepreneur, every move being regarded as a means to an affluent end. As *The South American handbook* advised immigrants: *An Englishman of modest means should conserve it (any capital) and acquire experience with a view to pooling his resources later. The days of big and easy fortunes are over, but good livings are still to be made by men of prudence, character, energy and skill.*

Indeed there was still much to inspire when Sam arrived back in 1936. The legendary Turkish-born Greek ship-owner and financier Aristotle Onassis (1906–1975), for example, had arrived in Buenos Aires in 1923 as a penniless refugee from the horrors of the Smyrna massacre. After reviving his family's tobacco fortunes in Argentina, Onassis bought his first ships in the 1930s and later entered the tanker business.

But for all such mighty success stories (in financial terms at least, for Onassis's private life was a mess) there were many thousands more who had no luck at all. Consider the tragedy of the great American playwright Eugene (Gladstone) O'Neill, who arrived a gentleman in Buenos Aires in 1907 and, being one of the greatest *chantas* of them all – a sometime seaman, prospector and newspaper reporter, as well as a future Nobel prize-winner (awarded in 1936) – was reduced to destitution within two years. At least John Turner Loader had made his own opportunist mark in reverse style: arriving poor and returning home much improved in station. Such is the luck of good timing and fate in combination. Maybe.

As the thirties drew to an end, Samuel C. E Loader was a Represente de Fabricas Britanicas, with a name card (dated October 1939 in his handwriting) and representing companies listed on the back: *in Shropshire, Stoke-on-Trent (sanitary wares and ceramic tiles), the Bilston Foundries also in Lancashire, and Glasgow (A.R. Brown, Macfarlane & Co), Etc, Etc.*

By November, just as he was settling in, the tide of fortune had begun to turn. He had written to my grandmother at the onset of hostilities between Britain and Germany, but to no effect. *I feel as you do,* he informs

117

my father, *that the War might bring laurels or wreaths to us all. I hope it will be the former... I bear no ill feeling to anyone in the world, except a fellow here who owes me about 100 pounds, and I am waiting and waiting to get it cleared up.* Then in jocular but still threatening tones: *I am afraid he is going to be out of luck if I do not get it in the next few days!* What was he implying? That he might thwack the miscreant with his cane? Or maybe punch him on the nose, as Barney had done to his own, just a few years before?

In general, business had slumped. *The bicycle trade is flat,* he tries to joke. *I have been with Duranona y Cia for two years now but have got nothing out of them. With the outbreak of war, things have changed. Their German sympathies have caused me to break with them... next week I am retiring* (from the company). With his own office, though, he is sure he will be fine: *in fact I shall do better alone.* He had just shipped thirty-thousand tiles for clients from the Campbell Tile Company in Stoke-on-Trent, an order worth 1,800 pounds, with a commission of 5 per cent minimum. Whisky sales are good but supplies slow. He is actively seeking new products... *Round Iron by the ton, also Steel and other metals.*

He wants my father to chase up the Triumph Cycle Company, having lost a lot of commission through the liquidation of Coventry Bicycles Limited: *Life is all ups and downs and grumbling not worthwhile. There is life in the old dog yet!* He knows for sure, however, that his son has other things on his mind. For this is the first letter in which my mother's name is mentioned: *I trust you will get married at the earliest opportunity, and am sure Gwen will be a good advisor and help you a lot.*

Sadly my mother was little equipped to offer advice other than to play safe. As with my father, her childhood had been struck cruel blows – tough times that, in breaking their families asunder, by many strange quirks of coincidence brought the two of them together – but from which neither would ever truly recover.

Like John Loader nearly a century before, my mother Gwendoline Edna and her sister Josephine Doris had started life in Shropshire. Their father, Joseph Edna Price (occasionally Edna was used as a man's name in those days, my mother insists) was a bit of a "chanta" in his own right. As the Registrar, in charge of recording births, marriages and deaths at Wellington Registry Office, he took advantage of this most reputable address to act also as the agent for the Pacific Ocean shipping line (often accompanying nervous passengers to see them off from Liverpool). He also acted in some capacity for a firm of local auctioneers.

Joseph was the youngest of fourteen children, not all of whom survived past infancy. His own father, Jonathon Price, was an Ironmaster, meaning he was master of a foundry, and indeed from photographs he looks so straitlaced and resolute as to be him self forged from stainless steel. Anyway, the family was comfortable and educated. Of the children who survived, the ones most relevant to this story are of course Joseph, James (Jim), Albert (known as Uncle Arcos and my Uncle Eric's father), Beatrice (nicknamed Beatie and one of triplets!), Lois and Margaret. The last three, known as The Aunts, were to live out their lives together in a state of Christian spinsterdom at Dove Cottage, Hadley, near Wellington.

Though my mother was born September 4, 1910 in Woombridge, near the border with Staffordshire, the family moved to Oakengates, Wellington when she was still tiny, so there are no memories. Jo was born near four years after, by which time their mother, Irene, was a very sick woman. She had first contracted tuberculosis at age fourteen, and once the children came along, the house was virtually run by maids and her own mother, Sarah Wagge. This remarkable looking – and sounding – woman, once in service herself, had become pregnant with Irene while working as a housekeeper. Though the name of the father is unknown, responsibility was accepted (a rarity in those days, when those in service to the gentry were regarded as fair game) in as much that Irene's education and general wellbeing were paid for through a firm of solicitors in London.

So my maternal grandmother was illegitimate. But this stigma did not stop Sarah from marrying twice thereafter, first to a Mr Lord, and after his death, a Mr Pickering. So little Irene – always dressed to the nines and studying dance and piano and French from the earliest age – was not short of paternal role models. If Sarah was a handsome woman, her daughter was nothing short of stunning, with a natural eighteen inch waist, fair colouring, blue eyes and long blonde hair. Quite the English rose, in fact. By all accounts she was also immensely talented – a natural mimic, whose sense of humour and beautiful soprano voice made her the life and soul of any party. (This is what my mother tells me, having no doubt embroidered her account over the years as painstakingly as she still stitches tapestry and appliqué today.)

While there was plenty of lively entertainment to be enjoyed in the early years of Irene's marriage, there was little to no mothering available for Gwen and Jo. When my grandmother was not in a sanatorium, she was living in a revolving summerhouse at the end of the garden, blowing kisses to her daughters when they were brought out to wave to mama early morning and before they went to bed at night, and popping ripe strawberries into their mouths through the hedge. When she died towards the end of the First World War, aged thirty-one, Joseph was devastated. He made no attempt to recreate his life, even for the sake of his children, succumbing to pneumonia within two years. My mother remembers her father's funeral: The Aunts told us to wave as the hearse drove away, but I just couldn't.

I wanted to laugh, she recalls. Then more reflectively: I didn't miss my mother, but I missed him. He missed her so much he died of a broken heart. (That's my mother: ever the escapist, the eternal romantic.)

Grandmother Wragge/Lord/Pickering somehow found enough strength to keep the household ticking over, but after her own death, the two little girls were left to the mercy of a succession of housekeepers and maids. My mother has no happy memories, and feels she hardly had a childhood, Not compared to what children have nowadays!

It was not until it looked as if they might have to go to an orphanage, aged near fourteen and eight, that Joseph's brothers and sisters came (with extreme reluctance, it should be said) to the rescue. By which time the girls were so neglected that they were virtually in rags – or so the story goes.

Gwen: Our mother was so clever with her hands. She made all our clothes – and loved shantung – always shantung. Also yards and yards of crochet. When our home was broken up, we never got anything; everything was swiped. We left with nothing but the clothes on our backs.

Having lost their mother and then their father, they then lost one another. Jo was despatched to live with The Aunts at Dove Cottage. Gwen was sent to live with Uncle Jim and his wife Ina, who owned a tobacconists shop in Aberystwyth, on the Welsh coast. Childless (and apparently perfectly content to be so) they gave my mother a roof over her head, food and an education, but that was about it. Love – even the smallest sign of affection or compassion even – was thin on the ground. It was even worse for Jo living with three unmarried sisters, their post-Victorian lives still ruled by church-going and related community events.

When Jo was fourteen, she left school with a pragmatic attitude and a sound grounding in Latin, Pitman's shorthand, and typing. Determined to be financially independent, she went to work for a local firm, and then gradually worked her way in upwardly mobile fashion towards Birmingham and eventually Coventry.

My mother set her sights on fashion in a rather different sense. At school – St Paddon's Convent, in Flambadon Road, Aberystwyth, which still exists today – she was spoiled rotten by the nuns, who constantly referred to her as "that poor little orphan".

They almost cried every time they looked at me, she recalls.

She was thus encouraged to assume pained victim mode, as well as to learn to paint, stitch beautifully, and study music like her mother before her. She had inherited Irene's natural soprano voice, which always drew much attention.

At age seventeen, she left Aberystwyth, and moved in with her uncle, Albert Price, the headmaster of an elementary school in Birmingham (who had remarried after the death of his first wife in childbirth) and her cousins, Donald and Eric. With a place at Birmingham Art School, she did a general year (the late 1920s equivalent of today's foundation course), and then specialised in dressmaking and fashion illustration. It was during this time that her own life became entwined in anthroposophy, and through this involvement she met my father.

In the cathedral on Plaza de Mayo, a wedding is in progress, and I tiptoe around (while trying to sneak a look at the bride's frock and the finery of all the other guests) to find two soldiers in traditional muster guarding the entrance to San Martin's tomb. It is a circular chamber faced with white marble housing a square monument in black marble, with a high dome overhead covered in mosaic. I note that the liberator of Argentina, and also Chile and Peru, was born February 25, 1778 in Yapeyu, and died August 17, 1850 at Boulogn sur Mer Ayayache. The quiet and dignified respect paid to his memory is remarkable; but I find myself distracted by the Argentine flag: in pale blue, white and yellow, with a sun (setting, I fear, rather than rising, though most surely it was designed with optimism) and a pair of all-seeing eyes. Trying to leave the building is as difficult as getting in. There are loads of people begging, and the babies and very old and handicapped especially make any style of escape an ordeal of Christian-inspired guilt.

Hearing the insistently hair-raising demands of *bombo* drums, I follow noise and a great swirl of people carrying banners. This is the second demonstration I have come across in three days. The first was with Maria-Elena on our day out earlier in the week: a huge gathering of predominantly native people and their families and supporters in front of a building concerned with social welfare. They want job or money, Maria-Elena had intimated, pulling on my T-shirt, desperate to get away. Today there is a flood of people walking arm-in-arm along the street, with banners, slogans, guitars and singing. But this is no excuse for festivity. Rather it's seething with anger, heavy with despair.

*Trabajo, trabajo* (Give us work!) shouts a girl at my shoulder. Aged around fifteen, she has wonderful eyebrows and desperately dramatic black eyes above a ragged washed out T-shirt and torn cotton trousers several sizes too large and gathered around her waist with what looked like electrical tape. Resentment is her second name. While her parents are off somewhere in the crowd, she has to care for a clutch of younger siblings, who stare at me and my camera as if I an alien from outer space. Maybe I am.

Traveling back to Caseros, I smile with relief (not for the first time) at a piece of graffiti on the wall of a coral-pink painted house in the playful shadows of some large broad-spreading trees: *Thelma y Louise*. Only to be brought back to reality by a genuine expression of discontent. In large block capitals, near a station where the seeded fruits of trees planted along the platform have turned the paved surface into a bloody, reddish-black stained battleground, *ARGENTINO DESPERADO.*

I buy a bottle of red wine from Mendoza for dinner from the wonderful Italian-style cheese shop next to Caseros Station. Julio accepts it with a smile and then gently (and ever-so politely) sets it aside, opening instead a bottle from his own home ground of San Juan, far to the west of Mendoza in the foothills of the Andes. How do I take this? As a rebuff or a compliment?

It is obvious my host has had a bad day, kept busier than ever but with little to no recompense. Since Caseros is a poor area, there is a great and urgent need among the children, he intimates. What can he do when their parents cannot pay? I am their doctor, he says, shrugging wearily.

We try to talk politics. I'm interested to know how he and my cousin coped during the Dirty War, when Julito and Pablo were small. From their gestures it was clear: kept their heads down. Now, as Maria-Elena lays out plates piled high with long rounded green bobby beans, sliced tomatoes, mushrooms, cheese, potatoes and fish – can she cook? she can cook alright! – Julio vents his frustration: Such a pity she (me) can't speak Spanish. We could have such interesting conversations.

Never mind that for his part he could try a little English. All I can do is hang my head, mutter *lo siento* (sorry), and join him in getting drunk.

## NOVEMBER 7, 1999

Again I wake late (after sleeping, waking with a headache, dozing and then reading until 5 a.m., I'm racing through Albert Speer's *Battle With Truth*), to find Julio on the back patio, wearing grey slacks and a bright blue sports shirt, preparing Sunday lunch. With a history of goitre and aware that he is overweight, Tarzan eats salads most of the week. Sunday, however, is beef blowout day, the one day in the week he allows himself to gorge on Argentina's prime product. The brick-built barbecue lies along one wall, over the top of which is the backyard of a martial arts club, which I keep meaning to investigate but for some reason have as yet to get beyond the front door. (Yes, all the way from Japan to find karate, judo and aikido on my doorstep. What is still called in the UK, bringing coals to Newcastle. The coal is still there, but British mines have been closed down one by one since the 1984 strike. Power struggles and profit margins rule. Ordinary people inevitably lose out. Something Argentina knows all about.)

Julio is very happy, messing about, heating up the charcoal in the *asado*, laying out the meat. (Krieger is beside himself with joy, not simply for human contact and a modicum of attention for a change, but the promise of scraps. The caged birds are also aflutter with excitement.) There is so much meat that I fear the family is planning to eat half a beast at one sitting – huge slabs of flesh, ribs, offal, sausages, and some mysterious objects wrapped in silver foil. When Julito and his family arrive – it's the custom for everyone to eat Sunday lunch together whether from free choice or not (I most certainly receive mixed messages) – everyone tucks in, and I try not to watch the trails of blood from rare-cooked steaks dripping their way from plate to mouth. Needless to say, my strange non-meat-eating habits have been accommodated. I had expected to be given a hard time in a culture where cattle are staple. Instead, I am invited to unwrap steaming silver torpedoes to find all manner of vegetables and seafood cooked to perfection. There are also stuffed tomatoes, more beans, and a plate stacked high with white asparagus drenched in olive oil and fresh herbs.

After lunch, we all cram into Julito's car (Julio excepting; he sleeps now until early evening – another ritual) and set off for a Sunday market in Mataderos, the Argentine equivalent of London's Camden Lock perhaps? Certainly it sounds just my cup of tea, and so it seems! We ramble between families eating ice-cream and people playing chess at tables set up on the grass, towards a small plaza that suddenly envelopes us in music and colour. There are musicians onstage, sounding more Mexican than Argentine, and there are more native families around than people of European extraction. The atmosphere is terrific and I rush around taking pictures – piles of functional leather goods (amazing silver-studded saddles, bridles, whips), stalls with bright checked tablecloths piled high with golden cheeses, *mate* (and the instruments by which to sup it), and custom-made *gaucho* jackets and trousers. God, I think, a *gaucho* outfit in Japan (preparing to be measured up) but then do a reality check and accept I am not the right shape; I would look as lumpy in boxy pants and *bolero* as I do in *kimono*.

Sides of beef are being grilled on all sides – my clothes already stink. Under a cool, arched stone promenade, children are being taught a traditional dance, waving coloured handkerchiefs with limp to cheeky flicks of the wrist. In a square, couples of all ages, shapes and sizes are dancing to taped music – not tango but something more measured and grave. It's immensely touching and I would love to join in if only I had a partner – and if only my feet didn't hurt quite so much!

When I spot my first *gaucho* (authentic or otherwise), I am rooted to the spot; then follow on behind, captivated by clothing swaying elegantly and charismatically to where compatriots on horseback are racing along a track scattered with sand – they have to reach up and pass a ball through a hoop just before crossing the finishing line. The horses are superb. So are the men! When I smile admiringly at one young handsome-is-as-handsome-does, he gives me a disdainful haughty look that speaks volumes: I don't believe you exist, but just in case you do, drop dead. It's another game, another act, of course; another device to prop up the smallest hint of a faltering ego. And immediately I am reminded of interviewing an Argentine in Tokyo (now a friend, especially since coming down off his own high horse) who explained with all seriousness that before we began conversing I should understand his exceptional superiority, being one of the most good-looking, sexually attractive and intelligent beings on the planet. I still don't know how I kept a straight face.

Julito thinks I will be interested in the *gaucho* museum, so inside we go. But I find it rather sad, reflecting a way of life that is near extinct. Maybe that is why the guys – misfits in the modern world – have to keep their end up; like American cowboys, they are a dying breed, performing for the tourists and helping further determine their country's folkloric mythology. As usual, photographs and illustrations are more informative than dusty riding gear in glass cases, and amateurish tableaux showing how families used to live on the *pampa*. When we come out, a galaxy of native children – Peruvian, Bolivian, Mexican, Paraguayan, from who knows where – cavort past wearing felt hats and billowing skirts in rainbow combinations that give my camera lens something to think about, even in terms of auto-focus.

This is the most fun I have had since I arrived, and for a couple of hours, I manage to put other global realities on hold: a daughter about to lose her home; a son about to represent his mum at the funeral of a great-uncle he hardly knows; yesterday's angry reaction from my cousin when I criticised her for not letting me know the arrangements as promised, the message on her part being that she had more important things to do than worry about me gallivanting around South America; she had, after all, just lost her father! She is right, of course, but also wrong: a bereaved person can feel as upset at long distance as close to home – and a lot more guilty and helpless.

It is only when I get back and look up the area just visited that I begin to feel really bad, deep down in the core of my being. Mataderos was the site of the municipal marketplace and slaughterhouse – so many cattle were ripped open, their throats cut, day after day after day that the streets were permanently awash with blood and the stench unbelievable. Cattle auctions were once regarded as one of the sights of the city (sheep were dealt with at Mercado Tablada) but not for me. It's interesting, of course, but there is just too much historical blood and guts for my liking. We will rue the day we took it upon ourselves to dictate and control the existence of other life forms on the planet. We will have to pay the price.

Mataderos is also where the first *frigorifico* was constructed. Before the technologies of chilling and freezing were introduced, meat was largely salted and dried. The resulting preserve, *tasajo* is what the industry used to call Jerked Beef, but now prefers the term Beef Jerky. Because salting and drying made even poor quality meat palatable, there was little incentive to improve livestock. This all changed with the construction of freezing plants, eighteen in total and largely along the banks of the River Plate. Realising that the technique demanded better quality beef, *estancias* began importing British-bred bulls.

The *frigorificos* purchased cattle and sheep directly from the owners or through agents, who sold their animals at public auction houses in Buenos Aires. Most however were bought onsite on the *pampa*, then shipped by the trainload from the *estancias* to the freezer plants – vast establishments where, after slaughter and preparation, carcasses would be loaded onto ocean liners bound for the US and Europe.

Argentina became famous for its chilled meat, transported at a temperature set at 29–30 degrees Fahrenheit. Arriving in soft condition, it could be eaten immediately. Frozen meat had to thawed out and lacked flavour. But as stock improved, and technologies became more refined, frozen beef, mutton and lamb became more and more profitable. Though there had been a French vessel named the *Frigorifique* in 1870, the first shipload of meat bound for Britain arrived January 1884 via the *Meath*, owned by the Houlder Bros. Line.

Quite apart from corned beef (dating from 1878) and meat extracts (Bovril advancing a technology first developed in London in 1865), the by-products of the industry were money-spinners too: inedible fats (used as tallow); edible beef and mutton fats used for lard and margarine (I never ate Christmas mince-pies once I learned that today's mincemeat is largely preserved with lard); the residue – incinerated bones and the like – used for charcoal in sugar refining, black pigments, poultry foods, manures, pottery and china. Hair, bristle, horns and hooves, ox-galls, dried blood, and intestines (for sausages), were all valuable sources of income.

I go to bed feeling sick.

## NOVEMBER 8, 1999

It is 6 a.m. on Monday, Be Nice to Feet Day, and I am giving myself a pedicure, trying to get a handle on my blisters and limit the damage (caused I suspect by sneakers bought in wintry Japan without taking into account that in the warmer weather of the southern hemisphere my feet would swell). Outside right now, however, it's overcast, rather like the day I first arrived, so I sit quietly, waiting for the house to wake. Julio is up first and I hear him greet Marta who arrives around 7.30. I wait for Maria-Elena to finish in the bathroom, then shower, wash my hair and explore the dressing room, looking for a bar of soap. I have never seen so many expensive cosmetics in my life! She must spend a small fortune. I think of my single jar of Body Shop moisturiser, mascara and all-purpose kohl pencil, and wonder what she makes of me, really.

Catching up with copies of the Buenos Aires Herald purchased over the weekend, I note (after getting past a picture of a giant panda on the front cover of the Saturday paper) that with thirty-four days left before President Carlos Menem (of the ruling Peron Party) hands over power to President-Elect Fernando de la Rua (of the Radical Frepaso Alliance), the transition period is dominated by – to put it politely – differing budget deficit figures. Menem (the report says) insists the budget deficit for 1999 will be around 5.1 billion pesos, and this will drop to 4.5 billion in 2000. De la Rua, on the other hands, reckons the deficit could rocket to 10 billion pesos. Bad news either way.

As I put my money on the more pessimistic projection, I note that de la Rua is off to Paris, where he will meet today with British Prime Minister Tony Blair (he who turned socialism into a brand product) and former South African President Nelson Mandela at the twenty-first congress of the Socialist International. Ah, Paris, I romance, and then remember once again that Europe is locked into midwinter.

Much cheered, I laugh a lot at Adam Freedman's Newcomer's Diary – Give us your huddled masses, yearning to be free... in which the young American describes the joys and woes of immigration, having to nip over the Rio Plata to change his visa status. (I know all about this irritating but necessary game from my early days of living in Japan!) Talking with his own local kiosk owner about the rising crime rate, Adam was told: It's the same in the US. Just as you have illegal immigrants from Mexico infiltrating your country, so we have immigrants from all over South America. They don't come to work; they come to rob.

After a sticky altercation with an immigration official at Colonia, which reminded him of Ellis Island on a bad day, Adam is exceedingly glad to be back. As he remarks ironically to the same kiosk owner on his way home: You know what? You're right. Immigrants are killing this country.

Maria-Elena has to go into the city to the bank. She orders a car (by this time it is after nine) and assumes I'll go along, so I do. My schedule is shot already, so what the hell. No Pablo this time but more a social statistic; a former high-level banker who having lost his job is now driving a taxi. He is luckier than most, he reckons, with a decent home and savings. Thirteen million out of Argentina's population of thirty-six million live in inadequate housing. In Buenos Aires alone, two million live in slum conditions, districts known as *villas miserias* (literally Misery Towns).

Dropped off somewhere that seems vaguely familiar, at Rivadavia 3800, I find I'm not only lost but off my map. So I take stock in a *confiteria/pizzeria* on the corner, which has a display on the wall describing its history, along the bottom of which it reads: *Almago de mi vida, lugar de Ensuinos y poesie, Asi cantaba, Carlos Gardel.* I have stumbled on another treasure: Cafe Tunin, founded in 1886. Revived, I track down the subway system, dating from 1916 and the first to be constructed in Latin America, and take a ride. I like watching the cooking show on the platform monitors as I wait for a train, but without really being sure what it is exactly I'm looking at: an actual TV programme or an ad of some kind?

Heading for my bank (as I have now come to think of it) to change more money, I see British influence on all sides. It has been said before but I shall say it again: the English invented Argentina, in large part because in the past at least they have always been quick off the mark where money was to be made. First the country was bound into a trading agreement that benefited Britain far more than it did Argentina. When the railways were built, it was for the sole purpose of transporting meat to Buenos Aires for shipping to feed home markets. Standing on an intersection, the wall of the building at Maipu 500 is customarily inscribed with the name of the architect: *Thomas Newberry*. And you can't get much more English than that.

Having spoken to my mother and sent my love to Jo (Eric is being cremated today, his ashes to be scattered I know not where) and dealt with a bunch of e-mail, I'm now on the line to Retiro's twin station at Plaza Constitucion on the far side of the city. This used to service the south of the country, just as Once served the west, and Retiro – actually three stations in one – was the starting point for the Central Argentine, Pacific, and Central Cordoba railways. At the subway station in San Juan, the walls are covered with beautiful mosaics – lyrical scenes of the city in its early days (at Avenida de Mayo, the illustrations are more obviously historical). At Constitucion itself, the theme is the *pampa* –

*gauchos*, bucking broncos, cattle being herded, that kind of thing – with the design accredited to F. Molina/Campos 40, but realised by IUNA (the city's Institute of National Ceramics) in 1998. Again, money is being spent, but on frills, not the basics. Still I guess they help cheer people up – or distract them from what really needs to be done.

I'm back in San Telmo, the oldest part of the city. Once known as Alto de San Pedro, horse-drawn coaches used to stop and rest en route to the port. Pedro Gonzalez Telmo was a seventeenth century Spanish monk of the Dominican order who took it upon himself to preach to sailors and fishermen from Galicia and Portugal. Since the earliest inhabitants of the area were all somehow involved in the life of the port, he became the protector of the neighbourhood. San Telmo soon became a popular residential area; being uphill it was moderately cooler than down near the shoreline. (There is a high area in Yokohama – Yamate, nicknamed The Bluff – to where foreigners escaped for similar reasons. In Liverpool too, the affluent sought high ground, as far from the life of the port where they made their fortunes, as possible. But also – as Andy once pointed out – so that owners could keep a weather eye on their vessels sailing to and fro.) After San Telmo was ravaged by yellow fever and cholera in the 1870s, wealthy *portenos* moved as high as they could go, to the north, slashing and burning to create room at the top.

Wandering aimlessly, I realise that the days are beginning to slide one into another. It is time to move on. And this is what I announce to Maria-Elena later that evening: I've decided to leave Buenos Aires for a few days (to take control again). Next stop, Chile.

CHAPTER 9

# NEXT STOP, CHILE

**NOVEMBER 9, 1999**

Though quite prepared to make my own arrangements, Maria-Elena has sprung into action. I have misgivings but leave her to find me a cheap flight tomorrow. This is one of her days for babysitting Santiago while Paula works, but she seems excited at the prospect of having something out-of-the-ordinary to do, perching her gold-framed glasses (normally carried around her neck on a chain) on the end of her nose, and getting down to work on the dining table with phone books and notepads.

If I begin the day with any similar enthusiasm, it swiftly peters out. I am tired and coughing, my stomach rebelling against irregular mealtimes and stress-refluxed acid offering up the most agonising heartburn. The museum in San Telmo is closed again – yet another wasted journey. And once more I consider the inherent madness of launching myself into yet another unknown country with no plans, and no contacts other than the list of names in the telephone book – most certainly no equivalent of Maria-Elena as a welcoming and magnanimous safety net. This time, really, what the hell do I think I'm doing?

Scanning the pages of my newspaper it seems the world at large is being far more decisive, for better, for worse. Australia has voted against becoming a republic. Mexico voted just yesterday to elect the ruling party's presidential candidate – apparently an unprecedented move for a party in power for twenty years and very much a test of its unity. While in Guatemala, in the first presidential election since the end of a thirty-

132

six year civil war, opinion polls are favouring the populist candidate of a party associated with state terror. Which naturally gives rise to the question: who can you trust these days if even supposedly objective pollsters are cooking the books. Maybe in allowing the whole stupid system to have its way with us, we really do deserve the patriarchal ego-driven leaders we get.

As the sun heats up towards midday, a deep fatigue descends. The plan to cut through Parque Lezama and look around the Russian Orthodox Church (I can see its domed roof, dating from 1904, down the hill to the left) falters and fades. Instead, with roses and a bandstand adding oh-so-English touches to an otherwise semi-tropical view, I lie down under a jacaranda with palms fanning in every direction, place yesterday's copy of the *Buenos Aires Herald* over my face, and switch off.

This is what my grandfather would seem to have done throughout 1940: switched off. There were apparently some letters going to and fro, but between whom no one will ever know. Certainly it appears there was no communication between my father and his own until mid-1941, by which time the war in Europe was well into its second year.

The missive dated June 3 is therefore significant in two ways: it reconnects father and son after a long silence; it is also the first letter addressed to my father and my mother as a married couple: *My dear Gwen and Bob...* My grandfather has heard of my imminent arrival (by the time he replies I am four days old) *and the good news made me feel quite happy again. You must be very pleased with yourselves, as for myself, I am like a dog with two tails, and the fact of becoming a grandfather certainly makes me look at the clock... In any case, although such an event should make one feel older, as a matter of fact I am just the same as I was twenty years ago, and as lively as a cricket.*

How did my parents' paths cross to result in my creation and subsequent safe delivery on Planet Earth?

We must return to my mother, leaving Wales for Birmingham in 1927.

She had scraped through her Cambridge Senior Certificate at Tanbank, a private school in Aberystwyth run by two sisters, the Misses Hilda and Muriel Garbett. Here she learned to write and add up and subtract, but admits she never made much of long division. (Another failing we seem to have in common!) Her strengths lay in music and art, which at age seventeen demanded decision: to study music she would have to stay in Wales; she was desperate to get away. So, art it was.

My mother says she was overwhelmed when she began studying at Birmingham Art School. She had never lived in a large city before, and the staff and students were all so cosmopolitan and (in her eyes) refined. She was also completely ignorant about sex, believing that a girl only had to be alone in a room with a man to become pregnant. Staying with Albert Price's family – he being principal of a school in Birmingham – she remembers First Cousin Eric coming into her room once to mend a window, and being scared to death until her next period, called in those dreadfully unenlightened days, "The Curse".

Was my father any better informed, I wonder? He and my mother allegedly courted for seven years and yet (according to my mother) they never laid a finger on one another. Was she lying, or were people so much more innocent in those days? A combination of the two, perhaps, aided and abetted by hung-over Victorian–Christian values of Guilt and Shame.

My mother had hoped to become an art teacher, but it was decided – by her instructors and/or the school authorities – that she was "Unsuitable". (She was to prove them all wrong.) Instead she opted for fashion, thinking to be a fashion illustrator, even though the pay was notoriously bad. In those days Jewish firms (who were predominant in the rag trade districts of the city) were paying 4 pounds and 6 pence for a drawing. She must have been good though, because in her first year, she was selected with another student by Lady Bird (of Bird's Custard Powder family fame) to do all the drawings for the Warwick Pageant.[26]

As my mother recalls: Nora (Gibbs) did the designs that ranged historically from the time of Cymbeline (40 AD) to Elizabeth I (sixteenth century); I did the drawings. We filled a whole book, got paid 30 pounds, and were a bit of a star in local papers.

My mother's best friend was Nora Jennings, who lived in King's Norton; but she also fell in with several metaphysically inclined students, including Gladys Bligh and Rhona Everett. After graduating, she messed around for a while, mostly doing bits of dressmaking. Luckily she landed a job at Ruskin Hall, Bournville, teaching day-continuation embroidery classes to young female factory hands, nicknamed the Cadbury Angels.[27] There were lots of free samples on offer, and soon she was carrying bags of chocolate to Gladys and Rhona (whom I remember especially well as she and her family lived just down the road from Eric and Kathleen in Love Lane) and other former art school friends who were working at Sunfield, an anthroposophical community on the outskirts of Stourbridge.

My mother began visiting Sunfield regularly at weekends. Then came the invitation to stay for two weeks. She was to remain there for six years.

In the summer of 1928, Friends House (the headquarters of the Quaker's Religious Society) played host to the World Anthroposophical Congress. Some two thousand delegates attended, including if not my grandmother, surely at least one representative of the branch she belonged to in Liverpool. Among the speakers, many brought from Germany by the dedicated anthroposophist Dr Ita Wegman, was Fried Geuter, an expert in Rudolf Steiner's Curative Education (better known today as Waldorf Education).

The following year, Theodora Wilson, a Quaker and a member of the Anthroposophical Society for over a decade, sent her son Michael to meet Fried (pronounced Freed) at Birmingham's New Street Station. A professional violinist, Michael was not pleased; he was due to go to the opera Lohengrin that evening. Still he did his duty. The two young men caught up with one another the next day (both proved to be addicted to Wagner) and before he knew what was happening, Michael was following

Fried to Berlin to attend the first ever Waldorf Curative Conference. It has long been said that opposites attract, and here was living proof: Fried the idealist and Michael the pragmatist, but sharing a love of music and whole-heartedly appreciating each others' gifts and capabilities.

Initially Michael stayed at Sonnenhof, the very first home to be established for curative medicine based on Rudolf Steiner principles in Arlesheim, near Basel in Switzerland. Here he became properly acquainted with Steiner philosophy, the care of children with special needs and the German language. He then joined Fried in England, at a children's home in South Darenth, Kent. Soon enough (records intimate) they were booted out for not agreeing with policy. Back in Birmingham and deciding to open their own establishment, they found a house in Selly Oak, which they named Sunfield, after the Sonnenhof and Elmfield, the name of the Wilson's family home. (Theodora was a councillor on Birmingham City Council. There was also a family connection with Bournville.)

In the summer of 1932, Michael gathered everyone together – this would have been about twenty adults together with the children in their care – and told them they had a new home. Using a legacy, he had put down a deposit of 3,000 pounds on a large house with three cottages set in extensive gardens and surrounding farmland – some 40 acres in all. Clent Grove, as it was called, cost 6,000 pounds, and repairs and alterations began immediately. (Already converts to the anthroposophical cause, the vendors, Hugh and Cynthia Chance, organised the sum outstanding as a mortgage.) The new Home, renamed Sunfield after the founding home in Selly Oak, opened officially on June 4, 1933.

My mother was not the only person to be attracted to Sunfield, beautifully situated as it was in rolling English countryside at the foot of the Worcestershire Clent Hills. Over the next few years, the trickle of visitors turned into a small flood, as word went out throughout Europe of the community's unique and spirited work. They included many refugees fleeing increasing intolerance and discrimination under Nazi rule. Jewish exiles in particular brought a welcome array of riches – both in terms of creative ability and practical assistance. There were doctors, artists, writers, musicians, dancers, actors and singers – a galaxy of talent. Yet painters and poets happily became teachers; care staff and musicians, cooks and cleaners.

Dr Wegman visited many times, especially after 1935. She likened Sunfield to Epidaurus, and gave the buildings Greek names such as Aesclepius and Hygia. Michael Wilson, Fried Geuter and his wife Maria were the lynchpins of the community. After the war began, however, cracks began to appear in their relationships; after Ita Wegman died, they fell apart. Still it was a remarkable period, and my mother was there almost from the start.

Once again, she felt overwhelmed by her new environment. She remembers hiding behind a curtain for the first few weeks darning socks, because some of the children were so frightening; many of the older autistic and brain-damaged boys were large and ungainly, and often unpredictable in their behaviour. But gradually Michael in particular drew her out, and as her talents revealed themselves, he put them to work.

There was his orchestra, for example. He had already built a theatre, to the same shape and dimensions as Covent Garden (where he often performed) but in miniature and in accordance with the anthroposophical rules of architecture – crafted in wood and organic in design: no corners or sharp edges. He sent my mother and two other musically inclined staff members to study cello under Johan Hoch, a conductor with the Birmingham Philharmonic. Her comrades soon hit the dust, but Herr Hoch kept my mother on. Soon enough, Michael (who was always intrigued by her, saying she had a good bowing arm – or perhaps he simply fancied her?) had his orchestra, which included two harps because one musician could not change pedals quickly enough to keep time.

When my mother first moved into Sunfield, she became quickly aware of one staff member much younger than the rest. Elizabeth (Betty) Loader had been seventeen when her mother sent her to Clent from Liverpool to work and learn by example, and she had already been at

Sunfield for eighteen months when my mother made her own move. My patriarchal grandmother, Sarah – with the nicknames Sal, or Primrose – was at this time living in a flat in Walton, Liverpool, and working at the local hospital.) Naturally enough Betty's older brother Samuel Robert, or Bob as he was always called, who was working in and around the Birmingham area, often came to visit.

The first time my mother became aware of my father was as she descended the main staircase and saw a long thin back sitting in the entrance hall, waiting for his sister: I was so relieved he didn't take much notice at the time, she says; I was suffering an attack of impetigo on my face – lots of spots and pimples – and looked an absolute fright.

Once my father did become aware of Gwen Price, he too joined the community, working mainly in the gardens and on the home's farm, run as it was according to Steiner's principles of bio-dynamic agriculture by David Clement. (He and my mother still communicate, all these years later.) The idea was that Sunfield should be as self-sustainable as possible without being cranky (though my father was to have strong opinions on this matter), eating vegetarian dishes created from organic foodstuffs off home-made ceramics, wearing clothing woven and dyed in the workshops. Little wonder that the father of Indian nationalism Mahatma Ghandi called in while on a trip to the UK; my mother recalls his visit with amazing casuality because, So many famous people – including Haile Selassie and Chad Varah – visited in those days.[28]

Life was poor in the material sense, but enriching in every other way. The only money coming into Sunfield was from the parents who placed their children in its care. If a family with a child with special needs proved too poor to pay the fees, staff would try to find a philanthropic sponsor. No one received wages as such. Instead everyone was fed and housed, though sometimes clothing ran second to the necessary payment of community bills. But there were study groups every evening after the children were put to bed, and the atmosphere was charged, both intellectually and creatively. Sexually too, I suspect.

My father left Clent on the declaration of war against Germany in September 1939. He felt he should be out in the real world, doing his bit, the intimation being that life at Sunfield was somehow not authentic, not legitimate. Not that the world outside jumped up and down with gratitude at his sacrifice. At age twenty-eight he was considered too old to be immediately drafted, and spent the next few years struggling to survive in a string of insecure and badly paid jobs – anything, anywhere that would keep him near Gwen and his sister.

He could have been a solicitor, my mother keeps repeating. By accepting the offer of that careerist boat to South America that sank, my father had missed another, one that might have kept him nicely afloat into retirement. The choice he made was not only to haunt him forever, but was to colour my mother's attitude towards my grandfather throughout my childhood.

My parents went through a civil ceremony of marriage at Coventry Register Office on August 24, 1940. It was a small gathering according to photographs – my father's landlady Mrs Batten, and her daughter Mary, his friend Bill Kidd, and Uncle Arcos (Albert Price) for my mother. My father (who was tall, well over six foot, and skin and bone from head to toe) wore a somewhat ill-fitting double-breasted suit with enormous lapels; my mother, a blue wool coat that she had made herself, with a matching hat. (She insists on maintaining nostalgic contact with this event every time she gets up in the morning and turns in at night; she claims scraps of her wedding coat are pegged into the rag rug beside her bed, though damned if I can find them.)

Three days later there was a full-scale ceremony at Sunfield. Photographs show it was a beautiful sunny day, with everyone outside on the front lawn – children dancing and singing, relatives and friends crowding around. My father wore the same suit; my mother another of her own creations: a dress of creamy white lace, nipped in and shaped to show off her own eighteen-inch waist and thirty-six-inch bust to best advantage, tight sleeves and a full skirt, all edged with ruched satin ribbons and rosettes of the same on ribbon streamers. Yet she insists it was not made as a wedding dress, but rather for a concert. How she got hold of such fabric and trimmings in wartime is a bit of a mystery, but again she swears she bought them by the yard, and cheaply, from the department store Owen Owen in Birmingham. Her veil was kept in place with small creamy-white rosebuds picked that morning from the arbour.

She had one bridesmaid, Ilse Germeiner (later Brice), whose dress she had also made, and with whom she shared a cottage on the estate. (This was before barracks were built to house staff, called The Watches.) Jo was there for the occasion, also Eric and Kathleen, Albert and his other son, Douglas. It was, my mother says, a wonderful day.

Such occasions were a relief from less happier times. As my mother recalls: Several of the staff – mostly German male refugees – were removed from Sunfield to detention camps, some as far away as in Canada. The police would come in the morning, and we would all stand in a circle with the children and sing The Quest of the Holy Grail before our friends were taken away. I remember a very young talented pianist being put into a car... also dear Roland Zader (who married Rhona Everett). He was an Oppenheimer, his father an eye specialist, yet at Clent he just laid tables and printed out music on the Gestetner.

My parents moved to the outskirts of Coventry, where my father eventually landed a job with Armstrong-Siddeley – by this time a round-the-clock Shadow Factory, having put the manufacture of cars aside to assist the war effort. He felt himself lucky, and I guess in those difficult times, he was. But he was never happy, bent over a desk, pushing papers, ordering nuts and bolts by the ton. He once told me that he had envisioned himself as a farmer or a racing driver. He was to come nowhere close to either dream.

My parents returned to Sunfield for my birth, and I was born in a beautiful wood-panelled room in the building at the back of the main house, called St Mary's. I arrived with a fine crop of dark hair, assisted into the world by one Nurse Skinner, with the occasion duly celebrated by the whole community. At my christening, Michael Wilson promised to act as my godfather; Jo, my godmother. (I am told Michael happily did the same for any number of babies over the years that followed, quite possibly forgetting their names as quickly as he forgot mine.)

It is at this point in their lives that Sam catches up with his eldest son and daughter-in-law. He likes my parents address – The Bivouak, Gipsy Lane – and is familiar with both the district and Coventry, having spent time there when last over on business. He stayed also at the Royal Arms in Kenilworth, and yearns to see England again.

There is, of course, no news from Liverpool. He had written several letters to and about his wife, the last mailed via the steamship *Andalucia* in March, concerned that she had been unwell: *It is distressing to know that she has been sick, and that I was not alongside. I have never fallen out with anyone, it was the other way around and I am always willing to get together again but somehow I get no response and therefore have to make myself content out here.* Also he knows that second son Barney (he of the well-aimed punch!) was safely returned from France. Such information was extremely sketchy, however. Sam did not appear to know, for example, that Barney had been at Dunkirk, standing in water for two days waiting to be evacuated. Interestingly Andy's father, a member of the King's regiment and a strong swimmer, was awarded a medal for saving someone's life during the evacuation from that terrible beach. My uncle's, I like to think.

For Barney's part, his health was irreparably affected. For my grandfather, ignorance is bliss. Because Sam remains at the Hotel Hispano, and very comfortable he is too. Having given up the whisky business – *which I dropped after losing $10 000* – he now has more freedom, crossing the estuary to Montevideo on a regular basis. *I am still in touch with Mr Downes, the Manager of the Triumph Cycle Co. Ltd., Coventry, who has been bombed out two or three times but comes up smiling every time.*

Indeed, he appears to know more about Downes than how his son was faring in the same city. During the final devastating blitz of November 14, 1940, my father left my mother's side only when the church near where they were lodging in Balsall Common received a direct hit. The curate, who had been taking a class and sent everyone underground when the sirens began their hair-raising wailing, lost his eyesight. Everyone else emerged unscathed, except for being filthy dirty. My mother – pregnant with me – came to in a local pub, with locals waving smelling salts under her nose: Jo, working in Birmingham and hearing that Coventry was under heavy attack, had rung Sunfield. Fried Geuter and Michael Wilson then came over from Clent, looking for us.

Whether my father ever went into such detail in his letters, I have no idea. I suspect not. As a young man of privilege (attending a minor public school in Liverpool that, until some still unidentified family ruckus pulled the security blanket from under everyone's feet, instilled strong values as to what constituted an English gentleman) his stiff upper lip, his determination to stay strong and suffer in silence, were engrained.

Sam to the contrary continues to bemoan his fate: *I live a quiet life, entirely on my own, as I don't go abroad very much. Just now when it is cold, after dinner, and coffee, I generally retire, and read in bed for an hour, and afterward sleep comfortably until morning. I sometimes go out to Belgrano for dinner on Saturday or Sunday, and watch a rugger match on Saturday. Also when there is anything on at the cine* (cinema) *I go along.*

Six months later, still self-absorbed and refusing to take any blame for the fragmentation of his family, he is noting even more peevishly how extraordinary it is that people will not communicate. *I reply at once to every letter I get, so as to place the responsibility upon the receiver to reply in due course.*

*It is the same with the family in Liverpool, they never write. They appear to think I have no interest, but I am worrying all the time, and waiting for some favourable sign that they might have come to their senses. On the 23rd instant, I sent a cable to Mother, reminding that I had not forgotten her birthday, and asking how all were, and to please write. On the 24th I celebrated, took myself out to dinner at one of the popular restaurants, and silently thought of all at home, including you and Gwen. I also bought myself a present to fit the occasion.*

He does hear from some people, but they are mainly business acquaintances: *Bob Hughes, Major Dromfield, Mr Cranfield, Mr Norcliffe and others in the South and Midlands, so I get what little news there is to give, or can be given.*

All this notwithstanding, he keeps quite extraordinarily well, he chunters on, barring trouble with his teeth, but is getting them fixed and longing for the day when he has *something really good to chew on.* Also, because business has done quite well over the previous eight months, with losses of 1940 recovered, he can now afford to do business further afield: *I go over to Montevideo, as I can always pick up orders there, and they pay my expenses for a short holiday down at one of the splendid seaside places on the coast. I am due to go over again on the 10th proxo, and am taking a bathing suit.*

He then provides a rare insight into his daily routine, reviewing what he calls a perfectly ordinary day.

*I get up at 7.30 and not liking the coffee in the hotel, usually I go across the road to a Cafe or Bar, and have Coffee and Milk, three crescents (light bread) and Butter with Dulce de Leche. After reading the newspaper, I enter my office, next door to the Cafe, and toddle about with anything there is to do. If the going is good I get orders for Sanitary Ware etc., which is enough to keep cash for hotel expenses, office, and a little more besides. I see a few clients, but as business is very restricted, I have plenty of time on my hands. I go to lunch at 12, and after have a rest, and perhaps sleep, an hour or so, and back to the Office at 2 or thereabouts. When five comes along I nearly always go to the Chinese cafe, The Pagoda, for Tea, toast, butter and dulce, and a few cakes. At six I close my office, and often read for an hour, or rest on my bed. As dinner at the hotel is 8.30, I often do not know what do, so perhaps go to News Cine. I am usually in bed by 10, to keep fit.*

While this paragraph makes me laugh, it is more than likely it made my father cry (or rather feel like crying). What was it like for him to read of such easy and idle gluttony, at a time when rationing was beginning to tighten and the very idea of *a few cakes* must have made his mouth water. He never showed his father's letters to my mother, and maybe (I am now moving to better understand) with good reason. She would not have been amused.

I myself am not amused to wake early afternoon and find my day half gone. And yet there are also wonders upon which to marvel. The newspaper shading my face may have taken off in all directions (accidental litter lout that I am) but my backpack still lies under my head and shoulders, one strap wound around my wrist, untouched. I have been asleep a good hour and yet remain unmolested. What a wonderful city this is, I think; what on earth are people talking about when they describe it as dangerous?

On this positive note, I decide to do something constructive, heading down to Azapardo 455, the address of the *Buenos Aires Herald* itself, as Founded (the sign outside proudly proclaims) in 1876. Unlike *La Nacion* and several other major papers, which hang out in monumental Baroque or Victorian splendour, this building is discretion itself. Flanked by trees, the ground floor glass frontage surmounted by a second floor fronted with modernistic Islamic-style arches, and with a modest entrance and quiet under-stated lobby, I feel immediately at home.

Despite my crumpled appearance, the receptionist at the front desk takes my *Japan Times* business card seriously and disappears upstairs. Before I know where I am, the lift is carrying me upwards to the editorial floor and a very nice man with rolled-up sleeves, a tired, gentle face and an equally tired, gentle demeanour is offering assistance. The editor is not in, but John is sure Andrew would want to help.

Of course you can go through the files, John says; I suggest you call us when you get back from Chile and we can set up a date and time.

Excellent, I say and bow out, gifting a scatter of grass and leaves in my wake. But it is good news. I have made a useful contact. Now, faced with hours of searching through back copies of the paper (as you already know, reading microfiche makes me feel hideously ill), I have to decide what exactly it is I am looking for.

I celebrate this small accomplishment around the corner, sitting outside a cafe and watching a choreographed dance that, while not the tango, is just as complex and dramatic. Men come and go, in and out, moving from table to table to table, exchanging greetings, news and gossip. And at the centre of the proceedings, a man of such vast proportions – rolls of blubber that overhang two chairs, half a dozen chins, a suit that surely required half a cotton field – that I find it hard to tear my eyes away from such bafflingly sad incongruity. I mean, how can he bear it? How does someone get to be like that? A heart attack is surely on the cards.

Aware that my own bits of unwanted flab are not assisting my poor sore feet in doing their job of getting me around, I walk back towards Retiro as far as I can (ouch! eech! ouch!), and then hail a taxi. Good idea, wrong taxi! The driver wears a singlet designed to show off a muscle-bound torso developed in a gym and tanned in a solarium. I can see him in the mirror, his eyes sliding up and down the top half of my body, but with a kind of contemptuous interest. And then he puts his foot down like the thirty-year-old macho-manic he undoubtedly is.[29]

As I tell Maria-Elena later that evening, still feeling half-sick with fright, it is a miracle I survived to tell the tale. And she gives me her own good-bad news: No ticket for Chile tomorrow. All flights booked. But definitely Thursday.

# PART 2

# MIDDLE YEARS

*Happy families are all alike; every unhappy
family is unhappy in its own way.*

LEO TOLSTOY

(Anna Karenina)

*If fortune turns against you, even jelly breaks your tooth.*

ANONYMOUS

(Persian proverb)

*To have to understand the living, you have to commune with the dead.*

ANONYMOUS

# THROUGH THE PAIN BARRIER

**40 RANULF CROFT, COVENTRY, 1944**

*When Eric and Kathleen used to bring me back from Stourbridge, where they lived, normally my uncle would park his splendid car (or so it seemed to me) in front of our house. I often stayed at their home as a child, in large part I think to provide my cousin Alison with company of her own age. She was almost exactly one year younger than me.*

*This time, however, I distinctly recall walking around the corner into the croft and crossing the road to reach for the latch on the front gate. I am wearing a tailored brown coat, made by my mother, with a darker brown velvet collar, and matching felt beret. (Think Harrods children's department and you get the picture.)*

*I climb the stairs and go into the back bedroom where my mother is sitting on the edge of the bed, her long hair flowing over her shoulders as dark as a raven's wing. (Usually it is rolled up in practical but unbecoming fashion, in accordance with hard times.)* Look, *she says, nappy in hand, her mouth full of safety pins,* Here's your little sister. *I look, and there she is: Bridget Anne.*

*I am told it was love at first sight. But that blind emotion was all too soon to become confused with responsibility. When my father finally joins the Navy towards the end of the war, he tells me to look after my mother and Bridget, for I am the man of the family now. (Well, he did want a son, and what he got was me.) I take this instruction very seriously, placing childish thoughts and needs aside to do my very best.*

*I think a lot about this responsibility in later years. I was after all, only three – or maybe just four – years old.*

## WALSGRAVE HOSPITAL, COVENTRY, 1945

*Pretty sickly as a child – what in those days was politely called "Delicate", though if you saw me now you might find it hard to believe – I missed a lot of school. Often my bed would be moved downstairs into the back – the dining room – so that my mother wouldn't have to run up and downstairs all the time. The family doctor was a constant visitor to the house. While considering him extremely old, I was always much amused by his name: Dr Lavorty.*

*It was so much prolonged time spent in bed that transformed me into an avid reader. Since I was too young to be enrolled, my mother would bring me a batch of library books once a week, and I'd skim through them at a rate of knots to decide which I wanted to read word-for-word and which not. The librarian was disbelieving, having never heard of a four-year-old reading so much so fast. How could anyone of my age get through half a dozen books a week? So one day when I was fit enough to accompany my mother into central Coventry – the library being alongside St Mary's Church, just in front of the bombed ruins of the old cathedral and the Golden Cross pub – the librarian put me to the test and I scampered through the outline of the story without hesitation. No trouble after that! By the time I started school, I was way ahead, hardly able to believe that most of the children in my age group didn't even know their ABC.*

*When I am nine, I'm diagnosed with acute tonsillitis and admitted to hospital to have the offending flesh cut out. I awake from the operation to hear rather than see in fuzzy fashion a group of nurses scoffing the contents of a box of chocolates brought to me as a present (still a luxury in those days). When I try to protest, my throat turns to acid and flame. Force-fed jelly and blancmange for days, I toss and turn in a tangle of feverish outrage, unable to comprehend such an act of deceit. Of course I have long since forgiven them, starved of sweet treats as they were in postwar Britain and no doubt thinking such sophistication would be lost on a child. But I have never forgotten.*

*Adults in general have no idea of the short- and long-term effect their actions have on children, especially when perceived as acts of betrayal. I think a lot about this too – especially in relation to my own children, wishing I had been more aware and considerate when I was younger.*

## 40 RANULF CROFT, COVENTRY, 1948

*On my seventh birthday, my mother takes us to Sunfield for the day. In the pottery I make a tiny figure of a man sitting on a bench, then paint it with multi-coloured slip. (I have it still.) My mother then leads me into the theatre, to show me where she used to work. As the doors of Wardrobe swing open, a deliciously foreign perfume wafts forth... Sandalwood, my mother whispers, intensifying the sense of mystery. Starting down the long, wood-lined corridor, she slides panels one after another and encourages me to run my hands through the hundreds of silk Eurythmy dance robes hanging within: feather-like wisps that she helped dye, cut and stitch in every colour of the rainbow, starting with white and ending far distant in an indigo so dark it is a deep purplish-black. My mother... as talented and good with her hands as her own beloved Mama.*

## GREEN LANE PRIMARY SCHOOL, COVENTRY, 1949

*I am sitting on a bench in the playground at morning break, observing my peers at play from the safety of a book. Part of me wants to join in... to be asked to join in... be as popular as Suzanne and as plucky as Sheila, my sometimes best friends out of school but not in. I don't know why, only that the discrepancy makes me feel twisted with unhappiness, as if I am out of kilter with the whole wide world.*

*As the bell is rung to denote the end of the rest period, I stand up and move to join the queue for my class. At that moment, a big boy – meaning he is nine or ten – runs straight at me and bashes into my side with a whoop of what sounds like victory. I hear a click, feel a sharp, excruciating pain, and* lift my right hand to see the little finger sticking out at right angles from the second joint.

I must have viewed it with a certain detachment, because I join the line, trail into class and sit through the next lesson without a murmur. When it comes to writing something down – a spelling test I seem to recall – I struggle and the girl sitting alongside suddenly sees the reason why. As she screams in horror, I smack the finger back into alignment against the palm of my left hand. By the time the teacher reaches our desk, there is nothing to see – in my eyes anyway.

Sixty plus years on the finger is only a little misshapen. But it's very good at telling me when rain is in the air.

## 40 RANULF CROFT, COVENTRY, 1951

(My mother considers we live in the part of the city called Stivichall, or Styvechale – the medieval spelling – as this is considered more upmarket; my father likes to bring her down-to-earth by insisting we live in Cheylesmore, but in some ways he is the more snobbish of the two.)

I have my own room now – the tiny box room above the hallway, next to my parent's bedroom at the front of the house. I have to clear out when my grandfather comes to stay, but that is such a rare occurrence it causes more excitement than resentment. My grandmother's visits are quite another matter. She would move in permanently if she could... if she was allowed.

I love my room, spending as much time as possible imagining myself locked inside. I would like to be able to lock my door as my parents lock their own, but am regarded as too young and irresponsible to have my own key. There is as much logic in this as my father hounding me to go to church on Sundays, when he hardly goes near the place himself, except in later years when he becomes ill. Or my being ordered to bed at 7p.m. even in high summer, when I can only sit on my bed and watch all the other children in the croft playing until nightfall. I am not encouraged to play with them. The implication is that we are somehow better than everyone else, a concept that, however hard I try, both aggravates and reinforces prejudice.

I love my room as much as the swing in the back garden, an enormous hoop *of iron set into concrete by my father, around the same time he planted two apple trees, one for me, one for my sister. My tree grows strong and prolific. I manage to shoot off the top of Bridget's with a homemade bow and arrow – two garden canes and a length of string – and it subsequently fails to thrive, as does she. Could the two matters be linked? Did I shoot down my own sister?*

*The blocks of concrete holding the hoop in place work loose so that the swing rocks backwards and forwards in a most comforting way, as I reach for the sky by day, and later, when allowed (or in secret) the stars by night. I would give anything to be able to fly away. I have a problem being anywhere inside the house apart from my room; sometimes I think I will die of claustrophobia, or end up killing someone.*

*It is difficult to argue my case on any point; my thinking is such a muddle that I do not know where to begin, let alone draw any conclusion. Most of the time I am too frightened to even try.*

## SCHOOL BUS, COVENTRY TO WARWICK, 1952

*There are three buses every morning, and more often than not I am running for the last one. It is quite a walk to the nearest bus stop and usually I leave the house with a piece of burned toast smeared with margarine and marmalade in my hand. (The sound of my mother scraping burned toast out the back door, and my father complaining bitterly about her dreamy carelessness, are seared into my memory. Her spirited apology, however, was always the same:* Charcoal is good for you!

*One day, a gang of girls sitting at the front of the bus pass along a whispered joke that involves sanitary towels and tomato ketchup. Sitting alone at the back, trying to catch up on homework – reading and writing, which I know from experience makes me feel incredibly ill – I am made to feel sick twice over. I have never been able to eat the sickly sweet pungent stuff since.*

## CALEDONIAN EXPRESS, BIRMINGHAM TO EDINBURGH, 1953

*I am twelve and my parents are putting me on the train to travel alone overnight to Edinburgh. Was it a sign of the times that they could be so trusting? Maybe they assumed me a well-seasoned traveller since I went to school daily on the bus. For they simply asked a couple with a dog – an old smelly spaniel with long, ragged ears – to keep an eye on me. I remember feeling sick with excitement (not fear). And going to sleep with my head on the dog's soft but solid rump.*

*At some point during the night I wake to find the compartment full of soldiers, drinking, smoking, playing cards and singing. I think, this is the life, and with a sense of pure contentment return to my slumbers.*

*Next morning, my father's elder sister, Catherine, meets me off the train in Edinburgh. She is tall and tweedy and rather forbidding, but kind. She takes me for breakfast in one of the big hotels, and I have porridge with brown sugar and cream. (At Forneth my Uncle Charles eats his with salt and milk. I know which I like best, but the difference fascinates.) We drive north in my aunt's ancient Morris Minor, breaking our journey overnight in Inverness where she has a little terraced house built in grey stone and slate, and then set off to cross Scotland east to west to the Isle of Skye. Along the way, in amazingly remote nooks and crannies of the landscape, we stay with friends – a couple of fluffy dizzy ladies, but also kind. At the Kyle of Lochalsh, I stay up reading through the night by light of a table lamp over which is flung a pink silk scarf, with beaded tassels around the edge. The book is one from the shelf:* The Hasty Heart. *All my romantic notions are fleshed out and satisfied. It does not occur to me that maybe my aunt is enjoying her own.*

*In the morning I play shinty on the loch-side road, with local kids, using my stick more to hook and drive debris from an overnight storm – branches and seaweed – back into the water than to hit the puck: a pebble I think.*

*On the ferry over to Skye (there was no bridge in those days) I lean over the side and one of my aunt's mittens falls into the sea. My hands had been cold, and she had taken off her gloves and put them over my own. Though a bit of a stickler, Catherine treated me above all else as if I was an intelligent being in my own right. She was not only extremely kind, she was also considerate and respectful. I sensed she saw me. I liked that.*

## UMBRELLA CLUB, COVENTRY, 1957

*My parents do something even more out of keeping. Knowing my keen interest in theatre and told that I have talent by a friend – the principal of Coventry Art School, and father of my best friend Sarah at The King's High School for Girls, Warwick – they take me along to the newly formed arts club in the city.*

*They push me through the door, enrol me and retreat. Leaving me among a group of people I assume to be at least twice my age, many of whom – straight and gay – regard me as jailbait. My terror is unimaginable. As always, I find a way to survive, adopting a posture and attitude of enormous sophistication, pretending to be all-knowing in the ways of the world. Half the time I have no idea what is going on.*

*I have this photo of a slim young woman with a pony tail and her nose in the air, in a sheath dress her mother has kindly made her (but in tweed, for God's sake), a stole around her shoulders, holding a glass of wine. It is the opening reception for* The White Devil, *the Jacobean tragedy by John Webster, being staged in Coventry's medieval Guildhall, in which she has – I had – a leading role.*

*For the first time since childhood I meet boys of my own age – three sixth-formers from King Henry VIII Grammar School in Coventry, roped in to play pages and underlings by one of their male teachers who is a member of the cast. Their names are John, Mike and Rick, and being far too scared to make the first move, I do my thing: assume the aloofness of Miss High and Mighty, while all the time praying like crazy to be liked, understood and fancied rotten.*

*Poor Angela – she looks twenty-five, going on thirty. In fact, she is just sweet sixteen and only recently kissed. (And not by John, Mike or Rick!) When I study her face now, there is no hint of what is going on inside her head, her heart, the depths of her soul: is she screaming again? No, I remember now; it was worse. She was wailing.*

# CHAPTER 10

# DEFINITELY THURSDAY

**NOVEMBER 10, 1999**

Don't ask. Disappointed, disconcerted, childishly resentful (if I'd had my own way, been allowed to get my own ticket, I would have got one) I lie in a slump past breakfast time. I know I should get up, go out onto the balcony, do a little yoga, attempt to rebalance the chemistry that brings me down into such a deep-seated dark and angry place. But there is no energy, no will. When Maria-Elena knocks on the door, concerned (as I would be in her place) I rudely feign sleep. In fits and starts through earlier hours I had finished Sereny's book and, while enthralled, now seem to understand little more of Speer's mindset than when I started. Whose failing is this? His, her's or my own?

I read two letters from Sam, the first dated July 4, 1942. Having heard from no-one – *denied information from any source* – his sombre self-pitying mood matches my own: *It is strange that whilst in England, and out here in business and private circles, and have built up a position where I am honoured by all, my family ignore me and treat me like a criminal, where as I have struggled all my life to help you to better positions, and in doing so and taking chances did not succeed at a time when a little luck, as you might call it, would have made all the difference.* This is the kind of statement typical of the betting man, every happy-go-lucky *chanta*; the gambler who never loses but ever-so-nearly wins. For the first time I feel a mild irritation, as if the man learned nothing from experience.

To the contrary. My grandfather is on the lookout for new business opportunities, going very shortly up north, and maybe visiting Colombia and El Centro, and Maracaibo, Venezuela: *For this purpose a new passport photo has been taken, and enlargements made of the best, one of which I enclose herewith, so that you may keep it, because in time I shall pass out, but if I feel as I do at present, I shall live for ever.*

He claims no ambitions for old age. *When the end does come I shall feel satisfied that I have always endeavoured to make up to you all again, but trust in the meantime I shall hear from you all regretting what has happened, and inviting me back, with the same love as of yore, because on no account am I returning on money conditions, and shall live my own life first if I am not assured of, first the love of my wife, and afterwards the love of my children.*

*I have always had high hopes of you* (meaning my father, heavily underlined in pen), *from the time I took you out to Colombia, but you seem to have been infected with the same malady. I am very soft hearted but it will require going all the way to make a cure.*

It will require going all the way to make a cure, I repeat, and somewhere deep inside, something resonates.


By May 1943 Sam has still not heard from anyone. Those of us at war in Coventry, however, are not forgotten: *I am thinking of you every day, almost every hour, wondering how you are getting along, and what you are doing.*

For himself he has little to say, little to grumble about, having been able to maintain good business and the previous year the best for many a long day. He shuttles back and forth between Buenos Aires and Montevideo, is in *splendid condition* and now weighs close on fifteen stone *without any superfluous fat to show.* Still lodged at the Hotel Hispano, his office is also very comfortable, being located in the late residence of one of the former Presidents of long ago, and for this reason the rooms are large, lofty and cool. It is not clear, nor ever becomes so, whether he is talking about the Calvet Building or some other premises he has moved to.

He has few friends, he claims, but *prefers to be alone* (again heavily under-scored; and not for the first time I fail to believe a word). He mentions going out to dinner with cousins (cousins? cousins in the plural? what cousins?) and heading for the *cine*(ma) when hard up for something to do. Watching rugby and polo also helps while away the hours. *It seems I am only wasting my time now, with no interest in the world, as my personal interests have gone stray, and nobody seems to care, so I keep my sorrows to myself, hoping that one day there will be an awakening.*

I awake a different person. Full of purpose I leap out of bed and into action. There is no reason as to why early morning appeared so bleak, and now I feel on more of an even keel. It happens every now and then (though not as often as in the past) and I am learning to stay low and not to panic; the clouds (depression, negativity, misery) will pass, the sun (energy, optimism, renewal) will come out again. Catching up on news clippings from 1992 (this file the thickest to date) while travelling into the city centre, the heat is promising and I make a note – listed after *Bank, Embassy & Clubs: Buy sun cream.*

According to a Gallup Poll published in early January, 1992, Argentina had suddenly become the most optimistic country in the world. Sixty-one per cent of those polled were upbeat because the economic plan to privatise state-owned industries and peg the peso to the dollar appeared to be working. And though torrential rains just days later left at least fifty-two people dead in Cordoba, the country's second most populous province after Buenos Aires, this did not dampen President Menem's confidence concerning the year ahead. Indeed, the world faced a flurry of government statements regarding the future of the Malvinas Islands, coming hard on the heels of a promise by Menem to visit the UK by the end of the year – the tenth anniversary of Argentina's defeat in the region by British forces.

At the same time, *The Washington Post* was enquiring, "Why Doesn't Latin America Work – Is its Economic Malaise Based on its Culture?" Every day in Argentina, it seemed, thousands of employees arrived late or failed to show up at all, thousands of appointments were missed, thousands of business meetings cancelled, deadlines allowed to pass, and golden opportunities irretrievably lost because those involved had to spend an hour or more waiting in line (somewhere, for something, even buying postage stamps).

To stimulate change (or add to the problem), the European Commission was considering sending hundreds of thousands of East European refugees to settle in the region. Argentina (meaning its government, members of which could afford to pay people to stand in line for them) was keen to fall in with the plan, because a) the country had a slow birth-rate and b) the economy appeared to be coming out of recession. As Diego Guelar, a fourth-generation Romanian and Argentine Ambassador to the EU told *The Times*: "Argentina has always supported this type of emigration."

In February 1992, one year on from Menem announcing that Argentina would open its archives on former Nazis accepted into the country after 1945, the government was being accused of staging little more than a publicity stunt. On March 17 a car bomb exploded, reducing the Israeli Embassy in Buenos Aires to rubble with many fatalities. Menem described it as a terrorist attack committed by, "Groups acting from outside of the country." Other officials thought it might be aimed at scuttling the Middle East Peace process, or simply to attack Israeli interests.

During March, newly released Nazi documents were, "Too late for justice". Argentine veterans were still bitter to be veterans: "A bad memory". Meanwhile, British residents who had found their loyalties divided over the Malvinas–Falklands debacle were shocked to learn that their children preferred to speak Spanish ("Anglo–Argentines bat on in defence of tea and scones", headlined *The Times*). As winter turned to spring, Leopoldo Galtierri and his generals continued to refuse to talk about The War, the UK Franks report indulged in a very British cover up of the political failures that led to The War, and an Argentine peace boat that sailed to The Islands received a very frosty reception.

By May, Menem was making waves abroad. He was describing Argentina's role in the Americas as, "A Canada of the South". July he made headlines in *Time Magazine*: "Menem's Miracle: A backwoods governor turned economic messiah, Argentina's president has created a free-enterprise success under the banner of Peronism." Inside the country, however, there was deep cynicism: while his personal life was shambolic, "With low inflation, Menem could wed ten women and dance till dawn and no-one would care."

Again all appeared to go quiet on the Argentine front until the end of the year starred the Robbery of the Century: three men posing as Central Bank Inspectors walked away with 30 million dollars worth of old bills collected for incineration.

In between Menem's waves and that great robbery? Maybe I just stopped clipping newspapers, for 1992 was a year of much activity and travel: Okinawa (May), Paris and the UK (June/July), Sado Island off Japan's West coast for a music festival in August.[30] It was also when Lee's marriage fell apart on Cyprus, and he painted the exterior of our house in London in exchange for a ticket to Japan to spend August in tropical heat licking his wounds. There was a lot happening, at home as well as abroad.

In the early summer of 1943, Sam experiences a change of heart of his own. It has at long last occurred to him that maybe letters are not reaching their destination because of the war, now in its fourth year: *I wrote you about three months ago, and at that time several boats were lost.... others may also have gone stray owing to the uncertainty on the high seas.*

Business continues to be very slack, owing to restrictions, and although commissions are still being reordered, it is not of the same volume as the previous three years. Buenos Aires, however, is still active, with few signs of the conflict affecting Europe: *everyone seems to have plenty of money, and the pleasure places are always full of people.* His great new amusement is a radio, because he can listen to the whole world, including Great Britain: *I had no inclination to purchase such a machine previously, but now find it an economy. Instead of taking coffees etc or going to the cine, etc, I now stay put, and smoke my cigars which, by the way is the only really wicked vice I have. I must have my box of good cigars every month.*

He is still in the Hispano, *which I have just about bought, having paid out some $10,000 since I came out here.* Then begins wittering on about the lavish nature of his wardrobe, apparently unaware of – or insensitive to – just how hard life was for my parents (no wonder my mother got so mad with him at times): *All my clothes, especially socks, come back from the laundry like new. I have a heap of clothes, about ten suits, all good, dozens and dozens of shirts, ties, collars etc, which I have bought when I had good months, and they have been quite a lot.* (Nothing like bragging to make a friend of a far distant unknown daughter-in-law, for sure.) *I have also bought a large traveling trunk ready for a trip* (back to England). He longs to see us all, and wants photographs of my mother and me to add to the one of my father on his dressing table. And as usual he sends his fondest love to us: *Mother (to whom I sent a cable on her birthday and at Christmas but no sound from the Western front),* and everybody else, *trusting that Barney is safe and sound.*

It amazes me that he could be so bound up in his own needs and neuroses that the reality of life, both abroad and at home, had so little impact and meaning. (And this with a radio to listen to.) For example, on June 3, 1943, the date he tapped out this last letter, the writing was on the wall for the Argentine government of President Ramon Castillo – a former Dean of the Faculty of Law at the University of La Plata, where fifty years later Pablo's girlfriend, Fernanda, was to study. Within forty-eight hours the government had been overthrown, defeated by a military revolutionary movement, a provisional junta in power, and martial law declared throughout the country. Now you would think such momentous happenings would warrant a line, especially with civilians being caught up in rioting in the Plaza de Mayo just up the street from his hotel. But no. He is in a small narrow world of his own making, where a suit count takes precedence over any body count, and he is more focused on the silence of family lost than the sounds of fellow-citizenry in uprising.

As a businessman, however, he would surely have belonged to the British Club and the British Chamber of Commerce. Most certainly he would be listed as a resident with the British Embassy. So this is where I head first.

At Palomar, an elderly man with an unfashionable but marked elegance bounces his cane up and down to the music of a *tanquero*, wafting out of a coffee shop. To one side, a middle-aged couple enjoys a smooch; they could of course be dancing the tango, but lips are busier than legs. Walking down Avenida Alvear, at 1585 is a hairdressing salon named Alfredo Takahashi. Now there's a Japan–Argentine-linked story.

Number 1693 is a building of unbelievably ornate beauty, but crumbling, in dire need of a coat of paint, with large hungry-looking guard dogs roaming the perimeter fence. Yet the area is exceedingly wealthy: here is Sotheby's, for example, there, Louis Vuitton; Polo is across the road. Versace, Hermes, all the brand names are roundabout. In the window of an antique shop, a ceramic negro in turban and knickerbockers, holding aloft a shell as an offering, is stood alongside two well-defined, near-naked negroes designed as bookends. I mean really, where was – is – the respect.

Compared to all this extravagance, the British Embassy at the address Dr Luis Agote 2412, is a model of deferential decorum, though housed in a building of such stark contemporary ugliness that it makes the soul cringe. My soul anyway. What did they knock down to build this, I wonder, turning my attention in the comfortable if clinical lobby to the Citizen's Charter on the wall: seems that if I am not satisfied with the service provided by consular staff I can complain to Her Majesty's consular representative, currently HM Consul Mr David Paginton, who is obliged to reply to my queries in three working days. To complain about the consul him- or herself, I must write to the Deputy Head of the Mission, in this instance the Right Honourable Dominic Asquith, who is obliged to answer in a similar manner. The Deputy Head of Mission – the Vice-Consul – is named Emma: my great-grandfather's counterpart, over a century on.

Or so I have been assuming. Months before I had faxed the embassy, asking for confirmation of Samuel Turner's diplomatic posting and my grandfather's own expatriate status. The woman with whom I have been communicating is here now but operating at a snail's pace with a vague half-knowing smile on her face, as if her mind is in large part elsewhere, which it most probably is. For this reason, having travelled God knows how many miles to meet her, I leave no better off than sitting at my fax machine in Japan. According to asserted searches, not only are the two men unrecorded, but the name Loader itself unknown.

It is the same bemusing news that I had received from a female civil servant woman half a world away at the British Foreign Office, also contacted earlier in the year. She wrote: *I cannot find the name of your great-grandfather, Samuel Turner Loader, in any of the Foreign Office Official Lists for that period; he is not listed under the staff in Argentina, or in Uruguay, or in the Statement of Services, which is a short career history of diplomats that accompanies each volume. I have checked in the* Times Index *for 1899 as normally diplomats would have an obituary in the* Times Newspaper, *but again there was no reference.* It was this kindly soul – a member of the Americas, Asia and Pacific Team providing Library and Information Services at the Foreign Office Library – who suggested I try the Family Records Centre at the Public Record Office, if I had not done so already.

Outside the embassy, on the street, feeling slightly hysterical, I burst out laughing. It is ridiculous. Did these men exist or didn't they? Lunch at a nearby pizzeria helps ease the anguish: it may be that I have come all this way for nothing.

I have extracted some small bits of information, however. Emma's secretary's phone number on a direct line; also two names: a David and a Rosemary. Heading in their general direction, I keep seeing red telephone boxes, even if they do say only *Telecom*. Also a taxi (rather too optimistically I feel at this point in time) passes with a sticker across the back window: *Diego Maradona: The legend continues...*

At the same time I recall this morning, looking at Maria-Elena's family photos from Chile, and hearing her think aloud along the following lines: What is it about this family that so many of the women don't want to get married. Why do so many remain single?

I walk into the first address on my list, number 586 on 25 de Mayo (having initially confused it with 556) and find the premises in the process of renovation. There are tarpaulins and debris everywhere, with the sound of hammering echoing up the stairs. Undaunted I ascend to the first floor, and just as I lift my hand to knock on a dusty door, it opens and a tall, rather elegant chap in a smart business suit peers at me over his glasses with quizzical good humour.

Well hello, he says, in dulcet English tones; And what can we do for you?

David turns out to be the Executive Director of the British Chamber of Commerce in the Argentine, as well as the Lloyds Representative. He reminds in looks, posture and well-modulated tones of a certain former member at the Foreign Correspondent's Club of Japan in Tokyo, but proves to be rather less pompous and awesome. David is kind enough to consider my family name sounds familiar, and even takes the trouble to note it down.

Then he comes clean: Look, it's really bad timing. You can see the state we're in. I mean, all our books and records are in complete disarray.

After saying this, he throws open double-doors to the main club room, with everything covered with dust sheets except for a dusty elderly man fast asleep in a large dusty armchair, with the observation, As you can see, we have many old relics.

I can see that, I reply tongue-in-cheek; He most certainly looks like an old relic.

David guffaws in agreement: You're absolutely right. He is an old relic.

Given precise instructions for my next port of call, I find Rosemary just a few streets away, on the first floor of 575 Reconquista. She is busy with an elderly man, who does not seem to want anything in particular, but just to chat. Occasionally he turns to me and makes pronouncements: I fought in the war, you know... I'm eighty, you know...

I am happy to confirm here and now that he has a place in the world and will never be forgotten.

When he leaves, a grey-haired woman of rather less-advanced years takes his place. She and Rosemary then discuss eye operations. Rosemary, it transpires, has had four, To repair retina damage.

Oh yes, the woman contributes eagerly; My husband had that a long time ago. He had to lie with sandbags on either side to keep his head still and stare at the ceiling. He became *so* familiar with the tunes on the radio at that particular time.

I feel increasingly as if I am in some kind of Woody Allen time warp, with Christmas cards and calendars for the year 2000 on sale, but surrounded by the type of paper chains I used to make for Christmas as a child, a Poppy appeal, notice of the Suburban Players performing Arnold Wesker's A Taste of Honey, and news of a Millennium Do at the Tigre Boating Club.

Asked the purpose of the club, Rosemary bridles, but in friendly fashion.

We're not a club, she corrects; We're a charitable organisation, founded in 1939 as the Argentine-British Community Council, to collect money to send to England for the duration of the war. Since then we've been taking care of widows or actual volunteers in the First and Second World Wars. We still look after one (volunteer) who survived 1914–1918. Leonard is one hundred and two, insists he is going to live forever, and next year his life will have spanned three centuries. I think that quite remarkable, don't you?

Remarkable, I agree; Not many people manage to do that... except in Japan on the Okinawa island chain, where men and women do it all the time. But I keep that to myself, just in case she thinks we are in competition, which we most certainly are not.

Rosemary and her voluntary band of helpers are looking after some ninety elderly folk even as we speak. They are taken care of either in their homes and given a stipend and/or medical coverage as proves necessary, or supported in homes for the aged.

As Rosemary further explains: We're a link between the British community and the Ambassador. The embassy is very good to us, holding fund-raising events in the gardens and residence. We organise all kinds of other activities to raise money, or bring the community together. No, we've no idea how many Brits still live in Argentina, or even Buenos Aires. We've never been able to count. We have three thousand five hundred listed in our computer, but not everyone registers with the embassy, so....

Did Sam not register, I wonder now. Did he have problems with authority, just as I do? If he had failed to sign up, he would have most certainly slipped through the net of support that BACC offered during his time there.

Rosemary has been in charge here since 1993 and really likes the job: It's useful, you know?

She came to Argentina in 1963: I came with someone who was coming here and thirty years later, well, here I am still.

Isn't it always the way, I reply with deep empathy.

Well, she elaborates, her children are around, and anyway she really likes the place: Argentina's been very kind to her, she says.

We get on well. After all, we have a lot in common, and I really like her calm down-to-earth nature and natural warmth. I envy her such fluent Spanish, but then it's obvious she has put in the work. She suggests I talk to the owner of a bookshop called LOLA, for Literature of Latin America; Colin has been in Buenos Aires forever, she observes; he knows everything about and everybody in the British community.

I buy a picture calendar to remind myself just how quickly the days are speeding towards Christmas and the end of the millennium: *gauchos* on horseback, naturally.

Then as if to celebrate contact with so many English-speaking people, I jump on a bus. It takes a while to get the hang of how to put the money in and get a ticket, and those queuing up behind are not pleased. But the journey itself is a trip; I love buses, trains, but less so planes. I mean, I like the idea of them and porthole views of the world, whipped marshmallow and cream cloud formations willing. But not the thought of all that space under the floor, below the cargo deck, beneath…

I spy a piece of graffiti reading Lady Godiva, which makes me think of Coventry when I do not want to be reminded.[31] I call by the internet cafe to pick up any e-mail: none today. Yesterday there was one from Louise in Sydney, another from a company in Hong Kong, about six or seven in total – which I found both astonishing and time-consuming. I write a long letter to Andy, then repeat much of my news to Canadian neighbours in Japan who were close to Kevin before he returned to Toronto. And pack mentally for tomorrow.

Back at the Caseros ranch, there is yet another surprise I could do without. I am going to Chile tomorrow, but not alone.

## NOVEMBER 11, 1999

What could I say when Maria-Elena produced two tickets instead of one, like rabbits out of hat. Thoroughly pleased with herself, she laid them down on the table with a flourish and then enveloped me in an excited hug: We go together, yes?

So here we are, en route to the airport, driven this time not by Pablo No. 2, nor the overweight hulk from the cab stand on the corner, but a sadly dignified man in his early fifties. Learning I am British he asks where I stand on The War. (This has happened several times before; the Malvinas–Falklands conflict is unfinished business here.) There is no aggression in his tone, though, only curiosity. After I state my piece – about how it was a disgraceful exhibition on both sides of political manipulation for personal gain, with no thought for the general populace, the people who suffer, he waits until we are stopped at a traffic light, and then reaches around to offer me his hand. From his conversation with my cousin, I gather that he was a banker until two years ago when the corporate rug was pulled out from under his feet. He has not been able to find alternative full-time employment of a similar nature – or indeed any decent job – since.

166

At the airport, I phone my mother to find her frantic, not because of Eric, but because three days ago Bridget had been rushed to Rheumatology Outpatients in Coventry. (Maybe seeing that spray-painted sign yesterday reading Lady Godiva was exactly that: A Sign.) I finally get through to Walsgrave Hospital to be told my sister's blood count had shot up to one hundred and nine, with fluid on her lungs together with kidney failure, anaemia and a bladder infection. Apparently she is also having trouble with her heart, but my mother is not to know this.

Yes, it does sound bad, agrees the Ward Sister in a broad Brummy accent, But she's stable and there's nothing you can do but pray.

Praying however, is Bridget's style, not mine; she is the good Christian in the family. I have always been written off as the unholy one.

When I rejoin Maria-Elena in the waiting lounge, I am shaking all over again, struggling to contain myself. I am beginning to dislike and resent the ease of instant communications: in many ways wish I was travelling in complete ignorance of everything happening to everyone everywhere else.

The *pampa* is not as expected – or rather the part of the country over which we are flying is not as imagined. I had visualised the Argentina's economic heartland, fanning out some 400 miles from Buenos Aires, as untamed scrubland inhabited only by cattle and *gaucho*, and the occasional oasis-like *estancia*. It is flat and seemingly endless, yes, but carved up into a patchwork of fields and pastures that seem large enough from up here, but which down there must be gigantic. The weather is good but hazy, the quilt below in soft-focus: an endless crazy-paving stretch of brown and gold, with only the vaguest promise of green. Seed may have been sown but the planting is yet to show. On those areas described as prairie, new grass ghosts growth; still Spring has a way to go.

We have a way to go too. The plane is following the route of the old rail track, and this in turn followed an ancient trail used by native people for as long as the region was inhabited and named by the Spanish conquistadors, Camino de los Andes. You can lay a ruler and draw a near straight line between Buenos Aires and Santiago, east to west, to predict the flight path of today.

Before 1855, the region was wild and untamed: grassland without a native tree in sight. After the land was liberated – stolen is a more accurate and honest word – from the indigenous nomadic tribes who roamed the region, it was quickly carved up into vast estates – pastoral regions called *estancia*. On these camps or ranches, farms were established, *colonias*.

The *estancias* were feudal kingdoms ruled by oligarchic landowners with the support of private armies made up of loyal *gauchos*. It was only after agrarian settlement began that these characters – now a symbol of folkloric romance – appeared on the scene. The lone figure on horseback, as depicted on the calendar bought yesterday, was a product of that era. To understand, consider living in isolation, with only a horse and guitar for company, working in a landscape that stretched into infinity on all sides under open skies. Imagine the sense of physical and spiritual freedom, the breathtaking loneliness.

The system of land grants established at the end of the nineteenth century to help immigrants get a toehold on the *pampa* failed to materialise. The oligarchs were just too powerful, unwilling to relinquish one inch of the *pampa's* three-metre-deep richly fertile topsoil (said to be devoid of any rocks or even pebbles), especially to poor illiterate peasants from Europe.

Soon a restless urban proletariat developed alongside an insecure middle-class, neither of which felt any allegiance to the ruling oligarchy. Their lives were literally miles apart. This being so, it is very easy to see the roots of the deep dissatisfaction in society today. (Today native Argentines are outnumbered by people of European descent, described by one wag as, A bunch of Italians who speak Spanish but think they are French!)

By the 1930s, the *pampa* – meaning literally "space"– was tamed even further, fenced off into pastures of between 100 and 5000 acres, called *potreros*. (Presumably these are what I can see down below.) The *pampa* my grandfather would have known, would have been the one described in Fortune magazine in 1938 – in a country where the railway stations come, "every twenty minutes as though laid out not by geography but by clocks."

By 1960, it covered one fifth of the country and was home to 80 per cent of its population and forty million cattle, its naturally productive earth still requiring no fertilisers, and continuing to make any kind of construction – housing, road, rail – a testing business. Except that by this time, the days of laying down infrastructure were long gone, and what remained was in an accelerating state of decline. There was an air service at that time but few could afford such a reckless indulgence; 675 dollars bought a return ticket via either Pan America Airways, or the Condor Syndicate.

Having not flown by any airline for over a year, Maria-Elena is beside herself with excitement to be Going Home. She leans across me and jabs her thumb, indicating that I look down again. We are over mountains, cruel-looking black jagged peaks that stretch boundlessly ahead (westwards) and to the left (southwards) and right (northwards), slicing and stabbing upwards through ice and snow. I have never before travelled over such treacherous-looking territory; if a plane came down here, that would be that – and I recall the movie made about the survivors of one crash – members of an Uruguayan rugby team I seem to recall – who ended up eating one another to stay alive.[32] I would make good steaks, I think in a rare moment of dark good humour; so would Maria-Elena.

What do I know of Chile, a country that rarely impinged on my consciousness until a few years ago? Well there is the extraordinary fact that it is the only country in the western hemisphere where divorce remains illegal, resulting in the most convoluted family relationships imaginable. Other than this only statistics and data: a coastline 2,800 miles long; a narrow strip of land averaging no more than 80 miles wide at any one point, stretching from the tropics to the far south; bordered by Peru to the north, Bolivia and the Argentine to the north east, and the Pacific Ocean to the south and west. There is also the fact that it is cut off from Brazil, most of Argentina and the Atlantic (and psychologically therefore, the European continent) by the gigantic land mass – a near impenetrable wall – of rock, ice and snow over which I am now flying.

Suddenly we are dropping down and the landscape begins to lose its ferocity, sloping ever more gently over swathes of grubby-looking snow, giving way to shingle and scrub, and an eventual sweeping panorama of vineyards and small white-washed villages. The plane circles and descends between small volcanic extrusions of mossy green with the snow of the Andes streaked white, yellow and pink behind, and the haze of Santiago ahead.

We arrive, announces Maria-Elena triumphantly, gathering her numerous belongings and still with a large suitcase to claim in Baggage on landing.

I fall in behind with a light backpack, a list of hotels to hand. I know where I want to stay and I have this plan. Even if it only takes me into the city – into the heart of the unknown.

# CHAPTER 11

# INTO THE UNKNOWN

**NOVEMBER 11, 1999 CONTINUED**

Santiago de Chile feels different. Home to one third of the country's entire population, with election fever in the air (according to today's copy of the English language newspaper *El Metropolitano*), the atmosphere is somehow more open and egalitarian. I felt it at the airport. I feel it now as our taxi speeds into the city centre, through which a river – the Mapocho – tumbles in icy tumult via a wide concrete conduit, all the way from the Andes towards the coast. Maybe the reason for feeling so refreshingly light-headed is simply that Santiago sits 1,706 feet above sea level.

The driver asks where I come from. Inglese, I reply, this time getting it right!

I see him stare at me intently in his mirror. Then he spits out the expected questions about Pinochet: Why should the former dictator be put on trial in Europe? He was Chile's dirty business, not England's, nor even Spain's![33]

Not wanting to be drawn further, I spread my hands as if in total agreement (which I am) and consult my list of hotels. Wanting to do something constructive to help (and he too assuming I would be traveling alone) Akii had drawn it up for me, courtesy of the internet. Already I have picked out four places that look promising – interesting architecture, light and airy-looking, window boxes brimming with flowers – the Espana (the cheapest at 19 dollars), Hotel Japon (for curiosity's sake), Libertador and Foresta (because I liked their names). Convinced they sound, above all else, full of character, I point out their addresses to Maria-Elena.

Non, non, she responds, waving the list away.

Si, si, I reply in kind, pushing it back into her eye line: I want to go here!

Non. non, we go my place, she states firmly; You will like.

Sinking back into the seat, furious, my emotions spin once again towards the childishly unreasonable. When will I get what I want, for a change? Am I never going to have independent control over my movements ever again?

We turn left off the main route, with the river flanked by parkland and fountains. Now we are among higher buildings, with tantalising glimpses up and down side streets to more green spaces, crowded plazas. At one point I hear shouting – a kind of repetitive angry chant – from which a name emerges: Pinochet! Pinochet! Then I become aware of the ebb and flow of a demonstration in progress, with placards held aloft. It's hard to know whether the demonstration is in support of or against Chile's ex-autocrat, because we are past by in a flash, turning this time again into a relatively wide road, but made dark and depressing by high-rising grubby redbrick and stone buildings to either side.

Here, Maria-Elena announces, paying the fare and sweeping ahead into an entrance, down a narrow corridor lined with bleary-looking mirrors and tired pot plants into a dismal cubbyhole of a lobby. Before I can protest, we are booked in, rising in a lift with threadbare carpet and lined in part with cardboard, and being waved into a room so small that the twin beds are a near joke. There is a wardrobe (into which Maria-Elena smartly begins to unpack an extraordinary number of clothes for a short visit), a small bathroom looking out onto a blank wall, and that's about it. Opening the shutters onto the main street, noise, fumes and uncontrollable rage drive me to just as quickly slam it shut.

Already on the phone, Maria-Elena looks up from the edge of her bed in some surprise.

This, I splutter... is absolutely horrible! Whereupon I make a run – an undignified scramble around the beds, more like – for the bathroom, where all my anxiety, disappointment, frustration and anger lets rip. Locking the door against the entire world, I sit on the toilet seat, and burst into tears.

Fifteen-minutes later, I emerge exhausted and shame-faced to find the room empty. Maria-Elena has gone.

Lying on the bed, I try to make sense of what is going on here. Apart from travelling with Akii, I have only ever twice travelled with anyone else; in both instances relationships soured. At the time I had rationalised such breakdowns as being at the very least equally the fault of others, never myself alone. I had wondered why it happened, and what it was that could possibly have proved so irritating to my women friends, but was never prepared to take sole blame. Maybe I should begin by doing just that, take full responsibility and work back from there, rather than the other way around.

What, I wonder, will I do if I have alienated my cousin to such a degree that she wants nothing more to do with me. What if she packs up and goes home? Well, then I can move to the hotel of my fantasies and take up my life from there. This is what I want, right? Well, yes, but also no. I don't want Maria-Elena to think badly of me. I am sure she is doing her best, within her own agenda; it's just that not knowing what this agenda entails I am completely in the dark. And I am more used to leading than being led. Best to apologise, I decide, then take it from there...

When Maria-Elena does eventually return, she enters the room quietly and continues with her unpacking, but I sense her careful sidelong glances; she is checking me out.

I'm sorry, I begin, the words sounding wobbly, strange and strangled as they meet the tension in the air.

Immediately it is as if air has been released from a balloon. Maria-Elena is on her feet, shaking her head from side to side, protesting my apology.

No, no, she says; You have hard time – Buffy, uncle, sister.... I understand. Emotion. Cry. No problemo, no problemo.

It is clear that on the subject of family she is far wiser than I. She has put my outburst down to a build up of pressure solely based on familial concerns. This is something she can understand, how is it possible for her to be clear on anything else; after all, she doesn't know me. My god, I realise with another insight of startling (if unoriginal) clarity, I hardly know myself.

Sam (dare I say) was even worse than me. There is little sign he ever questioned his own behaviour, only that of others. Everyone else is at fault; he a paragon of virtue, the self-prescribed innocent victim of a family drama in which, as the war in Europe drags on, he decides to play a larger part. In 1944, he writes seven letters, and it is clear that this is because my father is communicating more.

By March Sam has a two photos of me, one enlarged, *the other, although very good, has a shadow across the face, and it would be difficult to eliminate.* He begs for a photo of my parents, because *it is a long time since I saw you both in Birmingham* (when was this I wonder? My mother cannot remember) *and am anxious for the day when we can all meet and have a long chat, about all and sundry.*

He is feeling better than a few months previously. Having suspected he had high blood pressure, he has been trying to diet, and while still over fourteen stone, has lost a lot of weight. He encloses a photo of himself in Piriapolis, a small seaside resort north of Montevideo that he likes very much, pointing out in the distance the hotel where he stays. He was in Montevideo for the end of Carnival, but regarded it as too rowdy to be interesting: *mostly people dancing all night, and making merry generally.*

Spoil sport. Sounds great to me!

Business is quiet and there is not much news, he continues, *except that we have QUINS in B/Aires, belonging to a wealthy family. A lady friend of mine, Mrs Leila Drew, who is one of many who call me TIO SAM, and who is a reporter on the B/A HERALD, was the only one admitted to take the story, and according she is now as famous as the family concerned. Probably you will read all about it.*[34]

Quite out of the blue, he is talking suddenly of relatives – names I have never heard before. For Mrs Drew was apparently *a great friend of my cousin, Daisy Lee, and my niece, Winnie Howard Pheasant, nee Lee.* Lee, I note with more than passing interest: the name of the company in Liverpool's Dale Street, which he used as a business address in the past.

Then, a narcissistic distraction: *Being a good-looking man, I am generally admired!!!*

On a more serious note, he trusts that the war will soon be over. *My opinion is about June/July 1945. I have never foolish enough to believe that the Nazis would climb down in any way. They are in for it!!!! – and will get IT!*

Lastly there is the matter of my sister's imminent arrival. *For the sake of you both,* Sam jokes again, *I hope it will not be QUINS!*

In April he sends my mother a copy of Selecta, *the best fashion magazine out here. She might get some ideas for herself and others, as Buenos Aires, I should say is now the centre of fashion, as Europe for the present is out of the picture. This country has always followed the Paris and London styles, but now goes ahead on its own.*

For himself he has bought yet another suit. *An English cloth, after the style of flannel, but in fact a cloth with a flannel finish. It is a peculiar shade of brown, quite unusual, with a wide-ish stripe. I always try to get something different from the usual run, which are after all uniforms.*

In May he is wondering whether my father is considering joining up, or will choose to stay in his job, where he will be safe: *there must be many younger men* (my father is by now thirty-four) *and not so great a target, with your 6ft 4 and a half inches to shoot at!*

Business is quiet: imports are reducing every day; orders are few. *In Uruguay also it is very quiet.*

*Well, old man,* he closes, *do write to me more often, or get Gwen to write for you. I like to see a healthy family of happy children. I have lots of little friends here, and send you a photo, not of anyone I know, but children of Indian origin. It is really very amusing, though what the mother thought is another matter.*

Sadly this picture is lost.

By late August he has received news via his sister Bea in Wallasey of my sister's arrival on April 29. *I know you have given her the names Brigit Anne, which is nice and will suit a pretty girl.* (The spelling does not tally with that chosen by my parents; Great-aunt Bea most likely got it wrong at source.)[35]

My grandfather has just heard also (it being August 25) that *Roumania* (sic) *has turned around and declared war on Germany, and yesterday here in this City there was a huge celebration of the Liberation of Paris.*

*You are very lazy folks,* he adds. *Why don't you write? I have sent five letters now since I received yours.*

Regarding herself as a very unlazy-like person, Maria-Elena suggests we go for a walk, so this is what we do: turn right out of the hotel, turn right again at the cafe on the corner, cross over a road, across which to the right is a bright red-painted church, and then walk straight for another block or so. Here, the road widens curvaceously to form a plaza, fronting a small hill – a dramatic rocky outcrop covered in palm trees and flowering shrubs, with small paths winding up and around, presumably to the top. Many think this to be the prettiest park (for this is what it proves to be) in all of South America, so we take our time, Maria-Elena's arm linked companionably through my own. In my experience women tend not to show affection in this, or any other way come to think of it, either in the UK or Japan, so it feels uncomfortable, embarrassing even, but having pledged to do better, I relax, and try.

Rising two-hundred and forty feet above street level, Santa Lucia Hill is a living museum in that it contains two fortresses. It is literally the foundation stone of the city, since this is where Spanish invaders held out against the native Mapuche, formerly referred to (in more politically incorrect days) as Araucanians. Diego Almagro led the way in 1535, setting out from Peru on an exploratory expedition of the region. As with Argentina, such an intial foray failed. The following year, the boldest of Pizzaro''s captains, Pedro de Valdivia marched down from the north and began Chile's colonisation. In 1541, he founded Santiago (named after the Christian apostle James) and the war with the Mapuche began. Conception was founded in 1550; Valdivia, 1552.) Rebellion was not squashed on the central plain until 1820, when peace was made. Resistance continued in the south, however, until 1883, when the Mapuche very sensibly decided that everyone had had enough, laid down their weapons and went home.

So here we walk, on historic ground, climbing stairways cut into the bedrock and worn smooth over the centuries, resting on balconies, peering into caves, and taking in views either across balustrades or through battlements. The first governor, Don Casimiro Marco del Pont built the original fortress, Castillo Gonzales; the second, Castillo Hidalgo, was a complex of dungeons that now houses a historical museum.

It was Chile's own national hero, Bernardo O'Higgins, who had the bright idea of turning the hill into a cultural attraction. He tried building an observatory, and a replica of the Greek Parthenon, but for one reason and another never saw his plans come to fruition. It was not until the late nineteenth century that another patriot (this time of patriarchal Scots ancestry rather than Irish) picked up where O'Higgins had left off. Benjamin Vicuna Mackenna put convicts to work in 1872 and within two years had completed the job. But again on such a beautiful day, who wants to be reminded of horrors, disappointments and struggles of the past? Instead Maria-Elena and I share the names of flowers and shrubs, and even the scattered cloud formations in the blue sky above. O'Higgins and Mackenna have had their day, after all. This is our own.

Mackenna's vision, however, lives on: a miniature basilica at ground level on both sides, with statues and fountains, elegant curving staircases in white marble, flanked by towering palms and exotic vegetation. Pretty as a picture, I think, taking out my camera, and capturing amid this beauty a couple – appropriately enough, Lovers of the Day No. 13 – in mid-argument: he, arms folded, face like thunder; she cowed, pleading. Escaping, we find a grassy area on a higher level, with an even larger fountain fronting a modern museum of brick and glass inside a redbrick enclosure. Yellow banners flank the entrance, bearing an ad for a website: *www.terra.co.*

We climb higher, with views of the city to every side and the Andes in the distance. Disappearing around a corner, I hear Maria-Elena call my name. And there, on a rocky spur, stands a statue of a Mapuche warrior – the finest figure of a man. From one angle his feet are wide apart, solidly planted, readying for battle; from the other he seems more poised for flight, but not escape. Wearing a headdress that resembles the petals of a flower peeling back from his forehead, and carrying what I can only assume to be a bow-like weapon, the image suggests strength, independence, self-possession, and a near mystical courage.

The Mapuche were regarded by the Spanish conquistadors as the toughest and most resilient of the tribes they encountered in South America. No wonder they fought so hard to regain possession of the rock on which we are now standing: their ancestors had long ago dedicated it to Huelen, or the god of pain. They surely renewed all their pledges and battled even harder when they saw the Christian Cross of the Conquest raised on the summit. Still, they got their revenge. When they captured Valdivia in his secondary push to the south, they showed a grimly cynical sense of retribution in forcing him to swallow gold as his death sentence. "You came for gold," legend quotes them as saying; "Well, here it is!"

Mapuche, which means People of the Land, live in Chile to this day. Unlike Argentinians, many Chilean families are said to be proud of their native blood; whether or not any stigma is attached, I have yet to discover.

We sit down finally in a large open space where children are playing on grass and in sand; old men chat around the edges, smoking and playing board games. This area is less manicured than the rest of the hill, so relaxed and natural. By contrast, the walls of the sandpit, and the benches are hard-tiled in blue and white. And as always there are rocks jutting through the foliage, as if to remind that this is still a hard wild place beneath the cosmetic manicure. Never having been anywhere quite so different and lovely, I want to fling out my arms to my cousin to say thank you. I mean, if I had had my way – gone to another hotel – I might never have found my way to this spot. However, flinging my arms around anyone except my children has never come easy; instead I lean over and kiss her on the cheek, which seems to please her very much.

Resting on a bench, the tiles deliciously cool against my calves and through the thin cotton of my trousers, Maria-Elena asks whether I have many friends in Japan.

Enough, I reply.

Who is best friend, she asks.

Well, it was Nikolas, I answer; But now he is in Vancouver.

Akii, he minds? she says, looking puzzled.

Not at all. Anyway, Nik is gay, homosexual.

Maria-Elena glances at me sharply, looks away, and then stands up. Our mini-expedition, it appears, is over.

I am lying on my bed, wondering what I am here to do, and how to do it, when the phone rings. Maria-Elena is soon chattering like a demented parrot, but then suddenly hands me the phone.

It is Olga, she announces.

Olga? I take the receiver and hesitantly say, Hello?

Olga, whoever she is, speaks slow but very correct English and sounds utterly charming. She asks if I would like to go her apartment this evening.

Maria-Elena, I hiss, my hand over the speaker, Who am I talking to?

It is Pepe's Olga, she hisses back, indicating I should say yes, yes.

Completely flummoxed, I tell Olga that we would be happy to come over, and I am looking forward to meeting a genuine *Santiaguenos*.

Maria-Elena, I ask after replacing the handset, who is Pepe's Olga? Who indeed is Pepe?

You see, she laughs; You will see. And gathering up her bag and scarf, heads for the door. It is at this point I realise she has changed her outfit – from the short-sleeved beige-knit sweater and brown pants of her travels to a leopard print shirt and black trousers. With new make-up and her hair re-swept into a chignon, she looks readied for some mighty important social event.

It seems a long way. We traverse the length of the main downtown street, named Avenida Bernado O'Higgins, but known to one and all as the Almeda, and then begin cross-crossing into deeper and poorer suburban territory. The cab finally draws up in front of a low-rise block of flats in an area called Nunoa, which reminds very much of the government-built *danchi* (estate) I lived in for my first two years in Japan. Cast in concrete, the facade is just as dirty and rundown, but here people are standing outside in the warm balmy evening light, chattering and curious to see who has arrived. Drawn to one of the windows above by the sound of a vehicle, a head pops out and then another. Maria-Elena is waving and calling; they wave and call back. Olga? No, two men, so maybe Pepe and... Who?

The man who opens the door on the fourth floor is older than us, slight and very thin, wearing an open-necked blue and white striped shirt. Smiling shyly, but his beady dark eyes taking in every detail, he takes my hand and pumps it up and down. *Bienvenido*, he exclaims, over and over: Welcome.

Inside he draws me towards the window where a small pretty dark-haired woman in a V-necked print dress and wearing glasses sits in a chair: Olga. A young man with a neatly trimmed beard and moustache then walks into the room, and introduces himself in English as their son, Daniel. He is followed by a woman with a broad forehead and calm Botticelli-like features, framed by a halo of soft waving hair, also in her early thirties, and carrying a very new baby.

My wife, Cecilia, Daniel introduces proudly; And our daughter, Elizabeth.

After explaining that he is going to take his family back home – they live nearby – and he will then return, I am seated in the window recess, with Olga – a former English teacher – to my left, my back to the light. Now the room is a stage, but who are all these players? There is a lot of scuttling back and forth into what I assume is the kitchen, and eventually a plate of ice-cream is produced, for me alone. Maybe this is some Chilean ritual, some grand treat, I decide, and try to do it justice as Olga shyly but eagerly watches my every move.

Daniel returns. He is thirty-one, and an architect. His father works in a factory. Before I can find out more, there is further commotion as another family arrives, a couple with two young girls, also an older man. More introductions, but still I'm lost. Who are these people?

Daniel, I realise, is not longer at my side. He is behind me, backed against the wall, his eyes shifting from side-to-side and muttering under his breath. I catch his arm, ask what's the matter. There is something about a death list, and he being only fifteen, then he appears to gather his wits, and escapes into the kitchen.

The new arrivals are Luis, his wife Silvia, and their two daughters Camila and Javiera. The older man is Luis' father, Guillermo, or William. Daniel tells me that the two men are brothers: Guillermo was born in 1927, his own father, Pepe – whose real name is Joseph – in 1936.

And what's your family name? I ask Daniel, determined to get to the bottom of all this.

Why, Loader, he answers. We are all Loaders.

And then it clicks. Or rather something clicks. Pepe and Guillermo are two of Charles' sons, two of the twelve children sired by my grandfather's cousin. Just as this begins to sink in, another woman arrives, upon whom Maria-Elena falls with laughter and tears.

Our Betty, she introduces with enormous pride and joy: Beatriz Eliana Loader Becerra.

Now whose daughter is she, I wonder. Again Daniel comes to my rescue: her father is Federico (Frederick) Juan Loader Cruzat, Charles' third born. So, Joseph and William are my uncles, Betty another cousin.

Betty keeps looking me up and down. She is not very forthcoming, and keeps her distance. For my own part, I note (not quite as obviously I hope) that she and Maria-Elena might have been cast in the same mould. But unlike her Argentine relative, who by comparison is far more relaxed, Betty is coiffed and lacquered to her bottle-blonde hair; clothes just a little too small for comfort; plump legs and ankles squeezed into tights and heels, despite the heat. I get the feeling I am not approved of, for whatever reason. If it's for lack of formality, don't blame me, I mutter under my own breath. No-one told me that I was being brought here to meet Family.

Family. With regards to my own back in England, it is amazing that all those children of the Victorian age can have resulted in so few descendants living today. As a child I used to envy the warm and shambolic nature of large extended families. By comparison, my own seemed to be shrunk, dried up, desiccated, fossilised. I grew to hate its narrow class-confused confines, in which the eye of the storm always seemed concentrated upon my hapless self, and yearned to escape. Later, in my early twenties, my few remaining relatives (barring Eric and Kathleen) turned against me. Personal hurt aside, the sense of relief was enormous. Fuck family, I thought. And then having raised my own children to the best of my limited but creative ability, made my way to a country where, I quickly discovered, family was everything. I guess this is when I began to look at things differently: in Japan. Now I know, of course, that extended families of any culture have problems too. But it was because of what I learned and witnessed in Asia that my interest in Family was revived. That bundle of letters from my grandfather could not have arrived in my life at a more opportune moment. And see where it has led me: to a tenement in the capital of Chile, another half a world away, and a group of people who all seem to know who I am, but about whom I am completely ignorant.

It is dark when we leave. Silvia, who is small, pert and organised, has asked us to go to their house tomorrow evening. Twelve-year-old Camila is especially thrilled; she too has been watching my every move, her dark eyes sparkling. (Her lively curiosity reminds me of me at that age.) Everyone seems keen, in fact, except Daniel, who has become quite sullen. Olga too thinks she may stay home. She is disabled in some way, I now realise; unable to move around too easily. But her intelligence is a shining light in the clean bare room that does its best to overcome any financial limitations and personal difficulties with a lace tablecloth and a scattering of genuine artworks on the walls – prints, oils, and a charming watercolour of sailing boats. I do hope we meet again.

Readying for sleep that night, Maria-Elena suddenly proclaims: I hate gay.

With her hair spread around her head on the pillow, she looks angelic; the words that come out of her mouth are not. I know she is recalling our conversation earlier in the afternoon, and decide to take things easy. I tell her how important Nik is to me, what a good friend he was (and still is), describe his professional life as a dancer and choreographer, his personal life with his then Japanese boyfriend. Recall funny stories, sad stories, just as I might about any friend, male or female, gay or heterosexual. She is very quiet, listening. I don't know how much she comprehends, but something gets through, because after I turn out the light, she says through the darkness: Maybe I not hate gay, just not understand.

I cannot rest, so turn on the lamp. Maria-Elena has already fallen asleep. She is trying. So am I. But I bet I am more trying than she is.

By late 1944, Sam is trying too – to bounce back. Replying on the 21st to a letter written by my father dated the 10th and received that very morning, he is in fine spirits as a result, and very droll: *I'm pleased to know that Bridget Anne is going on fine and will soon be as big as her mother* (who in her prime was five foot two inches in stocking feet). *It is better so for a girl, as if she reached your height, she would be something of a novelty.*

He has recovered his health completely, regaining all the weight he lost plus more. He has been in Uruguay, where trade is slow but food still plentiful. In Buenos Aires also he is far from starving, having orders for fifty thousand glazed white tiles, and an enquiry for seventy-five tons of super refractory cement. An order for three hundred tons of firebrick is proving a bit problematical, but only because he's finding it hard to secure the cargo space for shipping from the UK. In the meantime, *I sold 1000 pieces of sanitary ware this month; in ordinary times I can get through a lot of stuff.*

His big news concerns a Eucharist Conference held the week before. *The town was packed.... at each meeting there were over 200,000 people present. The main altar was in the middle of this avenida, which is now crossed by a new avenida, some 200 metres wide, so at the crossing they had plenty of room. It was very impressive and I looked on with interest on several occasions.*

He is pleased to hear that his daughter-in-law had been to Gloucester to see Sal (Sarah, my grandmother), and that my mother also saw Catherine. What are they like now, he wonders, for they never write. He does not know where Catherine is living (Bristol maybe?), and has heard only that Barney was a lieutenant, either in France or Belgium or Holland. Most of all, he writes, he would like to hear from Betty: *She was told amongst other things that she was not wanted, which was a Scotch lie, and so far as I was concerned, I would not be so wicked to think such a thing.* She (Betty) *believes this still.*

It gets worse: *Any ordinary person* (a dig at his wife) *would have written giving me interesting accounts of my children, but in spite of my many letters written in a most friendly way, and the cables sent on the occasion of her birthday, and Christmas every year, have never been answered in any way. I think she feels guilty that she treated me badly, and does not want to own up, as all Scotch people are stubborn, and very many stupid, in fact, anyone's ancestors who were Scotch drapers, in other words Pedlars of the old Packers variety, could not have an honest strain.*[36] *Even Jews shine brightly against Scotch Drapers, which is about the meanest business on the face of the earth.*

What a relief, Sam lightens ups, that my father was married to a Welsh girl, *who are certainly loyal through thick and thin.*

Why I wonder, through Maria-Elena's gentle snoring, did Sam imagine my mother to be Welsh? Or was she Welsh by association only, Shrewsbury being so close to the border. And why would the Welsh be any better or worse that the Scots? More prejudices were floating to the surface like a toxic scum; they made as much unpleasant reading as listening.

The next paragraph, however, provides a fitting new piece to the family jigsaw puzzle. *My ancestors were nearly Welsh, or even might have Welsh blood in their veins* (ah, now I know why the Welsh are so superior to the Scots!) *as they came from a village on the Welsh border in Shropshire, almost on the site of the old Roman City of Uricornium* (sic), *a centre of Roman culture.*[37] *My great-great grandfather I know was in the Shropshire Yeomanry as a volunteer during the stormy days of the 1700s. I intend to investigate further when I come back.*

My eyes scan the rest of the two-page letter for any additional information, the name of the village, for example. Or more information on distant ancestors. But no. He comments only on the lifting of the blackout in England, and is happy the war seems to be coming to an end, *but I do not think we will have peace until the middle of next year.* Longing for the day when he can return, he is already making plans. *When in Coventry, I shall stay in Kenilworth, at the Royal Arms, and in Sheffield, at Foxhouse Hotel, on the border with the moors. Most of my stay will be in London and the Midlands, but I shall go to Scotland, and perhaps the North of Ireland.*

His days are declining, he notes, and he wants to make the best of what time remains. *My great hope is to be reconciled with you all before the end comes, but as Sal turned me out, I cannot but await a call, to return once more. In fact things said cannot be undone, unless I were told that they had no meaning, but all this time I have harboured bitterness at what Sal once said to me in the dark days of Upper Parliament Street. What an awful time it was for me. Has anyone suffered so.*

Putting the file aside, I turn off the light and lie in the darkness. Upper Parliament Street, to where my grandmother moved with her children some time before Sam set sail for South America. Maybe they had been there together, the Spanish house sold, to pay off debts maybe. What could she have said that caused such a rift, such furious pain on all sides? Sam's sole comfort in this sad and sorry mess was the fact that my father remained in contact. My only comfort is that I know more now than I did less than a day ago, when I arrived in Santiago. But what it all adds up to, I haven't got a clue. Hopefully today – for it is 2a.m. – will provide a few answers.

# CHAPTER 12

# A FEW ANSWERS

**NOVEMBER 12, 1999**

We are going to find Charles – Maria-Elena's idea, while at the same time very much against her better judgment. I have as yet not heard one good thing about the man – her grandfather, my great-uncle – and that includes comments made last night at Pepe and Olga's place.

I am surprised to draw up in front of Santiago's municipal cemetery, having imagined he would be buried in a plot – one of those corners of foreign fields laid aside by the British government for the expired expatriate community. The frontage is impressive, a long semi-circular wall with a large imposing entrance gate facing an open area of grass and trees and the road busy with a constant flow of cars and taxis. There are flower stalls to either side of the gateway – over a dozen by my count. At the far end, an elderly woman has been pushed out of the more convenient mainstream area. I go to give her some business, and then, as usual, find the amount of choices onerous. It is a familiar problem when shopping: I go into a store to buy say some shoes, and am out within five minutes, bored out of my skull and irritated beyond measure by salespeople who at best hover and at worst put me under the kind of pressure than can only be described as bullying.

So what do I choose here (under no pressure at all, it must be said)? Deciding that a man with such an obvious burden of bad karma in life needs cheering up in death, I buy a large bunch of bright yellow chrysanthemums. Maria-Elena looks askance, as if to say, *Why waste your money*. But the truth is that however much he hurt others, I personally have no axe to grind and feel it necessary to keep an open mind; therefore it is only polite to offer a token gesture of respect.

The cemetery office is large, old-fashioned, and surprisingly efficient. Maria-Elena has never visited her grandfather's grave before (which says a lot in itself) so we need to establish exactly where it is located. The middle-aged male staff in Records are very helpful. Down come cumbersome-leather bound ledgers, and once Charles's full name and year of death are established, they find his *niche* in no time at all, giving us a map and the necessary co-ordinates. Though burial is common, interments tend to be in the Spanish tradition, either in a large family mausoleum, or walls of coffin-sized niches, one atop the other. Once the coffin is slid inside, the opening is closed with an inscribed plaque set vertically in place.

To enter the cemetery we have to walk through the main office – a cavernous utilitarian space, with tables along one side and a row of officials making entries, issuing documents. Facing them, ranks of chairs, with sombre family groups come to register personal losses. People are visibly upset, weeping and supporting one another. It would be easy to forget on yet another lovely day, going about one's business, that lives are coming to an end (and elsewhere babies being born) with endless unknown repercussions for all concerned, destined to rattle on down through the centuries.

It is incredibly hot, Maria-Elena orienteering her way through a seemingly endless landscape of tombs and graves, shaded only in part by trees. Finally, we arrive in front of a two-floor wall of niches dating from the 1950s, with crumbling stucco and ironwork typical of the period, and descend a rusting metal staircase. Being below ground level it is damp and depressing, with leaves blown into the corners, mulched into stinking black pools. I shiver then pull myself together; no-one is going to walk over my grave.

Here, announces Maria-Elena; Here is Charles.

Here he is indeed, in a corner, closest to the concrete flooring, surmounted by Francisco Ibanez P., who died 31 enero (January), 1954. Unlike the other niches, which are all engraved in Spanish, Charles's six-line epitaph is in grammatically perfect English; it is also kindly worded for someone apparently so despised:

*IN LOVING MEMORY*

*OF*

*CHARLES JOSEPH LOADER*

*WHO DIED ON 30TH JANUARY 1954*

*AGED 74 YEARS*

*AT REST*

Why is he here? I ask. Why is he not buried in the British Cemetery here in Santiago?

Maria- Elena shrugs. Ill at ease, she watches me fill two glass jam jars with water, divide the flowers between them, and place them on the ledge, to either side of the inscription. Not knowing quite what to say or think, I cover my embarrassment (for I can only assume this is what I am feeling) and do something totally out of character: I lean forward, knock on the grey granite facing to the niche and say, Hello, this is Angela from England. Greetings from all ancestors and descendants. Hope you like the flowers.

Almost as soon as I have done it, I wish I hadn't. My cousin is shaking her head. Deeply superstitious I now realise, she fears I may have woken him from the dead, which in the light of his history, she considers a very bad idea indeed.

As we walk away, I reflect on having not named his ancestors aloud, and in my mind run through the list, back through the years, to Harriet. Harriet Loder.

I had traced my great-great-great grandmother in 1996. Since Andy had run out of both ideas and time for excavating John Loader's roots, and there was little I could do productively at long distance, I had handed the job over to a company in England specialising in genealogical research. Commissioned in September 1995, Windsor Ancestry Research promised an initial report by Christmas.

Having heard nothing by the New Year, I queried progress, and finally received an apologetic letter in February. Based on the limited information I had been able to provide at that time – John having been born in or around Shrewsbury in or around 1816 – research had not proven straightforward. WAR (an unfortunate acronym if ever there was one) had searched Shropshire parish indexes and found that John Loder (note the spelling) had been baptised at Shrewsbury St Mary on February 16, 1817, the illegitimate son of Harriet Loder. This appeared to put paid to Sam's belief – or fantasy – that he was of good yeomen stock, so deepening the mystery.

Since there was no sign of Harriet in the Shropshire section of the International Genealogical Index, WAR's research had concentrated on searching for mention of her name in the nineteenth century census returns. Starting with a recently compiled index to the whole of the 1881 census of Shropshire, there proved to be not a single Loder or Loader mentioned for the whole of the county, and this from a population of 269,000. Even more puzzling.

Thinking Harriet might have married after the birth of her son, a search was made of a privately held index to Shropshire marriages made between 1817 and 1837. There was no mention.

The indexes for 1851 and 1861 were then ransacked. The fact that the name Lo(a)der did not appear in either suggested that Harriet had either died by 1851, or she had left Shrewsbury. Information was then extracted from records relating to the 1817 baptism. This revealed that at that time, Harriet was a resident of the local House of Industry, or workhouse. Research, I was told, was therefore proceeding on two fronts: the original Shrewsbury St Mary parish registers, and workhouse records and records of bastardy examinations for the city.

Having provided WAR with the additional suggestion, as supplied by Sam, that his ancestors came from, or may have come from the small village of Minsterley, close by Shrewsbury (I had initially – and distressingly, this being the downside of skimming the written word – overlooked this vital piece of information) a full report finally arrived.

The earliest parish registers for England and Wales date from 1538, when legislation was introduced by Thomas Cromwell on behalf of Henry Tudor. This decreed that all baptisms, marriages and deaths occurring within every parish had to be recorded by the incumbent in a weekly register. Since the earliest entries were written mainly on paper, it was further decreed in 1557 that these all be copied onto parchment, and henceforth written on the same. Record keeping (in Latin until 1733) varied considerably from one parish to another, and there are even quite large gaps, notably around the time of the English Civil War. Luckily John was born in a city and at a time when such matters were taken seriously. His baptismal records therefore read:

*16 Feb 1817 John (base) son of Harriet Loder House of Industry*

Since extensive workhouse records for Shrewsbury survive, it had been discovered from the Alphabetical List of Paupers Admitted 1809–26 that a pregnant Harriet was first taken in on November 4, 1815. Her age was not given (most likely she did not know it herself, being illiterate), and her health described as Venereal (not uncommon in those days). Under *Remarks*, the recorder had written:

*Dis. (for discharged) Absconded 17th March*
*1816. Admitted again, (still) pregnant.*
*Harriet Loder's male child was born a bastard in the house 2nd February*
*1816, and taken by the mother. Harriet Loder's female child was born*
*a bastard in this house 9th September 1819, taken out by the Mother.*
*Admitted again 20th June 1819 (sic). Discharged 13th March 1820.*

It would appear that Harriet was alone in the world, otherwise she would have gone surely to family to have her babies. Since she had no means of support, it is not unreasonable to assume that the father – or fathers – were not around to take responsibility. Nor did she seek support; her name did not appear in the Shrewsbury Union Contributions (Bastardy Accounts) for 1812–24.

Sadly John did not have a younger sister for long. The Shrewsbury St Mary Parish Registers record that Jane Pritchard, daughter of Harriet Loder, House of Industry, was baptised on September 12, 1819. But she died in infancy, and was buried as Jane Loder in the Castle Forecourt, aged seven months, on April 13, the following year.

As for Harriet, there was no burial entry at Shrewsbury St Mary up to 1837; it was as if she had emerged from the mists of obscurity and dissolved back into the same.

Also where did the distinctive middle name Pritchard come from? Initially WAR had imagined it was a clue towards Jane's paternity. But a Bastard Examination proved otherwise:

*The examination of Harriet Loader (the re-worked spelling being most likely an error by the scribe; a common occurrence) of the parish of St Mary of this town.... this twelfth day of October in the year of our Lord one thousand eight hundred and nineteen who saith that on Wednesday the eighth day of September now last past at the House of Industry for the said parish, she was delivered of a female Bastard Child, And that the said Bastard Child is likely to be chargeable to the said Parish, and that James Stanley, late of Manchester in the Co. (Country) of Lancaster, Civil Engineer, did beget the said Bastard Child on her body. The mark X of Harriet Loader Taken and signed before Thos. Kynnersley and W. Egerton Jeffreys*

Was Harriet in a relationship with James Stanley, or was he a passing ship in the night? Was she a prostitute, or simply an ignorant country girl fallen on hard times? WAR could not provide such personal details. But they did find a later record of John, seemingly alone, back in the workhouse:

| Date | Name | Parish | Age | Occasion |
|------|------|--------|-----|----------|
| 25th Sep. 1826 | Loder, John | St Mary's | 8 | Son of Harriet Loder |

Also records covering the Weekly Return of Paupers and Costs to be Charged Against Each Parish 1826–28, listed the following:

| | Name | Age | | Total weeks |
|--|------|-----|--|-------------|
| In the house | Loder, John | 9 | Oct 1826-1 Jan 1827 | 13 |
| In the house | Loder, John | 9 | 8 Jan 1827-2 Apr 1827 | 13 |
| In the house | Loder, John | 9 | 9 Apr 1827-2 July 1827 | |
| In the house | Loder, John | 9 | 9 July 1827-Sep 1827 | 11 |

Price per head: 2s (shillings) 10 1/2d (pence)
Total due 1st Jan: 1 17s 4d
Date of discharge; 12th September, by vestry

Why was John in and out of the workhouse during this period of twelve months? Was his mother ill perhaps? Was he abandoned, an orphan, desperate? If so where did he go on discharge? And what or who brought him back? WAR wondered whether he might have become an apprentice on his final discharge, but there is no entry for him in the Register of Apprentices 1824–26. However, with John last put out on the street in 1827, this needs re-checking.

As to the possible Minsterley connection, searches of the 1841 and 1851 census returns for the village failed to locate any mention of a Loder or Loader. It was possible, WAR thought, that the family connection lay a generation back. Harriet was probably born before 1800 and this is not a period covered by the International Genealogical Index. The next step seemed to be to search the original Minsterley parish registers for traces of earlier Loder ancestry, together with Overseer's records, which included documents relating to settlement, examinations and removals; these all related to the process by which the movement of individuals was regulated in the eighteenth and early nineteenth centuries.

As WAR explained: The equivalent of social security was paid on a parochial basis and it was therefore important to establish the credentials of individuals arriving in a parish so that, if they became indigent and fell upon the parish for support, a removal order could be issued and they could be sent back to their parish of origin. Often at such times, paupers would be moved from parish to parish and families were even split up.

Is this what happened to Harriet and John?

Continuing: Possession of a settlement certificate, however, which clearly stated where a person originally came from, would often ease entry into another parish, for the Overseers of the Poor could be confident of relocating the new arrival if her (or she) subsequently fell on hard times.

Such documents, WAR concluded, related to the poorest strata of society; illiterate and untrained, little would be recorded of their existence. But if settlement documents or examination appertaining to the name Lo(a)der, in Minsterley or Shrewsbury, could be located, the prospects of further progress should be considerably enhanced.

Unfortunately this was as far as I could take researches at that point in time; too many financial drains on limited resources. I let the matter lie....

Harriet stayed with me, however. She is quite possibly with me now, in a cemetery in Chile, amazed to have laid such a long and winding trail. But – for the moment at least – her life story remains fragmented, with no clear beginning and no equally defined end.

Maria-Elena is hungry. So am I. There is nothing like close proximity to death to make one appreciate being alive, and all the sensations that accompany this quite splendid condition. I spot a pavement cafe that looks fun, and out we hop (of a taxi, naturally). The food is good, the waiters attentive but not in any obsequious manner, and Maria-Elena realises that she knows someone who lives roundabout. She is fascinated by my researches, by the family's murky origins and Harriet's less-than-illustrious history – or rather her-story, as I try to explain in feminist terms without making much headway.

I also have no father, she says suddenly, out-of-the-blue, once again proving to me that she understands a lot more than I am giving her credit for; Well, I have father, but my mother, she not married.

Ana was far too strong and clever to allow her child's biological father into her life, Maria-Elena intimates. And I feel a sudden pang. For all my noisy support of feminism, I have never lived more than a year of my life without some man around. I am not half as strong and clever and independent as I like to imagine. No wonder I became a professional editor in London; I've been editing my life story to fit my preferred image of myself for as long as I can remember.

Maria-Elena is having a nap, so off I go to collect e-mail messages. I had found an internet address on one of my earlier rambles, just past the Santa Lucia Hill. It is an odd place, but friendly, run by a Frenchman with a Japanese wife and a new baby. Upstairs it appears to operate like a backpackers' advice centre; downstairs there are computers and books – books left or exchanged by travellers in a variety of languages, but mostly French and English.

Discovering I have quite a lot of catching up to do, I am online for over an hour. Finally I sign out, and reach into my bag for my purse. It is not there.

I sit back, close my eyes, pray very hard (as one does in any state of emergency) and look again. I turn the bag inside out, literally. Still no sign.

Heart pounding, I sit there for ten minutes trying to gather my senses.

Maybe I left it back in the room? I fear not; this is the first time I have opened my backpack since traveling back on the metro.

The metro. Was it possible I had been robbed – dipped? If so, how? I had carefully positioned myself so that my belongings were not too conspicuous, my back against a pole, my arms around the pack itself, clasping all my worldly goods close to my chest.

For the first time I wonder why I am not wearing a money belt. Normally I carry money and passport around my waist when travelling. Why am I not doing so now? Why had it never crossed my mind, even when packing to travel?

Whatever, however, I have no money to pay the immediate bill, and can do no more than throw myself on the mercy of the owner. Sweetness itself, he says I can pay next time, even though he must acknowledge deep down that there is a fifty-fifty chance that as a complete stranger I may never return. Interesting, isn't it, that in order to survive some people decide they must harden their hearts against all comers, while others (even when possessing next to nothing) choose to remain open, optimistic and trusting. It is more than a simple matter of economics, when all is said and done. It is a matter of heart, as the Japanese say.

It is hard to tell Maria-Elena that somehow I have been robbed. I feel even more foolish. The cash itself is the last of my problems. So okay, it was my allowance for Chile – some 300 dollars in local currency – but I have more yen tucked away, both here (in my suitcase) and back in Caseros (in the wardrobe). It is the loss of my Visa card that deals the hardest blow. It is – was – my only credit facility, and without it I suddenly feel immeasurably insecure.

Maria-Elena's initial reaction is to tut-tut and wag her finger at me: You see, she says; I told you, he (Charles) bad man. You wake him up!

Upset and apologetic, she gets onto the phone on my behalf to cancel the card at source. It takes a startling number of international phone calls to the UK, via the US, and the bill is far from funny. I guess I will just have to go to the bank again, change more cash and cross fingers that there is enough to see me through back to Buenos Aires. In the meantime I go over and over the memory of my every movement, trying to make sense of the loss, trying to somehow make the situation come right again; as tends to be my way, I add this failure to a growing list. (Imagine penitents with large whips flagellating themselves until the flesh is raw and blood runs, and you get the picture.)

That evening I take a lot of photographs at Silvia and Luis' home. Like Pepe and Olga, they live in Nunoa, but in a house – a contemporary open-plan design that whispers welcome the moment we walk in the door. Javiera seems a little better, but still pouty compared to her elder sister, who eagerly signals me to follow up the open slatted staircase to show off her room. It's very pre-teenage; colourful, stuffed with stuffed toys and posters, still enamoured with the wonders of the world and filled with intelligent innocent curiosity, but with parental, social and peer pressures beginning to crowd in.

Pepe and his family are not here tonight. Rather there is a different crowd, and I have to begin again, trying to work out who is who. Alejandra comes to my rescue, speaking very good English. Her father, she explains, is Alejandro, the youngest of Charles's children. She has two brothers, but only Nelson is here tonight; friendly and curious, he speaks only Spanish, so his sister has to interpret. Their mother, Juana, has the prettiest face imaginable, framed in a cloud of dark hair; a large woman with ample breasts, she sits and knits and smiles a lot – dark eyes sparkling, watching me intently.

My mother wants to knit something for you, Alejandra explains.

No, no, I say; thank you but really there is no time. Best to knit something for her grandson. (Alejandra has a strong roly-poly son of around seven; I never do work out who the father is, or even if there is a father around. Shades of Harriet and John, I wonder?)

But unlike Harriet (who may well have been intelligent but most certainly was not educated), Alejandra is a professional woman. Or rather she is trying to be, having experienced a triple dose of discrimination that has left her reeling with anger and deep hurt.

I was called into my superior's office last week, she recalls; He told me that I could expect to rise no higher in terms of promotion because I was too short, too fat and too dark.

Having only just met her, I don't know what to say for comfort. I could mouth platitudes – How terrible! How shocking! How insulting! Instead all I can do is take her hand and suggest she leaves, starts something for herself. This is what women are doing in Japan when they come up slap-bang against the glass ceiling of male dominance, I explain, to which she summons up a wry grimace and shrugs.

Alejandra is right, of course; it's not so easy… especially if she is raising her son as a single mother. But I do hope she will think about it. She has a quiet strong resilience that I believe will stand her in good stead, whatever path she chooses.

As a marine biologist her brother Nelson looks envious at mention of Japan. I get the feeling he may be an unemployed marine biologist, but am hesitant to dig any deeper. Maria-Elena, alternately beaming with pride at so cleverly having brought so many people together to meet me, and relaying the tale of my lost/stolen purse with a look of shamed sorrow, draws me towards another older man, and a woman, who have just arrived.

Josefina, she introduces: Here too Eric.

So now I have met five of Charles' children. Josefina, who has a narrow face, full of character, with bright searching brown eyes and a strong quizzical smile, was born in 1931. Eric, three years younger, is dapper, in a black shirt and dark suit, with a neatly trimmed silver moustache. Everyone has a full head of hair – and good strong hair at that. The strong noses are there, also the well-marked eyebrows, and the large, prominent ears – a particular Loader trait. Alejandro, who is nearest to me in age, most definitely has the ears; also cropped hair, thick-rimmed glasses and a certain reserve. While observing that it is such a pity that Pepe could not come, Maria-Elena lines up her aunts and uncles – Guillermo Mario, Eric

Walter, Josefina Leticia, Alejandro – and I snap away with my reliable but weighty Nikon as if in a dream. William, Walter, Leticia... all family names with Liverpool connections. And yet none of these Chilean descendants have ever been to England, let alone to the city of their father's birth; nor can any of them speak a single word of English.

What on earth would Sam, let alone Harriet, have made of all this, I wonder. My grandfather knew that his first cousin was just across the Andes; they had corresponded. But there is no mention of Charles by name, nor indeed of Chile in any of his letters to England. But then I suspect there is a lot he is keeping under wraps, for whatever reason. The politics of his days in Buenos Aires continue to receive rare mention. Also there is little to no elaboration on the extent of family contact in the city or indeed any of the people he mentions in passing. In the letter of October 30, 1944, for example, he writes of *hosts of little friends, who call me Uncle Sam, or Uncle Loader, and for my birthday I go again to Nechones to stay there whilst two of my little friends are there, and we shall have a really good time. One is called Diana and the other Elinor (aged 7 and 9). They are children of a family who have a Textile Factory in Bradford, which I represent.* But that is that, no more, no less. Nor is there any mention of this acquaintanceship, delightful or otherwise, ever again.

What he prefers to do is turn over old ground, trying to make sense of the rejection he continues to grieve over, but in the process bringing up new material to the surface that more often than not serves to further confuse the issue. On the subject of his sisters, for example:

*I feel years younger to know that someone in the family sticks by the Old Pater. I cannot thank you enough. I am sure the others would have written but they have been led astray. I also could not believe that the rancour towards my sisters would be passed on to me, as it was through no fault of my own, as I was in Venezuela when the unhappy episode occurred, and then I tried all I could by letter to persuade Sal to forgive and forget, but the bitterness continued and increased until it reached me, and then I got it good and hot, but in a quiet but very nasty manner. I have written time and time again… and the attitude towards my sisters has not been assuaged in any way. It is beyond all understanding why this all continues.*

What on earth was this all about? When asked, my mother is vague. All she can remember is that my grandmother (whose family migrated to Liverpool from Kirkudbrightshire) disapproved very much when her brother, Alexander, married Sam's sister Beatrice. She seemed think it incestuous, somehow, even though they were not related by blood in any way. Was this the origin of the bitterness, the nastiness? Hard to imagine, but maybe in those days attitudes, social mores, perceptions of right and wrong really were so very different.

Still Sam rages on: *I have not contravened the law in any way, although I have done things that were not discreet, and have been blamed a lot without pity from my own. If I had been murdered perhaps I would have been treated better. Families stick to one another through thick and thin, but when the thin came to me, everybody left me to get along as best I could. I always knew that things would come right, but in my case I had a bad patch. After leaving Upper Parliament Street, and despatching me, within two months I was on my way to recovery. I had a tough struggle even after that as the luck did not seem to change, but now I am happy and contented.*

Ha! I am inclined to respond. If these are the words of a happy and contented man, I am inclined to eat my tape-recorder.

On the positive side, he is trying to endow my father with faith in himself and for the future. *Always step out with confidence, make your presence and quality known. Your ancestors,* he reiterates, *were of the old Roman colony of Uricornium* (sic) *on the Border of Wales, and your very British blood must keep you well on top.*

*Perhaps,* he pleads, *through your intermedium, the others will write to me soon. I actually wrote to Mrs Barney* (his nickname for his younger son's wife Sally) *but so far have no reply. I have no enemies in the whole world* (excepting his nearest and dearest!) *and very few, if any, who do not think well of me. I live strictly in a correct way, and help all those I think justly deserve it.*

Following on from this self-congratulatory consideration, he has no doubt that my father is a good father, who will do his very best see that my mother, Bridget and myself come to no harm. Then sentiment, homesickness, sadness again crowd in: *I do not go far in this city, but am extremely friendly with my radio, and every night listen to the very best music, both from here and London.* And he closes with a verse that is emotional enough to pluck the most cynical of heart strings, adding in a handwritten note that of course, in all honesty, *it is not original:*

*How I would love to visit you today,*
*To lift the latch and peep within the door*
*And join the happy company once more -*
*I think I'd try to catch them at their tea:*
*What a surprise for everyone t'would be!*
*How we would talk and laugh, maybe and cry,*
*Living our lost years, they and I;*
*And then at dusk I'd seek the well-know lane*
*To hear the English nightingale again.*
*That's the old country, that's the old home,*
*You can never beat it, where-ever you roam.*

Sitting cross-legged on the floor upstairs, Sylvia and the girls are wading their way through photograph albums while the noise of the gathering below swells up the stairwell to envelop us all in a warm embrace of pleasure and excitement. Seeing Javiera and Camila grow before my eyes, from babies to toddlers, first days in kindergarten and school, holidays and parties, with family and friends, I feel a sudden homesickness pricking behind my eyes. Why am I here with strangers when I could be with my own children, laughing our way through our own family snaps – the good times, the bad times, the ups, the downs, faces old, faces new… All beloved, with never a regret.

Back downstairs, for what is fast becoming the ubiquitous group photo, I am sat in the very centre, backed by a large contemporary oil painting on the wall and a stack of chrome system shelving. On the glass coffee table in front of me, snacks – crisps, nuts, bits of sausage on sticks – and soft drinks, all set out neatly on paper napkins. (I have been dying for a can of beer or glass of wine all evening but everyone seems to be tee-totalling.) Behind me range Luis, Alejandra with her son on her knee, Nelson, Josefina, a young woman who came late and to whom I have still not been introduced, with William standing at the far end of the sofa, then Maria-Elena grinning ear to ear, and William's wife, and Juana, their haunches spilling out of smart cane chairs. On the floor to my right, Silvia and her daughters; to my left, Carole, then Alejandro and Eric. Seventeen in all, with some people already departed.

Carole? She is Ricardo's daughter apparently, and another architect – or rather an architectural student. But who is Ricardo? Haven't worked that out yet, but I'm determined to get to the bottom of it; most certainly he is not here. Everyone grins and hugs one another like crazy when the camera remote flashes; the girls squeal deliriously, giving the ubiquitous V-sign. Then the talk turns to tomorrow. It seems that an outing has been arranged. As we leave, Silvia, her daughters, Carole and Maria-Elena are even more excited (if this is possible!); apparently I am being taken to Valparaiso.

# CHAPTER 13

# VALPARAISO

**NOVEMBER 13, 1999**

We eat breakfast in the cafe on the corner and I get talking with a British couple from Bristol. Small, fair, blue-eyed - he in shorts, she a pink print Laura Ashley-style cotton frock – they are driving down from Central America to the southernmost point of Patagonia where they will (somehow, somewhere) pick up a cruise ship to see out the old year and in with the new, in the Antarctic. Picking up the main points of this astonishing saga, Maria-Elena is full of admiration but also slightly stunned. She cannot imagine, and to be honest neither can I.

Have you had any trouble, I ask hesitantly between swigs of coffee, my mouth sticky with sweet flaky pastry.

The couple look at one another, then break out into peals of hollow laughter.

Trouble? the man repeats; Well, none at all really apart from being robbed eight times.

Eight times? Eight? Maria-Elena's eyes are possibly even larger than my own.

Yaas, he continues, with just a hint of that lovely West of England drawl; And two were on the same day!

The same day? (I'm beginning to sound like a parrot.)

It seems that in Peru (the poorest, most desperate country yet visited, they readily agree) some desperado smashed in the window of their rented brand-new four-wheel drive (just asking for trouble if you ask me)

203

and dragged out a bag containing most of his clothes. So he went to the bank to draw out cash to buy new togs, placed the notes in his wallet which he lodged deep in an inside pocket, and on the way to the store, was dipped and lost the lot.

Skilful, his wife observes.

Indeed, he agrees, but not in the least admiring.

We are standing on the edge of the pavement discussing the inherent dangers of travel when a car draws into the curb. Up until now I have had no idea who is involved in this recreational kidnapping. What a nice surprise, therefore, when down rolls the window and there is Pepe smiling, with Daniel behind the wheel. Apparently this trip was mooted the first night we gathered at Pepe and Olga's flat, but they received the call only late last night that everything was on and A-OK. I am touched that father and son should so readily drop everything to accommodate me, and want to say so. Daniel interprets, and Pepe takes my hands in his own and kisses them. Needless to say, I am touched all over again.

With me upfront with Daniel, and Maria-Elena and her uncle in the back, we set off for the coast, a distance of some hundred miles, give or take. The journey is a blur because Daniel and I are trying to talk above the rapid and increasingly noisy, incessant chatter going on behind us. Maria-Elena and Pepe do not break their animated conversation for one minute; it is extraordinary and after a while Daniel and I give up, offering one another amused glances. And then, I hate to admit, despite the interest of the landscape, I fall asleep. I do remember Daniel sliding over a package containing literature and drawings of his latest architectural project: a massive condominium at the famed resort Vina del Mar just up the coast to the north from Valparaiso. And me thinking it looked no different to any other similar resort project, which I tend to dislike on principle. Maria-Elena and her husband have an apartment in a condo in Mar del Plata, to the south of Buenos Aires. I have seen photos, and received postcards, so I have a good idea what that resort looks like, and what it comprises:

row upon row of concrete apartment blocks, shopping malls, restaurants, casinos. My idea of hell and I don't care who knows it. But I do not say this to Daniel. Instead I ask politely about environmental considerations, and am saddened not to receive what I consider to be an encouraging or even a very concerned response. He is young, with a young family, and ambitious; we leave it at that. There are lots of other things to chat about – for example he is very curious about Japan and the current state of its economy – if only I could keep my eyes open....

Valparaiso is quite an eye-opener. The marine front, where we park and wander to find somewhere for lunch, is affluently at play, with roller-bladers, dog-walkers and young people in designer sports clothes and beachwear. The beach is wide, the sea a pale-misted blue, and the sand dazzles under a white-hot sun.

I take photographs – first of Pepe in his grey shirt and peaked cap, Daniel in black from toe to toe, and Maria-Elena, today in black and grey. (They have a pack of stray dogs at their heels including, I note, a very beautiful Alsatian, but horribly thin.) Another shot: a circle of teenagers in jeans, cut-offs and T-shirts, girls and boys shoulder-to-shoulder on the beach playing ball (you wouldn't see that in Britain); behind them people are sunbathing, but no-one is swimming. The beach seems to drop very suddenly into the sea; maybe this is why? This questionable scene is backed by a pier that juts out into the ocean. Supported on massive concrete legs, it is the oddest mix of green copper-roofed turrets-cum-pagodas with dinky little white painted windows, and jerry-built buildings topped with what looks like a crane. Finally, I shoot through a row of interesting vehicles: double bicycles with seats front and back and a canopy overhead, operated by foot power. The girl who pedals the one in the centre turns and gives me a brilliant smile; plugged into a stereo-headset she is halfway through an ice-cream, enjoying the break. Beyond the pier, the beach is being pushed seawards by development – condos that give way to rocks, an outcrop of trees, more apartment buildings and so it goes on around the curve of the bay, merging eventually with mountainside.

Inland, the city rises with a startling rate of incline, but terraced, with neighbourhood *barrios* reached by *ascensores* – funicular railways that go straight up, straight down, and pray the cables are well serviced. It is a colourful scene, with houses painted the colours of the rainbow and all shades and tints in-between; very pretty – at long distance anyway, for this is where just about everybody lives.

Approaching by ship, apparently, you can see that the city – once known as the Pearl of the Pacific – sprawls over a number of hills (forty-one to be exact) backed by the Cordilleras, the Andes. It was from one of these natural vantage points that Bernado O'Higgins watched the Chilean fleet (under the control of a British admiral) set out to attack the Spanish in the 1820s. Founded in 1536, Valparaiso grew rapidly towards the end of the nineteenth century. Because little has survived the elements – any number of man-made or naturally-inspired Acts of God – only a fragment of the old town survives, centred around La Matriz, a low-built stucco church from the 1830s. As Chile's oldest and still largest port, the city is now home to over a quarter of a million, all crowded into a natural amphitheatre.

Somewhere up there, or maybe some place quite different, but most certainly within the environs of the city lives Toto. Toto is my friend Richard's mother-in-law, met several times on coinciding visits to the UK. On my last trip, Richard and his wife Noemi were up in arms. Toto had been held in immigration at Heathrow yet again and this time given a severe grilling: Why was she in the UK? She came so often! (Once every two years or so is *often*?) Was she sure she didn't want to stay, wasn't trying to creep in illegally?

So disrespectful, so blatantly rude, Noemi was raging: My mother wants to see me, she wants to spend time with her grandson, what the hell is wrong with that? God, I hate this country!

She didn't mean it of course; she was just furious that a gentle courageous grandmother should be so shabbily treated, as if she were some kind of criminal. Personally Noemi has always been treated well, but nowadays there are certain elements in government and the media that choose to portray the UK as an island under siege; times have changed.

Noemi's parentage is Chilean (her mother, with Spanish blood) and Bolivian (her father, who died in 1972). She was always political, becoming active in secondary school as a school representative and working on the school newspaper. At university she was attracted to the extreme left, which was committed to challenging educational policies.

It was a very exciting time, she recalls from her home in north London; We were making it up as we went along. I really identified with such activism.

After twentieth-century border disputes with Peru and Bolivia, Chile became one of the richest and most politically stable countries in South America. Following capitalist free-market principles, however, the benefits went mostly into the pockets of the rich; the poor simply became poorer. Revolution came in 1970 when the Marxist Salavador Allende Gossens was elected president, with an agenda for transforming Chile into a socialist state. Three years later he was assassinated as part of a military coup, led by General Augusto Pinochet, with the backing of the manically anti-communist US, and the close involvement of Henry Kissinger, America's National Security Advisor between 1969 and 1975. This is when, for Noemi – or Mimi as she is known to friends – and so many of her generation, the shit hit the fan.

Her university was one of the first to be targeted as subversive. It was closed down and a large number of students from a broad range of social backgrounds were arrested. In late 1973, she went underground, hiding out with her grandparents to give herself time to assess the situation. Soon it became clear that she would not be going back to university; also she couldn't bear the idea of her family having to protect her long term. So she moved far away and worked as a primary school teacher in a remote village. With 99 per cent of her colleagues students-in-exile, they made the best of it, developing what she describes as fantastic ideas about teaching methodologies.

Mimi: We were mostly women, working in a poor social context; my background was working class, but in this village there were people far worse off than me.

After a year, despite the chaotic and frightening political climate, she returned to Valparaiso. Her boyfriend, from Vina del Mar, had been arrested in Santiago where he was studying medicine. Released, but under surveillance, it seemed as if the best course of action was to get out of Chile and its immediate environs altogether.

Mimi: The only way to get passports was through embassies and the Red Cross. My boyfriend was lucky; he got one via a church organisation called Vicario de la Solidarite. I wanted to leave with him, but it proved impossible.

Instead she went back to school for two years of technical courses, developing a relationship with another activist. He also was arrested.

Mimi again: With his family already in exile, I knew that this time I had to get out, so I applied to go to Canada and also the UK through the same church organisation.

Accepted along with several of her friends, she applied to the World University Service, which offered scholarships to people unable to pay their way because of political reasons. It took six months to get the papers through, using pseudonyms. She was never able to give any genuine information; it was just too dangerous.

Mimi arrived in London in June 1978. Ironically, just two months previously, the Chilean government had offered an amnesty. But the rules were so open to interpretation that there was an international outcry; people still had no real protection from political persecution. Torture was commonplace, people regularly disappeared.[38] Although Mimi had visas and funding in progress, many people she knew were imprisoned, missing or dead. Luckily she was with her mother in Valparaiso when her new boyfriend was picked up; somehow she managed to keep one step ahead of military police until it was time to leave. (This boyfriend was eventually released and went into exile. He returned to Chile in the early 1980s and is now a furniture distributor – about as safe as you can get.)

Of Noemi's group of associates, eight went to the US, four to Sweden and Belgium, and four, including Mimi and her close friend Ximena, a medical student, to the UK. It was a well-organised exit from Chile, an equally well-organised arrival in London.

Back in Valparaiso – as two Chileans from Santiago, one Chilean living in Argentina, and an Englishwoman based in Japan return to their car and move off to destinations unknown – I am thinking of exile. Two Englishmen (my grandfather and his cousin) who, if they are to be believed, were more of less forced into exile in South America earlier in the century; Noemi who has chosen exile in Britain; I still "On Holiday" in exile in Japan after fifteen years; my daughter married to exile in Canada. Despite the free choices involved, we all suffer – or have suffered to a degree – the decision to move to another country. What does it mean, exile? Well, many things apparently – in extreme to be expelled from one's native country, but more commonly these days just a long period of absence spent abroad. For some exile is a painful experience, at worst impossible to endure. For others it empowers and provides a wealth of hitherto unimaginable opportunities. But even in the most positively endowed situation, there is always an ache of regret: a deep romantic longing for landscape, culture and people left behind, all the things *Given Up*. Best to remember that there is good and bad in every country. As Mimi says, she finds Britain ageist, racist and sexist. But as she knows only too well, the same can be said of Chile and indeed, virtually every other so-called developed country in the world today.

Above all, Mimi believes that exile has made her strong – far stronger than if she had remained in Chile. When she first arrived in the UK, backed by the Greater London Council,[39] she and other women in her situation formed a group, Avance, meaning Advance. A lot of outside political forces tried to infiltrate, manipulate and take control, but the women resisted; it made them mentally and spiritually very tough, she reckons. With a new and clear position, they began to take degrees, form new relationships, make babies. Inez is now an environmentalist. Patricia an accredited psycho-analyst. (Only one woman left the group early, before her time: Magdelena who died of skin cancer at age thirty-four.) Mimi had dreamed of bringing up a confident, happy, ambitious daughter like Manuela, whose diminutive but impressively energetic mother Ximena is now a consultant paediatrician in a major teaching hospital in London. Instead Mimi got a boy, which initially filled her with foreboding.

Boys are harder, she believes; they assume they have a rightful place in society on the planet.

Still, for both Noemi and Richard, Ben is their own Beautiful, beautiful boy; very confident, very happy, if perhaps not quite as ambitious as his mother would like. Sometimes she is very Latin in her ambivalence: driving him on in one breath, enveloping him in smother-love the next.


We appear to have arrived somewhere, but where? I am 9,000 miles from the country of my birth via the Panama Canal, 11,000 travelling the long way around, by the Magellan Strait. I'm also at an extreme north to south diagonal across the Pacific from where I have made another home. Across the road is a complex of impressive buildings in pale honey-coloured stone. It looks like the local government office it proves to be, and both dominates and shadows the divide between affluent and poor; the road up which we have driven. For this side, on which we are now parked, is a different world. As the others huddle on the pavement, talking, I wander off down a side street which widens to allow an open space. It is filthy, the gutters awash with garbage, flies everywhere. But the stores are full, and pavement cafes abound, with kids running amok and the adults displaying the curious mix of open friendliness and grim stoicism that so typifies the poor and disadvantaged. I stand for ages in front of a store, trying to identify the fruit and veg, my eyes dizzy with colour (though it may of course be the after-effects of the wine!) I move away only when a woman comes out and starts shouting. I don't understand the words but the message is clear: Buy something or bugger off.

When I get back to the car, it has doubled. Goodness, I think, did I drink that much? But no, there is a second car parked, and now a third drawing in... And who should tumble out of the first but Silvia and her family. I never do learn the names of the occupants of the second car, but they are large and bear-like – the man bearded, his daughters smiling – very warm and accepting and sweet. There is now quite a crowd on the edge of the pavement, consulting maps, exchanging hugs and kisses. But while his father is behaving like a needy spaniel desperate for attention, Daniel, I notice, does not join in; he hangs around on the edge in his black T-shirt, black combat trousers and heavy boots, hovering.

Well, we are all back in our respective vehicles and moving off in convoy. In no time at all we are out of the city – goodbye Valparaiso, goodbye Toto – and heading into scrubby open country, with foothills beyond. After about thirty minutes, deep into countryside we pass a priest playing guitar and leading a small congregation of elderly women and small children in song at the roadside, then two men and one boy on two horses, and finally screech to a halt across the dust-filled road from a one-storey stone-built house. The door opens and more people pour out, screaming and gesticulating, again with a motley collection of dogs barking at their heels. Maria-Elena is screaming Ricardo, Ricardo, and a short darker-skinned man with a strong face and careful smile allows himself to be enveloped in her arms. Everyone has now disembarked, taking over the road, and there is a new round of hugs and kisses. I don't know who anyone is, in large part because dust has drawn a veil over the immediate proceedings. Best to go with the flow, I decide, dying for a glass of water, a cup of tea, anything remotely wet.

So now we are five vehicles; it's all very jolly. The landscape becomes rougher, with rocks and trees, scrub and cactus. Eventually we draw up in front a gateway, with a sign reading Oasis de la Campagne; high fencing runs to either side, merging into wilderness. Passing through what appears to be quite heavy security (could we be going to *jail*? maybe best *not* to pass GO) we follow a winding dirt road that eventually draws up in front of some kind of reception area and club house, with seats and tables and a piped recording of birdsong. There is a fair amount of action-packed unpacking, with a fold-up chair produced.

You, says Silvia, smiling, taking my arm, indicating that I am to sit down.

*Para mi?* I reply, surprising myself with my knowledge of the language.

*Si, si,* says Camila, who skips up bearing a striped cushion on her head, then drops it onto the chair seat with a triumphant grin.

Food is laid out on a table – pasty-style rolls of pastry filled with meat that I recognise as *empanados,* the Chilean equivalent of England's Ploughman's Lunch, and Japan's *onigiri* rice ball. Also an array of soft drinks. For me though there is a meatless sandwich and blessings of blessings, a cup of tea. Sylvia has brought along not only a flask, but a china cup and saucer. Feeling a bit like the Queen on some royal picnic, I am both delighted and quite hideously embarrassed. All these people have gathered and this whole day has been organised for my benefit. With such thoughtfulness too – and still more to come.

Silvia and Luis are building a house in this protected rural retreat (for this is what it is), and we are going to inspect its progress. But first we take a look around the swimming pool and other club amenities – the piped birdsong is beginning to get on my nerves; where are the real birds? I cannot argue the siting of the pool, however; it is stunning, surrounded by shrubs heavy with clusters of bright yellow flowers, with tall pine trees and ridges of hills bearing scrub and forest, backed by a mountain range scarred by glacial activity and turning lilac to purple in the mid-afternoon light. The location of the house is impressive too - a ten-minute drive away and, with not another building in sight, surprisingly remote. The basic wooden structure is up, and the floors down, so we can walk around while taking reasonable care. It is at this point that Ricardo's daughter Carole – the lovely slim young woman of the night before – comes into her own because, as it is explained, it is she who has designed the house for her aunt and uncle. Still an architectural student, and this her first commission, she is shaking with nerves; certain aspects of the design are causing such anxiety that she wishes (she confides in fragmented but perfectly understandable English) she could start all over again. When I tell Daniel, he says he does not know Carole, nor her siblings – a boy of about fifteen (who reminds me strongly of Richard and Noemi's son) and a younger brother so ravishingly beautiful that for the first hour I assume him a long-haired girl.

I don't know most of these people, Daniel adds, showing no real interest and making no attempt to alter the situation.

By the time we leave the house it is dusk. The hills around are closing in, black-on-black, like a layering of filmy cloaks one upon another, with bats swooping over the roof of the house. There is a final watering of trees recently planted – Pepe has much enjoyed pottering; a pleasant change from high-rise city living I guess – and rolls up the hosepipe with studied care. (Daniel, who puzzles me more and more, is nowhere to be seen.) Having chatted with everyone, Maria-Elena is well into a second round of talks. The children – the younger members of this large extended family – are played out, panting with excitement and exhaustion; it is a great place to explore, roam free. A second round of snacks and drinks is cleared away; everyone agrees that despite Carole's fears it is going to be quite a splendid house; and people begin to drift towards their cars with thoughts of the drive home. There is a final group photo, the kids sprawled on the ground, rolling around like a clutch of happy puppies; some adults have already left, so once again the picture is not complete. Still we have William and his wife, Silvia and Luis and their children, Ricardo and his three, Pepe and Daniel, Maria-Elena and half a dozen others whose names I have forgotten. I'm sorry about this, but so much has been thrown at me in the last few hours, with little to no explanation; I think everyone takes so much for granted that they forget that I am a stranger here – they assume maybe that Maria-Elena prepares me step-by-step, when in fact she is enjoying not my discomfort or confusion but the simple pleasure of presenting me with surprise after surprise. She is like a conjurer producing one rabbit after another out of a hat, with me as the goggling mystified audience.

I do not remember much more. Just that several hours later my baffled and bemused head hits the pillow in our hotel room and I am out like a light.

**NOVEMBER 14, 1999**

I wake early. Maria-Elena is still sleeping, snoring gently, her hair spread in a halo around her head on the pillow. So I return to Sam, lapsed into the self-pity of exile in Argentina in the last days of the war. But I must not be too hard on the old man, having to admit that whenever I read that poem he quotes about *The Old Country*, it always raises a lump in my throat. Whether it be for the image of *Lifting The Latch* (having yearned for a stable door all my life) or *The English Nightingale* (as if I have ever seen or even heard one!), or simply the thought of a man sitting in pained and uncomprehending isolation in a hotel room night after night listening to the BBC service, I am not sure. A mix of the three I suspect. That's what happens to people in exile: the grass always seeming greener and sweeter back home, we get soppily – soggily – sentimental.

By late 1944, Sam's mood has changed completely: he is ebullient. It seems that my father had broken all records and written twice in one week. *Considering this,* Sam writes, banging so enthusiastically on the keys of his typewriter that they puncture the light but inherently strong airmail paper, *I think I am entitled to pour letters on top of you in an unlimited wave of optimism for the future.*

He then proceeds with some excitement to talk business, describing orders received and transactions underway. Although there is little being imported still, he believes prospects are good, and is looking ahead to the end of hostilities and a return to the *Good Old Days*. (Importing 35,000 bikes in 1937–1938 to the value of 125,000 pounds sterling, and that just a small part of his wheeling and dealing, there must have been a considerable profit.) He then runs through a list of companies in the Midlands making motorbikes and bicycles, wondering if my father knows of any more. *Are there any firms in Coventry* (for instance) *that are not fixed up* (with representation)?

The day being All Saints Day and a national holiday, with all the offices closing after lunch, he plans a nap and then to stroll along what he calls the *sea avenida*. With a trip across to Montevideo booked for the coming week, he is in good form: a positive note on which to end a generally downhearted and angry year.

Why then did he write only three letters in the whole of 1945? To be fair, I clipped less than half-a-dozen newspaper items with regard to Argentina in the whole of 1993 – one in Spring and the remainder towards the end of the year. So, yes, I do understand how life impinges, time passes...

Just as I finish flipping them through, I spot a small entry on the same page under World Briefs (sic), about a 300 kilogramme man living in La Plata, 65 kilometres from Buenos Aires, who was in intensive care after eating a whole piglet for dinner: The man was identified as Alfredo Rosales, thirty two; The exact size (and age) of the piglet was unknown.

I am laughing when Maria-Elena wakes up. I laugh even more when she announces, glory be, that there is to be another party tonight, again at Silvia's, and that I will meet even more family.

More? I query, near hysterical with disbelief. (Maria-Elena has that look in her eyes again – twinkling, positively wicked with delight.)

Someone come to see you, she says, taking urgent control of her hair and securing it neatly in place with a comb; We are one hundred and forty-four Loaders in Santiago – maybe many, many more. He will tell everything.

Ricardo?

No, no, Claudio.

# CHAPTER 14

# CLAUDIO

**NOVEMBER 14, 1999 CONTINUED**

Maria-Elena has arranged to go with Betty to see her cousin's father in hospital. Federico – Frederick – is Charles's third child and second son, born in 1919, and he has Alzheimers. I offer to go along, but it seems that Betty would rather I did not. Nothing personal, explains Maria-Elena, but Betty's father is in a very bad way, and she believes it would be upsetting, for all of us. So after breakfast Maria-Elena hops into a cab, shouting back out of the window that she will see me tonight, and heads off in a cloud of fumes. I have absolutely no idea where she has gone, or how we will meet up. All I have is her assurance that Claudio exists and will somehow materialise.

I use the next hour or so to do chores, exchanging a few of my remaining bank notes into pesos, and then checking e-mail. The money situation is a potential worry. I'm going to have to be very careful. On the way back to the hotel, I pop into that startling red-walled church (Iglesia De San Francisco) passed so often – one of the oldest in Santiago and find myself in the middle of a communion service. Of course, it is Sunday. I had completely lost track. I am drawn to religious buildings – the architecture, the peace, the rituals, the sense of spirituality realised, of being centred. I have been into one church at least every day of my travels here in South America, and whether Catholic in Spanish or Italian tradition, they all seem immensely foreign and intriguing.

First I must light candles. I am not a Christian in the sense that I am a believer. Though I was surprised in Japan to realise just how much of my behaviour, how many of my attitudes, were directly linked to my Anglican upbringing. Over and over again, when faced with Japanese thinking, rooted as it is in Shinto, Chinese Confucianism and Buddhism, I would find myself questioning why I thought this and that, and indeed why I felt so strongly. Charity, for example, does not come naturally to the Japanese; even their kindness – extreme kindness it should be said – tends to be rooted in politeness rather than heart. Would charity come naturally to Europeans, I wonder, if it was not a part of their cultural – meaning essentially biblical – indoctrination: *Thou shalt love thy neighbour as thyself* (Leviticus 19: 18); *And now abideth faith, hope and charity, these three; but the strongest of these is charity* (Ibid.13:13). It's an interesting thought.

So, I light candles for Lee and Buffy, also one for Eric – and one for my sister, recovering now in hospital with, *Too many Get Well cards* (from the congregation of her evangelically-inclined Anglican church), *bouquets and pot plants, bunches of grapes and boxes of chocolate, to count.* (Her own words, over the phone, just this morning.) It does not worry me that I choose to light candles with equal gratitude and solicitude in Christian churches High and Low, Buddhist temples and Shinto shrines. As far as I am concerned, people the world over are acknowledging the existence of the same Higher Being, Source of Power, Energetic Force, call it what you will. It is the complex belief systems compounded (in large by men) around basic spiritual acknowledgement that create the problems, so setting Christianity against Islam, militant Shinto against the rest of Asia, Fundamentalists against anyone in disagreement, and just about everyone against the Jews.

A single tenor voice – a man not a boy – fills the church interior with heart-rending beauty – a sliver of glass in sound, pure and clear, slicing air and space. After ten minutes or more of this glorious morning song, the choir joins in, and then the organ for a final flourishing crescendo. It is very beautiful, genuinely uplifting – so uplifting that I empty my purse of small change into the waiting palms of those begging outside before remembering, Oh dear, maybe I can no longer afford the luxury of charity.

I am sitting on my bed in the hotel, wondering *what next?*, when the internal phone rings.

Hello, says this disembodied voice; I am Claudio. Is it okay?

As I arrive down in the lobby, a young man of about my height with an endearing gait and glasses, turns, and a smile splits his face from ear to ear. Hello, he repeats, I am Claudio, Claudio Loader Garrido. I am Alejandro Loader Cruzat's son, Alejandra and Nelson's brother and I have travelled 400 kilometres overnight by bus to come and take you to lunch.

His English is excellent, if heavily accented, and I have to listen closely until my ears become attuned. I am bowled over to receive so much concisely pertinent information in the first few seconds of meeting. Equally bowled over that anyone should take the trouble to come so far at no doubt some cost and great discomfort to meet a complete stranger. Also I warm to the fact that he has brought me a bottle of spirited Pisco, Chile's national firewater, to help break the ice; feeling that I know exactly where I am with Claudio, I happily place myself in his hands.

We come up into daylight from the metro and within no time at all have a table on the pavement in front of a lively little restaurant. I like everything about it – the cheerful tablecloths, equally cheerful waiters, the food (when it comes – bread and olive oil, soup, pasta and lots of it), the young and funky clientele. Claudio – who blends in perfectly, being in jeans and white T-shirt, his dark curly hair cut short but not too short- has already agreed (with some relief I suspect) to my picking up the bill. As I rationalised, he may have come to take me to lunch but that didn't mean he had to pay for it. It was only fair considering how far he had come, and on his day off too.

So, he is Alejandro and Juana's son, their youngest. There was an older brother, Boris, born after Alejandra, but he drowned in 1992. He had bought some second-hand diving equipment in a flea market and it let him down.

I ask questions. Claudio answers as best he can. Certainly I feel no sense that he is holding back, except maybe when we move into especially sensitive territory. For the first time I am enabled to get the family into some kind of perspective, and tell him so. I acknowledge Maria-Elena's kindness, while at the same time admitting that it is hard for me to know where Pablo is coming from because he himself appears so confused. On the one hand, he talks of being a new kind of politician dedicated to help the poor, while relishing in his membership of a shooting club. He is sweet and caring, responsible on many levels but... It seems to me that he exemplifies the confusion of Argentines in general. And I tell Claudio about my contact in Tokyo, the one who introduced himself by saying, I am an Argentine and I am very superior. Claudio wonders if maybe I misunderstood, that the guy was joking: You know, so many people say that we Chileans are the British of South America that a British friend of mine told everyone he was Chilean when he was traveling in Europe.

We laugh a lot at this, also the difficulty of penetrating accents. Chileans always know where Maria-Elena has come from; she sounds like an Argentine. The reason Claudio's own accent is so thick is that he spent ten years in Bolivia: Now my own people often say that they can't understand me, he laughs.


The bread is delicious; virgin olive oil helps smooth the way.

Claudio, I say; Why did I sense at Silvia's that your father and your siblings are somehow different, set apart?

He looks thoughtful, replying that any difference lies perhaps in Alejandro being the youngest. (Alejandro was born in 1934, which means that though technically he is my uncle, there are just seven years between us in age.) Also, Claudio adds, Alejandro was still a small boy when his father left.

Left?

Oh, Charles walked out on everybody. I thought you knew that. It meant my grandmother leaned on my father a lot. He left school to help her, taking jobs here and there, experiencing poverty and disappointment, growing up among working men. Recognising the many injustices that existed in society, and wanting to help in his own industry, he became something of a leader. This was when the family began to separate from him.

Separate?

When Pinochet came to power, Claudio continues, pouring me a glass of wine, Even my father's own brothers and sisters turned their backs on him. He had this opportunity to leave the country, go to Australia, but my mother refused. She said, No, we should stay and fight in our country. My mother, Juana, has both Spanish and native Indian blood. Many Chileans have Mapuche blood; you can see it in our faces.

So saying he pointed to his own, explaining that sometimes it is hard to know a person's background in Chile. The Arabs were in Southern Spain so long – eight centuries – making Spanish people a blend anyway of North African and European; Claudio doesn't know whether his looks and colouring are from native blood or that Arab ethnicity of long ago.

His aunt, Josefina – You met her too! – enjoyed relationships with two men, one of whom died at sea and the second was Brazilian, by whom she has three sons. One of these boys, Claudio explains, is blonde with blue eyes, the two others are black.

My eyes are out on stalks. Thinking how interested George would be in all this, I tell Claudio about walking around Buenos Aires looking for signs of African blood. And recall standing in a queue in the bank one day and becoming fixated on the kink in the hair of the girl in front, and the lovely curve of her neck, and my recognition of African ancestry in her own looks and colouring when she finally turned around.

We are now into the first course.

Claudio describes how when his father married his mother, the family was askance: They said, How can you marry her, she's dark-skinned.

Have her as a mistress, but not a wife! When Alejandra was born, our own problems began. She was so dark-skinned the family nicknamed her Tinto. Nelson was also dark. Because I turned out fairer, with blonde hair – for a while at least! – my aunts and uncles – like Silvia Rosa, Pepe – made a great fuss of me. Among the cousins, my sister, brothers and I were always on the outside because of the political differences. We were on the Left, but not extremists. The family however branded us Communists. I was at university when Pinochet was in power. I distinctly remember one of my uncles (he does not say which and I feel too shy to ask) asking my father, his brother, why he was still alive; You and your fucking sons! It was at this point that my father stepped out of the family circle.

I check that the tape recorder is working, recalling how I had met predominantly Pinochet supporters over the last three days. Thursday night I had met twelve family members, Friday fourteen and yesterday, around twenty. There were always new faces among the increasingly familiar, and it was not easy for me to understand who was who and the inter-relationships. Also those present did not always know everyone there; I remember in particular Daniel at the picnic saying, Who are all these people? When I joked with him about Carole being another Chilean Loader on her way to building the world – being an architect – he said he didn't know her and when I laughed and said Oh, you know, Ricardo's daughter, he turned away, saying he didn't know Ricardo. Also there was that funny thing on the first night when he muttered something about being on a death list, and only fifteen. Daniel has been great, really kind and supportive, but Alejandra was the first person I felt wholly comfortable with. I don't know what it was, or why; we just clicked.

The only times Claudio had met family other than his own was at funerals. For example, when his grandmother died, he saw a great many people he had never seen before. The only people he knew on any intimate level were Luis (Silvia's husband) and his brothers, also his aunt Silvia Rosa and her sons.

You know, this weekend is amazing, he says, mopping up remnants of oil and soup with bread and washing it down with another slug of good red Chilean wine; So many people coming together, sometimes for the very first time. You really started something with that letter you wrote Maria-Elena, you know.

It isn't sinking in. I am too busy slapping my wrist for not putting two and two together earlier. As I have reminded myself many times in my life, life is politics, politics is life. How could I have been so slow? I guess it is simply alien to me, something I have read about and heard about happening in other peoples' families – brother against brother – but here it is, showing its ugly face in my own.

I ask, What are Daniel's politics then?

Having met him only twice in his life, Claudio has no idea.

That first night, I push, Daniel said something about he and his father being on a list for assassination, I guess that puts them on the Right, right?

For the first time Claudio does not reply.

Okay, I say, I give in; Tell me more about your childhood. You talk, I'll listen.


Even when Claudio was small, his parents were constantly warning him not to talk about politics. They said, Don't talk about it at school, playing with friends out on the street, anywhere. It was hard for him to understand, but he could sense the fear that lay behind the words. His family faced a lot of criticism and prejudice, and not only among family, but among friends and neighbours even.

When I was at school, he says, everybody was either Right or Left. There was no freedom of expression; if anyone offered an opinion, they were expelled. It was very hard. Secondary school was the same.

Nelson was at university when Claudio involved himself in the first anti-Pinochet demonstrations, and was implicated as a result. This was when accusations of "Communist" began to be hurled at the family and life became tough: I had a friend on the Right. This was when right-wing students were persecuting other students for having a different viewpoint. It was impossible for our friendship to continue.

I ask how Chile is now?

Still difficult, there's no trust, no real trust, he replies, watchful of three addicts in need of a fix fooling around among the tables, looking to cause trouble. Once they have moved on, the sun emerges from behind a passing black cloud.

When he was twenty, Claudio left home to study tourism. Living in Bolivia opened his eyes, and when he returned to Santiago he realised that while there were improvements, nothing had really changed. Told of Mimi's feeling in England – that the Chilean people should decide what is to be done with Pinochet – he agrees: Such a move would be very painful, open lots of old wounds, cause a lot of trouble: The Right says, Oh the terrible British, why are they meddling in our affairs, but maybe it suits them to have him out of the country; they can blame the UK and avoid taking responsibility. On the other hand, the Left is unsure whether Pinochet would receive a fair trial if returned here. He has too many powerful friends. But on the whole it would be better for him to be returned for trial in Santiago: Everyone will have to think about and face what happened during those terrible years, and ultimately that has to be a good thing.

The main course arrives.

When Claudio lived in Bolivia he came to know a great many native people, whom he calls Indians, so I will too. Now he is living in the north of Chile, in the Atacama region, assisting a tribe in its fight for recognition of land rights and to retain its indigenous culture. The two-thousand-strong Diguitieoeas are not recognised by the government.

We do studies, offer spiritual support, Claudio says; But it's hard for them. Children shout after them, *Indios, Indios*. If you read Chilean history, native people don't exist. The very worst kind of racism, don't you think?

I tell him about Marta, and how surprised Maria-Elena was that I was at all interested in her maid's ancestry. Also I recall how yesterday in Valparaiso, walking along the front, I stopped to look at some crafts being sold at a stall, and Maria-Elena commented loudly, Oh, look at those Indians! I turned round, really embarrassed and said, Please don't do that. It's so rude. And do you know, she just laughed, using exactly the same words as her son: Angela, you are so funny!

Apparently there is a lot of racism in the south of Chile also. When Claudio is down there, he is often asked if he is German. When he explains the name Loader is actually English, people turn away. Why? Well, because they are German. Remembering the letters I am reading from Sam, written towards the end of the war, hair stands up on the back of my neck. The timing is uncanny.

I recall a conversation with Pablo's brother, Julito. He was moaning about Argentina, and I said Look, this is a rich country, a beautiful country. Why can't you be proud to be Argentine? Everyone living here should be proud of their country, whatever their race and ancestry. You are all together now, so be proud, show dignity. And he said, Oh, you don't understand, we are Europeans and there are all these Indians and robbers, so much shooting, so many guns. The gap (between us) is huge, huge...

Claudio shrugs. Currently British people are having a bit of a rough time in Chile because of what is happening with Pinochet in the UK. When people ask him how he feels, having a British name, he says it means nothing: he's Chilean. When the same people say, But you have British relatives, he answers that he doesn't care: he's Chilean.

Still on the main course...

The people Claudio is supporting live in twenty-one little villages in a valley. Since the inhabitants have only native names, he is trying to help them prove they have always been there, pre-colonisation, pre-republic;

that the land is their own. Before the Spanish conquest, traditions were oral; it was the Catholic church – Jesuit priests – that began providing documents for births, marriages and deaths. This particular area was administered by a single Spaniard through *ecomomderos* (a precursor to the *hacienda*) until the beginning of this century. After agrarian reforms, others could legally own land – but not the indigenous population, who according to Authority, did not exist.

Most of the Argentine *pampa*, Claudio adds, is owned by English people; Do you know that?

I'm not surprised, noting that I seem to have spent my entire time in Argentina and Chile apologising for one thing or another.

Claudio laughs; No need, he says.

I ask who pays his salary.

Well, he replies, my brief from the Ministry is to prepare a plan for expanding tourism, but I'm also working as a volunteer for a foundation called Serviciodis, concerned with poverty.

Asked where he is based, he points on my map to a city called Ballanari and then between two distant rivers, saying, Here, El Transito. There is another tribe in the parallel valley, with quite a lot of inter-mixing.

Claudio wonders how much I know about Bernado O'Higgins (the illegitimate son of Ambrosio O'Higgins, governor of Chile from 1789 to 1796).

Very little, I admit. I know with rather more certainty that there are many places in Ireland beginning with the letters "Balli", or "Bally" from where the name Ballanari might have originated.

Asked what he did in Bolivia, Claudio does a double take.

Bolivia?

You said you lived for ten years in Bolivia.

No, no, he laughs again; *Valdivia.*

Settling the confusion with another Salut! I remember that Valdivia – named after he who was forced to eat gold, and a port as far to the south as Bolivia is a country to the north – is in the German region.

Claudio knows about the town in Argentina where high-level Nazis and their families settled after escaping Germany at the end of the war, and how several journalists who tried to penetrate it have not come back.

But it's in Chile, not Argentina, he corrects; It's near San Carlo and off limits to Chileans. I've seen it on TV. The German immigrants in the South, Valdivia, have no connection; they came last century, many escaping persecution and the Bismark Republic. They hate the postwar German influx, well you can imagine.

Salad arrives, plus another basket of bread.

I show Claudio a book of postcards showing Liverpool in its heyday. He has seen similar pictures, and recalls a photograph taken when Charles first arrived in Valparaiso in 1909: There had been a huge earthquake and all the buildings were destroyed. Maybe that's why he moved on to Peru.

Peru?

Yes, then he met the mother of my grandmother.

I'm lost: The mother of your grandmother?

Oh, you didn't know. He had two women. There was Sara Cruzat, and then there was her daughter, Mercedes.

I am goggle-eyed all over again. I had heard there were two women in his life but not that they were mother and daughter.

Sara was single, Claudio continues. Despite having a daughter, and two children with him, Carlos and Alicia, she never married Charles. Then she died.

I stop Claudio here, having heard at some point over the past couple of days, that she had somehow disappeared.

No, he states emphatically, she died; And after that he made a few babies with my grandmother, who was just fourteen when her mother passed away, so she brought up her half brother and sister.

A few? *Ten*: Federico Juan, Ana Luisa (Maria-Elena's mother), Arturo

Eduardo, Adela Rebeca, Guillermo Mario (William, Luis's father), Silvia Rosa, Josefina Leticia, Eric Walter, Jose (Pepe), and Alejandro.

Well, it's a Catholic country, Claudio observes, amused by my bemusement. Except his grandfather was *atheos* (an atheist), also his father, and Boris before he died: Me too, he adds; My mother is very Catholic but our parents always gave us the independence to find our own way of thinking, politically and concerning religion.

I feel very quiet and still, wondering how to describe old feelings about family that I hoped to somehow reconcile on this trip: For reasons I am unable to fathom I was very bad with my own relatives, Eric and Kathleen apart, always pushing them away. My idea – inspired I believe by Joanna, a German friend in Japan who had made a shrine with photographs and mementos to the memory of her parents, parents-in-law and recently deceased Japanese husband to help with the grieving – was that by coming here I could somehow change things around. In that sense I am beginning to think I must be on some kind of pilgrimage. I don't really understand the whys and wherefores; it's just something I feel I have to do.

Claudio twists his glass in his hands, calls for more water and orders coffee: You know, some years ago, we had a meeting of the cousins. It was after we heard about your letter to Maria-Elena. Our parents, they never wanted to meet one another, but we felt differently.

How many of you met?

Twenty-five to thirty people, aged from fifteen into thirties. It was not the whole family, but enough. We got together on September 19, 1997, two years ago, at Everil's house, one of Carlos's daughters. She lived in the north, where Carlos is buried, but came back to Santiago in 1995.

Just social?

Just social. It was a real Chilean party. I was in Valdivia at the time, so came back specially.

Valdivia, I note; Got it.

Claudio asks whether I knew Charles had founded Chile's boy scout movement.

I had heard this, yes, but was unsure how it fitted with the story of him having murdered someone on the Atlantic crossing.

Claudio laughs, relating how that bit of news had really stirred things up! Some relatives had been deeply upset, including Pepe. Nelson has promised to look into Charles's past a little more deeply from this end, and then confer.

Claudio says that he, Nelson and Alejandra were all scouts as children. They had only heard of Charles's involvement three years before: Our father never talked about his father. Never, ever.

I relate how a brief visit to the British Embassy in Santiago on Friday had resulted in no trace of his name; the same story with Sam in Buenos Aires. No records, no death certificates, nothing. Which is especially strange here because everyone in the family says the embassy paid for Charles's interment. I wonder also why the stone was so different to every other stone – the typically perfect inscription in typically perfect English, and all the others in Spanish. And why in the public cemetery? If the embassy had paid, why was it not in the British Cemetery?

Claudio has an answer: In the 1950s everyone was buried in the public cemetery. Only people with money could be admitted into the British Cemetery.

But you say he was a professional man, teaching English at the embassy, founding the Scout movement and so on...

When he died, he was alone. He had no money.

With twelve children?

Yes but, oh, they didn't tell you what happened? My grandfather fought with my grandmother. I think he went crazy. He punched her and Carlos fought with him and said *guba* (fuck off!) This is why none of my uncles and aunts talk about him. All his children hated him. That's why he is alone in the public cemetery and not in our family grave in the Cemetario Metropolitan near my parent's house.

Amazing. (Amazing indeed. The hair is standing up on the back of my neck all over again.) There are so many parallels with my own grandfather's life, it's more than uncanny, it's bizarre.

I tell Claudio the story of Sam and Sarah, and Barney punching him on the nose, and how he came out to Argentina alone, with everyone back home thinking the worst of him, barring my father whom I suspect was subject to horribly mixed feelings.

Claudio: My grandfather lived in a boarding house until he died.

Me: Mine too. He had a room in a hotel in Buenos Aires. But died in a hotel in Uruguay.

Claudio: Charles was alone but had many fine things, furniture, a coin collection... many collections. After he died, my Aunt Silvia spoke to the people who ran the boarding house and they said he left nothing. She thinks they took everything. I know he died in the street. He was picked up by a member of the Salvation Army... a black guy, who took him to a hospital where he passed away. The embassy paid for the funeral and sent a message to my grandmother. No one went to the funeral. No one ever goes to the cemetery.

He doesn't know why Charles was fighting with Mercedes. Pablo had sent me a photocopy of them standing together and they look quite amiable, but then you never know do you, what is really going on in other people's relationships. Claudio has been told his grandparents were always fighting: When my father was small, he remembers Charles even shooting at him, screaming *Get out!* He was the same with everyone. More often than not he ate at the table alone. Now maybe you understand why Maria-Elena's mother Ana was so keen to escape, get as far away as possible.

Coffee arrives and I play mother.

I bring out old photos of the family in England, including one of the house in Liverpool where my own father grew up. When I explain that it no longer exists, most probably bombed out during the war, Claudio stops stirring his coffee.

Incredible, he says; My father said Charles always cried when he saw fiery-red clouds in the sky at sunset; they reminded him of war, maybe in Liverpool, maybe in London, maybe somewhere completely different. We'll never know now, will we?

I show pictures of my own family, including Akii who is nine years younger than me, and the kindest of men. Claudio laughs gently, declaring that the island near Toronto, where I had stayed with Buffy and Ross just two weeks before, looks just like Valdivia: Can you imagine, he said. I lived ten years in a beautiful place like this, and now I live in the desert.

Blowing kisses to a photo of Lee, I explain that he is *Doing the Knowledge*, hoping to become the first non-racist, non-sexist taxi (Black Cab) driver in London.

Good, Claudio responds; Good! Then: You know, whenever people asked my grandfather if he was English, he would say No, he was British.

A Colonial thing, I explain; To do with the British Empire. Nowadays friends from Ireland say they are Irish, from Scotland, Scots, Wales, Welsh. If anyone asks me, I'm English.

The coffee pot is replenished.

Claudio is talking about his Aunt Silvia. Married twice, she had two children by Alfonso before hitching up with Jorge. Jorge later had a child outside the marriage, named Christian, and the woman who was his mother brought him to Silvia Rosa, saying, This is your new son! Silvia took him in, and Claudio says he was more a brother than just another cousin. When told at age fifteen or sixteen that Silvia was not his birth mother, he ran away and lived on the street. It was hard for Silvia, hard for all of us. Occasionally he is sighted, but basically Christian has disappeared from our lives. I think it all goes back to when he was a child and one of his brothers used to tease him, saying Silvia was not his real mother. When he learned it was true, that he was a bastard, he went crazy.

There is another story about Uncle Jorge. That he was mixed up in something strange, working as a driver between Chile and the Argentine.

The family thinks he was a bandit, smuggling drugs maybe. Anyway, he was in jail for five years. Silvia sold everything to get him out, even the house. When he was released, he moved back in with her, then phutt… off he went who knows where. So now she has nothing, no husband, no home, no Christian. Fortunately, everyone loves her… everyone tries to help.

Will I meet her?

Oh yes, tonight. I heard she's coming to the party. I last saw her two years ago at my cousin's house, so I'm really looking forward.

The waiter hands me the bill.

My problem, I explain, rummaging for cash, is that Maria-Elena tells me nothing. Every day is a complete mystery. I get manipulated into these situations, with all these strangers – with many of whom I share DNA – standing there looking at me, connecting me with Charles, and I think Oh dear! At least I should have worn a nice suit. I have nice clothes in Buenos Aires, but Maria-Elena never said anything about all this socialising and the day after tomorrow I'm taking the bus over the Andes back to Argentina, so I never thought to bring anything smart. I should have got a clue from Maria-Elena's baggage – for her every day is a fashion show.

Claudio shrugs, saying he thinks I look just fine: Argentines think a lot about clothes. I have many Argentine friends and wherever they go, whatever they do, they always dress up.

I recall meeting Betty the first night, and how I thought I was seeing double, she and Maria-Elena being similar in size and image; It was like seeing twins!

Clones!

We laugh again. We are laughing a lot, and it's not just the wine. We really like one another; I can tell.

I remember, I say, Maria-Elena taking me into a restaurant in Buenos Aires and it was full of clones, all sitting like this (stiffening) with faces like this (critical, judgmental) and I said, No, please, not here… So she led me into another place and it was full of men standing two metres tall and breathing heavy-duty machismo, and again I said, No, please! I could see how disappointed she was. With Betty, I could see her looking me up and down thinking, Strange woman, what is her culture? But it's not culture alone, is it? Many women try to compensate for ageing and a general lack in their lives with clothes, jewellery, makeovers. Maybe it's to do with insecurity. I don't feel like that, at least I don't think so. My insecurities lie elsewhere…

The bill paid, we gather our belongings and thoughts to leave.

Lovely place, I say; Thank you for bringing me here.

Only now do I learn that the area, Barrio da Vista, is special. Once quiet and run down, it was used as a hideout from Pinochet's thugs. Dissenters survived by constantly moving from one safe house to another. Also many of the bars date from this period – gathering places for illegal protest meetings.

As we cross the road – to the house of Pablo Neruda, whom I know to have been a famous poet but not much more – Claudio is already plotting ahead: I can show you the offices where Charles used to teach, now part of the University of Santiago. Maybe you would like to see them?

Well, I reply, I'm not sure now that I know what a sad, damaged and damaging bastard he was. Anyway, what about Claudio getting his bus back? He says not to worry; there's plenty of time to buy his ticket and get to Luis and Silvia's home for five-thirty: This party is important for me too, you know, he adds, grinning.

This is the most concentrated and prolonged conversation I have experienced in two weeks. Near three hours have passed, with Sam and any vague purpose to this trip falling into place within a far larger picture. For better or worse, there is a sense, an awareness, of family coming together in more ways than one.

La familia.

Mi familia.

# CHAPTER 15

# MI FAMILIA

**NOVEMBER 14, 1999 CONTINUED**

As we pass by an awe-inspiring tree on a street corner, massive yet blazing an ethereal meteoric red against a brilliant azure sky, I observe (tongue in cheek) that Claudio is still unmarried. I feel his sideways glance, as he denounces this fact as a family obsession: It's a big thing with Chilean Loader men to have sons. Everyone says, You must marry, you must have sons! But I say, No, I don't want to get married, I don't need sons. If you want sons, have one for me.

Ah, machismo, I murmer.

Yes, a lot of pressure, he acknowledges.

Do you know how I found Maria-Elena, I ask, relating the story of Jerry and his trip to Buenos Aires, and how Maria-Elena had responded to my letter, saying that the family had always been looking for someone like me.

Yes, my aunts and uncles were always waiting, Claudio interjects; Sometimes Silvia would lose hope saying, Maybe there is nobody there...

Where?

Liverpool. There had been no contact in decades. When my grandfather was living with my grandmother, sometimes he would receive postcards from his sister, Alice. She used to send him money, I don't know why.

Maybe because it was so easy? She ran a post-office, you know.

Claudio asks me to go back through the generations, explaining exactly who was who. So I do a quick re-run, back to Harriet, and since this link is unknown to him, explain what has been learned to date and how the family name may have evolved.

What does this mean, he says, looking puzzled.

It is fun to reply: That our family's known recorded history began with the name Loder, not Loader, and with a woman, not a man.

But men do not like to take second place for long. For just as the existence of Harriet is sinking into Claudio's consciousness, that of Pablo Neruda surfaces in my own and I'm ready to learn more. For we have arrived at his home – one of Chile's cultural treasures.

Pablo Neruda – a pseudonym for Neftali Ricardo Reyes Basualto – won the Nobel Prize for Literature in 1971 and yet, amazingly, his poetry was banned in Chile until 1990.[40] A schoolteacher from the north, who wrote under the pen name Gabriela Mistral, received the award in 1945. As the first Nobel prize-winner for literature in the whole of Latin America, Gabriela – like Neruda, a career diplomat as well as a poet - deserves a book in her own right. Pablo, however, has the house.

And what a house. We stand before a low reception area, the upper part painted a lovely periwinkle blue. Above two identical doors, with a sign of the sun and the name *LA CHASCONA* (meaning – delightfully – *Dishevelled Hair*) hanging in-between from a fantastical curlicue of a hook, are spaced three small square windows under tiled eaves, curtained with white-painted ironwork. The sun motif is echoed elsewhere, peeping out as a grille between the shutters of an upstairs window for instance. It is a marvellous building, as original and contemporary as when first constructed in the 1950s.

Now I learn that Neruda did not design and build this unique and lovely pad for himself, but rather for his third wife and the last great love of his life, the artist and singer Matilde Urrutia (1912–1985). She was thirty-seven when they met in 1946, inspiring Neruda's famed *One Hundred Sonnets of Love*. A stunningly beautiful woman with sweeping brows, dark eyes and a sensual mouth, she took over the role of rebel and poet following his death from leukaemia (this just twelve days after the defeat of his country's democratically elected regime in September 1973), and establishing their home as a foundation and library in his memory.

The house is designed around an inner garden for complete privacy, with inter-connecting stairways and balconies laden with vines and creepers. Along with half a dozen other visitors, we congregate in the living room and begin the tour; being in Spanish, this does not make life easy and I feel immense frustration. Claudio tries to pass information to me in whispered asides, but I feel it is unfair to expect him to spoon-feed me, so tell him not to worry. He grins and says he won't.

I have had the most lovely day, I tell Claudio, as we stand – tired but near bursting with content – on the platform of the metro; and it's not over yet.

Me too, confirms Claudio, who has become very quiet, contemplatively studying his feet. Suddenly, hearing the train approach and appearing to have come to some kind of decision, he raises his head, looks me straight in the eye and says he wants to tell me a secret. No one in the family knows, he adds; It's part of the reason I live so far away.

Then he tells me, and I am not at all surprised.

When we get to Silvia and Luis's house, it is full of people. Claudio disappears into the crowd and I search out Maria-Elena, throwing my arms around her and thanking her for bringing him into my life. She is happy for me, but also sad, she admits; it was hard to see her uncle in such a bad way, not knowing what day or year it was, where or who he was, or even recognising his own children: I no want to grow old, she says, and we hug all over again, this time to combat the cold and shivering forecasts of Old Father Time.

I spend most of my time at the party in a daze. Or rather separated in some strange way from my physical body. As I move from room to room, I meet those people I recognise and stop to embrace or shake hands, whatever seems appropriate. Pepe is here, with Olga at his side looking very pretty and dressed up; she has a shining quality of essential goodness about her that I like very much. Of Daniel, however, there is no sign.

My sense of detachment increases as I realise that most people around me are strangers. I see them fall back as I progress, looking towards me, smiles blurred with curiosity. They do not know me of course; they are basing judgment simply on what they see. And what *do* they see? A middle-aged woman in what to their eyes must appear strange clothes – an old but much loved Issey Miyake soft cotton scarf in white, mauve and dark grey stripes draped over a white T-shirt under a black silk jacket with loose matching trousers, ankle socks and flat pumps, silver jewellery including four different earrings – with grey-blonde hair cut shorter than anyone else's in the room (and this includes most of the men!) What can they possibly make of me? I have no idea and retreat deeper to protect myself from signals of vulnerability, sharply bleeping their arrival of the horizon of my equilibrium.

I smile, I talk (I guess), acting my way through the event, the perfect party animal. When Josefina arrives, there are exclamations of delight and disbelief as people drag us together, laughing, marvelling at the likeness they choose to see between us – the shape of our faces, noses, lips. We face each other, taking each other's hands, scrutinising up and down. Yes, we agree, maybe.

Immediately I am reminded of the day in Walthamstow, earlier in the year, when Lee and Buffy's father arrived from the other side of London to say hello. He walked into the front room and reeled at the sight of Lee and Pablo sitting together on the sofa.

My God, Roger said; You look like brothers!

Describe them separately and you would have had two completely different young men – Pablo darker, more stockily built. And yet, with their hair cut short, and identically styled goatees, synchronistically sitting with their hands and legs just so, they looked amazingly alike.

It is the same with Josefina and me; different, and yet somehow the same. Our ancestral heritage showing through; maybe even Harriet herself offering us hints and clues as to how she looked, near two hundred years ago.

The crowd swells and diminishes, as people come and go. There is a point at which I realise that Claudio has disappeared, and feel a genuine pang that he did not come to say *adios*. Of course it is perfectly possible in the midst of the excitement he glanced at his watch, guessed he would miss his bus and fled in panic. But still a voice in my head cites desertion, for whatever reason, and in my imagination I pick petals from a daisy, one by one: maybe he liked me, maybe he did not?

A woman arrives and again there is a flurry of excitement. Older, wearing a black and white crepe dress with a brooch covering the top button, her white hair parted on one side and cut in a simple bob. Silvia, I hear people whisper; Silvia – the beloved aunt that Claudio so admires, and by leaving early (presumably to catch his bus) has missed meeting. She clasps my hand in her own: *Gracias, muchos gracias.*

She is thanking you for coming to find her, find the family, says a voice in English behind me, and I turn to find a tall nice-looking darkly bearded man in his late thirties or early forties standing at my shoulder.

My name is Jose, he adds; I'm so sorry my own mother is not here. As for me, my wife is over there… (and he points to a gently smiling woman in a simple cotton frock with her hair tied back, standing on the far side of the room). I teach at the university here in Santiago. My English is not so good but if I can help, please use me.

Suddenly there are calls for hush (the same in any language, maybe, sounding like the sea: ssh, ssh… and people sit or lean against walls as Ricardo moves to the centre of the living room, with something in his hands. He clears his throat, turns to me, smiles shyly and begins to speak.

He is saying (Jose interprets softly) that everyone welcomes you to Chile. We were all so excited when Maria-Elena told us that a Loader from England was coming to Chile. It brings past and present together. It makes us remember our ancestry and wonder about Liverpool and how we came to be living so far away. It is many years since our family here in Chile has come together in such numbers and in such happiness. From the information you have given us, he has been able to create a family tree. Here is a printout, and here is a floppy so you can read it on your own computer. Please come again anytime. Your family will be waiting. And thank you. Thank you.

Feeling suddenly graceless, with a lump in my throat and close to tears, I open out the spreadsheet and there we all are: with Charles and all his children and their spouses in pink, and the second generation and beyond in green. Silvia Rosa Loader Cruzat, I see, was born in 1929, making her a strong and dignified seventy, though I have to say she looks older. As for Jose (Carlos Ampuero Loader), he is the eighth child – there are three more around, somewhere – of Adela Rebeca, born 1924, following her brother Arturo Eduardo (born 1923, died March, 1992) and preceding Guillermo Mario – William, Luis's father. But the page – all the names, all the dates – is beginning to spin... it's all too much to take in. God, I need a drink. But there is nothing to drink – no alcohol, anyway. I wonder how the Chilean Loaders became tee-totallers? Or is it simply that Luis and Silvia do not encourage alcohol into their home? Unimportant queries tangle with vitally important questions, creating an intellectual backlog, so I ask, say, nothing. Some journalist, huh!

When we gather late in the backyard for the now requisite group photo, the surrounding redbrick wall topped with spikes and with what appear to be factory buildings beyond, we are a happy smiling hardcore band of just thirty. Everyone is dark-haired and, overall, pretty dark-skinned too. Josefina, seated alongside me in another rattan chair, has a beautiful child of about eighteen months on her lap, but I have no idea who his parents are. Everyone has their hand on someone else's shoulder, or around someone else's waist; there is a strong feeling of unification – or should that be re-unification? When the photographer signals Cheese (*queso*), we all break out in one DNA-ruled collective family grin.

Do not ask about the journey home, or my feelings on going to sleep.

Exhausted – physically drained and yet emotionally hot-wired – my brain finally pulls the plug in pity: Over and Out.

## NOVEMBER 15, 1999

I am into the second half my trip here, and Maria-Elena has gone.

She left for the airport (after going with me to the bus station, to help buy my ticket for tomorrow) to catch her flight back to Buenos Aires. Suddenly I am alone, struggling (much to my astonished pride and chagrin) to re-adjust. First I change rooms – no point in staying in the twin, wasting money I haven't got. So now I am on the far side of the building where it is not only much cheaper, but quieter. Being a single, the room has a monastic quality, which I like. Or I think I like; I seem to have forgotten momentarily how to be alone, having been caught up for three days in Maria-Elena's perfumed, hair-grooming, clothes-changing world – the close proximity of another woman's carefully strategised femininity. For a while I sit on my bed, waiting – I acknowledge eventually – for someone to call and maybe suggest meeting. But the phone does not ring. It is Monday morning and family life has resumed normality, going about its business elsewhere. Is it I who have moved on, or they?

Not wanting to be left behind, I go out into the warmth of mid-morning, and find electioneering in progress. I have not bought a newspaper since *El Metropolitano*, purchased on the day of my arrival in Chile, which ran a headline concerning "La Crisis Electrica", with the related editorial on page 10 illustrated with a photo of a dejected family sitting around a table in candlelight. Blackouts are a recurring problem in the capital, it seems. Now I learn that on December 12, Chile is due to elect a new political leader, with two main candidates in the running.

Ricardo Lagos – bookish, well travelled – flies the red flag of the Socialist Party. Yet he is described as amazingly moderate considering the SP once sent guerrilla fighters to join Argentine-born Che Guevara in Bolivia, declared its over-riding philosophy in 1967 as being Marxist-

Leninist, and accepted help from East German intelligence agents to spirit away surviving leaders after the coup of 1973. Now, Lagos says, in the face of alienating the popular vote and business leaders alike, The world has changed and we have all learned. (Shades of Tony Blair's new style of Labour government in the UK, I note.)

Joaquin Lavin, a youthful nerdish Christian Democrat, is the main conservative candidate. A low-level economist in Pinochet's government, he too is attempting to play a moderate game, chasing the all-important 10 per cent vote that could take coalition supporters either way. The Christian Democratic Party and other voters to the Right all fear a victory by Lagos; they see him as a threat to the country's stability. Those of a more Liberal persuasion are infused with memories of leftish-dreams dashed by the Pinochet dictatorship. Even though Lagos is trying to keep his distance from the SDP's former president, blaming the country's hyperinflation, shortages and economic collapse in the early 1970s on his party's radicalism, there are banners everywhere bearing the message, *With Allende Always.*

Right now, it seems, the two leading candidates are running neck-and-neck, hard on the heels of outgoing President Eduardo Frei of the CDP. If Lavin loses to Lagos in the second round on January 16, Chile will have its first Socialist leader since Allende died in the ruins of the presidential palace twenty-six years ago. A fresh start to the new millennium in more ways than one.

Everywhere I walk, though especially conspicuous in precincts and plazas, a political battle is in progress to win hearts and minds. Stalls laden with literature, banners and loudspeakers vie for attention. Party workers load me with leaflets, trying to tuck flags – both red, and pale blue and white in my pockets and hang streamers around my neck. Any attempt to create a carnival atmosphere on the Right is dampened by the Left, with billboards showing photos of those who suffered the military clampdown of near three decades before. Santiago's Catholic Church has compiled files listing 114,000 tortured, 1,700 murdered and

1,200 disappeared. These figures, insist many on the Left, remain grossly down played.

In the central Post Office, there is a poster showing pictures of lost children, serving to mirror the anguish on display in the streets outside. Issued by the National Centre for Missing and Exploited Children, it shows photos of little ones vanished into thin air for one reason or another between 1981 and 1990, but some from as long ago as 1966. All gone, spirited away. Since my own children were born in 1963 and 1965 respectively, I wonder how I would feel to see their images similarly frozen in time. Even the pain of trying to imagine such a situation is almost too hard to bear.

I have found a book in a *libreria* (book store) about a female *bandero* (bandit) once operating in the Andes. A compilation of documents, testaments and photos, with a prologue by Francisco Colane, it holds my attention for a full ten minutes as I try to puzzle out the Spanish. Some hope! A dictionary of Spanish and Mapuche is also eye catching, compiled by Felix Jose Deaugusta, published by Edicionnes Seneca. There are a lot of books about the Mapuche, but mostly wrapped in cellophane, so I can't evaluate what is inside. Great way to sabotage a potential sale, I think, cursing in frustration.

Today is Eric's funeral and I have not been able to send flowers because I have not heard from Alison. I'm deeply upset with her now. There is no excuse. All she had to do was mail the details of how and where the funeral was to take place. Checking my hotmail a second time, still there is nothing – except a message from Noemi (in Europe), saying that Akii (in Asia) is in a panic about my losing my purse (in South America). I can imagine.

Changing another 10,000 yen note, I count just three remaining. At least I have my ticket to Mendoza, over the Chile-Argentine border, the other side of the Cordilleros. My bus leaves at 8.45 a.m. so I must be there early, just in case. One problem: how will I wake up? I have no watch – have not worn one for years – and no Maria-Elena!

Still trying to get my bearings, I find myself in another church, synchronising with yet another communion service, this time being conducted to the sound of a single, high, pure voice chanting in Latin. Imagining Eric being cremated roundabout now, I allow the hypnotic flow of notes and phrases dissolve my stress and sadness, remembering my uncle's kind and gentle nature, giving thanks for the loving support he provided throughout my life, and wishing him well. I want to call my mother and Jo, both of whom I know will be feeling totally bereft, but where to find an international phone? What are the codes? And do I have the right change? Not for the first time, I feel useless, a complete and utter failure.

This little corner of the city – a few streets in either direction from the hotel – has become my home, my safety zone. Time now to strike out, venture across the beautiful Avenida Alameda de las Delicias that runs two miles through the heart of the city, and explore the hillside park of San Cristobal, on the far side of the river. A steep funicular railway carries me straight up the side of the hill, allowing time to compare it with the near vertical track up to the Peak in Hong Kong, and similar engineering feats in Japan. From the top, I see the city spread-eagled far below on a flat plain – a marvellous view. To the left, the Andes, which are hazy but still the snow shines through; in every other direction the cityscape dissolves into a more subdued yellowish mist of pollution. Three of the Andean peaks rise above 22,000 feet, with Mt Aconcagua (to the southeast) the highest mountain in the western hemisphere. At 6,292 metres, it dwarfs Japan's highest mountain, Fuji-san, which can see seen from Tokyo some 100 kilometres distant just as Aconcagua can be seen not only from Santiago, but from as far away as the coast.[41] From this side of the Andes, the name Aconcagua derives from the Mapuche (Araucanian) expression Aconca-hue, meaning River From the Other Side; in the Cuyo region of Argentina, where I will be heading tomorrow, it translates as Stone Sentinel from Ackon Cahuah, in the local Quechua language.

San Cristobal is a pretty nice place, except for the piped music. There appears to be a twenty-four-hour pray-in in progress, with robed priests taking it in turns to conduct musical prayers from the stage of an open-air Greek-style auditorium to a congregation of a few dozen stalwarts. Above there is another altar, with a large statue dedicated to Maria de los Andes. It seems appropriate to thank her for my time here, and ask for safe passage tomorrow, after which I sit on some steps and take my time.

I make a note of my belongings – camera, bag, sunglasses, and jacket. Moving off finally I walk right around the peak and begin to descend to the next level before noticing that I am without my Nikon. In a complete flap, hyper-ventilating in disbelief, I half-run, half-walk back to where I was seated, and there it is still, waiting, grumbling, as pissed off with me as I am with myself. How lucky I am; another few seconds and it might well have left on a permanent walkabout. How could I have been so careless, I angst. Am I unravelling, losing my marbles? With no one to depend on now, and apparently displaying all the early classic symptoms of senile dementia, I feel suddenly even more unsettled, a discomfort bordering on fear.

To calm down, I concentrate on the vegetation and in particular a tree burgeoning with what look like avocadoes, but they are smooth and shiny, hung on long thin stalks. To the right is a conifer, with branches that stick straight out ending in clusters of pale green tentacles. To the left is a specimen with the copper-coloured leaves of an English beech, but with seeded fruit the size of apples but maroon-coloured and glossy. I stand and stare and then gaze even harder, as if time and concentration will supply answers, because not for the first time in my life, I am completely stumped: not only have I no idea what is going on my head and my psyche, but I have absolutely no idea what I am looking at.

Thanks then to the gods for the familiarity of sunset, which is magnificent.

Back across the river at twilight, and down towards the Teatro Municipal, a sudden gust of evening breeze carries the sound of orchestral music in climax, followed by rising and falling waves of clapping and cheering. I arrive in front of the theatre across the road from which is a small open plaza, just as some kind of performance is coming to an end – musicians putting away instruments, volunteers folding chairs, while to one side, a young male dancer lifts a ballerina gracefully into the air with skilful ease and, as colleagues cheer them on, she stretches her body into the sky like a bird taking flight.

Grabbing the arm of a passing woman in the desperation that can only arise from acute curiosity (nothing ventured, nothing gained), I ask, What's going on? Why are you on strike?

Well, she replies, surprised but in perfectly understandable English, We have two young *amigos* here from the United States. Stay (here), I will find (them).

So I stay, and soon enough, they emerge from the crowd – early thirties maybe – in jeans, with jackets and knit hats pulled low, instrument cases under their arms.

Kevin, the smaller, skinnier and more vocal of the pair, is from Massachusetts. His friend Jeff, quieter, more careful, from New York originally...

We've been on strike for forty-eight days, explains Kevin; Yeah, a long time! Why? Well, a lot of stupid reasons. On Saturday a temporary agreement was made between lawyers and intermediaries. It was a pre-agreement, signed by the Labour Minister. Yesterday, while contracts were being drawn up, Management reneged, saying "No, we don't agree after all".

But why did you come out on strike in the first place, I ask.

Kevin again: Because we were suddenly offered a collective contract that gave us half of what we were getting before.

Yes, Jeff elaborates; Various things that had been in our contracts were completely omitted. Also looser matters that had never been written down – concerning benefits, practice and so on – were suddenly in tightly scripted black and white.

The pair inform me that I have just missed the entire company of some three hundred and twenty members performing for free: the full orchestra, complete corps de ballet, solo singers and chorus, plus all the technical and administrative staff.

Bugger, I say with feeling.

Yeah, continues Kevin through his teeth, bitterly angry; Management want us to work December 24 and also until midnight on Christmas Day, after which the plan is to fly us by cargo plane to perform at some army base. They want to take the money the government is paying us as strikers to pay scabs willing to go inside the building. And there's another thing....

Jeff suddenly flashes with anger: They just want to do us harm...

They just want to do you harm, I repeat softly, in solidarity.

Jeff plays the tuba. Kevin the trombone, But I cut my lip, he grimaces. They have been giving free concerts every day, to thank the public for its support and so as not to waste their talent and keep in trim. In fact, Kevin adds, we've played more concerts in the last month than the theatre had organised in five years; And I'm not joking!

When I ask what they are living on, they look at one another, grin wryly and state in unison, Air!

And how will they survive through Christmas and New Year? The answer is the same: On air.

The air must have been good up on San Cristobal. Or maybe I am just incredibly tired. Despite feeling terrified that I will not wake up in time, for the second night running I crash as soon as my head hits the pillow. The last image I recall from my day? Snow-capped ranges, cast in a rosy light, spinning into rainbows.

## NOVEMBER 16, 1999

I dream that I miss the bus, and wake at 6 a.m. in a complete sweat. Too late to return to sleep in safety, I switch on the side light and catch up with Sam in Buenos Aires in January 1945. He has not heard from anyone back home for six months, *with all news of old England gone off the air... I would like to start a string of correspondence, gaining in each letter more confidence, and warmth, so that we could exchange ideas of all that is going on, and what is to be in the future. For instance, I am building a good business here, and in due time, when I drop off this mortal coil, someone unknown will take up the continuance of the same.*

The truth is that business is slow, but he refuses to be down-hearted, listing orders he has received. *From this you see I am going to be very busy when trade becomes more fluid.* In the meantime he is off to Piriapolis for three weeks, *the longest holiday taken for years and years, with good bathing and plenty of country to roam about in.*

He lets drop that he had heard from Barney's wife, *but not a line yet from Gwen. All the other members of the family are still smouldering, and when the fire will assuage I do not know. In fact I have given up all hope of getting closer to them again. I have done my part and can do no more.*

He writes on September 1 that since in a day or so the surrender with Japan will be signed he is thinking ahead, of the world returning to normality, returning to work, *with each country doing its utmost to recover its stability and economy. Outside Europe there is more transport than ever, and the great flotillas of merchant ships will be released and will soon stock up the great markets of the world with whatever is required. Argentina is no exception to this state of affairs, although it has built up quite a large industry. In fancy goods* (for example) *important progress has been made, and the fashions are in the front of any country.* (Not surprising since Europe has been out of the couture picture for some time.)

He trusts that my father is still with Armstrong Siddeley – a company formed in 1919 and best known for producing luxury motor cars and aircraft engines – and has not joined the Navy. In the meantime, he hears from old friends and business colleagues on occasion, including one Tom Pears, with whom he hopes to stay when he comes to England next year. His plan is to take a ship in late April, *most probably accompanying a client who will also be visiting Italy, as he is of Italian descent and has relations there. He does not speak English so I will act as interpreter.*

By the first week of December, he is even more optimistic. He is expecting to be very busy, *as I am now controlling the buying of the largest importer of Cycles and Accessories in the country, with a business that grows day by day, and adding Sports Goods to their line. I believe in 1947 I shall sell them 15–20,000 cycles and large quantity of Chains, Freewheels, ball Bearings, etc. I have orders now for about 20,000 pounds, or more.*

He uses the company A.R.Brown, Macfarlane & Co. Ltd of Glasgow as his intermediary, and just that morning, a business colleague, Senor Gori, had remarked *that it would be a fine thing if one of my sons could look after this part of the business in Birmingham and District, the centre of the trade. All is bought on a Letter of Credit opened in London, and the job would be to place the orders, find sources of supply, new goods, and a constant contact with me here. This job would bring in 500 pounds in an ordinary uncomplicated year and probably a lot more.*

Once again he is planting a seed in my father's mind. For the first time, I wonder how my life might have turned out – or redirected itself – if he had jumped at the chance, or indeed, taken more carefully considered time to make a career change.

Time for me, however, to jump out of bed and get going. I have a bus to catch, and then another journey of a lifetime to make, across the Andes.

# CHAPTER 16

# ACROSS THE ANDES

**NOVEMBER 16, 1999 CONTINUED**

If yesterday my heart was palpitating, right now it's racing – beating fit to bust. Any moment now I expect my chest to explode and turn the interior of this coach into a location worthy of Tarantino's *Pulp Fiction*.

Everything had been going so well too – a sedate classic breakfast at the hotel, where I received the full attention of the under-worked waiter; smiles in the lobby that accompanied me all the way to the door; and a taxi that just happened to be passing and knew exactly where I wanted to go, *no problemo*. The difficulty – and a near insurmountable problem it turned out to be – was that I could not find the bus, or the place from where it was supposed to leave. On one side of the bus station, I was pointed to the other; there the same thing happened. I tried again, to no effect. I tried each and every bus stand asking, Mendoza? Sometimes people would shake their heads, others would point elsewhere and off I'd trudge, my bag increasingly burdensome.

As the minutes ticked by, I began to worry. Then worry turned to panic, and I was literally running around the station concourse, shrieking *Mendoza, Mendoza, donde esta la autobus por Mendoza?* (About the longest sentence I had managed to dredge up in two weeks.) Then with five minutes to go, an official – bemused rather than irritated – appeared from nowhere, grabbed me by the arm and frog-marched my bulk across the plaza to a different location altogether, an area I had assumed to be a car park. As the second to last person was climbing aboard, and with the second to last bag winging its way into the cargo hold, he laid his hands on my shoulders, faced me towards the door and gave me a shove with the encouraging words, Mendoza, okay?

So finally here I am, and I know I'm in the right place, because a very sweet young man, dressed like an airline steward, checks my ticket and shows me to my seat. The relief is not just tremendous, it is for several minutes at least, overwhelming.

At some point – most likely after being served a cup of hot sweet coffee that lifts my spirits again – I begin recording the journey... and do not stop (except for the most obvious of breaks) until we reach our final destination:

(switching on)

– walking along the side of the road, indigenous women wearing brightly coloured skirts in decorative floral fabric, pleated so there's lots of fullness, swinging as they move, with long glossy black hair in two braids or a single plait down the back, carrying posies of multi-coloured flowers or baskets of small goods. Really rather splendid... it's not just dignity, there's a bravado in the way they hold themselves; Shoulder Before Wind, as Maria-Elena would say...

– lines of workers in fields, bent double, collecting potatoes, loading horses, a near-medieval landscape... just passed through a toll that cost 3,500 pesos and three *carabineri* (local police) got off the bus, without paying...

– orchards, low hills to either side, covered in grass, scrubby trees, bushes... grape country: contrary to the French style, branches of vines are trained horizontally overhead as in Japan so that the bunches of fruit hang down for easy plucking... smoke rising from a field... a poster – bizarre – promoting surfing in Maui, Hawaii...

– beginning to climb... a sign for Los Dios 123 kilometres... painted on a wall, *Con Lavant Vivo la Canbera*... we're behind a Pullman bus... another sign, and suddenly the turning for Los Andes, where the train line from Buenos Aires used to end, and Ricardo now lives... *Ricardo, donde esta?* As if in answer we turn, going in search...

– the landscape is brown (barring trees and flowers growing wild along the edge of the road) stretching into blue between two hills, through which the crags and snowy peaks of the *cordilleros*... cows and horses grazing – eating what? innumerable and quite indeterminate large clumps of fur on the road, quite impossible to imagine what animals they might have been...

– have just been handed some kind of bun, plus another cup of coffee; feel rather elegant to be addressed as *Signora*... field of cactus with bright yellow flowers... signpost pointing into hinterland: *San Francisco*... a statue that resembles a tall geometric skinny Statue of Liberty, holding aloft a shining sword in place of a torch. Who? What? Why... – up we go, exiting tunnel No. 1 into La Provincia de los Andes, with Chilean pop music playing in the driver's cabin, the radio just loud enough to be pleasant and fun rather than annoying...

– rounding a corner, above poplar trees, a black barrier of rock punctuated by snow blown into nooks and crevices rears into blue, both part of the earth and part of the sky yet wholly its own; read somewhere that the Himalayas are endowed with a male energy, the Andes, female. Does this somehow mean I am coming home, or that I'm about to bring some part of myself into balance? Either way, it's thrilling...

– a fertile landscape once again – this keeps happening, one stretch passing through wilderness, the next back in so-called civilisation;

luxuriant sweeps of willow hanging into the road, well-manicured gardens and homes. Are we going through the town of Los Andes, or have we by-passed? the driver has a crucifix twisted around his windscreen wiper, the cross hangs down, swaying to and fro... made of glass it's really rather pretty...

– Calle Largo – a rather pretty place! Laval is here with flags and posters, his money (electioneering funds) stretching pretty far... yellow taxis, a long red wall topped with tiles that reminds me of Japan, but for the life of me can't think why...

– 6 km to Los Andes; we *are* going there!

– a woman just got on the bus, is declaring, very politely, her right to sit beside me with the ticket she has purchased. My grumpiness at having to share space made my own transforms into a sneeze, to which she responds with a generous *Salut*! accompanied by a smile of such sweetness that all resentment dissipates... the local newspaper here, *Le Mercurio*...

– magical flowers growing along the verges, giant harebells... cyclists cling to the shade... branch of an overhanging tree just smacked the front window, causing the driver automatically to duck... and here we are in Los Andes, with banks of yellow broom, as in Scotland; little town, low whitewashed stone-built houses, very quiet... *Ricardo? Donde esta*... or ought that to be *estan*? I forget...

– after a brief stop, we're all handed an orange ice lollipop... pass an army base... Mendoza: 266 kilometres, not as far as I thought, and yet... a railway line, where did it come from, where is it going? Another wide fertile valley with yet another river of down-pouring snow melt; signs for Champagne, and vineyards to every side: Valle Verde... the back and front windows of the bus are decorated with frosted stencilled bells and candles, reminding that the countdown to Christmas is in full swing... decorating the verges, little whitewashed shrines to the Virgin Mary...

– tethered horses with gleaming coats... stone walls and lines of cactus marching up mountainsides... a muddy swirling river, replicating that forcing its way through the centre of Santiago, and reminding this time that Maria-Elena will be home by now, and all my Chilean relatives enjoying *siesta*... there are graves along the side of the road, victims of accidents...

– must have day-dreamed in a semi-doze (in sympathy with *siesta* time), returning to the present amid fantastical rocky landscape... the train track now the far side of the river, disappearing into a tunnel... a waterfall gushes from a cleft in the mountainside and despite the distance is breathtaking... have never been in any terrain so wild and inhospitable; it makes the Scottish Highlands tame beyond all imaginings...

– rounding a corner, going down, and it's green again; the contrasts are extraordinary, bizarre...

– another barren stretch, relieved only by a shining metallic pipeline

– carrying what? water, oil? – snaking down one mountain side and up another; guess it goes under the road... Portillo, 27 kilometres (like suddenly I'm in Italy?) have lost the train track; where did the line go...

– another stop: Campeneros de Chile Biaja Guardia; more papers checked... now entering Las Desea la Region...

– waterfalls both sides, the last of the winter snow... this part of the

road is roofed, with rock face on one side – an open view the other and
a river far below – to protect against falling rocks... painted in large
letters on a massive boulder: *Las Strada Frontiera*...

– more mountains ahead; no trees, no cactus, simply powdered *macha*
tea green as if with a large feather duster... vast stretches of scree...
pools of mud, iced water, all on a previously unimaginable scale... wish
I could read the landscape in the same way that NASA trains astronauts
to read the surface of the moon; the colours of rocks and strata must
give so much away, but being geologically illiterate, I'm unable to read
the signs...

– level with the snowline, with water literally spouting out from
under the edges of the fast-melting snowfield... and so into a series
of incredible horseshoe bends that navigate an otherwise impossible
gradient with my ears popping like crazy; everywhere I look, only black
and white, no shades of grey: up or down, forwards or backwards,
succeed or fail, live or die; no place for half-measures this...

– we would not be allowed to die, of course – huge container trucks,
gears grinding, crawl with a snail-like slowness in both directions,
carrying meat and grain to Chile, wine and whatever to Argentina – but
unfortunate travellers would be solely dependent on the kindness of
strangers; despite alleged feminine energies, this part of the world is
harsh and unyielding, severe to an extreme...

– we have stopped... Chilean passport control... outside the wind is
freezing, but also fresh and bracing and indeed (for this female at least)
energising... we are in a weird high place – the Paso los Libertadores,
3,200 metres or 16,800 feet above sea level – surrounded by rocky
peaks, intense quiet broken only by the sounds of vehicles starting up
or slowing down, the eerie wailing of airstreams in turmoil...

– inside a hangar-like building, we line up for scrutiny... a guy I know
to be British, with a terrible cold sore on his lip and looking in dire
need of motherly love (or any kind of love for that matter) refuses
to meet my eyes and sticks with a trio of male Spanish-speaking
acquaintances met on the bus; well, that's fine, his prerogative... my
papers stamped, I'm free to go... imagine working here; what a hard,
disconnected life...

– the conductor returns, screaming at us against the wind to get back
on board... having just decided to stick to the *banos* on the bus for
my ablutions, I choose instead to brave the public facility and swiftly
scrunch my way across the roof of the Andes for a pee... re-emerging,
a conveyer behind a cab roars past bearing six bright red brand-new
Chevrolet trucks on their way to the wild west... now a second one...

– wheels officially leaving Chile behind, I fall again into a reverie,
surfacing only as we exit Tunnel del Christa Retindor, into La Provincia
de Mendoza, Republica de Argentina... but with Mendoza itself still 191
kilometres to go...

– this is undoubtedly the closest I will ever get to a lunar landscape... or
maybe I'm on Mars? The surface, red, bright red, now pink, then orange
through to red again...

– still high at 3,151 metres but starting to descend... that tiny place,
La Cuevos, was almost a village, with what appeared to be brand-new
buildings all falling down; did idealistic inhabitants swiftly give up?

– La Rio de la Cuevos running ancient and bloody through a landslide
of mud and shale; above, rocks and shingle are coloured in bands of
grey, green, yellow and rust, red, grey, white, beige and black... on
the other side of the road, roofed structures march in lines across the

mountainside, built maybe to halt landslides or possibly at one time for human occupation; all I know for sure is that everything man-made – excepting the road, and hopefully me – is falling to pieces...

– such a beautiful stretch this: though not a tree or blade of grass in sight, an impression of great softness and delicacy; for mile after mile, swathes of shale drifting down on either side, like pale grey veils...

– the official Argentine entry point (I'd assumed the first was for leaving Chile and entering Argentina, but it seems we've been in no-man's land for quite some time)... our luggage gets scrutinised here more than we do... this border post serviced by Puenta del Inca, but when native riders gallop past with no saddles I feel I might as well be in Mongolia...

– a cemetery, so people do live and die here... this part of the journey reminds of Asia; could the movie *Seven Days in Tibet* have been shot here? Maybe: China refused permits for filming in occupied lands... a settlement named Puquois; sounds native American Indian... and there, between two peaks, an incredible sight: army-like columns of granite in fierce formation, on the march...

– Los Pentitentos: a much larger settlement with – believe it or not! – a hotel and a restaurant; I wonder if there is skiing, being closer to the city, and yes, suddenly there is a ski-lift, and a flurry of pensions with red roofs, green roofs... a rail track again (maybe the same, maybe not), even a station, but derelict... trees, a gendarmerie, three policemen disembark (they came aboard at the Argentine border post), another gets on...

– an even more dramatic stretch, if this is possible: one side of the valley is yellow, the other red, while up above, grey... the hillside ahead resembles a zebra's hide, with horizontal stripes of blackish-brown and creamy-white... just so beautiful, so spirited... sweeping down now into Pulvarados, still 2,400 metres above sea level...

– a couple crawl by in high gear on a tandem bike, flying the flags of many nations (now there's a story)... huge sheets of white paper flying all around, like gigantic snowflakes; fallen off the back of a lorry?

– wake from yet another light doze (in which I semi-hallucinated about being lost in a snowstorm but feeling perfectly secure and at home) to find it raining... very surreal but it appears we all fell asleep en masse; there's magic for sure – some strange witchery aboard! Just 53 kilometres to Mendoza, yet a mile or so on another sign claims 64! Seems time and space play tricks here too...

– we're dropping down noticeably now; it's flatter without being at all flattering... passing through debris left from some gigantic construction project and now sand dunes, really weird... good God! I think I just saw my first gaucho (but in this rain, in this strange place?)

– a child is fretful, bored and tired... the mountains are to our left now, falling behind... scrubland... telephone poles march into the distance (hundreds of miles across the continent towards the east coast)... a petrochemical complex... horses grazing by the road move back warily, one trying to bite a chunk out of his companion's backside... the first sign of organised farming since Chile with an orchard, then the first of Mendoza's famed vineyards...

– dropping down onto a motorway, with shanty towns all around... Rio Mendoza, but with so little water it causes alarm...

– a sign for *Godoy Cruiz* makes me wonder whether a woman named

Godoy is still living in Kita-Kamakura, Japan; haven't thought about her for years…

– so far Mendoza is a dump, a travesty of so-called human development compared to the astonishing unblemished beauty and power of the region just travelled. But give the town time, Angela, give it time…

Later that evening, I learn from my precious file of letters (copies, not the originals; they are back in Japan) that throughout 1946, my grandfather was giving his family all the time in the world to get in touch. He wrote to my father only once, on April 12, acknowledging that at the advanced age of thirty-five, his eldest son had been drafted into the navy, and was based down south in Devonport. Sam has strong feelings on the subject too: *I think it wrong to take married men away, especially after being given special permission to remain on specified work.* (Quite what this assignment entailed I have no idea. As far as I know, my father worked as a buyer for Armstrong Siddeley until his death. All I know about his exploits at sea is that he was a purser and saw no action, other than one mine being blown up.

At age sixty-five, Sam is busy as well as opinionated, consolidating for the future and *sees no possibility of starving in the near future.* I smile ruefully to read that he has links to a firm in Glasgow that before the war made dry docks for the Japanese government. I smile more broadly that my grandfather *is not getting any thinner over the lack of contact from other members of his family.* All those cakes, perhaps… Promising to send word by airmail before he leaves, he is planning now to travel to Britain in late May or early June, and sends love to all as usual, *including the kiddies.* (That's Bridget and me!)

For now, however, I'm sitting on the main street of Mendoza, enjoying pizza, having booked into the Hotel Du Sol. It's a very pretty place and my room – just behind me, up above my head – is large and comfortable, with big shutters that open up onto a view of pavement cafes, but not at all noisy. I'm paying 40 pesos a night, which may be stretching my remaining money to the limit. When I go out into the street, however, I find lots of people far worse off, which places my situation in far better proportion. Also all attempts to find an internet cafe in the immediate vicinity fail. Tomorrow I really must take a good long hard look at my financial situation, find a tourist information office, make some decisions.

While eating, I'm accosted by a dramatically dressed and made-up woman of indeterminate age who begins telling me a fascinating story in a mix of English and Spanish about meeting extra-terrestrials and visiting other worlds. It takes a full ten minutes for me to realise she is raving mad. Either that, or she is the sanest woman on this particular planet.

## NOVEMBER 17, 1999

I was out like a light by nine last night and have woken at eleven, once again the day near half gone. Why am I so tired? I look horrendous, like a shattered ghost. Had the eight-hour trip from Santiago really been so exhausting?

Clever of me though to have found my way at dusk last night to the centre of town, if this is what it is, and if not, who cares. Walking from the bus station, I'd found the streets green and pleasant, buildings rarely above two or three stories, and people friendly in a reserved laid-back kind of way. I could gather myself back to myself in Mendoza, I'd decided.

Yes, I need time, space, quiet, because despite being welcomed in Chile with warmth and so well looked after, I feel as if I have been dragged through some hugely emotional trauma: the family, the politics, the loss of cash and credit card, the shadow that I fear Charles has somehow cast on my progress, my confusion to find so little of Sam in Argentina and yet (at the last count) one hundred and forty-four unexpected relatives turning up just over the hill, so to speak. Which reminds me: Mt Aconcagua stands invisibly tall somewhere eastwards between here and San Juan, which is where Maria-Elena's mate Tarzan hails from. Many people assume Aconcagua to be in Chile. In fact it stands proud – about the only thing that does! – in Argentina. Funnily enough, I feel closer to the peak here than I did in Santiago, from where it was clearly visible.

Mendoza, I now understand, having read up on it last night after bringing myself up-to-date with Sam (whom I am trying to drag back into view now that I am back on Argentine soil) is a miracle of survival. This side of the Andes, the Cuyo region, is as naturally dry and arid as Santiago was lush and fertile, but since Mendoza was founded in 1561, huge efforts have been made to create an oasis by means of a constantly expanding and improved irrigation system. After a massive earthquake in 1881 – the whole region is prone to rockin' and a' rollin' – *Mendocinos* (as locals describe themselves) rebuilt for safety. This explains why it's low-rise, with relatively narrow streets for quick escapes, sycamore trees planted to protect passers-by from falling rubble, and a park located every fourth block with yet more greenery. (According to Fodor, deep-rooted trees don't begin toppling until about 7.8 on the Richter scale. Japan, take note! )

Also Argentina is one of the world's largest producers of wine, and much of it comes from around Mendoza, thanks again to the miraculous greening of the desert. The high spot of the year is the wine harvest festival Vendimia, held on the first Saturday in March.

I like my street, with the familiar sound of carpets being vacuumed; being both downtown and uptown, it's interesting. Breakfast is still just about available, and just about affordable: special service Promo 9, which consists of *una* (one) *cafe du leche* and *dos* (two) *medios lunos tortias*.

Just around the corner, on yet another street named San Martin, I wander into the Mercado Artesanal Mendocino, which promotes local crafts. A charming woman named Emiliano introduces herself, explains that she works here, and offers to show me around. Textiles are a passion, I inform her in return, delighted to have stumbled onto such treasures. There is a lot of leather, which personally does not attract. But the basketry is very fine, pretty and immaculately woven, and in normal circumstances I would have bought at least one example. Still the textiles are irresistible. Unable to risk more than a few pesos, I buy two small simple geometrically patterned pieces, one in red and cream wool, the other green and orange, woven in Lavelle Province by Susana Barroso and Maria del Carmen Barroso. (Sisters? Mother and daughter? Cousins?) I have this information because of the Certificado de Autenticidad attached to each mat. It's depressing not to be able to buy more, for the makers' sakes as much as my own. Weaving is not to everyone's taste, and I strongly believe in keeping traditional techniques and designs alive and kicking.

I'm looking at some of the natural dyestuffs that the indigenous population has used over the centuries. A tiny bright yellow spiraling seed pod is extraordinary. Hold it to your ear and shake, invites Emiliano, who laughs at my obvious surprise and pleasure. When I move to hand it back, she shakes her head saying, Keep it, keep it! By the look of the textiles, most are coloured with minerals or bark and seeds. Noting the lack of blue, I ask about indigo, which is the classic dyestuff of Japan and Asia at large. I recall reading in a book in Santiago (luckily one not wrapped in cellophane), that Mapuche did not use blue because they feared they might be stealing from the sky. Emiliano had not heard this, and like me, considers it a moving notion. The artisans that supply this outlet are Huapes, native people from roundabout who now extend their movements to the south and into Chile and north to San Juan and San Luis on the other side. There is nothing celestial in their work either: Huapes are just as earthbound.

Across the road, I wander into what appears to be some kind of tourist secretariat, but no one speaks English. On the steps outside, however, I bump into someone who does: Lydia. Born in Mendoza, but visiting, she knows her way around well enough to lead me around the corner to the right address, where I pick up maps and names of coach companies for the return trip to Buenos Aires. Lydia, who is well turned out in a casually interesting way, not only has a son working in Ottawa, Canada, but she has been to Japan once, conducting research into gifted children. Scribbling down her address, she declares it a shame that I have to leave so soon: I'm off to a hotspring in the mountains, and you could have come with me.

Yes, a great pity, I agree, meaning every word but quite unable to admit there is another reason why I cannot change my plans: I have next to no money.

I'm taking the bus tomorrow night, I reply apologetically, And as you know, we do have loads of hotsprings in Japan.

Not like the spas here, she counters; They offer the most amazing massages!

True, I think. About the best massage you get in Japan is when someone offers to scrub your back in the local bathhouse, or you get a neck and scalp rub after a wash and dry in a hair salon. Thailand is *the* place, or so I've heard.

I walk the five blocks back to the bus station, across another of those mad dashing muddy rivers being carefully channelled by concrete, and buy my ticket for tomorrow night. I'll get into Retiro at 9 a.m. Thursday morning, having crossed the *pampa* from one side to the other. Another exciting thought. This is only slightly dashed by finding the Savigliano International Hostel opposite the station; I could stayed here for half the price – and invested the rest in a rug!

Plaza Carlos Pellegrini is typically spotlessly clean, with a bandstand surrounded by palm trees in the centre of a small park, and indeed – as counted out – located just four blocks from the last. But this is especially pretty, with green-painted ironwork wreathed with flowering vines and the scent of jasmine near over-powering. The downside, and inevitably there is one (or is this just the way I perceive the world?), is that every seat is occupied with native youths at *siesta*, limbs hopelessly sprawled or bodies tight-curled like babes returned to the womb.

Passing the offices of Los Andes Dario on St Martin, dated 1882 and with a polished brass plate alongside the door that states so, I turn right and off to the left find a marvellous arching arcade, with a wealth of antique stained glass. At the end, around the corner, an internet cafe, and at one of the computers, the guy with the cold sore from the bus.

261

We exchange surprised glances, then grins of recognition; he had seen me, he did remember me. He is Welsh, has been traveling for months, and says that while the centre of Mendoza is Okay, the outskirts are a disgrace: I just went on a tour of a vineyard, he explains, And you should see how the workers are forced to live; disgusting.

I e-mail neighbours of my mother and aunt, to relay my whereabouts. Anne and Gordon live up the hill behind Forneth village, at Roughstones, a former farm on my uncle's estate. Anne is especially close to my sister, and very supportive. I then answer a message from an old friend in north London, which Akii must have passed on from Hayama. I haven't heard from her for months, and it is uncanny that she finds me here, because Anna is a crafts specialist, and how she would love to share what I am seeing. I spend nearly an hour at the screen, trying for much of the time to understand why one message keeps bouncing back, and then hand over five precious pesos for my trouble.

The place of legislature in Plaza Independencia looks near edible, built in creamy marble with white and cream and pale blue accoutrements and a brass trim. Also it is thrilling to find trees being allowed to grow as nature decrees, cascading over thoroughfares, paved open spaces and fountains alike. So different to Japan, where everything is cut back hard in the ongoing battle for control. On one side of the square stands the Legislatura Mendoza, on the other, Camara de Deputados. While on the corner of 25 de Mayo (a familiar address if ever there was one), Park Hyatt Mendoza is under construction as Hotel y Casino. With a mock Colonial frontage, it's going to be quite something, especially since an architect's drawing shows it rising seven floors. This will surely make it the highest building in the city, with presumably new technology inbuilt to keep it swaying upright in a quake, rather than falling like a house of cards. Park Hyatt is not a company to cut corners in my limited experience. The architectural practice? Mario Roberto Alvarez y Associados ...as marvellous a mouthful as a Spanish omelette.

I enjoy this gentle meandering, noting that while pavements are less than perfect, they are in infinitely better nick than those of Buenos Aires. As in the capital, streets are marked on every corner, with direction of traffic indicated together with the numbers of buildings in the block. For example, standing where I am now, I have this information: traffic is moving from left to right, Peru 7 Est, 1000-1200. It makes finding addresses really simple. Take note Tokyo (where not even taxi drivers can find their way around)!

Enjoying a welcome coffee on another corner, a woman passes carrying a large cardboard box containing an artificial Christmas tree. Fleetingly I feel disorientated, to be here, in this climate, with Christmas just five and a half weeks away, the end of the century six weeks distant, and a new millennium on the virtual doorstep. Time I know is immeasurable and such artificial counters yet further attempts to control the uncontrollable; but ritual markers can also be comforting, can calm the emotions, nurture the spirit, help us mark our progress along the timeline of our lives.

Sam was much preoccupied with marking his own days of import on Planet Earth. His first letter of 1947 made no comment at all on the war having ended, or that amid a devastated landscape and ruined economy Britain had just experienced the worst winter for decades. Rather he admonished my father for having sent the letter to the wrong address, so that birthday wishes arrived late, and then set out in detail how he had marked yet another lonely self-absorbed ritual of passage: *I did not hurry in getting up, and had my coffee about nine, afterwards taking a quiet stroll along the sea front which is a promenade after the style of New Brighton.*

*I took the car up to Florida, walked its length to the Avenida de Mayo, where at about 11.45 I had a glass of Quilmes beer, with its always accompanying Pea Nuts and Wafer potatoes, enjoying a few minutes of resting before lunch. I say lunch, but when lying on my bed fell asleep, and woke at 2.30, so lost (missed) my lunch, which really I did not feel like taking after the nuts, etc. I lounged in my room, and listened to some local radio music in English, and then at 4.30 p.m. wended my way to a Tea Room, The Copper Kettle (underlined), another quiet spot in a busy street, and in a very subdued light took tea, sandwiches, cakes, toast and preserve* *to the accompaniment of a piano soloist who plays very well indeed. At about 5.30 I entered the <u>Monumental</u> (underlined) Cine, and saw the film <u>Lady Hamilton</u> (underlined), with Vivian Leigh in the title part, which I very much enjoyed, as I had seen Vivian Leigh in the flesh is the play <u>By The Skin Of Our Teeth</u> (underlined). We were out by about 8 p.m. and I strutted to the Hotel, and had a light meal to the accompaniment of a bottle of Cider, which was my champagne of the day. After I sat on my balcony, watched the people, and jumped into bed shortly after 10 p.m. And that was how I spent my birthday.*

I am not in a hurry in my wanderings around Mendoza, and my own birthday was back in May. Turning fifty-eight seemed an important factor in making this trip – a case of now or never, while still fit and mobile – but also linked strongly to the symbolism of the millennium – however unnaturally devised – as the end of an era and the commencement of another.

Even as this thought shapes up mentally, I am raising my camera to capture the image of two pigeons, one black, the other white, sitting on the heads of two statues in another of the many lovely leafy spaces that scatter the centre of town. Yes, these two brave men of two brave nations – O'Higgins and San Martin – stand side-by-side just as Argentina sides with Chile (unless they are at war, that is, which they only just managed to avoid last in 1978 after the Church's intervention in a dispute over three islands just south of the Beagle Channel).[42] A hefty sword plunged in between the two figures into the plinth, symbolises what, I wonder: shared interests, combined strength, the Cordilleras?

Best not think so much. By the time I press the button, one of the birds has flown. It's heading east, I note, by my handy compass – the one thing that travels with me in my pocket. Lee gave it to me when I left England for Japan: So you don't get lost Mum.

It has helped me find my way ever since. It helps keep me heading in the right direction. It helps keep me on the road.

CHAPTER 17

# ON THE ROAD

**NOVEMBER 17, 1999 CONTINUED**

It's nearly impossible to get anyone's attention this evening. I'm in the plaza just around the corner from the hotel, sitting in front of one of the restaurants, and all the waiters are inside, glued to the box. It's football, of course: Argentina playing Spain.

When a young guy does scuttle out to take my order, champing at the bit to be back inside, all the things on the menu that I can eat are off. So I'm stuck with salad and fries. Never mind; the bottle of wine – making up for the lack of alcohol in Santiago, I rationalise – compensates: a delicious 1994 Vinca Famosa by Bogedas Lopez, a local winery founded in 1898.

The soccer score is still 0–0. Just an amateur match, the waiter says, meaning maybe a friendly game. As he far less reluctantly hops, skips and jumps back inside, I feel something, someone, at my shoulder: a boy sidling past, carrying a walkie-talkie, looking as if he might be sussing out opportunities to better himself. So far Mendoza has been a good experience, and I don't want to kick that feeling in the head. So I come down on the side of optimism – the boy's a nice kid who just happened to brush up against me. At the same time, I find myself winding the handle of my bag tightly around the arm of the chair. I hate to do this, but...

Hey, I've discovered a great way to eat shredded red cabbage. You twirl it on your fork, like pasta. (This salad by the way is a South American tour de force, with shredded lettuce and carrot accompanying the cabbage, together with cucumber, tomatoes, tinned palm-hearts and hard-boiled eggs, the yolks pinpointed with peas.)

This is the life, I reckon. Sam Sam Sam the Mystery Man (as I scribble on the edge of a paper napkin) must have enjoyed a similar lifestyle in Buenos Aires, though back in his day it would have been significantly more laid back, rather like Mendoza is now. As if to mirror this thought, an elderly man leaning on a cane hobbles past to an empty seat, dusting off his light-coloured suit and with trembling hands laying a battered but clean Panama hat on the seat alongside. It could be him, I think. It could be my grandfather. I know he is not, and maybe nothing like. But he could be.

Sam was an observer of life, choosing to sit and watch the world go by rather than actively participate, just as I am doing now... Smiling at the sight of a construction worker who in turning his hard hat back to front resembles a Trojan warrior... a small boy struggling with a live palm tree in a pot so large it is three times the size of his own head... the realisation that the blue of this restaurant's umbrellas and chairs match the corporate design of an adjoining city bank. Far too coincidental to be accidental, for sure.

A group of boys saunter by, scrapers at the ready to clean car windows. (At least they are wearing shoes on their feet, which is more than can be said for many of the kids doing a similar street trade in Buenos Aires.) A scary-looking woman with mountainous breasts and a monumental bum rolls past – such a lesson in obesity that I eat all the salad and leave three chips. Now two more independent Sam look-a-likes, ageing, colonial, trying to keep a good front but fraying around distinctly unloved edges. Most probably they live alone, not through choice but circumstance, happenstance; resigned to live in minimal comfort with as much dignity as they can muster. Maybe this is why my time in Mendoza is so important: I need to pull back, reconfigure to regain my equilibrium; in Japan I'm used to spending time alone. I'm scribbling madly here, because I've just realised there is a big difference: I stay in Japan by choice. And I am loved.

But wait. Something is going down. A drug deal, perhaps? The men at the table alongside are in perpetual motion: as one moves in, arriving with papers to be read and signed, another carries off files and binders. A constant stream of phone calls – all in all the choreography of business. Yet this dance of wheeling and dealing is in public, so if not drugs, what? The action appears to revolve around a guy in his thirties, dressed in denim from top-to-toe. But here comes that older man in the blazer with his orange file, again! A lawyer perhaps? The moving and shaking shifts to another table, with a lot of whispering, again an exchange of seats – three tables now involved! Any number of men now, spiralling between tables and chairs, standing up, sitting down, handshakes, circling, more handshakes, amicable pats on the back with one hand while the other slides down and around to check on wallets in back pockets.

Everyone is scrabbling to make money, keep money, turn money into more money. Areas like this operate on two economic levels: the restaurants and shops where people offer and buy services, and the other world that lives on the scraps the system throws their way. The haves, the want-to-haves, the have-nots. Without my credit card I feel psychologically like a have-not. But such a selfish, indulgent thought makes the contents of my stomach curdle. There are adults here desperate to sell a single plastic pen or shine a pair of shoes – or indeed clean a car window – to help put a scrap of food on family tables.

Here comes a desperado right now: a woman carrying a small child – always a good ploy. But I say no, because I cannot say yes to everyone (or can I?) and she is far too well made-up, groomed and manicured to be in desperate need. Though how am I to know? Who am I to say? Does it make it worse that I make such judgmental observations while continuing to slug my wine and ordering dessert?

So I am a little kinder to the next needy cause, which comes easy because she is cuteness personified, in jeans and a white sweater with long hair pulled back, hand outstretched, going from table to table, begging. It is her knowing flirtatiousness that sits uneasy, the way she coyly pats men on the knee or slides her hand up their arms, while twisting her head and body in appealing fashion. She is, after all, only seven or eight years old.

Even as I watch her work her way from tables to those of the neighbouring restaurant, a small quiet voice behind me says Hello, and an accordion draws breath. Not stridently, to capture my attention or bully me into listening, but to draw me gently and politely into her world, which she does very well.

Maria, aged twelve, arrived in Argentina from Bosnia three years ago. I ask whether she learned her English here or in Bosnia.

Oh here, she replies.

It's very good, I tell her (at which she blushes and smiles); Do you remember your own language?

No, no. I forget.

That's a pity, I say.

Well, I no speak my own language so much now. I hear only Spanish and English in places like this. (She means places where the haves hang out – well-to-do locals, and western tourists like me.)

I ask if her family is here.

In Argentina yes, but in Buenos Aires.

When I explain this is where I will be heading tomorrow night, she is thrilled: My father is here to work but it is difficult because he no speak Spanish so good yet. I try teach him, but I must work, so no time.

I tell her to take care, press coins into her hand, and she moves on, turning once to wave. Maria fills me with admiration. She has a skill. Performs with dignity. Displays a lot of talent combined with a lively intelligence. I wish I could help, but this is assuming she wants or needs my help. The wine is making me both sentimental and pragmatic. Not liking myself at all, I finish the bottle and unsteadily head for bed.

**NOVEMBER 18, 1999**

I have a splitting headache, with no one to blame but yours truly. Reluctant to leave the security of my room for the soon-to-be open road, I return to Sam's letter of January, 1947, in which he is looking beyond the immediate postwar period: *The Government at your end seems at all sixes and sevens, and the same here, and all kinds of controls of import and export tend to make things more and more complicated... Now that you are through the winter things will not be so grim, and I think from now on you will find things improving so far as food is concerned, and general activity.*

There is a distinctive shift in this letter. Sam makes jokes – asks how my sister is getting on with the British language (Bridget was slow in speaking), and notes how wonderful that my father bought an Argentine chicken! After signing off, he adds in a pointed postscript that Airmail Postage is now (the heady sum of) *one shilling – expensive!* Also, for the first time he signs off as *Daddy*, first typed, then in pen, followed by his usual signature.

As for the letter of May 8, there is an outpouring of affection and information. *About the middle of last month,* he begins, *I sent you a parcel of foodstuffs through Mitchell's English Bookstore of this City... It is only a small quantity, but all I was allowed to send.*

He goes on to explain he is enclosing an enlarged photo of himself, and another of his own father, Samuel Turner Loader, taken in Buenos Aires roundabout March, 1895: *He was an exceptional man in many ways, one of God's own, and never had an enemy in the whole world, being as you know* (a fact I was unfamiliar with until reading this) *an employee of the Bridgewater Canal Co, Salop,*[43] *as a youth, and on advice received from a friend set out for Uruguay, and was there from 1865, which resulted on my appearance on the earth, as also my sister Florence as Uruguayans.*

This I had known already, of course, from his passport. Now I want to know more. As if in answer to a prayer, Sam assists as best he can:

*My father soon entered into business for himself as Importer, and joined another friend, Hoard, and the firm became Hoard Loader & Co, somewhere about 1872. He returned to England with all the family, my mother (Martha) and sister and self, and with the Uruguayan connections formed an associated firm, Johnson Loader & Co., exporting and importing from the River Plate, i.e. Uruguay and Argentina. He became Consul for Uruguay in Liverpool* (Liverpool? *Liverpool?* I am slapping myself again for having missed this; all that wasted effort just because I read too fast) *and remained until the Uruguayan Government decreed that only natives should occupy Consul positions, and immediately he was nominated Vice-Consul for Argentina, which he carried on until his death in 1899.*

As an afterthought, possibly after reading the letter through, he types three lines down the side of the page: *Johnson did not play the game, and my father left him, and then called the firm Samuel T. Loader & Co. (\*Turner was an old Shropshire name also.)*

Great-grandfather apparently had friends in high places, *and his greatest was Sir Charles McIver, one of the originators of the Cunard S.S.Co Another was Edward Whiteley, who I think was M.P. for a Liverpool Division.*[44] *My name Edward came from him. Samuel came from Samuel Smiles, then an idol of all young men, and Charles was my Uncle, then a Cotton Broker.*[45]

Now comes background on my great-grandmother, Martha Jane Newbould: *My mother was one of five daughters of William Newbould of Intake, Sheffield, a family mixing with the county folk and relations of the well-known families Watson and Cadman, both names appearing prominently in the history of Sheffield. Both were Knighted, and Sir Cadman was a Chairman I think of the Shell Mex Oil Co. Ltd. My mother often said she would receive an inheritance from the Watson family, which never came off.*

*My grandfather, that is my mother's father, was a Colliery Proprietor, and was comfortably living in a country house at Intake. My father's father was John Loader, who came from Minsterley, Salop., which I visited on my trip last year.*

Despite the fact that I was already aged five, I have no clear memories of this visit, only images with a romantic dreamlike quality. But obviously this is why he is connecting emotionally: he has at last met me, Bridget and my mother, and on some level improved relations with my father. We are now his immediate family.

*So to Minsterley: It is a village about 12 miles from Shrewsbury, in wonderful country. I had lunch in the old Inn, Crown and Sceptre, which consisted of a good portion of tender chicken, etc., etc. One of the best meals I obtained whilst in Old England. I walked about the village, in a circuit of about two miles, and looked around the old church, but only discovered one family name, i.e. Whitefoot, and another which I now remember, Hope. I cannot say whether this is a family name, or the name of a village, but there is a Hope Mountain thereabouts.*

He describes other travels around the UK, to Sheffield, Hull, Bakewell in Derbyshire to stay with one Tom Pears, even getting as far north as Loch Lomond in Scotland. Already planning to return in April, 1948, he fills in my father as to his background, in case he does not know or has forgotten... *I was educated at Fairfield High School, then one of the best Boys Schools in Liverpool* (well of course), *and as a very small nipper but tall, I played in the school team on a few occasions, and remember playing against Birkenhead School, and Wirral College, long since defunct. Later I went to another very good private school, Elm Park College, and when I left for a trip with my father to South America in 1895, was somehow second boy in the school. I was Captain of the Football team, and Cricket team for a year or so.*

*After returning from S. America, I went back to school but could not stick it, and my father put me into the South British Fire and Marine insurance Co. where I stayed until his death, immediately entering my father's firm. I encountered a lot of trouble from the new Managing Partner, and put up with a lot of barging and interference. Eventually I took over. If I had not been overanxious to make a fortune <u>for you all</u>* (the last three words underlined), *things may have been better, or may have been worse. Merchants Export trade was by then on the wane, and I always considered myself well out of it, but would have preferred to retire another way. I consulted with my friend Wilfred Clothier K.C. and he advised me to get out, although I could have arranged for another firm to take over.*

*Cheerio,* he signs off. *Write soon, Yours lovingly...*

Something brushes my cheek, encouraging me to sign off for a while. A sudden breeze has set the voile curtain in motion, signalling it is midday and time to leave. Down in the lobby I pay up, leave my backpack behind the desk and go out into the world near broke and empty-handed. The manager has been kindness itself, helpful but not intrusive. Perfect.

I only just manage to catch the market, where mountains of food make me wake to just how hungry I am. Surrounded by multi-coloured (green, yellow, black) and multi-sized olives and as many grades of mate yerba from all over Argentina – labelled Misiones, Comuesta, Taverde – as there is green tea (o-cha) in Japan, I grab a seat at a stall and order beer and a deep-fried breaded thing. The guys alongside begin to shift as a bell begins to ring, and I realise that everyone is packing up. Following the crowd, I'm captivated by a stall of Italian-style cheeses, above which hangs an old photo – a group of young men in 1920s fashion, playing guitars and named Los Chalchaleros. I imagine they all worked here once in the market, perhaps on this very stall, their descendants happy to hang onto this memory of a gig at the Teatro Rivera Indate Cordoba.[46]

When I turn to leave, it is to find all the main doors closed... Everyone has vamoosed for *siesta*. Hunting up and down the aisles, I find one elderly couple padlocking their moneybox in slow motion, and waiting until they leave, follow-on like a needy stray. It's interesting to go out the back way, where I find cleaners and porters sprawled and most already asleep.

It's interesting also to tour the souvenir shops – the only places open – with nothing to spend. It's only just after lunch and the streets are nearly deserted. Even taking *siesta* into account, I don't remember it being like this yesterday. Half-day closing, perhaps?

Finding a cafe which allows me to hang out over a single cup of coffee (to counterbalance the effects of the beer) and endless jugs of iced water, is a joy. The waiter – half asleep but still on the job – brings me a newspaper, and despite it being in Spanish, I am informed that the news this morning is good. *VICTORY*, reads the headlines: *Spain 0 – Argentina 2.*

Later – much later (I fell asleep, my head on my arms on the tabletop) – I make my way up La Antigua Calle las Heras de la Mercado to La Calle de Heras, and so to Calle de los Immigrantes. This road leads to the train station, which was once the end of the line for immigrant workers crossing the *pampa* from Buenos Aires to find work. Half closing my eyes, I imagine crowds of weary, impoverished families with bundles and cases making their way towards me, hear their shortness of breath and hacking coughs, feel a stale heat and catch the stink of over 800 kilometres of slow bone-shaking travel on their clothes as they shuffle by.

I want go to the station, take some pictures, but I'm too weary; it's too damned hot. Instead I hang around the small free-standing exhibition behind glass in front of the old theatre, Teatro Maria Mazzarello, organised by the Association de Amigos de las Amigos Heras, showing scenes of early life in Mendoza. September 18, 1956 it reads: *La fueton dada con los objectivos essential de propender a la union de los commerciantes en defensa de los interests communes.* (Even I can vaguely work out what this means!) The first ever chairman was Jose Fa. The last – un-named – claimed no fame for the post in 1984.

I'm sad to leave this place, but also I am ready. I feel not only reconnected but better connected with Sam now that I know so much more about him. I want to thank him for passing on so much detail about his early life, telling me about Martha, fuelling me with renewed enthusiasm to get to the end of his story, pursue the Loader line. Thank you.

Waiting for the coach to open its doors in the bus station – I have been here for what seems like hours, initially wandering about like some homeless person but now determined to employ myself – I re-open Sam's file to his last letters of 1948.

May 18 begins with an observation of his lonely life (*I have lost count of many of the things that gave me pleasure in the past*) but having sent my father some cigarettes, which cheered him up no end, Sam then engages in happier talk about his fondness for cigars: *I get now and again a 25 box of Commerciales which are Brazilian, but I like them more than* (Cuban) *Habanos.* He then sinks again, going over old ground as regards the family situation, feeling as if he is *in the wilds... Betty is the one together with yourself who I take an interest in, as Betty had nothing to do with affairs, but was led by the nose, and that is all.* He then mostly makes comments on the business situation, ending – and once again this really makes me sit up – *I hear that Eric Loader may be coming out here to have a look around.*

Who?

Early September he notes that surely another parcel of foodstuffs has arrived by now. (I put his grouchiness down to having fallen in a swimming pool earlier in the year, and his elbows still ache. He fell on one and then the other came out in sympathy!) He continues: *Here business has been upset by a withdrawal of import permits, and for the moment new orders cannot be taken... The stoppage on the exchange of the pound sterling has been withdrawn, and the government has stated that applications can be made for import permits of chemicals, etc., but that does not help me.* He then mentions a letter received from Paysandu in Uruguay, from a cousin, *the wife of Roberto Catterick who died about two years ago. I called upon them long ago, and they have two daughters, about 40/50ish, apparently old maids. They are very nice, and the old lady has written me several times.*

So many new names: Whitefoot. Hope. Eric Loader. Now Robert Catterick. Catterick... sounds familiar and yet I'm not sure.

By late November, Sam is observing that *it is very hard luck on everybody* (in the UK, that is) *that the rationing continues in a still more acute form. Our Colonies will help reconstitute Great Britain, and according to accounts the people are doing all they can to put things right by increasing production.* For his own part, health is a concern: *Old age is always subject to ups and down. For the last three months I have been limping about with slight but awkward rheumatic pains in my left leg, which has always troubled me since I was continually getting wet whilst parading the streets* (of Liverpool) *as a policeman. As far as the other parts of the frame are concerned, I am alright, and cheerful, and don't intend to be worried by anyone if I can help it.*

Staunch words at the end of a trying year. It helps perhaps that *The British Commission will arrive next week to try and fix up the difficulties, and permit trade to run more freely.*

By the time the coach draws out of Mendoza, it is already dusk and night is falling fast. There are few passengers, so we spread ourselves around, make ourselves comfortable. Across the aisle is a university law professor, bearded, kindly, in his late thirties or early forties, heading back to teach. He lives in Mendoza and commutes.

I used to fly, he says, with a wry smile; But with the cuts they make me go one way now by road. Argentina is broke you know.

So am I, I reply, only half in jest. I tell him my story and he is interested enough – or simply being polite – to stay awake right until the end. After we exchange names and contact numbers, he wraps himself in a blanket and quickly nods off.

I cannot sleep. Rather I think I cannot sleep, when in fact I do, again fitfully, waking periodically to a vista of darkness beyond my small moving world, but above which the sky is dazzling with stars. Occasionally my eyes flutter in a semi-focused state of half-sleep and black forms – maybe trees, maybe buildings – pass as flash cards, leaving an impression but no more. More likely I am dreaming in various stages of consciousness, some providing more clarity than others. When I do surface, I rest easy, knowing I can return to exactly the same stage of the dream as where I left off. No trick, just a technique honed by long experience. And in many respects it is the perfect dream – a journey within a journey – covering the same ground as I ranged over in the summer in 1996 when I went in search of Harriet.

I love Shropshire. It has always drawn me, and now I know why: ancestral roots are planted deep. My own son was conceived in the county, in his paternal aunt's cottage just beyond Burwarton. And we all spent many happy hours in Ludlow, especially after Lee and Buffy's paternal grandmother Florence moved there from the Black Country after her husband died in the 1970s. British Poet Laureate John Betjeman (1906–1984) described Ludlow – with five hundred listed buildings, and a medieval layout of streets surviving near-intact – as "the perfect historic town", and he could be right.

Driving a rented car, I stayed overnight with my ex-mother-in-law – by this time known affectionately by all her grandchildren as the Incredible Shrinking Grandma. It was to be my last time to see her, spend time with her, but I was not to know that. Simply put, I loved her. She could drive us all nuts with her fussy ways and dreadful cooking, but also I acknowledge that Roger and I could not have managed without her help and unconditional generosity when Lee arrived on the scene in 1963. I believe it was her sense of nurturing that helped develop my own. My own mother was in Scotland, choosing to define the limits of her own world, which at that time did not include me or my family.

Florrie's sixteenth century house in Lower Raven Lane had become as eccentric over the centuries as she in her own lifetime. It was narrow and crooked and not at all convenient, and it quickly became clear that she was not managing half as well as she used to. Taking her out in the car, we stopped off at her favourite spot on Whytecliff, which offers a fine view of the town, the castle and the Teme and Corve rivers that encircle its battlements. It is the perfect spot to place such a fortification. Dating from 1086 AD, it was built as one in a string of castles along the Marches, to keep out the Welsh.

Later I climbed the nearly impossibly steep stairs to her attic, where the floor was so uneven that toes often stubbed in the night to an accompaniment of curses, trying to find the way to the loo. The walls bulged and heaved, and the window looked drunk. Not an especially comfortable bed either, but piled high with Florrie's famed crochet blankets, all made from carefully unravelled hand-knits. She never

believed in throwing anything away that could be useful, and for a long
time regarded me as a wholly unsuitable wife for her son because I never
kept rubber bands and used string, and had flagrantly extravagant habits,
such as cooking with cream.

I set out next morning, heading north. It was hard to say goodbye,
and I vowed to see her again, soon. Another broken promise.

Quickly enough the landscape distracted, capturing my attention. So
green. So quiet. So mysterious. I say this because the road almost runs
parallel with the giant earthwork built in 780 AD by the Mercian King
Offa to keep even earlier Welsh at bay and create a territorial border.
Eighteen feet high and stretching 140 miles, Offa's Dyke took fifteen
years to build, with each locality responsible for its own section.[47] Once,
long ago, I took Lee and Buffy to Clun in my beloved green Saab 95[48]
just across the border from Bishop's Castle and the location of many a
battle, to look at a cottage for sale. The house was a tip, but beautifully
located, overlooking a valley filled with forest. Yes, said the agent when
I observed strange vibes; It's said that you can hear the voices of dead
Roman troop movements at night, wailing down over the centuries.

Determined to find Harriet, I headed for Minsterley and was soon
passing beneath the arching trees of Hope Valley. Which instantly
reminded me of the name Sam had found in the graveyard. Also that my
Aunt Kathleen's maiden name was Hope, but she came from Warwickshire.
And this in turn conjured up a sudden memory of riding a rollercoaster
with her brother, the concert pianist Eric Hope (he wearing a bowler hat
and carrying a rolled umbrella) at the Festival of Britain in 1951. Funny
how the mind leaps about, taking us here, there and everywhere.)

Hope Valley is a nature reserve conserved by the Shropshire Wildlife
Trust, not only for its flora and fauna, but its geological importance.
According to a pamphlet on the subject, this area – designated SSS1 – is the
junction between older Ordovician shales and volcanic rocks and younger
sandstones, and siltstones of the Silesian period. I even stopped for a quick
peek behind the bus shelter at the junction of the A488 and the road up to

the village of Hope (that name again), where rocks pressured by enormous earth movements ripple in violent convolutions. They continue in this fashion all the way into Wales, where during the earliest part of the Stone Age they pushed upwards to form the Welsh mountains.

Before I could catch breath, I was in the heart of Minsterley, which was part of Westbury until 1910 when it became a separate parish. I parked near The Cross, hewn out of Cornish granite to commemorate local men who fell in the Great War of 1914–1918. I sat on the stone wall of the central arch of the bridge over Minsterley Brook, the largest tributary of the Rea Brook, which runs into the River Severn. A flood here in 1811 left 3,000 acres under water, and nine dead in nearby Pontesford.

Built in 1240, the Old Crown and Sceptre remains the oldest of four alehouses built at the crossroads, and where Sam ate the best meal in Old England six centuries later in 1947. Old Yew Cottage, Brook House and Minsterley Hall all proved to be splendid historic buildings. But there was settlement here long before the founding of Ludlow Castle. Saxon invaders, attracted by the rich fertile soil of the Welsh Marshes, overcame resistence by local tribes people, called Ordovicians, and put down their own roots. The name Minsterley was from Menestrelie, menestre being an early word for a minster of a church affiliated to a monastic establishment, and ley from the clearing in which such a minster was founded.

It was the possible site of this Olde English mynster to which I was drawn. In 1634, the local fat cat family – the Thynnes of Minsterley Hall – funded a church to be built on what were reputedly the remains of a far older place of worship. And what an extraordinary church it remains; I'm not alone in never having seen any example of Christian architecture remotely similar. The Saxons used stone, and twelve centuries later, the Victorians brick. Nothing new here, for sure. But the style in which they are combined – brick walls sloping inwardly from the perpendicular with seven buttresses and carved stone cherubs as keystones – are eye-catching. Even more so, the decoration above the porch and around the eves: an hourglass, and skulls and crossbones, surrounded by a festoon of scrolls. Never had I ever seen anything so macabre and direct in its message: life is short.

Life had been short for local maidens – spinsters of the parish – who lost husbands-to-be ahead of marriage. Never before either had I come across Virgins' Crowns, and inside this Church of the Holy Trinity I found seven. Standing just inside the doorway, taking in the delicately tinted original glass and simplicity of the interior – whitewashed walls, dark wood – my eyes were drawn upwards, to strange faded headpieces of decorative flowers and paper gloves mounted on short metal rods, each ending in a heart-shaped escutcheon, bearing a woman's initials, age and the date of her death. The earliest read 1724, the latest 1794. Seven is universally regarded as a lucky number, but not for these unfortunates – unless of course they escaped making marital vows for better rather than worse. I found a replica of such Crowns, under glass by the bookstall. The ribbon rosettes, withered roses in decomposing tatters, were originally in patriotic red, white and blue. It was customary also to hang each Crown above its owner's pew; a strange, sad custom now almost forgotten but that William Shakespeare knew all too well. Remember the lines from Hamlet with regards to Ophelia's funeral, referring to Maidens' Crants? One and the same.

Already spooked, but excited rather than scared, I walked up the aisle, scanning the plaques on the walls for my family name. Nothing. Perplexed and disappointed – I had already explored the graveyard outside, finding – just as Sam had recalled – only the surnames Hope and Whitefoot in any significant number – I stood before the altar and murmured in what I thought was *sotto voce*: Harriet, I'm here, looking for you. Please give me some help. Where the hell are you?

No sooner had the words left my lips, than there was the most terrific crash behind, to my left. Turning, I found the vase of flowers on one of two plinths flanking the aisle had somehow jumped off and shattered on the tiles below, scattering flowers and water everywhere. For the third time since passing through the thatched porch way into the ground of the church, I felt the hair stand up on the back of my neck. Okay, Okay I responded: So you are here. But what am I supposed to do now?

First I went to the vicarage, and the friendly fresh-faced woman who came to the door fetched her husband, Bill, who walked with me back into the scene of my crime – or Harriet's desperate attempt to get attention! He was surprisingly open and philosophical, saying that a lot of weird things happened in Holy Trinity, and that I should not take it personally. He would clear up the flowers later; in the meantime why didn't he walk me around the graveyard again, and maybe he could come up with ideas of how to help. It was odd that my grandfather was so sure of the Minsterley connection. He personally had never come across the name Loader anywhere roundabouts, including in the parish records. Now Pritchard, he noted (the recorded name of baby Jane's father) was – like Hope and Whitefoot – common enough. A local haulage company of note went by that name. But Loader, never.

Maybe you should go and look in churches of some other local villages, he advised; I also minister to St Luke's, Snailbeach, and St Mary's, Habberley. You could also try Pontesbury.

So that is what I did. With a great deal of enjoyment on a beautiful English summer afternoon, but the ever-increasing confusion of one hundred and one red herrings.

# CHAPTER 18

# ONE HUNDRED AND ONE RED HERRINGS

**NOVEMBER 18, 1999 CONTINUED**

I stayed that night at Cricklewood Cottage – an eighteenth-century find at the foot of the hill known as Stiperstones, not so far from Minsterley and close by Plox Green. (It seemed appropriate since I had begun my adult journeying life in 1962 in London's Cricklewood NW2.) As a classic B&B, CC proved to be a gem, not only for the warm welcome, fresh ruffled bed linen and an unparallelled English breakfast, but the lovingly designed garden at the back. With a trout stream running parallel to the road, the land in-between cottage and water was planted in such a way that one section grew naturally into the next: a woodland patch and fernery, bog garden, herb garden...

Having booked in, I raced up Stiperstones to watch the sun set over a patch-worked merging of green and gold into purplish shadow. Seeking silver roundabout here, the Romans had found lead in quantity. They built a road from the richest mine at Snailbeach all the way to Uriconium, as ruled over at long distance by Hadrian (Publius Aelius Hadrianus, AD76-138) – the Roman Emperor who also ordered the building of a wall across the width of what is now northern England.

After dusk swallowed the last detail (and swallows on the wing the last insects) I drove around to find a good place to eat. And ended up (unlike Sam) at Stables Inn, Hopesgate, where I tucked into three courses with a hunger born of frustration but softened by sunshine, pastoral views and, inescapably, my own good humour. Because believe it or not, I had found John Loader, though sadly he was not at home.

Having nearly exhausted Bill Rowell's suggestions, I had driven mid-afternoon to Pontesford, lying as it does in the shadow of Shropshire's sleeping dragon (Pontesford Hill and Earl Hill). . Unlike Holy Trinity, I got no vibes at all from the church or its graveyard. On the verge of giving up, I circled the village, crossing the ford en route, to find a garage. Filling up the car with petrol, the chatty owner asked where I was from and where I was heading. In a nutshell, out came the purpose of my mission and, backing up what Bill had told me, I was informed that Pritchard was a common enough name in the area, but Loader? No.

Where upon a woman's voice commanded attention from inside the garage office.

Yes, there is, she shouted; There's a John Loader up the hill. And then she emerged, grinning from ear-to-ear to have put her boss right, with the address scribbled on a scrap of paper.

I found the house – you cannot conceive such a heart-pumping stomach-churning level of excitement – but as I said, no-one was in. (After returning to Japan the following month, John Loader was kind enough to reply to a written enquiry. The oddest coincidence, he agreed, but without foundation: no known connection at all.)

According to another red-herring of an imagined relative – a lawyer in Toronto who replied to an e-mail of 1999 – there are more Loaders in Hampshire and Wiltshire than any other county. Lisa Loader (her mother was Japanese, from Niigata of all places) had never heard the name in connection with Shropshire or Liverpool. As if to bear this out, the John Loader of Pontesford was an immigrant, from the South of England.

If I had not been given a parking ticket – my own fault for being too impatient – I would have left my ever-curious literate heart in Shrewsbury. Originally the settlement was called Pengwern, and then Scrobbesbyrig, from which the present name is derived.

Clive of India (1725–1774) was both a local MP and Mayor. Charles Darwin was born in the town. Mary Webb (1881–1927) – whose novel *Precious Bane* (one of few books my mother ever owned) was to stir deep passions in me as an hormonal-struck teenager of the 1950s – is buried in Shrewsbury Cemetery. Other locals of note: Brother Cadfael, a twelfth-century fictional monk brought to life by Ellis Peters (actually, the author was Edith Pargeter, writing under a pseudonym), and then adapted into a radio and TV series; and Percy Thrower (1913–1988), the former superintendent of local parks who had filled me with a passion for plants through his long-running radio show, *Gardener's Question Time.*

Yes, what a lovely, interesting place – England's first Tudor town! Yet Shrewsbury Castle dates from 1080. And the church of St Mary The Virgin, in the very centre of what is now considered the capital of the county and with one of the highest spires in England, stands on Saxon foundations. Today it incorporates just about every European architectural style, including Norman doorways, German stained glass and a famed Jesse window.[49] The interior proved gloomily rich with atmosphere, the past manifesting through the centuries to appear totally in the present: I could imagine Jane and John being named at the font; Jane's tiny coffin being genuflected over, amid a general fatalistic sadness and a mother's veil of tears. Buried in the forecourt, soft baby bones long returned to earth beneath neatly mown turf, old gravestones are mostly dug up and ranged against walls. Jane, my great-great-great aunt... long lost but no longer forgotten.

In one of the side chapels, two volunteers were serving tea to visitors. Asking how I could obtain a copy of a portrait discovered in a gallery of former vicars, a woman with an excess of costume jewellery told me (virtually) to get lost.

We don't do things like that, she said, smugly, pulling on her hat to quit her shift.

I had seen her colleague wince with embarrassment and, once alone, this second woman called me back, offering to copy the picture personally and send it on. When asked what I could do in return, Phyllis was promised as good as she gave: used stamps from Japan for her grandson. It took her a year but she fulfilled her pledge, posting a carefully packaged picture of J.B. Blakeney, incumbent from 1794 to 1826. By my reckoning, he would have been vicar when Jane and John were baptised. Did he also read funeral rites over their mother? There is no record of her death at that time, so what happened to Harriet? Where did she go?

Tearing my parking ticket into shreds (a useless exercise in the long-term but immensely satisfying at the time) I drove across the river that all-but-encircles the old town and its original layout of streets – Raven Meadows, Milk Street, Shoplatch, Dogpole, Swan Hill – and up to the site of what is now Shrewsbury School. It was this impressive collection of buildings that once housed the poor and destitute of the county. Ignoring all *PRIVATE* signs – it was a weekend, with few boys or staff about – I drove inside and toured around, even parked and enjoyed the view from the terrace down over the Severn to The Quarry, now one of Percy Thrower's public parks of yore, and the town. Again I found myself waiting, expectantly, for Harriet to offer up further clues and signs. But no, nothing. Not even half a red herring.

Still seeking a miracle, I spent an hour in the Shropshire Records and Research Centre at Castle Gates.[50] WAR (Windsor Ancestry Research) had already conducted an intensive study of all local records, so instead I based myself in the Reading Room, concentrating my attention on the institution in which Harriet and her children found refuge. A book, *Kingsland And Its Associations*, proved helpful, and I was allowed to copy as many pages as I liked. SRRC: what a marvellous resource, with the most helpful staff imaginable.

Okay. How many know the name of merchant seaman Captain Thomas Coram? Not me, for sure. Born in or around 1668, he criss-crossed the Atlantic between Britain and North America until retiring to London's East End. Far from falling asleep into old age, he awoke to the horrors of early eighteenth-century poverty in that part of the city, and more especially the plight of abandoned children.

In 1739, after strenuous lobbying and much hard work, he obtained a Charter of Incorporation for the Maintenance and Education of Exposed and Deserted Young Children. The aims of his London Foundling Hospital, which opened in 1745, proved so popular that funding poured in from philanthropically-inclined institutions, their only condition being that no child be turned away. A basket was hung at the entrance of the London Foundling Hospital, where a desperate mother could leave her baby and ring a bell to alert staff inside. (Hospitals have since started doing this again apparently, even in Japan.) Also she was expected to leave a personal token of some kind, to help identify her child if reclamation proved feasible; babes were given a new name on entry.

When it was decided to extend the service beyond the capital, Shrewsbury was selected because of associations with the textile and clothing textile industry. In 1758, a ninety-nine-year lease was granted by the local corporation for a site known as Kingsland, with central government agreeing to buy adjoining land.

The first intake of foundlings – twenty boys and twenty girls – was initially housed in Dog Lane because Shrewsbury Hospital (as it was first called) and was not quite ready. By 1758, however, it was caring for fifty-six children with 163 *Out To Nurse*, meaning that they were being nourished (for a pittance) by mothers with a plentiful supply of breast milk. Children under four were usually placed with families in outlying villages; from four upwards they were cared for in the central building to be employed in woollen manufacture and later apprenticed, mostly to mills. Vile though this system was, being open to the worst forms of abuse, a visitor to the hospital in 1766 observed in a letter to a friend: *The neatness of the wards and the healthy looks of 500 children just setting down to dinner in the open air on the finest natural terrace in England formed a most picturesque scenery.*

In 1784 the hospital was renamed the Shrewsbury Union Workhouse – commonly known as the local House of Industry – and opened to provide destitute adults as well as their children with the basics of life. This was the period when Harriet – and later John – found relief. The SUW remained so named until 1871, when there were so few residents left that Poor Law officials decided that the upkeep of the place was too much of a burden on parochial rates. The buildings were converted into classrooms; the old Shrewsbury School in the town below moved to higher ground in 1882.

Founded as a Free School in 1552 by King Edward VII, Shrewsbury School was inaugurated by Queen Elizabeth I nineteen years later. Listed by the Clarendon Report on British Public Schools as *One of the finest in England*, it is now a private educational establishment (meaning it is far from public or free!) boarding 720 boys aged between thirteen and eighteen.[51]

What would John have made of this, I remember wondering.

Mid-afternoon found me pointing the car northwards to circumnavigate Liverpool for Formby. With Andy away on business, his wife Joan and I had the chance to get acquainted. It was the first time we had met.

The next day, I moseyed around the city by bus and taxi, taking a closer look at addresses with family connections. I walked Thomas Lane in Broad Green where my grandparents, my father and his siblings and beloved Spot the Dog had once lived; the original house had long gone, most probably bombed and long since redeveloped. I recalled Andy telling me of a stroll he had taken down the road and how a neighbour had indeed recalled the address next door – Las Piedros – as having Spanish connections! Alas, like John Loader back in Pontesford, friendly Elsie was not at home.

I took the train from Broad Green station into the city centre to find 44 The Temple, a fine redbrick Victorian pile now renumbered 42–46 Dale Street, under the wraps of refurbishment. I marched into Liverpool City Hall to mooch with mock bravado before the great fireplace, pretending that I had the right to be there even if I did not actually own the joint. Going outside, the river was in one direction (I could smell it, and there were seagulls), and Castle Street the other. After vegetarian goulash and fruit trifle in the Pudding Bowl, my next port of call was Upper Parliament

Street, which is where my grandmother took her brood after Sam had left for Argentina in 1936. Or maybe even before.

I like taxi drivers (mines of information and usually happy to talk) and this big-beer-belly – who like most Liverpudlians have always been able to temper the deepest depression with upbeat comic wit – was no exception. When asked if his job is dangerous, he laughed so much the whole cab shook, recalling: Once an accountant got in, bleedin' like hell. I said, you want an ambulance mate, not a taxi! Less than an hour later a young girl, only seventeen, flagged me down, slashed across the face. Apart from things like that I get no trouble.

Number 138 Upper Parliament Street must once have been a stunningly elegant address. Now it was closed up, black with grime and totally dilapidated.

Lots of pros (prostitutes) hang around, using deserted joints like that, instructed my tour guide; Which makes me have to ask, me love, what the hell are we doin' here?

I checked Moscow Drive where Sam once lived; the handsome double-fronted house proved a badly painted bright red – which while I approved (it helped cheer a long drab street), I was quite sure he would not. What a pity that all the photos I was shooting on the trip were in monochrome – why was that? – because soon after processing the negs went missing and now all I have is a single contact sheet, making all such colourful allusions a disputable memory rather than in-your-face fact.

Next stop: Anfield Cemetery, to pay my respects amid a littered landscape of damaged gravestones. Uniquely the Loader family tombstone faces a side road, and though covered with moss and lichen and somewhat eroded by time, remained undamaged. Also, once cleaned off with clumps of grass, it proved relatively easy to read:

*IN LOVING MEMORY OF SAMUEL TURNER LOADER, ARGENTINE-VICE-CONSUL, DIED 30TH MARCH 1899, AGED 57 YEARS.*
*PEACE PERFECT PEACE.*

*ALSO OF MARTHA JANE, THE BELOVED WIFE OF THE ABOVE,*
*WHO DIED 12TH OF FEBRUARY 1915, AGED 66 YEARS.*
*THY WILL BE DONE.*
*ALSO GERTRUDE MARY LOADER, DAUGHTER OF THE ABOVE.*

Simple words, simply designed, being quite plain but for a Grecian-style border along the base.

I looked, walked around, paid witness, left. Sadness overwhelmed, not so much for those I had come looking for, but the desecration all around. Stumbling between shards of glass from stoned stained glass windows, I came across a series of vandalised angels with their heads bashed in and wings knocked about. For the first time in months, I found myself in tears.

As usual, I found solace in a place of worship: the new Liverpool Cathedral, approached by flights of concrete steps a-swirl in waste paper, with whole newspapers being catapulted into orbit by wildly violent winds off the river. How come so many contemporary architects refuse to take Nature into account in their designs?

Inside, however, I discovered conductor Simon Rattle – he of the equally wild hair (a force of nature in itself) and awesome baton – putting the Liverpool Philharmonic and a soloist on the cathedral's magnificent organ through their paces in preparation for a concert that evening. I listened to the organ and strings converse and then begin to argue, alternately melodic and discordant. The orchestra was like a patient mother trying to placate an irritated child who progressively became more and more angry. Finally the organ lost the plot completely, shrieking and stamping so hard and loud, all stops out (or maybe that should be in?) that I feared the ceiling would come down. But no: one final demented primal screech and then silence, followed by a gust of expelled breath all around and the tap-tap-tapping of bows on music stands – the classic appreciation of a magnificent performance.

Next morning I said *sayonara* and *arigato gozaimasu* (thank you) to Joan, and headed south. First stop, the Liverpool Record Office of Local Studies, where, again unsure of what I was looking for, it seemed best to ramble along alphabetically-labelled shelves – Argentina, Buenos Aires, Montevideo, Uruguay – and await revelation. Eventually – in another part of the room entirely, a card – Ref. 1920/MD-399 – relating somehow to South America – suggested I dip into the archives.

Oh, noted the clerk, I don't think we've ever been asked for this before. I wonder what it is?

Quite some time after, she approached solemnly with a trolley, on the top of which lay a small flat object covered with a cloth. I lifted it off, hardly daring to breathe, to find a small leather-covered book. Settling at a desk, I began turning hand-written (the ink only slightly faded), illustrated pages (the colours still bright, as if painted yesterday). A journal, written by traveller Thomas Gibson, it described a voyage that began in Liverpool in 1837 and ended in Monte Video and Buenos Ayrez (sic) the following year. There was a little drawing on the first page, showing the brig *M. M. Waters* being tossed on huge waves far out at sea – and this despite being loaded with 40 tons of copper dross for ballast and a cargo of general goods.

*Sailed 26th of December, at 10 o'clock in the morning, our intrepid voyage began; I have a state-room all to myself. The other two gentlemens' berths are together... It is only my second voyage... I had waited a week in Liverpool with my brother for the sailing of the vessel. A fine breeze with the flood tide carrying us down the river at a rate of five knots an hour. It was at first foggy but soon cleared, and from the number of vessels going out with us, counted at one time 70. The scene is most animated and beautiful...* Hey ho, this diary ended 64 days later; *Upon the whole it has become a very pleasant voyage. Finesse. Finis.*

I loved the index, quote: *strange flat or low rainbow*, page 62; *flying fish*, page 63; pages 114-115, little painted drawings of flags showing how to identify vessels of other nations...

Then right at the end, I found pages from another journal stitched in, started in March 1936. This was written by some bright spark – no, not Sam, that would have been just too much to expect – on the way to Argentina, with a longer section covering the voyage of eighty-seven days back.

Approaching Liverpool, Anon. writes: *We are off Point Linus lighthouse, about halfway from L'pool to Holyhead. I forgot to say we lost two of our ducks. They and the fowls were about the decks, and in the hurrying of making sail, had not been put in their pens and got overboard by a small hole in the bulwark. The mate's name is Thomison, the steward a* <u>black</u> *(underlined), Archer. The captain has a very fine dog, Carlo.*

On this canine note, entries ended. Watching the log being carried away, maybe never to be asked for again, I had the oddest sensation: as if I had touched something of enormous import, without really understanding what or indeed why.


Port Sunlight, across the River Mersey via the tunnel not the ferry, is another fine attempt to create the perfect community.[52] But I had no time to spare other than trawl the most obvious streets making appreciative noises. I had an address to find in Wallasey, where the occupants of a semi-detached address in Prince's Way were waiting: Joyce and Alison Loader.

Andy had found them during his initial researches and even taken the trouble to visit to add information to my family tree.

In her seventies, Joyce was warm and animated, despite being slowed by arthritis. Her daughter Alison – another cousin named Alison – already had the kettle on and made tea, which we ate in the front parlour (what my own mother used to call in Coventry, "The Lounge"). The first thing I noticed was a photo of a man looking remarkably like a Loader, complete with jug-handle ears. Remember Sam saying that an Eric Loader was coming out to Buenos Aires to have a look around? Meet Eric, only child of Arthur Loader Price (in Spanish style) and Margaret.

Joyce had faxed me in November 1994, filling me in on her husband's family background, and amusing reading it proved to be. She could not vouch for the accuracy of my family tree's early cast of characters – John and Susan, or their son – but knew far more than me about his son William, daughter-in-law Sarah and their offspring, starting with Walter: He did marry Millicent, but they separated after a couple of weeks, Reading between the lines, Joyce had written, I gather the gent (to put it tastefully) was not the type to marry! Then there was Arthur Ernest (1883–1926) who married Margaret Macmillian (1897–1981). The others – Charles, Anne, Alice and Herbert – are as you have them listed.

Chattering on: Referring back to the top line (of Andy's family tree), Samuel Turner who married Martha – their daughter Gertrude lived in Wallasey when I (Joyce) first moved here in 1944. She was the oddest old duck (so many ducks on the same day...) you could ever have met, but kind-hearted. The story goes that she had a troublesome toe removed, and kept it in brine or pickle in a small jar! Mind you, anything I know was passed on to me by my mother-in-law, known as Madge, and she didn't exactly run a Loader fan club.

Joyce had also met my grandfather, When he was visiting this country from, I think, Monte Video (sic). It must have been the mid-forties, for there was this talk of Eric and I joining him in the business. On the strength of this, Eric and I took a Spanish course, and a fat lot of good it did us! The only bonus is that when holidaying in the Canaries, or Spain, I can ask for a cup of tea or coffee and shower the waiters with my grateful thanks.

Joyce and Eric had known one another since childhood, growing up in Hightown, a small village outside Liverpool. They married in 1942, when he was a captain in the Queen's Town Cameron Highlanders, and she was a land army girl stationed near Chester. Their first child, Ian, born in 1944, proved to brain damaged, and thereafter needed twenty-four hour care. Joyce: If I had not had Madge and my own mother to give me support, I think I would have gone under.

Second son Neil was born in 1951, and Alison in 1956. After Eric died of a sudden massive heart attack in 1978, Neil insisted that his mother agree to Ian going into residential care; he was becoming harder and harder to look after at home, Madge was failing and Joyce's own mother was in her late eighties.

Joyce: Being only an hour away, we were able to visit him every week until (having deteriorated over the years) he passed away in 1990. I was so thankful; his quality of life was very poor.

Neil had divorced and was now sharing his life with another Angela! His two girls, Joanne, fifteen, and Katie, thirteen, were with their mother but seeing their father every other weekend.

Joyce: Alison lives with me, and we get on very well.

Being inveterate travellers, they were both enthused at the idea of my going to South America, To find out more. And so we spent a couple of very happy hours looking through old photos, pondering on the eccentricities of the Loader clan, and marvelling on the fact that neither side had known the other existed. I had only distant memories of once visiting my grandmother's brother Alex and his wife Bea (Sam's sister, but I didn't know that then) in Hoylake, a small seaside resort on the Wirral peninsula. I remember the back garden as a very steep rockery, and a beach so far away at low tide that even in the distance I could not see the sea.

## NOVEMBER 19, 1999

I wake to the coach attendant tucking a blanket under my chin; despite the heating there is a chill in the air – that deep clean cold that sprints ahead of dawn. Outside there is only darkness and a sense of time and distance spinning by unseen, unknown. Maybe out there, somewhere, people were watching us flash by in sudden unexpected streaks of warm light, leaving only a haze of fumes to momentarily warm night-cold concrete. What might they be thinking? Certainly it would not cross their minds that they had just witnessed the night passage of a mad woman, hurtling from one side of South America to the other, chasing ghosts.

Is that what I am doing? Not for the first time on this trip, I wonder why I'm more preoccupied with the dead than the living. My aunt – Jo – thinks I am obsessed. Angela, she wrote ahead of my leaving Japan three weeks ago: You've had a bee in your bonnet for years. I do hope it will have stopped buzzing by the time you get back.

So do I, and replace Sam's writings on my lap, to see how far we still have to go, how much longer this is all going to take. He is writing more and more as old age begins to catch up and my father presumably takes pity…

In January 1948 my grandfather says he was thrilled while staying in Piriapolis to receive a letter and a new photograph of Bridget and me on Christmas day, and signs off as *FATHER* (typed), followed by *Daddy Sammy* (handwritten).

By the end of the month – yes, two letters in one month – he is *dog tired* of the to-ing and fro-ing by plane across the River Plate, but still finds enough energy to mail off another small food parcel to help keep us alive in postwar rationed Britain: *I am glad to hear you are getting a bit more bacon, and a further ounce of margarine.*

He describes a possible trip back in the summer to help keep two Argentine clients on the straight and narrow in Italy, France and the UK, and business orders that are just about keeping him afloat: *Special kind of Needles. Grinders, Breast drills, Bicycle saddles, and a lot of other stuff that gives work. I don't suppose the whole lot is worth more than a thousand pounds. Montevideo I took orders for Sanitary Ware, which has commenced there again but not Argentina. Cast Iron Porcelain Enamelled Baths, and receptacles for Shower Baths. The Cycle Trade is quiet just now, but a lot of machines are on the water.*

He feels time passing slowly in Buenos Aires. *Prices keep going up. For a few days, there has been no Ice, owing to a strike, and now there is no Milk, or Butter, for the same reason. There is much prosperity here, but things are beginning to rock, and people are afraid that one day there will be a sudden falling off in trade, with all the consequent troubles of labour, etc... The British Mission is getting along slowly... Problems are difficult to settle. Cheerio. With love to you all, DADDY SAMMY* (typed), *Father* (handwritten).

Late February he is making plans to leave for Europe in April, expecting to arrive in England in August. Then: *How are the two kiddies, who stare at me from my dressing table where they are fixed. I always smile at Bridget, who looks as if she does not care a toss for anyone. I enclose a pound note to buy them some sweets.*

There is no sweetness and light about a letter dated March 1st; rather he gives a rare insight into the internal politics of his adopted country, because: *This is the Day on which the British Railways become Argentine property, in exchange for what we might call a fair deal. Most of the material is hopelessly out of date, and must be renewed at enormous cost, which in British hands was impossible by reason that the Government would not allow any increase of rates or tariffs. Now the people will have to pay heavily, and whilst there is plenty of money about, it is easy, but in a year or two when the inevitable depression takes place they will be in queer street. It is practically a general holiday and at this moment 5.45 p.m. all the PERON element is en route to RETIRO STATION, or PLAZA BRITANICA where ceremonies will take place, and a lot of speechmaking by Peron, his ministers etc etc, whilst the crowd will roar themselves hoarse with the cries of PERON, PERON, PERON, and anything they can think of. Most calm and decent people* (he is talking about himself, presumably) *have gone to their homes where it is quiet. The others, mainly the lower element of working classes do the shouting.*

*Below my window in the Avenida there is a HELL of a lot of noise, of people shouting on their way to Retiro. Excuse the word HELL, but it suits the occasion extremely well. This is the main route for all processions, demonstrations, and anything else of a political kind. It is all or mostly all propaganda for the Government, and also for the coming Elections for new candidates for the coming Congress. Now below a man is howling at the top of his voice from a car with a Loud Speaker. The call for Vivas is strong, but not always gets attention...*

I try to catch the attention of the coach attendant, but he is glued to the ceiling-slung video screen which is showing a British movie with Spanish sub-titles. I begin to watch, but a picnic scene beside a river and the dulcet tones of standard English begin to fade before the far noisier and potentially more volatile images that Sam is describing... I come to again (the file of letters closed and placed alongside, and not by me) to the gentle.sound of assorting snorings against the background of engine and wheels in concert. Outside, the wide flat agricultural plain mists into early-morning infinity. I have missed the *pampa*, with still no sign of a real working *gaucho*. And in less than an hour we are swallowed up by the outskirts of so-called civilisation – the sky behind a pure pale duck-egg blue, with the far less promising haze of pollution looming ahead. As we draw into the bus station alongside the battered broken sooted pile that was once beautiful Retiro, I suffer another fleeting confusion of emotions: regret that this part of the trip is over but also relief to have made it in one piece.

I am back in Buenos Aires.

# CHAPTER 19

# BACK IN BUENOS AIRES

**NOVEMBER 19, 1999 CONTINUED**

My step is light. I'm on familiar ground. It's only when I try to pass Retiro to check how far the trees have come into leaf in San Martin, and find a freight train at a standstill on the track crossing the road, with crowds of irritated commuters trying to get to work by scrambling over and under in any way they can, that I remember: this city has troubles of its own.

Still, there is a bitter-sweet pang of pleasure at seeing Caseros lurch into view; the tower block panelled in red and yellow that has become such a cheerfully familiar eyesore; richly depraved aromas from the cheese shop just outside the station exit, making me salivate like crazy (after a constant supply of buns through the night I'm hungry for decent food); and when the Leaning Tower of Pisa comes into view through morning rush hour fumes along the main road, I have to laugh. LTP is quite a pile – a four-storey-high 3-D billboard for some local industry hammered out of steel and painted like the Italian original, but now weathered and peeling. Also the height and angle seem extreme enough to be potentially very dangerous indeed, but I'm not arguing. Turning off into the side streets towards Avenida de la Torre, a couple of familiar faces smile and wave, calling *Buenos dias*. My goodness, it feels like home.

Everyone, it seems, is pleased to see me. Maria-Elena hugs, Tarzan pecks my cheek and grunts. Marta tries to wrestle my bag away but loses. Even Krieger wags his tail from the patio, which is very nice of him considering his pitiful state. His winter coat is so matted and clumped that he must be as hot as hell, poor thing. And as for the barking... it is clear to me – if no one else – that this animal is going stir-crazy. It is at this point that I decide not to be scared and somehow come to his rescue (but not today, because it has to be a covert operation). Right now I need to wash my entire wardrobe, sort myself out and Make A Plan. *Another* plan. I also need to catch up on Sam, big time – a whole clutch of letters fired off with varying degrees of optimism towards the end of the 1940s.

It is not Spring of course when he writes in April 1948. It is the beginning of the Argentine winter, and he is booked to sail in June, thus escaping into an English summer of roses, strawberries and hedges running wild with honeysuckle and Queen's Anne Lace. Not that MV (merchant vessel) *Devis* would have had any sail, of course, but old terms die hard.

Having recently posted two parcels, and set himself the task of bringing over any bits and pieces that might help a family in hard times, he focuses on his old Eiderscutum overcoat *which I have carried all over the Americas, but never worn it, but the moths have used it as a larder, and eaten quite a lot of it... It would cost 50 pounds to buy the same thing today in England, as it came from Aquascutum in Regent Street.*

Also he describes a letter received from Wilfred Price in Bogota, written *a week before the tumult... .*[53] *I wrote back straightaway to find out if they were alright.* Wilfred again, the dapper chap posing in a photo from Sam's trip to Colombia in 1935 it is assumed. Of course I am left in the dark as to who "They" are; did my father know?

*I cannot make up my mind if the troublemakers were Fascists or Communists, and perhaps both were in it,* Sam reports, while admitting to getting a lot of fun out of the whole political farce. *It looks like fascist work to me... You will see that in Argentina the main instigator, with its fascist crowd, are stirring*

297

*trouble for themselves in JOE-BROWNING the South American Colonies in South American countries, as also the Falkland Islands. Joe Brown is of course the U.S. comedian with the big mouth.*[54] *We should blow all the Spanish heirs of Spain to Hell, as we did at Trafalgar. I cannot see what rights the Franco lot have in these parts at all. They rebelled against Spain, declared Independence, and now call Spain the Mother Country, which they love so much, murdering at the same time as many natives as they could... We have as much right to it as they have.*

The trip in late May is off, having too many bits and pieces to do. *My visit is postponed until next year, unless I get restless, and make a dash about September...* Busy with woollen and cotton goods and Excelsior motorbikes, he is at a crossroads with bicycles, but still hoping to sell *a minimum of 5,000 this year.* He is fit but still limping with spasmodic rheumatism, but always finds that a trip over to Montevideo cheers him up. *This time, I had to return by steamer, as the sea was too rough for the plane to rise on the surface of the water...* Being Sunday he is off for a stroll along the sea front, before lunch, then *after a* siesta, *will go to the British Hospital, to visit a sick man.*

He adds a second page soon after, pointing out uncertainties in the future. *There is a lot of intrigue against Great Britain from this country, especially as regards trade, which Argentina is endeavouring to fully control, both import and export, and I suppose eventually the result will be a bust up. Uruguay is better, but of course a much smaller market. There are controls there also with import permits difficult to control.*

Poor Sam. Having changed his mind yet again about making the Atlantic crossing, he is juggling bookings on various ships while packed ready for any availability that comes his way. He worries about his wife, who has been ill, noting slyly that *she is lucky to have her children to look after her.* He likes the sound of my father's garden: *I am longing for some good cabbage, which we don't see here.* His own gesture towards growing things consists of two *macetas, or fancy, large (very large) plant stands, which I have on the balcony...* He is sorry to hear I have been out of sorts, but is quite sure I will be back at school soon. Of my sister he writes: *I can quite understand why Bridget does not worry, and her looks in the photograph show this quite clearly.* His only other news is of stamps, which my father collects. From where? Japan of all places. *This very day I received a letter from Browns House in Tokio* (concerning bicycle accessories) *and I enclose the stamps which are something out of the ordinary, as very few Japanese stamps are as yet coming along.*

My father obviously takes his time to reply, because at the end of July Sam fires back: *I WAS BEGINNING TO THINK YOU HAD EMIGRATED.* He apologises for any typing errors, but it seems that in the first week of July, walking along Calle Canglaao (sic), *a private motor car mounted the pavement and skittled me out.* His left arm is now in plaster, with a double fracture of the elbow. It must have been a nasty break, because the bones had to be screwed together. He has to return to the British Hospital – ironic that so soon after being a visitor to the sick he is now the patient – to have the screw removed and begin rehabilitation. The most difficult thing is to dress. *My tie and left shoelace give me the most trouble and in the morning I roam all over the hotel trying to find someone to help me out.* He is sorry that he will have to leave the subject of bikes (as gifts for Bridget and me) for the moment. In the meantime he encloses 10 pounds *WHICH WILL NO DOUBT COME IN USEFUL.* It is at times like this that I really admire the old bugger. Self-pity has largely gone by the board and he seems genuinely to be trying in his own characteristic self-centred way to be as helpful and generous as possible.

By autumn he is on the mend, and greatly pleased to be able to report that he just fixed his own tie for the first time since the accident. *I feel as proud as Punch... my spirits rose 50%.* He is delighted also to hear of *happy family picnics*, and recalls being in Leamington, Warwick and Stratford two years previously. *What glorious country!* He wonders if Barney is being faithful to his mother, and hopes Betty is keeping in good touch, Catherine too. Also he is especially pleased to have received a letter from me. *I shall compose a few lines to her and hope some time or another she will write again to say what the cockerel tasted like out of the pot.* Tomorrow he goes to the Uruguayan port of Colonia *and thence by omnibus about 100 miles to Montevideo.*

Colonia, I ponder. And look it up on the map. It is time to start thinking about Uruguay – the next – and final – stage of my odyssey, and I have to time it perfectly in order to be there on the right day.

For now, however, having turned back the clock, best to take the opportunity to catch up with my own family in postwar Britain.

My father had escaped the draft until the very last months of the conflict when the authorities were getting desperate for manpower – a final sweep for military fodder. Enlisted into the navy, he was ordered to Devonport, to join HMS *Demetrius,* and through one of Sam's letters I know he was there in early 1946. Appointed Purser, a below-decks-desk-job in deference to his advanced age (thirty-four), a photo of the crew shows him standing to one side, as scrawny and gangling as ever but also a bit sheepish, as if embarrassed by the comparative youth of his crewmates. I don't remember him leaving us, his absence, nor indeed his return. I have only my mother's word for standing on the window ledge of the back bedroom and seeing him striding across the fields at the back of Ranulf Croft (in those days we were right on the edge of countryside), kit bag slung over his shoulder. This gap in memory is interesting surely; I was well on my way to turning five and can remember any number of other things.

Life cannot have been easy. But I think we were protected to a large degree. We had good neighbours – Welsh Florence and her suave husband Reg to one side (the house beyond their own flattened by a bomb but later rebuilt in similar style), though my parents seemed to think Flo a little odd. Also the Bell family, who lived on the other side of the croft, with blonde daughters... Mr Bell was the local grocer who brought supplies in a box once a week; my mother would write a list, which I would often pop through their letterbox. The Starks (who lived next to the Bells) were interesting... Mrs Stark lived alone with a teenage daughter whom my parents regarded as "fast" (which in those days meant promiscuous though I never saw any hint, let alone proof). The Hammonds had a daughter of my age; Gillian and I lost touch when she got into grammar school, became close again in later years, and then drifted apart again. There were other young people too: the boy whose hair turned white in his late teens, the Smiths – bullying twins whom I feared. And the Palmers: a warm, tumbling, noisy lot that I was discouraged from associating with because they and their children were deemed Common. My parents obviously saw themselves as a cut above the rest in social standing, though if the truth were told we were poorer than most, in love and money. Not that my mother and father did not love us; I know for sure they did. But it was a desperate conditional type of love founded on their own losses of the past and fears for the future.

Our only regular visitors – those that I can remember – were my godmother, and Eric and Kathleen who would come by car to scoop me up to take me back to Stourbridge as company for Alison. A mysterious elderly woman known only as Auntie Winnie – some distant cousin on my mother's side. Oh, and Granny.

When I think back now, I consider my grandmother to have been a major influence on my mother who, as she herself became older, took on the role of Sweet Little Lavender Lady (while concealing a spine of steel and a Masters degree in manipulation). This is how I remember Sarah Primrose, always appearing so soft and sweet with her white hair caught back in a simple twist and a hair band, but inside as tough as old boots. She must have known that she projected mixed messages, causing much upset, because her letters inevitably concluded, *from Your Nice Old Primrose*, or *Dear Old Primrose*, as if trying to convince us (and herself) that there was a gentle soul beyond the critical face she so often turned towards family members. It was a pity she did not look inside herself for answers concerning Life and Death and the Great Beyond; instead she sought solutions in books, seemingly incomprehensible tracts concerning mysticism, the occult and science.

I remember thinking her Very Very Clever to be studying higher mathematics in her eighties, but also feeling Very Very Afraid: not only of that very cleverness, but the relentless attacks against her absent husband, a clear disappointment with my father, and her much-voiced disapproval of me and the way in which I was being brought up. For one thing, she would have liked me to go to a school based on anthroposophical principles, not the State's idea of education. As Rudolf Steiner once wrote: "We shouldn't ask: what does a person need to know or be able to do in order to fit into the existing social order? Instead we should ask: what lives in each human being and what can be developed in him or her?"

It is not clear in which year Sarah left Liverpool. But when her younger daughter left Sunfield, they moved together to Gloucestershire. Betty had a job teaching at Wynstones, a Steiner Waldorf school based in another fine stately home, Whaddon Manor.

Wynstones was the second school to be opened in the UK. Sunfield may have been the first Special Needs home founded in Steiner's name, but it was not the first educational establishment. This position is claimed by Michael Hall, the first English-speaking Steiner Waldorf school in the world, which opened in East Sussex in 1925. In 1936–1937, Michael Hall held its first teacher-training course, and I am thinking (since records do not appear to have been kept) that maybe Betty was one of its graduates. Wynstones opened in the Cotswolds in late September 1937, and one term into the academic year, two young teachers joined the staff: Renate Talmon-Gros, responsible for Handwork and the anthroposophical dance form Eurythmy, and Elizabeth Loader, Gym and Riding. Where or how my aunt had learned to ride I have no idea, but there you are. Miss Loader (reads page 3 of a published record: *21 Years at Wynstones School*) became a class teacher and remained for many years: a most gifted and artistic member of the College.

The war years were not easy for Steiner establishments, with local people and the authorities deeply suspicious of any links with Germany.

But in 1946, another Steiner school, Elmfield, opened at the far end of Love Lane (where Eric and Kathleen and my cousin had their home) in Stourbridge, just a few miles from Clent. When Alison was enrolled, I could only stand back in envy (a ruling characteristic of my personality), because her parents were relatively well-off – Eric was CEO of the company producing electricity for the Midlands – and my own were not. So that was that. Instead – much against my grandmother's wishes, but then she had no money either – I went to what was then known as Green Lane Primary School, the far side of Stivichall. It was down along a green lane, which amazingly still is! Green, that is. Anyway, here I did well enough – in reading and writing at least – to be moved up a year ahead of my actual age, give assistance to the school choir with the soprano voice I had inherited from my mother, and help found the school orchestra with a descant recorder.

But back to Betty at Wynstones, where my grandmother was employed as Matron to the boarders. During that time, many letters passed between my father, his sister and their mother. Only a few have survived, but it is easy to read between the lines. My grandmother was "difficult". When asked about Primrose – an unforgiving bully disguised as a sweetly fragile old lady – my mother will only say vaguely, Oh, she was nice. But Betty – who was far more grounded and honest (with herself as well as others) – had to bear the brunt of her mother's moods and manipulations, and often came close to tearing out her lovely fine, fair hair.

Over the years, my grandmother covered innumerable small sheets of plain notepaper in a largely illegible loopy scrawl. In June, 1946 (the earliest communication I can find) she informs my father that Catherine is back in Edinburgh, Rachel (a sister, cousin, friend?) is much better, and Betty's name is now Mrs John Elwell, address Michael Hall, Kidbrook Park, Forest Row, Sussex: *Cath likes him, she writes; And I'm sure you will…* Then somewhere buried in all this, the seemingly casual enquiry: *Have you heard from Ted* (her name for her long-absent husband) *again?*

Ten days later, she writes once more, describing a midsummer festival at Wynstones, With fire and singing. She plans to go to Michael Hall, *For the official opening of their new place*, then go to see my mother, *And the two babes!* She is having difficulty spelling with her pen (I have to smile here) and writing is hard because, *My hands are awful.*

Two years later, in mid-summer 1947, Betty is writing to my father from Michael Hall to explain a previously sent urgent telegram: *Mother must leave Wynstones as she is getting really ill...*the Wynstones people have written to me saying they can no longer accept the responsibility for her.

She plans to bring Sarah down to Sussex when she and her husband have found a place, and in the meantime suggests that my grandmother stays in a guesthouse near the school, which she must leave by September. Betty is cross with her brother Barney, settled back in Liverpool, whose reply to a letter on the subject she describes as impertinent: *He seems to refute my observation of the facts of the case as a responsible authority; his answer to the matter seems to be to put the entire responsibility for Mother on to Catherine as, to quote him, She has the least other responsibilities and here lies the solution.*

*Unfair*, says Betty; *impractical too*, as she knows her mother would never go to Edinburgh: *The Weather for one thing!* Anyway, my aunt does not consider that differences of age or sex determine any degree of responsibility, and tells her brother so. Better that all four siblings share financial responsibility, adding: *For my part I am only willing to pay one pounds to ten shillings a week, though I might say I earn only 230 pounds a year and John is at Oxford* (University) *on an army grant! Catherine is ready to contribute 30 shillings a week, and if my father can help, I am prepared to meet the expenses of the Guest House.*

Always fair and solicitous, Betty speaks supportively of her elder sister: *Catherine is not as well off as Barney seems to think, and in any case, not being married and having the society and joy of a home, she needs the little extras in life.*

Betty pleads with my father to help fix something up for their mother within the next two weeks, ahead of consulting her: *She is really very fragile indeed and believe me, I am convinced her health is in a serious state. I think she has some illness of wasting of muscles disease, and if it isn't dealt with soon will need a nursing home (much more expensive!)*

Fragile? Excuse me while I snort disbelief. My grandmother was to live many more years, and never struck me as being seriously sick in any way whatsoever. But how am I to know.

In 1949, writing from Kingston Road in Oxford, Betty is again writing to my father, and this time it is her husband who is ill: *Possibly cooking for a flu, but I think he is just tired and rather tense about his exams in the coming term. Now, about Mother...*

Sarah has been living in Bath, and whoever is caring for her, no longer wants the job. Betty is trying to get her into the New Nursing Home in Stroud – maybe another Steiner institution, most certainly one run according to anthroposophical principles. Betty adds: *Dr Glas (the woman in charge) has a knack with her.*

*I'm so tired of all this,* Betty continues; *The best I can think is we fix her permanently at the Nursing Home and have her to stay with us as often as possible. But I can't have her as a fixture with us... we are unsettled (there are plans to return to Sussex if John cannot find a job roundabout after he has graduated) and I have had two miscarriages, the last very serious, brought on entirely by worry about her; it's not fair to John. Mother* (her continual grousing) *just makes me ill, and John has to bear the brunt of it all.*

Money continues to be a problem: *Catherine has been very good and I've used all the money I saved at Michael Hall to buy* (Sarah) *clothes she needed. I heard from Mother that Father was coming to England again in July. I would like to meet him. Can you arrange it for me? Is there any hope of his helping support her... do you think it's possible for me to talk to him about it. By the way, I rather like him. I'm sure he isn't as bad as he's been painted... tell me what you think. Did he like us, or didn't he say?*

For sure Sam/Ted loved, even liked his children – what he knew of them, that is. But did my own father ever pass on that simple and clear message to his brother and sisters? Remembering my father's inhibited and repressed character, I'm not sure he ever did. Which in large part is why I am here, in this city, this country, right now.

## NOVEMBER 20, 1999

Information given in my grandfather's first letter of Spring 1949 meshes with the one Betty wrote to my father in the March. Sam is glad my family went to Bath to see Sal and quite understands her being lonely. But at least she has the chance to go stay with family for variety and new views. *My lone sojourn is permanent, but make the best of it.*

He is sorry there has been sickness in the family, and recalls his sisters all having whooping cough when he was around ten, *which I escaped and was sent to my cousins, the Crawfords, to stay with them about a month, and had the time of my life. And that,* he adds cheerfully, *is all I know about whooping cough!*

Grumbles about business still being slow apart, the only news of any import is that, *The bicycle will be delivered to Angela about the second week in May, and will be sent from Messrs F. HOPPER and Co. Ltd, BARTON-on-HUMBER. Carriage Paid, etc., with Lamp, Bell, Pump etc. It will be 20" frame, with 22" wheels. If you want 24" wheels please inform me at once.*

And suddenly, for no reason at all (other than to answer his daughter's painfully sad question about parental love) and after a strings of *XXXX* for kisses to me and my sister, he signs off *GRAN DADDY SAMMY.* (In fact he signed it *GRAND.* but struck off the *D* with another *X.*)

Seeing the name Crawford provides a relative focus to my day; what am I going to do about hunting down all these cousins that fifty years ago seemed to litter Argentina – and if we take Wilfred Price into consideration, other parts of South America too. To assist my brain in concentrating along such a track, I take the train and go for a walk. Pure escapism, of course.

Remember Sam promenading the sea front? Okay, I'll try to follow in his footsteps, passing through Madero towards the estuary to find the old municipal bathing resort. But negotiating the dockland complex of canals and bridges and locks to Costa Nesta Sur is no mean feat... There is so much construction, pounding pneumatic drills, dust, and it's hot, hot, hot. I find a coastal road of sorts, but still I am nowhere near anything remotely resembling a beach; rather a marshy wetland pool with ducks and herons foraging among reeds and water lilies. Still, the open view of water is pleasant, with a raft for swimming, and a waterfall. Was this it?

Then ahead, I see a fountain – encaged in scaffolding for renovation, but wonderful all the same. Carved in white marble, Neredias is a positive orgy of voluptuous naked sea nymphs, a celebration of the sacred feminine, no holds barred. Designed by Lola, the nickname of Dolores Mora (1866–1936) who hailed from Tucaman, the sculptor/tress had made waves at the turn of the century with an impassioned depiction of joyous sexual freedom (all entwined limbs and spouting conches). As one report reads: "(It) caused consternation in the quiet timid society of Buenos Aires due to audacity of its theme and the realism of its execution."

Good for you Lola, I cheer, and move on.

Sore feet temporarily forgotten, I head back towards the city, flanked by innumerable casinos. Did Sam ever drop in for a flutter, I wonder, turning left towards the old port. Faced with a gigantic rusting crane that frames the view like some monstrous desiccated insect, marooned at the end of a track that cuts across the road, I cut inland to make the walk less post-industrial. Entering a residential area of old houses and tiny green parks shaded with ancient trees, I turn a corner, and am stopped in my own tracks.

Buildings are painted in a riot of colour combinations, but gently weathered. Here, lower walls are painted ochre, with dark blue and sky blue doors, windows framed in red, and a thick red line painted horizontally to differentiate the ground floor from the apartment upstairs. There, lemon yellow, with green awnings, and a metre-wide band around the top of the flat-roofed building decorated with triangles that link the overall colour scheme.

On another block, each family has painted its own outside wall a different colour: bright yellow above white; to one side grey, and above orange; the other direction, chocolate brown and sky blue. It is original, lovely and I am charmed. My eyes then take a break by focusing on a white cat sitting on a white stone doorstep before a white painted door in a whitewashed wall – all slightly grubby but what the charismatic hell. I have reached the outskirts of La Boca (literally *the mouth*, or *entrance*).

Between 1880 and 1930, with the country flush with wealth and confidence, Buenos Aires was rebuilt, with old colonial one-storey buildings and narrow streets swept away to make place for wide, tree-lined boulevards, parks, and buildings inspired by Italian and French architecture. (This was the period when the French quotation "As rich as an Argentine" came into common use.) Only La Boca survived to allow any comparison of old and new. Around the city's original harbour, the main stretch of decoratively painted homes – Caminito – is full of artists hawking their work, most of it predictable in being nearly 100-per-cent tango-orientated. For this is the area where Argentina's most famed dance form is said to have originated. Guidebooks (and others) tend to take the easy way out by explaining its birth as a blending of sailor's dance with Genoese dance tunes played on a German accordion. There is of course a lot more to it.

The Viennese Waltz was the first dance that involved what was called "A Close Hold". When first demonstrated in or around 1850, it caused a scandal in Europe.

In Buenos Aires, couples began to first dance together in the late 1800s in bars, cafes, gambling houses and *quilombos* (brothels). Lonely sailors deprived of female company took the dance to new levels of physical desire, and lyrics of songs of the period were full of references to sex and obscenity. A favourite ballad, *El Choco*, meaning corncob, was a direct phallic allusion. As for men from so-called Respectable Families, they had no option than to dance with other men! (There is no record of what the women were up to, one with another. Though for sure Lola and her nymphs could have told us. )

The next phase of the tango saw it adapted by the thousands of immigrant families from mostly Italy and Spain living in the areas of boarding houses in La Boca and St Telmo called *conventillos*. These were open areas bordered by rooms and kitchens with shared toilet facilities. It was here, taken up for weddings, christenings and other festive occasions, that the dance became "purified of sinful moves". Among low-lifers, however, the tango, as it was called, was still, "The bastard son of pimps and prostitutes, dressed like a poor *compadrito...*" It was also full of *lunfardo* expressions – an in-house language; jargon more like – that developed within the confines of prison. By this time the tango had inspired a whole vocabulary of its own: *pista*, for dance floor; *abrazo*, meaning to embrace; *sandwicho* (a favourite of mine, since it sounds like the Japanese loanword for sandwich) but which in this case referred to one dancer's foot being sandwiched between those of their partner.

In early 1906 the singer Saborida sold one hundred thousand copies of sheet music for his tango, *Yo soy la maracho* (I am a brunette). After Flora Rodriquez recorded it, first on disc, from where it was transferred to cylinder and then paper rolls played on pianolas, the tango spread into most homes, becoming Acceptable.

Where did the word tango come from? Well, there was a dance that existed in South America long before the tango came along – the *milonga*. Nowadays this word equally can mean an establishment where the tango is danced; fanatics tour the *milonqueros* (*milongas*). The most likely explanation is that in its etymology *milonga* derives from the African expression *mulonga*, meaning *word*. Among tribes from the Congo, Gulf of Guinea and Southern Sudan, tango referred to an enclosed space, circle, or a private place which required permission to enter. Since slave traders called the places where slaves were held tangos, and this was both in Africa and in the Americas, it is easy to understand how the word came to mean any place where blacks gathered to dance and drum, and later the name of the dance itself. Maybe.

By the time I reach Caminito, I am as much attuned to startling theories as colour theory, about which (thanks to my mother) I know something. But this is tourist stuff, and I take the new paint and carefully designed geometrics at face value, with a pinch of sea salt. Yet this is where the art form took off, so I swallow any scepticism and make my way along the main drag, down the centre of which a rail track used to run. Now it is paved over, and a mecca for artists to sell equally gaudy and fanciful work to visitors.

This is where the painter Quinquela Martin stood and had the bright idea to enliven the homes of the poor backing the railway to either side, clad as the buildings were in rough and ready jigsaw patterns of rusting corrugated iron. The resulting colour schemes ran riot. (He also had the seats of the nearby Teatro de la Rivera painted in different colours, where I learn Tom Stoppard's *Travesties* played for four nights in 1974.) A photograph of the period shows Martin wearing what appears to be a very sombre outfit for one so joyously and eccentrically-inclined: dark suit, white shirt and black hat, posing roughly where I am standing now. But then it is from a black and white print, and a photo-copy at that.

At the end of the street I turn left and find myself amid a wide expansive tangle of rusting rail tracks. It was along here, at the peak of Argentina's prosperity, that the non-stop flow of cargo trains used to carry meat and grain for export from the heart of the *pampa*. The contrast of a powerful industrial past at the end of the road (in every sense) with the street of artists could not be more vivid, nor more heart breaking. Like the port of Liverpool at its lowest economic ebb, this once thriving area is now dependent on handouts, with pockets of tourism to service the notion of redevelopment.

With money in my purse again and happy to be taken for a sucker, I had decided earlier to buy a painting – a couple dancing (black and grey, white and red, very slick) – but later, on my way back. Mistake. By the time I return, having taken far too long in a bookshop (buying postcards, checking through second-hand titles) it is being wrapped for two Japanese girls. And while kicking myself, I really should not be surprised. Just days before I had been told in the Tourist Information Office of plane-loads of Japanese tango fans booking for five days (and four nights) of lessons and guided tours of *milonga* clubs and cafes. No wonder I have been picking up business cards for sushi bars and noodle shops!

Soon enough I come to understand why that painting was not for me. Because turning around, I come face-to-face with Celeste. She is small, and far from young, with a mop of salt and pepper hair held in check with a headband. Bright blue eyes twinkle quizzically from a face weathered to the colour and texture of old cow-hide and creased with smiles. Fizzing with energy, she offers me a card painted with a snake logo, and I point at this and then myself, saying Me too; I'm also a snake. I write 1941; she writes 1929, and we share a good laugh. There are twelve years of the zodiac between us and we both know our Chinese calendars.[55]

We communicate in an inarticulate but perfectly comprehensible kind of way, and I buy three small paintings: a *bandoneon* player, the entrance to a bar, and a portrait of a small black girl with plaits standing out like a halo around her head. (For George, without question.) The style is naive but full of vigour, the colours sensitive and vibrant. As an artist, she knows what she's about.

Celeste, I learn from a leaflet in Spanish, was born in Paysando in Uruguay. She had her first exhibition in Montevideo in 1956, and came to live in Buenos Aires in 1969. She is especially interested in religious themes, also memories of the city's once lively African community drumming and dancing – in tangos! Pragmatically, she paints what will sell to make a living. Sensible, I think, and kiss her cheeks in Spanish style to say goodbye. We are delighted with one another – I love her work, she is apparently more than happy to pocket my 35 pesos. A great exchange.

Flushed with success and a sense of adventure (which tends to inflate my ego to such an extent that I think I am invincible and can go where I please in complete safety), I make another detour. This leads not back to the main coast road and that impossible-to-miss signpost of a crane, but into a slightly intimidating wasteland of warehouses and blank-faced business premises. Ahead, a fluttering dance of pale blue and yellow catches my eye: a shop spilling souvenir goods onto the pavement, and opposite, across the other side of the road, a tantalising glimpse (between two buildings) of the corner of a stadium, and those colours again: geometrics of pale blue and yellow, on concrete.

Consulting the map I realise I have stumbled onto the home ground of Argentina's most famous football team (outside the national line-up, that is): Boca Juniors.[56] Rifling through fan-club memorabilia, a hat proves tempting, designed like a medieval jester's cap but with the ends knotted rather than hung with bells. But who to buy it for? Santiago is too young; nor do I have any nieces or nephews of the right age. And for the first time ever I feel a small but distinct pang: I would not mind being a grandmother.

Consulting the front page of today's newspaper on the bus back to El Centro, ostensibly to check the date, I see: "Britain Amazed: Blairs' Pregnant". Far more worrying is the report that none of Argentina's five traffic control radar systems are Y2K – Year 2000 – compliant. The scare tactics of the media at large seem set to make us not simply afraid, but very afraid indeed, as if some unsubtle globalisation of terror is underway.

Drawing out of Retiro, I am more happily reminded of my Lovers of the Day project as a couple emerge from a railway carriage abandoned in a siding. Hand-in-hand, with sweet shy smiles and distinctly crumpled, it is clearly obvious what they have been up to.

Oh, I think: such days are past and, on reaching Caseros, eat in a local restaurant to cheer myself up. Being a Saturday there is a birthday party in progress, but despite being alone, I do not feel lonely; after all, I have my emotional twin-self for company. When I finally reach home (as I have come to think of it), there are stuffed tomatoes for supper. Maria-Elena made them for lunch but I never turned up. Guilt pushes me back into regret. The realisation – that I have had my chance, had my family – comes as an aftershock to unexpected broodiness, grandmotherly notions inspired by Santiago's better moments. I sense a sudden unexpected regret of the past and dread for the future: youth to middle age flown; another step towards the grave.

# CHAPTER 20

# TOWARDS THE GRAVE

**NOVEMBER 20, 1999 CONTINUED**

Last night, Tarzan drank a *salut* to the Land of the Rising Sun, to which I responded with a *salut* to the sun rising over Argentina – and as speedily as possible, please. Maria-Elena clapped and said *Claro* (a favourite word of agreement in her vocabulary). After which Julio and Santiago took me back to their flat, to wait for Paula's return. Filled with primary-coloured plastic toys and soft Disney characters, it was the light, bright place I remembered, but small, and with few signs of adult interests and pleasures.

I'm desperate to move, Julito said. And from the balcony gestured into darkness, towards the lights of central Caseros, whilst explaining that there was a site down there he was thinking to buy. Measuring eight metres by thirty-five metres, it was on sale for 45,000 pesos.

My parents have two apartments in my name, he said thoughtfully; I'll sell them both to purchase the land. To build a house though I'll have to go for broke.

When Paula returned, she began to prepare a meal. It never seemed to cross her husband's mind that he could have started to cook; rather he was much more interested in my adventures – in his eyes an ongoing Comedy of Errors. This time, he was amused to hear that today I had missed the stop at Caseros and gone hurtling on to Hurlingham, where I had found myself on the return platform amid a sea of beautiful boys, all being trained to kill people at the nearby College Militaria de Nacion.

What were you doing, he asked; Dreaming?

Noting down graffiti, I replied.

Like what, he asked again, now totally bemused.

So I read out my list, starting with *Grunge Trio*... and soon after, *Iron Maiden, How About You?*

He looked even more baffled; Go on...

*Einstein, La Renga; Becinos Rock; Chacarita Puco Boca Tapo; Mario, Juan, Victor, Loro* (four names); *Chaos* (besides a man's toilet); *Snoopy People* (which might sound funny in North America but not in Japan); *Novutar Resistianca Luta; Platense Puto*; and that familiar refrain everywhere I go, *Argentina Desperado*.

Julito pulled a face and gave me an odd look. An even odder look passed across his features as he gazed at his wife's backside in the kitchen. And I remembered Maria-Elena telling me how she had picked out Paula for her first-born son. It appears that while she was at college, Paula Fernandez Romero participated in a TV show, which involved students competing in teams. At one point, to demonstrate her team's extraordinary wealth of talent, Paula played the piano; she was studying music with the idea of becoming a concert pianist. The Bustamante family was at home, watching the show, and Maria-Elena swiftly became infatuated with the pretty pale-skinned girl with long red hair who showed such proficiency. Since Julito was attending the same college, she asked if he knew Paula, and told him he should invite her out on a date. (Pablo says this is normal behaviour for Argentine mums; they like to do the choosing!) After that, Maria-Elena would not/could not let the matter lie. She nagged on until poor Julito befriended Paula to keep his mother quiet. Time took care of the rest.

Inspired by that wonderful statue of yesterday, I'm off to find LOLA – nothing to do with anarchic architecture, but the abbreviation of Literature of Latin America. It's at Viamonte 976, and is run by an Englishman – Colin Sharp, whose name was given to me long ago (or so it now seems) by Rosemary Morton. Pressing the well-polished brass button, a woman snaps back in Spanish. I begin to speak in English and the front door swings opens with an equally irritable automatic buzz. I climb up the winding stairs and again have to gain access through a secure door. I hear heels click-clicking across the floor to let me in, and determine to keep up a brave front in the face of language deficiency.

She is formidable. Dark-skinned, dark-eyed, dark-haired, her grim face says it all: I have no time for you. The words that follow are similar in meaning, I guess, because having explained that I want to find out about the British Cemetery, she sinks out of sight. Helpful, I think; what a great way to run a business! But then she rises up again from behind the desk, and hands me a phone. Alfonsin, she announces rather than introduces.

Alfonsin not only speaks English; he has written a book about the earliest graves in the British Cemetery, dating from 1812. But this is not the period in which I'm most interested. While Tarzan and Maria-Elena were still sleeping this morning, and even before Marta arrived at seven-thirty, I had snuck into the good doctor's clinic and run through the city's telephone directory listings. I was looking for the names of Sam's elusive cousins: Crawford, Lee and so on, and Crawfords I found: Elsa, Louisa, Maudio and Raquel, at four different addresses. The greatest surprise, however, was Cook, which I had looked up with secondary interest, because while not a relative, Horacio C. had worked closely with Sam for a number of years. Twenty-three Cooks were listed, and one – you could have knocked me down with a feather – was named in clone-like fashion: Horacio M. Cook, with an address on Ayakucho. Now there was a phone number – one that I scribbled down with both alacrity and a distinct sense of deja vu!

As I look through Alfonsin's book – which is amazingly interesting but not especially relevant – the gorgon behind the desk waves the phone again: *Senor Sharp.*

LOLA's owner and inspiration introduces him self in clipped but dulcet English tones and asks how he can help. With regards to seeking help from the Embassy, he thinks I won't get much support; But they do have ledgers in which people have signed in over the years, and you should ask to see them.

He informs me also that he – LOLA – is about to republish a book about the British in Buenos Aires called *The Forgotten Colony*, and that if I come next week, I should be able to see a copy hot off the press.

We sold out during the Falkland crisis, he explains; And then we had great difficult in getting permission from the English publisher, Hutchinson in order to reprint. It's by Andrew Graham-Yool of the Buenos Aires Herald; maybe you've come across him?

Indeed. And here is his name on a set of proofs proffered by Colin's gruff but – I now must accept with a softening of my own heart – exceedingly helpful assistant.

*Gracias*, I manage to mutter; *Muchos Gracias*. To which I detect a hint of a smile. I tell her also that I will be back, because LOLA has wonderful first editions, by Hudson and others... But a dismissive wave of the hand suggests that on this occasion at least, my time is up.

At my (by now, regular) internet cafe, the cute curly-haired owner Luis and I get talking. Appearing a basic racial mix of Spanish and native South American (*mestisto*), he has the uncommon privilege of Murray as a surname: I think one of my grandfathers was Irish.

His family lives in Mendoza – another coincidence – and he left home in 1996. Now he feels he can't go back, because everyone he knows is married and everyone has changed, including himself. We shake hands on this.

In a wine shop nearby, I find a bottle labelled Aberdeen Angus, bottled by Finca Flitchman in Barancas, Maipu, Mendoza, and with a picture of a prime specimen – a cow or a bull, on the label. It reminds me of a story in family lore of when my aunt Jo was first married: her husband bought a prize Aberdeen Angus bull for stud on his estate. But the silly thing, being top-heavy and muscle-bound, fell over into a puddle and drowned. My Uncle Charles – the kindest and sweetest of gentle men, but not a business man – nor it seems forty-years down the line, much of a farmer.

I buy a paper and see that the headline has Menem wrapping up his last visit to Europe as a head-of-state. Inside there is an article about Argentina exporting Aberdeen Angus embryos to Scotland. This coincidence also does not escape my notice.

Seeking to satisfy a long-standing desire to visit one of Sam's regular haunts (he used to go there after sea-wall walks) I find the Confiteria Ideal at Suipacha 384 in San Nicholas fallen on hard times. Built in 1912, the exterior is fabulous, the lower part in marble, the first floor a row of arching windows either swagged with garlands or in unusual semi-circular bows of fine glass, and with the French fleur de lys a predominant logo. It's mostly in white stucco and very fancy, like an over-the-top wedding cake.

Inside, though, I am brought to a disappointed full stop. It is cavernous, grungy and near empty. The long bar is vacant and ghostly. Mirrors are, without exception, spotted and pitted with age. Likewise the waiters who look half dead on their feet. Once the Ideal must have been just that: perfection. Now it's eighty years old and, if someone does not resuscitate the patient very soon, the end is surely nigh.

Sitting near a pillar so as to keep watch on the entrance, I become aware of a young couple nearby. He looks like Julito, a handsome be-suited young businessman, quite possibly also a lawyer but maybe a banker. She is petite and could be Spanish or even Indian – an Indian from India, that is. Seeing me looking at her, she blushes, looks furtive and whispers to her companion. They continue doing whatever they are doing, but self-consciously. Which makes me wonder what on earth is going on, because she appears to be giving him an English lesson, and her accent sounds more than a little familiar. She's just asked her student in a rather long and convoluted sentence to recall a happy day spent

318

in London and unsurprisingly he's gone completely blank. Simplify, I think, simplify...

A waiter as old as Methuselah and eons of centuries grumpier than LOLA's book seller, lurches towards me; he looks ready to collapse, and so will I if I don't get some food in my stomach pronto. It's producing acid at unprecedented levels; I'm stinging with heartburn and coughing again. I order prawns, and then wish I hadn't but don't dare summon him back. Maybe the snail pace service is supposed to be charming? The tourists who keep popping in through the main door to take a cheeky snap seem to think so.

When her student leaves, the woman – pretty, vivacious, short dark hair – takes a deep breath and approaches.

Are you from Immigration?

I look up at her, stunned – what Andy in Liverpool would call gobsmacked: What, me? Do I *look* as if I'm Immigration?

Well you could be, she backed off; You might be in disguise.

I burst out laughing and tell her to sit down, have a glass of wine, or something. With luck you may get it by early evening, I mutter unkindly, as Ancient Waiter dumps down a salad with no grace or favour whatsoever.

Karen was born in Muswell Hill in North London to Anglo-Indian Catholic parents, and she's been traveling for a decade. She met an Argentine guy in Thailand, with whom she stayed friends for several years but then they lost contact. When she met him again in Rome in 1997, on her way back to Australia where she had lived for a year and a half, he had moved back to Buenos Aires.

Basically, she explained, He invited me to go and take a look before I went back Downunder. So I came for three months and here I am still. But I'm going home for Christmas, and one reason, apart from seeing my family, is to go on to India. I've been there three times and it's my favourite country. From the UK it's cheap to fly, but not from here.

When she first arrived in Argentina, Karen cried for two weeks. The first week was for Lady Diana, when she died: I saw her once. She came to Planet Hollywood where I was working, and when she smiled, you melted. I loved her. I went to the Embassy here when I heard the news; I needed to cry with the people of England.

And the second week?

I cried for Mother Theresa. (When she died!)

We talk about how both women, with strong personal agendas, had manufactured and manipulated images to their own ends.

Never mind, says Karen cheerfully; Cherie Blair is pregnant. There'll be a baby in No. 10 (Downing Street) for the first time in one hundred and fifty years. I think that's lovely.

When I tell her that I'm going to Uruguay on Wednesday, she gets excited: Oh, you must go to Colonia, that's lovely too!.

I tell her my story (in an ever briefer nutshell), explaining that that I still have so much work to do because to date I haven't had much luck at the Embassy, where it turns out she has friends. Told I am trying to find family records, she pulls a face: So much disappeared during the dictatorship, you know.

Karen and I talk for well over an hour; she has another class coming up so she can't stay longer. It's a joy to be with someone who knows better where I coming from, culturally, and with whom I share in a common language. At age twenty-five, working as a finance manager in the restaurant trade in London, she was shocked to be out at dinner socially with a group of Australians and feel so out of the conversation.

I'd been to Europe and even Egypt, she explains; But in terms of living, surviving, the way they were talking was just so different. I'd decided to travel rather than go to university: the University of Life. Then at age thirty I got engaged and lived in Darlington in the north of England for a year – yuk! Yes, it's true, once you have gained a wider more worldly perspective it's hard to go back and pick up where you left off. Impossible in fact (and especially in Darlington!)

Realising marriage was not the next stage, she travelled through Peru and Bolivia: Stunning!

I tell her (rather to my surprise) how much I want to see Lake Titicaca – the highest landlocked-lake in the world and quite the mystery.

As for this place, Karen says, I love Buenos Aires. I have my own school on Condova Palermo, sponsored by companies. I charge $25 dollars an hour to my rich students, who help sponsor the poorest of the poor who learn English and to draw and paint to help express their feelings and dreams on paper. I have this little house – like a youth centre for kids off the street, where we have no chairs but sit on the floor. One of my very first students now teaches adults, which is really rewarding.

Karen does not reside at this address, however: I live in Belgrano – a lovely place. Calcutta is poor beyond belief but you get there by plane. Here in Buenos Aires, Third World is just around the corner. This makes Argentina Fourth World. It's unique in this way. Here in the centre of this beautiful city I'm in Rome, Madrid, Paris and New York. But as I said, around the corner... it's very easy to remain blind to the poverty and problems. In fact, most people choose to remain blind. It's easier that way.

But the cost of self-delusion is high, she adds; Twenty years on from the Dirty War, people are very depressed within themselves. The women are all anorexic and so disturbed.

All her male friends are gay, she explains: The culture makes it impossible here to have a straight guy as a platonic friend. Once a guy gets a girlfriend, our relationship has to stop; she would see me as competition and not allow it (to continue). In this sense I feel as if I am going backwards, so I tend to hang out with foreigners because they are so much more open and interesting. On the other hand, here I'm political in a way I never was in London. I march and lobby because this country is so divided and human rights a joke. Argentina's history is so sad. You can feel it.

She enjoys teaching, because for one thing it is proof that she can;

she had to teach her self in order to get work. Leaving school at sixteen, she had no qualifications and survived as best she could, dishwashing, waitressing, whatever.

At age thirty-four I had to buy myself a book to study English grammar, she laughs; I hadn't a clue.

It is the work that keeps her here: Rich and poor, all my students are doing well in their own way. One is living with my parents in London, in my very own bedroom; another is elsewhere in the city. A third is going there to study acting. I tell them, go out and live on your own awhile to understand yourself better, because here – in Argentina – you will only get married.

Although she lives in Belgrano (with friends; a home of her own is next on the agenda, when she comes back from India) she hangs out mostly in Palermo, from Paradine down, because this is the heart of the city's gay scene. A lot of straight guys go there for a laugh and regard the women who hang out with gay men as easy lays; They have no respect. Once forty of us went to a restaurant there for my birthday, and at dinner the waiter said he had never served straight and gay people together before, and of so many different nationalities. He'd never felt so, Accepted.

She asks what I am doing tonight, Because I'm going out for dinner with a gay group and you could come along. There's no fag-hag hang-up here; you'll have a good time.

Now I'm the one who feels Accepted; a good feeling, but I find myself surprisingly hesitant. Explaining that I have been warned not travel back to Caseros in the dark, I realise that the protection of Maria-Elena's home, and the family's paranoia is making me more dependent and less confident. This worries me, and despite having been told Uruguay is Very Safe, and being so near the end of my journey, I'm not prepared to take the risk.

So Friday, Karen suggests.

I'll be in Montevideo, I reply, returning Saturday and then I have only three days left to accomplish a miracle.

What kind of miracle, Karen asks.

And I have to admit, I haven't a clue; There's just something fizzing, bubbling away at the back of my mind, like yeast fermenting... a kind of whispering to Keep Going, Not to Stop. It's driving me crazy, crazy... We wish we had met before, but agree with the novitiate wisdom of student travellers that, "That's Life": we're but ships that glide by mid-ocean, usually stopping to wave, more often drawing close enough to pass the time of day, occasionally colliding (as we so nearly did). I suggest that if Karen is in London for Christmas, she call Lee, tell him she met his Mum in Ideal circumstances, maybe even get together for a drink. She seems genuinely enthused at the notion and surely he will be too; he likes bubbly interesting fit young women, and Karen is all of these and more.

For one thing, she is informed. I know now, for example, that from 12.30 p.m. every day, there is a *milonga* upstairs, and anyone is free to go and watch. So that is why people have been dribbling in... not to eat or drink, but dance.

I leave my prawns – decidedly whiffy and not to be trusted – and mount the staircase to the first floor, from where the sound of tango escapes every time the door to the dance hall swings open. No live music; taped. But this makes no difference to those on the floor, dipping and gliding in dignified style. Most of those attending are middle-aged and upwards, though there is a scattering of youth. Around the edges, they sit alone, ever hopeful of a partner or gossiping in-between tracks. Once on the floor, however, there is only serious concentration; no one makes eye contact, let alone speaks. The dancers and the music are somehow at loggerheads; where, I wonder, is the joy, the sheer sensuous pleasure that I feel in watching and listening. I want to dance, but I am an outsider. Which brings me down.

Ten days into 1950, Sam – or granddaddysammy, as now refers to himself – is delighted to have heard from his sister Bea in Wallasley that Betty has made him a grandfather again... *she has brought into the world a strong and hefty daughter, and this has added to my happiness in a selfish kind of way.*

*Please ask her to send a few lines...* On the downside, his sister Gert is now in a nursing home: *She is still very ill and am afraid it will take a long time to get over the stroke that laid her low.*

Still, he notes cheerfully, there is an election coming up in the UK and he trusts for everyone's sakes that Churchill will be returned with a good margin over the Labour party. *It will be a good tonic for trade.* (In the meantime) *I hope you are getting through the winter without too many blowing noses and hot water bottles.* Then he signs off, *With fond love to the chicks...* He writes again on his birthday, having celebrated turning sixty-nine with the habitual hearty breakfast, eaten while reading his usual copy of *La Prensa*, and feeling himself to look very fit *with a new suit, made from cloth brought over from England, a Lovat Tweed, green-blue and not too striking, well made up by an Argentine tailor.*

In February he notes that my mother (who as well as being equally pre-occupied with clothes and teaching dressmaking at Coventry Art School , is also still playing the cello) *is now a member of Halle's Coventry Orchestra, and if you* (my father) *get the fiddle, then we can at least compete with the cats next door, and in the neighbourhood.*

He hopes I am getting on at school, and that *Bridget is setting the Thames on fire with her intellect and wisecracks.* He also wonders how Betty and the new baby are getting on. *You didn't tell me her name. When I come to England next year, I shall of course be in Glasgow, and can see them, as also Bea's daughter's family, and also my sister and her family tribe.*

I know nothing of Bea having a family and grandchildren. Nor these days would I know where to look. But I do know my Aunt Betty's daughter's name, which is a good start: Genevieve.

## NOVEMBER 21, 1999

The house is empty. I am empty. Why do I feel like this when I finished last night on such a positive note? I stay in bed most of the day, getting up only occasionally to roam around, as if trying to prove to myself that I exist, that I'm still alive.

Early evening I make an effort when told that Patricia has arrived. I don't know who Patricia is, but drag a comb through my hair and go downstairs anyway. This much I owe my hosts (plus so much more...)

Later I toss and turn into the small hours.

Patricia, who spoke and taught English, was nice enough, and friendly, but as she looked me up and down, again there was something unspoken. When she asked me whether I liked Argentina, I felt obliged to say something, but what... While waiting for me to reply, she asked what Japan was like.

Well, what is Argentina like, I heard myself snapping back and then hated myself for being so rude and difficult: giving her such a hard time.

Is it arrogance on my part? It's just that her English felt pushy, aggressive somehow. Really, I don't know how to explain... English with attitude, perhaps? Argentine attitude.

**NOVEMBER 22, 1999**

The morning newspaper fills me in about a hijack exercise staged yesterday at Ezeiza International Airport. Also recession-hit Argentina posting an October deficit of 837.7 million pesos, triple the 279.9 million of the previous year and, quote, "Mostly due to heavy public debt interest payments."

On the train, amidst an open discussion about literature, and the work of Borges in particular, I realise I have eight days only remaining to accomplish my mission. I note down the word, because it has never come up before, and then stare at it. So I have A Mission. But what is it? And what then? What comes after? In the meantime the patient courtesy of the elderly man selling books, who is presumably encouraging discourse in every single carriage in order to afford a modest breakfast at Retiro, makes me feel very small and ashamed: I know nothing about human dignity.

Now here I am wandering among the dead. The British Cemetery in Buenos Aires is part of Recolata, where Eva Peron is said to be interred, its interests overseen by two remarkably polite and patient retired English men. Despite the fact I have not called and made an appointment, they sit me down, listen to my story and make a note that I am looking for Lees, Crawfords, Cattericks, Prices, maybe even Loaders – though I think this more and more unlikely.

The person you need to talk to isn't here today, says a gently plump and balding, slightly florid gentleman in tweeds and moustache; He has business at the law court – some inheritance problem. Now, how do we get in touch with you after you leave this office?

I apologise for having taken so long to get here, blaming closed museums, suburban living and just about everything but the real problem: me.

Well, he says, fingering his facial hair contemplatively; As you may be realising, Argentina is not like the rest of the world. In fact that is Argentina's burden, to regard itself as somehow fallen off the edge of the planet. There is both an emotional and physical disconnection; we have short-circuited and no-one seems willing – or perhaps remembers how – to mend the fuse.

There is a moment of reflective silence, then: Early records describe a Dissidents Cemetery, that is non-Roman Catholic. What is now the British Cemetery contains not only Brits, but Germans, Americans, Jews. Until twenty years ago, there were sections for different nationalities, and you had to prove you were not Catholic...

So, I butt in, why was my grandfather's cousin Charles interred in the Catholic cemetery in Santiago and not in that city's British Cemetery where he surely belonged.

Two possibilities, I am told: Charles was a Roman Catholic, or he converted to Catholicism in order to marry; in those days the Church insisted.

It seems that fifty to sixty years ago, many RCs were buried in this part of Recolata, but then Protestants began to lease plots and could bury who they liked, with no questions asked; as converts began to creep it, it became known as the Dissidents Cemetery.

So anyone who was not Roman Catholic was a Dissident?

Right. Until the 1860s, many Jews were buried in the British cemetery because they had no burial ground of their own. They were classified as Dissidents. Actually before General Roca's time, Jews could not be buried per se.[57]

Edward recalled the struggle he had had to get a certificate of burial for the British Cemetery for his own father – an accountant for the railways who died in the 1960s; He'd not been to church for so many years.

Rather I think this is what he said, because it is at this point that I notice that my tape recorder isn't working – or rather I had neglected to turn it on properly. Ronnie thinks it very amusing, and chortles on: Edward here is an engineer, as I was too – Nottingham University.

Railways?

Railways, all my life. My Dad came out in 1912 to work on them, and I followed suit. I've been all over – Brazil, Costa Rica... Went to the war, of course, 1941–1942, and came back married to an English girl, a teacher in Cheltenham. Produced three daughters who are all over the place – Chile, Eritrea, and Frances who is teaching languages in Plymouth.

When I tell them about meeting sixty of the one hundred and forty-four Loaders in Santiago, he shakes his head: How very industrious, very moving... There follows a quizzical look: Is there a goal, he enquires; A book perhaps?

I nod but purse my lips... Um, links between Liverpool and Buenos Aires? Slave trade? Similarities and differences? Why several generations of men would come this far to seek their fortunes... But there's lots of family stuff, lots... I just have to piece it all together.

Are you trained? (An odd question, but maybe not in the face of my hesitation, what sounds to my own ears horribly like a lack of conviction.)

Actually my training is in theatre. (A long time ago, but true.)

Ronnie snorts: Now why am I not surprised? (I feel doubly disconcerted. What does he mean by this, I wonder.)

I ask Edward – small and thin and quite the civil servant in a neat dark suit – if he has been here a long time.

It depends what you mean by "a long time". I was born in Argentina but took this job over when I retired, he replies; Ronnie insisted...

Ronnie takes back the reins: This is the oldest cemetery office in Buenos Aires; we opened for business in 1871. Not me personally, of course.

Then to his associate: Give her a brochure...and let's put her name card on record; we'll need to know where to fax when we've had a good look around for all those long-lost cousins.

If they exist, I add, suddenly not at all sure of anything. Am I even getting the names right of this enchanting two-some right – a Laurel and Hardy combo if ever there was one. Is Ronnie Edward or is Edward Ronnie?

Also I'm wondering why they are here on a Saturday. Or is time playing yet another trick on me?

Doing a little research of my own, I find the cemetery – founded in 1821 and now part of the British Cemetery Corporation – not dissimilar in its history and layout to the *Gaijin-bochi* (Foreigner's Graveyard) in Yokohama. For Japanese this is quite the sightseeing spot, moving between so many graves and tombs with strange writing and symbols and statuary from all around the world – Jew next to Hindu, Christian alongside Muslim, all with death in common so far from home. Also the wildlife is uncurtailed, with trees growing to full size and birds and butterflies in profusion. Buddhist cemeteries tend towards neatness and control in the name of over-riding convenience. But as with everything else in Japan – wonderful country of contradictions as it is – not always.

As in Yokohama, here everyone is crammed in side by side, with little room for intolerance. My eyes flicker from name to name, wondering, daring to hope that they might alight on something recognisable, personal even. It is a beautiful day with a gentle breeze; leaves and flowers dance – waltz rather than tango – all around, scattering dappled light and shadows over rambling roses and engraved headstones, careful plantings and less-well cared for plots.

My feet scrunch gravel paths as I read off the names of British counties and towns that brave immigrants once called home: Lancashire, Birmingham, Bristol, Yarmouth, Oxfordshire... Then a string of Russian, Polish and Jewish names: Edenheim, Spitz, Rosenthal, Meyer, Kopmann, Reinstock... Some of the inscriptions bear literate but fearful witness: *Thomas Eastman, a native of London, died Jan 2, 1844, aged seventy-four: Upright and honourable in life, he bore his final illness with dignified resignation. Not even the dread of something after death, the undiscovered country from whose bourne no traveller returns, could daunt his spirit; conscious of his impending dissolution he saw his last hour approach with calmness and fortitude.*

Others are more straightforward and upbeat: *Robert Michell from Argyllshire, who died in 1841 aged forty-two: A kind husband and a loving father, a generous friend and an honest man.*

Here a strange symbol: masonic perhaps?

There, Robert Read, another Scot, this time a doctor from Abbotts Hall in Fifeshire who died aged thirty-four.

A flurry of Taits from Edinburgh.... which is of interest because of knowing three generations of Taits on Orkney – Orla, Ingrid and Cara – and their ancestry is Norse, not Scottish at all.

Followed by several Stars of David. Then a grave containing an enormous family from somewhere no longer legible; mother, father, children, babies – so many babies... But no burial site stops me in my tracks. No name connects, sings out to me. The only echo I hear – if I hear anything at all – is from far, far away, in yet another country.

# PART 3

# FINAL HOURS

*Every generation revolts against its fathers and*
*makes friends with its grandfathers.*

LEWIS MUMFORD

(The Brown Decades: A Study of the Arts in America, 1865–1895)

*Dream sequences all, they are playing with you, they the cat,*
*you the mouse. You don't know what it is that is being stretched*
*in your guts, your vision. The word, the idea of travel would not*
*even be a bad joke at this point, it could make you vomit.*

ELEANOR CLARK

(Tamrart: Thirteen Days in the Sahara, 1984)

*There is meaning to every journey that is unknown to the traveller.*

DIETRICH BOHNOEFF

(1906–1946)

# NEARING THE GOAL

**COVENTRY, 1941–1946: SNAPSHOTS (IN COLOUR!)**

*A clump of Michaelmas daisies in our back garden, the mauve petals and yellow sepals aquiver with fluttering wings. I know they are Red Admiral butterflies because my mother tells me so…*

*Our pet white rabbit disappears from its cage. Postwar years pass before I make the connection with a rare and no doubt highly nutritious stew…*

*A Christmas present from my father: a train set – a green engine on a single circular track, going nowhere; a Christmas present from my mother: a doll, exquisitely dressed – pink wool bonnet and coat over a green and white gingham dress sprigged with roses; lace-trimmed lawn petticoats; silky knitted underwear and socks; cream felt shoes with rosy ties, and every single item made by hand with tender loving care. Unlike my mother and her sister who were bought dolls but only allowed to hold them once a year, I am encouraged to play with Rosemary. But I've never been comfortable with surrogates, and every time I pick her up, she whimpers…*

*My mother begging my father not to trim the Rowan tree planted too near the house: It's magic, she says, well steeped in Celtic lore and believing herself a fairy; to cut a Rowan is bad luck…*

*Turning somersaults down a grassy bank at Baginton, my father calling, Be careful, and me landing in a happily dizzy green-stained un-ravelled heap on the edge of the River Avon, with only dragonflies and reeds between me and untold depths. Always desperately taking risks...

*My mother losing her wedding ring – then I finding it twenty years later while weeding the rockery; See, she says, I knew it was your fault...

*Chasing after any horse-drawn vehicle that enters the croft: my mother scoops up droppings for garden manure; my sister and I compete with other kids to collect any bits of coal that fall out of sacks piled on the back of the cart, but being Sort of Upper Middle-Class Fallen on Hard Times compared to the rest (for this is how my parents see themselves), fail miserably...

*My mother directs my father to mix paint for the front room, adding colour drop by drop into white for a perfect pale mauve. When we come down the next morning, the paint has dried and the room is purple. My mother screams Oh no! but is smiling: purple (which I now understand to signify wisdom) is her favourite colour.

*Punting en famille with Aunt Winnie on the River Avon in pouring rain. My father is in charge of our progress. The punt glides forward, he is left clinging to the pole mid-river... Who was Aunt Winnie?

*I like Mark the boy who lives in the rebuilt house beyond Flo and Reg. (It suffered a direct hit in the year I was born.) But his younger brother David is the more outgoing. We play a variety of games that our parents know nothing about: Cowboys and Indians in the back field (I'm always the one to be tied up); walking blackened timbers above gaping cellars in bombed out houses near St James; practising wicked but wildly exciting expressions, like Bloody hell! and Bugger off...

*My father takes me to see Coventry City playing a match. (This is long before Coventry became the Sky Blues, a football team worthy of First Division status.) My father is Up There, with all the other Men. I am Down Here, and cannot see a thing. I am aware only of smells: a masculine blend of dirt, wet tweed, sweat and cigarette smoke, which both excite and disgust. I feel very small – forgotten, not at all important...*

*I want to be like my Aunt Jo: independent, with her own flat, her own money. There is a pool in the park near her home, and my father buys me a small yacht to sail from one side to the other. In my imagination, it becomes the size of the Titanic, and I emigrate. Only Josie is with me; we are among the survivors.*

## 40 RANULF CROFT, COVENTRY, 1947

*Cold. Cold as never ever before.*

Terrified of running up bills he cannot afford to pay, my father forbids heating in bedrooms. Every morning, the inside of the windows are fantastical forests of trees and ferns and flowers in icy riot. You can pick it off the glass with your fingernails, except I don't have any, just bloody cuticles! (My toes are bloody too, with chilblains – another eternally painful curse.) When the snow comes – and what snow! – tunnels are dug to reach neighbours and the street. There has never been such a bitter winter in living memory, and coming so close after the end of the war, it must have been especially hard for the adults to bear. I just shivered and vomited in physical distress, vowing never to be poor and cold again. Poverty may have become my father, but it never became me.

## 25 LOVE LANE, STOURBRIDGE, 1947

While admitting that I am appallingly ungrateful and horribly disloyal, I grow progressively sure that I am not – cannot be – my parent's child. I dream that Eric and Kathleen will adopt me, as they adopted Alison. I never feel as comfortable, as naturally at home, in Coventry. At Love Lane I feel calm, nurtured, supported. I seem to know better who I am, remember who I

*am. I love the order, regular meals at appointed times in the Breakfast Room;*
*Christmas dinner in the Dining Room. Being sent to my room after lunch for*
*rest, meaning privacy, quiet and access to Alison's entire Enid Blyton collection*
*of* Famous Five *books. It also means comics and chewing gum, consumed in*
*secret with the curtains drawn against the sun and the world at large. At home,*
*I am allowed only* The Children's Newspaper *(educational, so exceedingly*
*worthy if unbelievably dull) and* School Friend *(a comic designed with nice*
*middle-class girls in mind). Staying in Stourbridge I can tickle myself to death*
*with Beano and The Eagle's Desperate Dan.*

*I love the exotica of Eric's pickled walnuts, harvested from the huge tree*
*outside the kitchen door. I love to join him on walks with Benny, the family's*
*romping Airedale. A dog – heaven! (My parents did take in a puppy once, Sally,*
*but she caught distemper and died. Despite my parents' undoubted sacrifice,*
*nothing seemed to flourish in any healthy manner in that house, come to think*
*of it.) I love to help my uncle in his greenhouse, potting seedlings, fertilising*
*tomato plants. Nothing died here; nothing withered on the stem... but mostly*
*due to the finishing touch of Kathleen's talented green fingers. Most of all I*
*love the way he makes me feel safe – just as I love the way she makes me*
*feel special. They can never understand me, of course, but they do try. In fact*
*they make me feel Extra Special, because while I am always treated with great*
*affection and consideration, Alison is always in trouble; often I hear my cousin*
*screaming as her mother comes down hard...*

## THE BULLRING, BIRMINGHAM, 1948

*As we pass through the Bullring in the centre of Birmingham on our way home*
*from Christmas in Stourbridge (now an annual event, with a full-scale Nativity*
*Play after the Queen's Speech on Christmas Day afternoon, written, directed*
*and starring yours truly) my father buys ten chicks from a farmer with the gift*
*of the gab. Fresh eggs for breakfast, my parents are assured, believing every*
*word...*

*My mother rears them with care, and most survive, scratching around at*
*the bottom of the garden, where my father builds a coop. Each and every one*

*turns out to be male, a cockerel. As my mother complains, we don't even get to benefit from the meat. (This is because my father is too soft or scared to break their necks; he can't even find it in his heart to strangle them. I think they must have died of old age). For years after, though, we grew grandiose vegetables where the birds used to hang out, keeping neighbours awake from the crack of dawn. Imagine radishes the size of cucumbers... Now that was quite the bite!*

## 40 RANULF CROFT, COVENTRY 1949

*I have a bike – a Hopper, upon which I hop as often as possible. It is indescribably beautiful – black and red and chrome and shining. My grandfather sent it to me all the way from Argentina (or so I like to imagine). It carries me far and wide, exploring Baginton, Stoneleigh, the Avon, Warwickshire at large. Not as far as Stratford-upon-Avon; that comes later when I bunk off school and hitchhike to see Alan Badel as Hamlet (and other dramatic heroes of the mid-to-late 1950s) at the Royal Shakespeare Theatre. No, Hopper helps me find horses, horses that I can clamber on to from the tops of fences and learn to ride bareback, clutching their manes. I yearn for riding lessons, but my mother is firm: Not until you/I have stopped biting those nails. The psychology was not good: I simply tore at them even harder. Eventually a pair of beautifully elegant custom-made jodhpurs did arrive, but at age sixteen they were too late. I had moved on to boys.*

## 40 RANULF CROFT, COVENTRY, 1952

*Despite teachers saying I would sail through, the pressures prove so huge that I fail my eleven plus examination to get into Grammar School. My father shouts and slams doors. My mother can hardly bring herself to speak to me – for several weeks! It is decided I shall go to a semi-private, semi-state school in Warwick, as recommended by Kathleen, who went to school there. Thus I become the reason the poverty of my family deepens; my parents have to find the money to pay my fees, uniform, books, travel costs, and I am never allowed to forget it. First cold, then money. Finally, hunger. I am always hungry, and often driven to steal from the larder. Food becomes a minor obsession: I eat too fast, I eat like one ravenous; there is never enough, of anything. Yet I remain stick thin. And was as tall at age eleven to twelve as I am now. Friends of my father would make me squirm on seeing us together, commenting that they would surely have to drop a brick on my head if I didn't stop growing. I learned to stride with him, trying to keep up. But I know he was unhappy with me, disappointed. For one thing I hated maths, and something inside me turned first to molten lava and later stone when he tried to teach me chess, or any other left-brain game for that matter.*

## 40 RANULF CROFT, COVENTRY 1952

*We are eating Sunday dinner. At her anthroposophical nursing home in Stroud, my grandmother has to be vegetarian, but when she comes here, she transforms into an eager carnivore. Today, she is not only attacking the miniscule-sized joint but picking on me – the way I am sitting, the way I am eating... She goes on and on until my father loses his temper. But rather than turn on his mother in my defence, he leans across the table and swipes me good and hard into the tiled fireplace. Mother picks me up, calls Bridget and takes us both to the park for the rest of the day. It is soon after this that my father becomes ill, is diagnosed with angina and, by refusing to change his lifestyle – stop worrying, stop smoking, resign from the Conservative Club – turns with increasing rapidity into an even more fearful and angrier sad old man. Except he was not old. Only middle-aged.*

## 40 RANULF CROFT, COVENTRY 1953

*Grandaddysammy is coming to England again.*

*Am I excited? At age twelve I guess I'm pre-occupied. So easy to look back now and be sorry. About many things...*

## 40 RANULF CROFT, COVENTRY 1962

*My mother is crying. Bridget is hiding somewhere upstairs, also weeping. I can hear her sobbing, Stop, stop...*

*My father is shouting, lashing out at me, flailing in furious desperation. We are in the tiny hallway, and I am trying to get my suitcase out of the front door. I have a train to catch for London, a job and an audition waiting. It was* always the plan (having been away to college for two years and completed my probationary year back home as promised) but the fact that I am going with Roger and a group of other students from the art school, bound for The Slade and the Royal College, is apparently all the proof my father needs that I have gone to the dogs. My parents always feared I would become A Scarlet Woman (whatever that was) – would shame them before the whole world- and here now is the evidence that I am one. They preferred Gerry, and it's true he was very special to me. But by now we had both moved on.

While my father is trying to bang my head against the wall (to see sense, I assume), my mother is screaming at me: You're killing your father, you're killing your father...

Because it's all too complicated, I harden my heart and leave all the same. I never see him alive again.

# CHAPTER 21

# ANOTHER COUNTRY

**NOVEMBER 23, 1999**

I have my ticket to Montevideo, leaving tomorrow. It took ages to find the port office, which is not located where presumed (further along the city front) but virtually opposite Retiro Station, behind the Sheraton Hotel. Wandering further along into El Centro, I'd met a sportily dressed American woman, also lost. But she was meeting a jogging partner near the Catholic University in Madero, so it was easy to put her right. (Look at you Ange, I think, preening: quite the tourist guide these days – except when it comes to finding anything new and then I'm as clueless as the date I arrived.)

It is interesting to observe how I appear to be slowing down and losing energy as time speeds up. I think back to the detailed records describing my early days of travel; though trying to keep up the momentum, it is now almost impossible: I am writing less and less, making mistakes in recording, feeling a new and very different kind of pressure. Yet on this last leg, I really will be on my own, so very much need to keep my wits about me.

Quite on the off chance, I rang Horacio Cook earlier in the day. A woman I can only assume to be a maid answered in Spanish and went off to find someone, who turned out – astonishingly, though perhaps not really – to be Lucas Cook, the grandson of my grandfather's one-time business associate. (The company Sam left because of alleged pre-war sympathies with the Third Reich.)

My father is named after his father, Lucas explained in good English;

But my father's not here, he's down at the *estancia* and won't be back until the weekend. Call on Sunday when you get back from Uruguay; maybe we can get together to talk.

This unexpected connection has quite made my day, with the larger part still to come.

I am off to Olivos, to have tea with Molly Hampton. It has taken some perseverance to pin her down, but she seems quite happy, not at all put out: I know who you are, she said the first time I called; Chloe told me all about your expedition. I have to say, I think you're very intrepid.

But then she had to cancel. The next time I called, Molly told me why: I had to take my friend to the hospital and then had to wait ages for the doctor. I could kill her (the friend) sometimes. I'm fond but basically I've heard her story over and over again... She's forgetful too. This time she swore she'd left nothing behind, and we got as far as seeing the doctor before she realised she had left her X-rays at home.

I could have killed her... *killed* her, Molly reiterates. But then she laughs: Don't worry. That's how we talk in Argentina.

Chloe Lola (that name again) is Molly's red-haired brown-eyed grand-niece, and the daughter of friend Frances in England. In 1997, having just graduated from Oxford University (which she found far too snobbish and unfriendly to make it any fun), Chloe made a big trip, staying with us in Japan before heading down to Australia and New Zealand, and then across to Argentina to see her great-aunt. Having known Chloe since childhood, and always liked her vibrant ever-questioning personality, her visit was a great success. When she left, I gave her Pablo's contact number, and they did indeed meet up. Taken to a club in Buenos Aires, she could not believe how subservient Fernanda became to her boyfriend who, Chloe said, only had to click his fingers for a cigarette to be lighted or to be handed his wallet. Chloe was also invited to Caseros, and found it hard to put her reactions into words that did not sound churlish or ungrateful.

340

Pablo's father was in his vest and hardly took his eyes off the TV screen, she told me, much embarrassed; They – the family – didn't seem to be very... um...well, you know, cultured?

Well, I had said at the time, it takes all kinds and they are exceedingly kind and hospitable in their own sweet way. To which she could only agree. (We are a snobbish lot we English when all is said and done. And when your father has remarried into the family of the poet Robert Graves, as in Chloe's case, one's view of the world is surely even more rarefied than usual.)

Travelling to Olivos is a new experience, and quite delightful. For one thing, it's another spanking new train, and the items for sale carriage to carriage are again relatively upmarket: calculators, plastic cigarette lighters, tourist postcards. We pass through Belgrano, where my grandfather often hung out and today Karen hangs her clothes – and very classy and expensive it looks too; one tennis court sports the name Club Harrods.

Olivos was inaugurated in 1863 which means it celebrated its centennial in 1963, the year my son was born and I was living in complete ignorance of Sam, Buenos Aires and one hundred and forty-four relatives across the Andes. I call Molly who says she will come and pick me up. In the meantime, I walk down to the waterside and out along one of the many little quays, lined with men and boys drowning disappointment and fear of failure with meditationally baited lines. To my right, I can see the glittering corporate towers of the city rising out of smog; ahead there is only an ocean of swirling red upriver water. This is what I will cross tomorrow, to the far side.

But here comes Molly, driving a somewhat battered sedan car and looking as down-to-earth colonial as you can get. I love her on sight – faded blouse and dirndl skirt, youthfully bright blue eyes in a make-up free face, unconditional smile and all. She lives on the top floor of an apartment building built forty years before, and she and her husband were the first people to move in. Being the highest building around they had a clear and uninterrupted view all the way to El Centro. Now, she laments, there are high-rises in the way: I must take you for a drive, show you the area.

She and her husband never intended to buy the top floor apartment at all - a complete misunderstanding... And look at all these bills, she exclaims, misjudging a pile of promotional fliers on a table.

A wide verandah, canopied with a striped awning runs the full width of the apartment, and there are ferns and plants in pots in abundance. The whole flat has a feeling of genteel permanence. After four decades, of course, this is not surprising, but there is something else – an element (cultural connection maybe) or atmosphere that Maria-Elena's own home somehow lacks. Molly is off making tea, and I nose around, leafing through the *Lyell's Official Antiques Review*, a Webster's dictionary, and a poster of the Kings and Queens of England – a present from two grandchildren, apparently – with equal interest.

Which dynasty do you think you are descended from, I ask, as she carries through a plate piled with thin brown and white sandwiches, their crusts cut off in time-honoured tradition.

Oh most definitely Henry the Eighth, she answers cheerfully, tweaking the tablecloth unnecessarily into line. Because all too soon it is hidden beneath (sandwiches apart) buttered fruit bread, small patisserie cakes, and a flowery teapot with a chipped spout kept warm under a funky hand-knitted tea cosy.

Pouring tea, she worries about a son who had been recently robbed, They took everything: They went upstairs with baskets, emptied all the cupboards of clothes, linen, everything... took the safe, the car, even my grandson's moneybox.

It got worse: My son, an architect, was at his office. Only his wife, their little son and the maid were home. These four chaps (who had followed them up from the garage, having slipped in unseen as the car was being parked) came in with guns, told them to sit down, shut up and be quiet. My daughter-in-law lost her voice from fear, her own mother

342

also became speechless. Now we're all so worried about how it will affect the little boy. But what can we do? These things are happening all the time. This new president is promising security, but you can't promise things like that. How can you make things safe? And now this great lady (the daughter-in-law's mother) has asked me for tea next week, and what am I going to wear?

Molly breaks into gales of laughter – a device for dissipating stress? – then steers the conversation this way and that, often neglecting to provide the connections that allow me to keep up with the whos, whys and wherefores, but entertaining all the same. My goodness she loves to talk, but whether this is because she is a natural chatterbox, or taking advantage of a rare visitor, I'm not sure. I suspect the former, because there are no sign she is lonely – indeed she has grandchildren staying – what she calls Lovely young people! – and is expecting them back any minute.

Returning to Molly's fashion problem, I ask if she cares what people think.

Not lately, she replies; One of the advantages of getting older perhaps. If they don't like the way I am, well *alla ellos* as they say here. (Tough shit!)

I bring out a fast-fading fax that Chloe sent me long ago – It's about Chloe's paternal grandmother, Alex Christie Riess – and show it to Molly. Ah, says Molly, Alex was my cousin. When she was living in Peru – Chloe's father Frank would have been very small at the time – her brother Roy went to visit, and the family boxer dog jumped at him and ruined his suit. Sister and brother never spoke to one another again.

Am I to take this seriously, I ask, incredulous.

Oh yes, Molly continues, thoroughly enjoying herself; They had this rich aunt Lola in the US. When she died she left a fair bit of money to her brother and her sister Elena (Alex's mother). When Elena died, her share was passed to Alex and Roy. When he died, Alex got all of it. I always thought Roy must be turning in his grave to think of his sister coming into such a fortune.

Although Molly herself was born in Argentina, her parents came from Boston, and from the bits of family history she has accumulated in a file, she believes her father's ancestors were Flemish weavers.

Ah, so that's why you have so many nice pieces, I note, pointing as an example to the lovely hand-woven native rug in front of the fireplace.

Molly recently celebrated her eightieth birthday in grand style: The boys (her sons) gave me a big party and invited everybody. Afterwards I realised there were dozens I hadn't invited, but then you can't invite everyone can you?

Depends on how many people you know, I laugh.

We were one hundred and fifty already and you can't go on and on... Well you can but... Oh, something's burning!

An empty kettle, water evaporated and red hot: I advise her to leave it to cool down and she fusses back and asks where she left off...

One hundred and fifty guests, I prompt, and she picks up seamlessly: I'm still meeting people who say, I heard you had a party! But it was marvellous, you know. We had a tent and everything. Look, here's the photo...

And here they all are, one hundred and fifty guests and Molly, all wearing cowboy hats, and all 100 per cent white Caucasian stock. I ask her to point out her sons...

Well, he's the oldest at fifty-seven and an agricultural engineer. Then there's John, fifty-two. And Sandy, forty-seven. I had a daughter in-between, Molly adds quietly; She would have been forty-eight now.

After topping me up with tea, she is back to how her family, the Jacobs, emigrated south from New England... and so she rambles on down memory lane: My great-grandfather was very wealthy and something to do with the navy, yes, that's right, and a son deserted his family – nine children, the youngest of whom was my father, were dispersed among different relations. But my father and two of his siblings, all in their late teens, decided to go off to the Boer War. Oh, look at that bird!

Yes, I agree, you have some amazing birds here. There was one sitting while you were on the phone, yellow, quite big, about the size of a jay – oh look, there's another one.

Molly has no clue: I've never seen one like that before. Must be the rain or something.

The rain? I decide not to pursue this line, but she quickly offers an explanation: There are so many insects on the wing; see all those little bugs? Oh, they've gone. How strange. There are so many birds from different provinces, I can never remember their names. The same with plants – and I've been a member of the Garden Society for years!

Molly tells me all about her father's safe return from the Boer war (during which he realised he was fighting on the wrong side): He and his brother got sent to England, and only returned to Argentina after Queen Victoria died and the country plunged into gloom. He did various jobs and was managing a sugar plantation when he met my mother. She was from Mold, in Wales, and came out to see her sister who had married an engineer here.

And that was that?

Well, it very nearly wasn't, Molly recalls; My mother was pretty and charming, and one day wrote to her own mother and said she was going to have tea with a grumpy old bachelor named Enke Jacobs, and in no time at all was sending more letters and cables saying she was going to marry him. My grandmother in Mold was frantic, but it all worked out. Mummy had had a boyfriend in England, very nice, and we all met him before he died at age ninety-nine. When she went back to buy her trousseau, Mummy was supposed to be going to some big dance at some club, but got raging toothache. The boyfriend was waiting there to see her, and just moped around, not dancing with anyone else.

What would have happened if she had gone?

It would have been a different story, like I wouldn't be here talking to you now. Still they kept in touch. Even Daddy liked him very much. Funny how things turn out, isn't it.

Molly began life in the Chaco region, then was moved to an

experimental station in another province, and from there to Louisiana in the States: Daddy was trying to introduce a new strain of sugar cane to that part of the world. My mother had another daughter there – everyone was very surprised, as I was six, my brother nine.

When her father began travelling the world as a consultant, he sent his family to Wales, where one year turned into five because of the Wall Street crash of 1929. Enke Jacobs lost his money, got back onto his feet to make more, then lost everything all over again. Eventually he returned to Argentina, bringing his family with him. That would have been in 1934, Molly assures, having counted out the years on her fingers.

She remembers, she says – and here I jump to attention! -that before they left England, on a visit to the Argentine Consulate in Liverpool to organise paperwork, a very nasty little man – the consul himself – began speaking to her in Spanish: When Mummy told him I didn't speak the language, he laughed and told me how I would be an outcast in my country.

Aha, I think. Sam had informed my father that my great-grandfather *was nominated Vice-Consul for Argentina, which he carried on until his death in 1899.* Now I am wondering if this is why Samuel Turner did not show up in records here: he was a consul in Liverpool, not in Argentina itself as I had first assumed on my initially excited (and obviously superficial) reading of Sam's letters. Most certainly I like to think he would have been kinder to Molly than whoever was in office in 1934. But there is the distinct possibility that Sam would have known this "nasty little man", since it was only months later that he left for Buenos Aires, and would have needed paperwork of his own.

Anyway, back to Molly's story: We came out on a cargo ship, My father was working on a ranch in the Province of Cordoba, owned by an English couple. They planned to build us a house, which never happened. In fact I wouldn't be surprised if the bricks are still not there, sixty years later.

346

Because things were not working out between the adults, we came back here. Mummy, my little sister and I got digs in Belgrano. My brother was already working on one ranch, my elder sister was working as a governess on another.

Asked if it was a happy childhood, Molly reflects: When I look back, I think I just accepted everything. I don't think children would now, but I was fourteen and dumb. At English school, we talked about the Argentines as Natives. Terrible when you think about it, but we so looked down on them. In those days, it was unusual for an English girl to marry an Argentine, but now most of them do.

Whatever an Argentine is, I reply archly.

Indeed, says Molly; Exactly...

She thinks of herself as Argentine: Most of her father's brothers married Argentines; his sisters married Spaniards. We are considered to be the Ingles of the family, she says; The English! But nowadays I have Argentine cousins who don't speak a word of English, and even the English schools accommodate Spanish language lessons in their curriculum. My grandchildren can speak English, but amongst themselves and their peers, they speak Spanish.

Observing that Molly has lived through some extraordinary times, she nods: One of my grandchildren wants me to write a book. Well, I have kept a diary since I was thirteen – though I'm sure it's very boring really. And I copy all my correspondence. Just the other day, tidying up, I found copies of letters I had written to my husband, and letters he had sent in reply whilst travelling, and before I knew what had happened, four hours had passed. Towards the end (of his life) when he wasn't well, he changed. It was good to be able to balance out that difficult period with the letters we'd exchanged earlier.

She has been on her own since 1981: He was sixty-seven. His sister is still alive and ninety-one, but in a home, her mind gone completely.

Molly holds up her hand: Still listen to me, rambling on... this tea has turned nasty. I'll make a fresh pot.

Fortified with a new brew, and remembering (quite out of context) how she was sick all over her future father-in-law while living in Tucumán, Molly voices strong views on schooling: In those days. English people used to send their children to school in England, which I think is terrible; they grow up without parents, a family. I can't understand what the parents were thinking. There were good schools here... my own brother went to a boarding school in Hurlingham. Imagine a child making that trip across the Atlantic twice a year...

As the afternoon whiles away, Molly becomes emboldened by memory. She remembers being in her house Don Torcuarto on the outskirts of Buenos Aires when a nephew came to call: Actually he was a terrorist but we didn't know that at the time. He said to my husband – it was a lovely day and we were out in the garden – Aren't you ashamed to have all this when so many have nothing? And my husband replied, No, I don't. I've worked like bloody hell for everything I have.

I mean, Molly continues, How can people judge when they just don't know. They just think everything has been handed to you on a plate.

I encourage Molly to write her book, and she says she will start... but not tomorrow because she will be counting cows and weighing sheep out on her son's ranch: I said to Charlie, What have I got to do when I come? And he said, A lot! When I asked if I could go riding, he said No! But that's only because the last time I rode was for two hours, and when I got off the horse I staggered into the house and there wasn't even a hot bath ready. What an old fool!

When the phone rings, she is quickly embroiled in a conversation about dogs.

No sooner has she replaced the handset, than she is off again, talking about one of her sons: You like that picture (hanging on the wall)? George did it, with Nescafe. He doesn't paint anymore, but he was always different to the other boys – a real-life hippie with a long drooping moustache. When he married his first wife – she was an architect – they chose a registry office ahead of a church wedding, and she turned up wearing hot pants and a cardigan touching the ground, and I said, Cora, you're never going to be allowed in looking like that. But all the guests looked the same.

Ah, we sigh, the 1970s; all that Love and Peace and Revolution. Yes, Molly says, cackling with laughter. Now he (George) wears a sports coat and trousers. His eldest daughter was born in London... and once he said he'd hitchhiked, and I said Hijacked? and he said No, Mummy, that's different... When they were in Guatemala there was that awful earthquake... and then there was that time in Ecuador...

Walking me to the station through dusk, she apologises for not taking me for that drive.

Never mind, I say; We saw those birds, that spectacular sunset, laughed a lot and I met one of your beautiful grandchildren.

Kissing goodbye, Molly says she'd love for me to come again before leaving for Japan: You could stay for dinner, come out to the farm. Then I really will take you out for a drive and of course you must stay the night. You must, you must... it was so very nice and really all I did was jabber jabber on...

The city looks very beautiful this evening as I return to Retiro – all the lights, the sky a deep indigo blue, and all these clouds, low and full, very tranquil.

The train to Caseros is another matter, and I am reminded of Karen's words, about how Argentina is Fourth World, with the haves (like Molly and myself) so easily colliding with the have-nots – like the woman who through accident or design tried so hard just now to ruin my day. Really, people have no manners; they treat one another like shit. Looking remarkably like Hilda Ogden from vintage Coronation Street, she sort of plonked herself down beside me and in doing so sat on my backpack. When I pulled it away, saying (in English, which I guess was asking for trouble), Excuse me, you're sitting on my camera... she flew at me, shrieking in Spanish. To which I replied – internally that is, being a terrible coward in matters confrontational: Well, if you're going to be like that... All you had to do was be polite and I would have lifted my rucksack out of the way. As it is, if my camera is in any way damaged I'm going to sue you for every peso you've got from this end of Argentina to the other. So get off your fucking backside, you rude old bag!

### NOVEMBER 24, 1999

I feel increasingly at sea. I am also in debt, having borrowed two hundred pesos from Maria-Elena; embarrassing to say the least, but there is a deep terror of being caught short of cash once I cross Rio de la Plata, the River Plate. This stretches before me, the strangest waterscape ever experienced in its powerfully swirling nature and exotic but slightly frightening ever-changing colour combinations: right now the river-sea swims all around in that familiar muddy pale terracotta but overcast with a glittering yellow under a sky that runs through slate to grey to white. I have never seen such a tumultuous scenario of colour and light – a river of gold, not of silver at all. Obviously those early explorers of old had either very different eyes, or they were here at another time of year.

As I was saying, I feel more and more at sea. What am I doing here, sitting on this splendid state-of-the-art Buquebus (promoted on the ticket as Ecologico, Veloz, Silencioso) in the middle of this chaotic waterway – the widest river estuary in the world – without sight of land in any direction? (Leaving Puerto Madero at 11.15 a.m. on the dot, Buenos Aires quickly fell behind.) I try to imagine the physical volume of the 2 billion cubic feet of silt that is carried into this estuary each and every year, where the waters are further churned up by the collision of river and ocean, tidal movements and passing traffic. The central channel is being constantly dredged to enable vessels ease of passage; like painting Edinburgh's Forth Bridge in Scotland, it's work that never ends, a genuine job for life.

Hanging off the guard rail, I seek signs of aquatic activity – a rare sighting, for example, of the La Plata dolphin (*Pontoporia blainvillei* in Latin, known locally as Franciscana). Small, grey-brown in colour, with long beaks for scooping up fish, shrimp and squid, it is unknown how many such dolphins there are in the wild, and very little is known about their behaviour. Sadly, they often die caught in fishermen's nets – unlike the humans Disappeared during the La Guerre Sucia, who hopefully were dead before they hit the water, dropped out of helicopters in the dead of night, but not necessarily. No-one knows how many men, women and young people were disposed of in this way, discarded like garbage, with no consideration of anyone's humanity or feelings – victims, families, lovers, friends. It makes me shudder this fearful crossing of water, an all-too-real unfathomable maelstrom, the mythical River Styx. Shudder and turn cold. Have those Halloween spirits again caught up with me? Or is it Chilean Charles dogging my footsteps?

In Greek mythology, Styx is both the name of a primordial goddess and that of that river which formed the boundary between earth and the underworld, Hades. (The Buddhist version of this river is known as Sanzu.) In the thirteenth-century Florentine poet Dante (from Durante) Alighieri's version of the myth, Styx is guarded by Phlegyas, who passes the souls of the newly dead from one side of the river to the other; in more recent times the ferryman Charon was given this responsibility. Dante made the Styx the fifth circle of Hell, where the wrathful and sullen are punished by being perpetually drowned in the muddy waters. If so, I am thinking, why did the victims of military persecution die rather than the perpetrators? Or was it simply a matter of karma – that word again. To be honest though, I'm none too hot on how karma works, and make a mental note to wise up in the next millennium.

Molly and her family's adventurous wanderings has set me thinking about Martha, my great-grandmother. For the first time I wonder if Samuel Turner met her in the UK or South America? Most certainly she accompanied him on at least one of his trips, which in those days was no mean feat. Imagine dealing with Victorian clothing and laundry in mid-Atlantic storms, the simple daily matters of hygiene and sanitation. Which leads to considering the other women in my family, whose courage and intelligence more often than not seem to outshine that of the men upon whom I have been concentrating my attention. What do I really know of Sarah, who raised four children alone? Her daughters, Catherine and Betty. My own mother, who becomes more of an enigma every day. Every time I go back to see here, there is less and less in the cottage. Like a snake readying to shed its skin and move into a new phase of evolution, she really is preparing to shuffle off her mortal coil! Bridget, even; how much do I really know about my sister's life, what makes her tick so courageously through all her pain and suffering? And then of course, going back full circle, there's Harriet. It seems that the more I learn, the more I do not know. An unending quest that, if I am not too careful, may drive me witless, loopy, around the proverbial bend.

Down in the restaurant, I chat with an African-Brazilian doctor bound for home. I ask her why there are so few remaining trace elements of African history and culture in Argentina, and she shakes her head, admitting to never having really thought about it before. It's true, though, she muses; It's true.

All those making this crossing are relatively well heeled and there is no-one under forty. This is in stark contrast to the staff, all of whom are under twenty-five. Those with nothing pressing to do are mesmerised by a video onscreen: a full-length feature film about a Danish youth who skips probation, hitchhikes all the way to Morocco, falls in love with a girl (surprise, surprise) and then gets hauled back by the Danish ambassador. An unlikely tale made all the more bizarre for being shown here.

Since the plot requires no more than half an eye on the screen, I'm numbering Sam's letters from one to one hundred and seven, something I have been meaning to do for months. Imagine coming all this way to do something so mundane.

Much of the content of his correspondence from 1950 onwards – a stream that evolves into a torrent in the last years of his life – leans to the mundane. As he struggles to maintain a positive front on the business side of his affairs, he becomes more and more involved in the daily goings on of family life on the other side of the Atlantic. With the war over, everyone more relaxed and secure and mail moving smoothly once again, my father warms to his father and shows more willing to communicate.

From the first letter of 1950, Sam signs off by typing GRANDADDYSAMMY, followed by Father and then an official signature in his usual small firm handwriting. He writes sixteen letters over the following twelve months, and at some point in Spring moves from the Hispano to a small room (temporarily he is told) at the Novel Hotel, Avenida de Mayo 915: *I would like it better if it has more space. (But) It is light, fairly cool, and away from the street traffic. With my office here* (across the road at 840) *I have a large balcony, where it is cool, and it is well-furnished with good carpets, and I have my easy chair, also the radio, which is at the moment pouring out classical music, which I like, as often it is Argentine music, which melody is strange to me and not, I think, pleasing to the ear.*

He mentions for the first time Howard Pheasant, with whom he is sharing the office and handling an increasing amount of business with Japan. This *nephew politico*, as Sam calls him, *will forward mail if I am away, does most of the spade work, and consults with me when necessary, so it relieves me of a lot of work. He is extremely efficient, and I am very lucky to have him alongside me.*

Howard Pheasant: a nephew by marriage to that vaguely referred to Winifred. (Nothing to do with my Aunt Winnie, who I am now reliably informed was a relation on my matriarchal grandfather's side, a housekeeper somewhere in the North of England, with no immediate family of her own.)

In early March my great-aunt Gertrude dies, and there is no doubt the news rocks her brother to his core: *She is buried at Anfield with your Grandfather and Grandmother. It is a sad business, but I must confess that I hardly expected to see her when I came again to England, as she had fallen away a lot since three years ago. My other two sisters are 71 years and 63 years, and I am on the verge of 70.*

Though returned to the Argentine only six months since his last trip to England, he is already planning the next. With business still sluggish, he spends an increasing amount of time in Montevideo, and the coastal resort of Piriapolis, which he has always loved for its fine air and bathing. Though troubled with various aches and pains, he passes the time writing letters and asking for news of my sister and myself, and Betty and her baby daughter. With only the occasional business-related cocktail party to look forward to, life is quiet and while still sending my father the occasional cheque, money seems tight: *I am now cutting out all eating between meals for economy reasons, and it does not seem to affect me very much, as I often go on strike against such things for self-control. I cannot really say I smoke, but like a good cigar, and bought a dozen or so in Montevideo, of Brazilian variety, which cannot be found here. These I do enjoy at times.*

The end of the summer brings news of our family holiday in a caravan in Brixham, Devon (two weeks spent in a tin can in the pouring rain and my tall long-legged father going spare with discomfort and frustration). Sam thanks his son for a photo of me: *surely the daughter of her father. I have never seen such a resemblance.* And encloses, *A sprig of violet root, which may be kept alive, if you nurse it well. Get Angela to look after it, and keep it watered and protected from the frost.* (This proves to be a fad of his, sending seeds and plants to people. Customs were obviously a lot less strict in those days.)

In all respects, life is at a standstill: *Nephew Howard comes to the office most days, but business remains slack. Even Japan has fallen away for the moment.*

Towards the end of the year, he is pleased to hear that the family back home is being more pro-active. My mother had been to see Betty, John and the baby: *a good move.* Also Catherine had looked us up: *It is pleasing she is happy and contented with her interesting job with the government.* My aunt, who spent much of her career teaching physical education in women's colleges, was by this time attached to the Scottish Recreational Board, advising on the development of a new winter sports centre in the Cairngorms. An active observer of the great outdoors, she was always very much the outdoor jolly-hockey-sticks type.

As the year comes to an end, Sam has his ticket to England booked for April 20, 1951. Japan is back in the corporate picture; Koria (sic) a new player – and he is once again asking my father to chase up business for him. (My father dutifully obtains and posts catalogues, but all to no avail.) At the same time Sam is offering my father advice about changing jobs – to Rootes, *helped perhaps by the influence of Gwen's sister.* (Nothing comes of this blatant piece of attempted nepotism either.)

In his last letter of the new decade, he leaves off his signature, and instead adds a flourishing row of kisses: *XXX*

I'm back on deck, watching a wild sea that is one moment the colour of spew and the next a brilliant jade, rampaging by as we approach a coastline emerging to the left. As Uruguay provocatively lifts her veils one by one, shadows transform into trees, misted geometrics reveal themselves as buildings, and in no time at all a detailed cityscape rolls down into port: Montevideo. The city is not large; I can see that. Nor does the port appear especially active, but oh how interesting, with a quaintness that enchants. Before I can say *Hola*, I am scooped up by a young cab driver who seems to know where I can quickly find a bank. Slickly dressed he drives a hard bargain, but I am not in a position to haggle. He then drives me no more than a few hundred metres up the hill, which really pisses me off. When I say, Oi, I could have walked it, he shrugs and shoots off; *mi problemo.*

The relief to have some local currency is immense. Now I can set about finding a hotel. Nor is this task so irksome, because the heart of this El Centro is really quite compact; I feel I am in Buenos Aires in miniature, somehow. It is an easy walk; my backpack is not so heavy and there's a sense of relief to be on dry land again. I cross Piedras, Cerrito, Avenida de Mayo (what, here also?) and finally reach Plaza Interpendencia, and the Tourist Information Office. Staff recommend the Hotel Los Angeles, just a short walk away at Avenida 18 de Julio 974, and in no time at all I have a room. The manager is all smiles and the price is good. Sorting out my stuff on the bed – secreting what remains of my Argentine money under my mattress, and my precious

Filofax at the very bottom of my backpack – I feel a sense of achievement. I've got here, have cash and a roof over my head and can now afford to relax. Tomorrow I think, really can look after itself.

Heading back to the tourist office to ask how to reach seafood restaurants on the quayside via the original part of the city, the girl behind the counter draws a route on my map – through the port to Mercado del Puerto – and off I go. The oldest part of Montevideo is fascinating but poor. Very poor, I swiftly acknowledge. It does not scare me, but rather causes unease; I feel out of place, disconcerted. Snapping a photo of a plaque that reads seventeen-something, a young man (handsome, mixed blood) approaches, shows what I take to be genuine interest, and speaks to me in Spanish. My ignorance of his language results in a casual shrug and he leaves, but as he resumes a lounging position across the street, I feel him watching. It is, I feel in my bones, not the best place to be, so I determine to get the hell out. I turn a corner, get my bearings towards the ocean and begin to walk with calm determination along a long deserted rundown street, bleached near white by sunlight. I wave to two small girls playing on their doorstep, but fail to raise any response, not even a smile.

It is then I have the strangest feeling, as if a ghost is on my back. Realising within a fraction of a second that there is in fact something far more concrete behind me, I begin to turn and catch a hand in my backpack, which swiftly pulls away and shakes me off. Sensing I am suddenly a kilo lighter, I realise the hand – young, brown, male – is clutching my Filofax. Screaming, I try to grab it back and fail. The thief – wearing jeans, hooded fleece and sneakers like a billion other young men the world over – lopes off into the distance while I – trying to run in pursuit but for the first time ever really feeling my age – shout through distraught tears: No, no, please, just take the money, not the book, that's my life! Please, please…

He turns a corner and is gone.

I am at a crossroads.

With no one else in sight, I start pounding the ground, swinging my arms, howling.

# CHAPTER 22

# HOWLING

**NOVEMBER 24, 1999 CONTINUED**

I am spinning in the middle of the street, throwing myself this way and then another, ricocheting off walls and tree trunks. Anyone watching would think I had completely lost the plot, and so I have. The anger that comes rip-roaring up from deep inside is both red-hot and polished blacker than sin. Yet, typically, I don't feel angry with the perpetrator but with myself. When a woman emerges from the shop on the corner with a drink of water and tries to establish the source of my rage and grief, I take the glass and dash it to the ground, only to start spinning all over again.

A small crowd gathers. A police car arrives. By now I am exhausted, but stand gulping hysterically while the driver resorts to his mobile phone. A second car drives up and screeches to halt beside me. It is white – a dirty white and much dented, I seem to recall. Suddenly a young woman in a cotton dress and sandals is standing in front of me, yelling in good but broken English: You idiot! What the hell do you think you're doing in a place like this! Look at you! Look at your clothes, your hair... a woman of your age just asking for trouble. Are you insane or simply stupid?

I go rigid with shock, momentarily come to my senses and then start shaking all over again. This is the last thing I need for fuck's sake. Who is this bitch? I want help, poor-me style commiseration, not this merciless tirade. But then I realise she is shaking too, and it is only when she puts her arm around me that we both let go of our emotional extremes.

At last I can explain what happened: I've lost everything – well, not quite everything; there is some Uruguayan currency tucked away in my room – but family photographs, passport, UK driving license, all my Japanese papers (visa, ID, etc.), most of the money loaned by Maria-Elena, plus all the names and contact numbers and business cards gathered over the past three weeks.

I don't care about the money, I tell the policeman through Kareen (for this is her name); I understand being robbed of cash. I understand the extremes that the poor can be driven to. But I do care about the other stuff, especially all my notes and my entire address book. Some kid has run off with my life and all my reasons for being here, and most of it is of no interest to anyone but me. I'd gladly give up the cash to get the rest back.

The small crowd that has gathered begins to disperse, slipping back into shadowed entrances and alleyways; the police leave; and shamefaced and apologetic I offer to pay for the broken glass. I still have a few coins in my purse, thank God. The shopkeeper waves me away, as if to say, Don't be silly (you poor pathetic creature). And Kareen orders me into her car. (It is only later that I wonder what on earth I thought I was doing, putting my trust in a complete stranger.)

Kareen is an architect, and her office was on the second floor, just above where I was robbed.

I heard you scream, she said; It was a scream like I have never heard before in my life. It came from deep underground, from a frightening place, like a wounded animal roaring. I'm used to life around here, and also I've lived in Berlin, so I know what it's like to be a stranger among poverty and violence. I was robbed many times in Germany. That's why I felt I had to come and help.

Asked whether I think I might recognise the thief again, I explain that I never saw his face. It might have been the young man who spoke to me, and then cut a diagonal dash through familiar streets to come up behind me, but I can't remember what he was wearing in any useful detail and can offer no proof.

358

I know everyone around here, Kareen declares matter-of-factly; I'll drive around a bit, ask some questions...

And so we navigate a maze of dusty and impoverished streets, with Kareen stopping every so often to disappear behind a ruined wall, or enter what appears to be an unoccupied building.

No luck, she repeats each time (having spoken to mostly local drug dealers and gang members); Usually a thief just takes out the cash and jettisons the rest, but nothing has turned up yet, and news travels fast around here. Still I've put out the word that you just want your personal stuff back and won't make a fuss, so we all reckon you could well be lucky. Now, where are you staying?

She drops me at my hotel, explaining that a female officer who speaks English will be by within the hour to accompany me to the police station.

Call me, Kareen calls back over her shoulder; Let me know how things go.

The manager of the hotel – who reminds me now of the Hardy-half of the duo at the British Cemetery in BA, complete with tweeds and moustache – is horrified: I was going to tell you to leave all your valuables with me in the safe, he says; But we were having such an interesting conversation going up in the lift to your room, that I quite forgot. I feel totally responsible. I'm so sorry.

I try to dissuade him otherwise, but it is a hard task, and soon I give up, and wait in the lobby in a state of ice-cold suspended animation. For the moment, I am out of tears, just a long way from home and wondering what on earth to do. My legs are too wobbly to carry me upstairs so I just sit, feeling pathetic. Guests come and go, wondering perhaps at my ravaged appearance – swollen eyes, and a tear-stained face that no cold compress seems ready to repair. But no one comes near me and I feel more and more alone.

The policewoman is small and young, squeezed voluptuously into a uniform at least one size too small, with baby blonde hair plaited into the nape of her neck under her official hat. Rather to my surprise, she is sweating profusely and shaking with nerves. Indeed she is in such a state that I find it necessary to offer her some comfort, rather than the other way around. Any facility in English is being sabotaged by an overdose of jitters; she can hardly communicate a word in her own language let alone a second without being overwhelmed by tremors that run vertically from head to foot, threatening to reduce her height even further.

She hands me a note with her name and a scrawled message: My name is Adriana... I am a police officer. I am working in a police turism (sic).

I am your English police friend, she adds, squeaking while trying to draw in large gulps of air. Please, she gestures towards the door, and stumbles sideways into the glass. As I catch her and set her upright, my arm around her shoulder, I feel her relax; she looks at me, and blushes, eyes shining. It is her first job, she explains; I am her first distressed foreign tourist.

And you, I reply, are my first distressed rookie Uruguayan policewoman. But I'm not sure she got the point.

Most certainly this is my first ride in a police car – a police car in any country. The siren is going full blast, as if I am a major emergency, and the street clears as we progress at phenomenal speed. My chaperone is clutching my arm now and making soothing noises; I suppose it's in the manual: Step 1 – Hold distressed foreigner's hand. Step 2 – Calm them down as best you can...

The police station lobby is ill-lit and painted a murky utilitarian grey-green, the staff on duty are hulking, uniformed and chillingly armed. They do what they are supposed to do – go through the motions of form-filling in a bored and desultory kind of way; questioning me through my chaperone, who very sweetly does her best. I wonder what she will be like in a few years, when the system has had its way with her innocence and charm; a sobering thought on top of all the others that crowd in right, left and centre.

360

What was I doing in that part of the city, they ask. Don't I know there's an election in the offing, and that for the first time in decades there was a strong possibility that the Left might put flight to the Right? Slum areas are in a state of high excitement – people at the end of their tether sighting a tiny pinprick of hope at the end of a forty-year long time tunnel. So dry is the political tinderbox that officers have been withdrawn from patrol; there is little to no policing, especially where I was walking.

My case is nothing special, worthy of interest only because I am a tourist who just happens to be a *peridisto* (journalist) and therefore might doubly cause trouble at some unknown worrisome level. Papers are completed. I sign everything, and when I think about this later, realise I have no idea what I signed or in what language. The attitude and posture of the men fascinate; when a young man is dragged in and taken through for questioning, the handling is rough and threatening. Now I just want to get the hell out of here fast; I need the friendly bright-lit safety of the Los Angeles to feel human again.

I can't believe any of this is happening. Am I dreaming? If so, I'd like to wake up, please.

Lying on my bed, I am beyond tears. Is Maria-Elena right? Did I wake her grandfather up? Is Charles shadowing me, dogging my steps. Certainly I feel as if I am drowning – as if those awful waters I crossed have somehow caught up with me and closed over my head, with phantoms besieging me on every side. But I am not ready to pass over; I'm too close to my goal, have come so far I have to keep going. Instead I count my money, call Kareen and tell her I'd like to buy her a drink to say thank you.

I'll be round in thirty minutes with my boyfriend, she says in that slightly slurred fashion that suggests she might have been smoking. Is that okay?

Okay? I reply. It's more than okay, it's great!

Kareen has let down her hair, which now sits around her heart-shaped face in a soft, dark cloud. She has changed her dress too; another light printed cotton. Her partner, Carlos, reminds me of cousin Jose in Santiago: heavily bearded, with kind intelligent eyes, a warm dry sense of humour and also speaking English, I like him immediately.

We drive to the beach area and draw up outside a lively bar-restaurant with Christmas tree lights twinkling in time to a disco beat – mindless but energising music designed to drown out the worst of any day. A young woman screams with pleasure when she sees Kareen and asks if I'm her mother. There is a great deal of heavy-duty cheek-kissing and bantering laughter, and only I remain un-amused. Given a table on the terrace upstairs, with a view across the beach road – *La rambla* – there is sea and stars, and I feel my psyche, wound tight as a spring, begin to relax: this is how I had imagined my journey to progress. Only starting earlier, without the trauma of violation and loss in between. Just revisiting that sensation of suddenly not being alone, of there being an unknown entity behind me, makes me shiver and tense up all over again.

I don't feel like your mother, I say, trying to change the mood.

Kareen laughs: How about sisters?

How about friends, I reply, and she likes that.

You had such bad luck, she reflects, ordering a jug of sangria and some snacks; We want you to experience another side of Montevideo.

Suddenly I realise that I'm starving, but there is little food when it arrives and I dare not order more. Luckily there are questions and answers and stories to take my mind off my stomach. So I switch on my tape recorder.

Carlos is trying to explain the meaning of the word Uruguay, and he and Kareen are switching back and forth in English and Spanish. It means, he says, The river of birds and coloured shells.

What are those animals, like this, interjects Kareen, sticking up a finger on each side of her head.

Snails, we chorus.

Si, si, river snails, *paracoles* in the language of the Quechua native people.

Then she begins to talk about family. When calling earlier and asking if she was busy, she had started to tell me about her own grandfather, and a ritual she had conducted at his grave two years before. My quest – however I had described this journey to her – had reminded her, touched her heart, she says. It seems she and Carlos are off up along the coast tomorrow to their holiday hideout. Actually it belongs to some German guy; they're housekeeping until he returns to Uruguay.

It seems that Kareen had met a young German (one and the same? I never did find out) in Berlin and got pregnant. She continues: I didn't realise until it was too late that he had a problem with alcohol. But he dried out, so we got married, and our daughter Lara had her eighth birthday just two days ago. I came back here with her three years ago. I didn't like Germany, and I didn't like the Germans.

In the beginning she decorated the facades of buildings to make a living. It was wonderful work and very well paid, she recalls: creating wonderful multi-coloured effects for house owners who wanted something special. I guess it was this talent that enabled her to buy her own place in the area where she also works. Later on the way back to the hotel she takes a detour and shows it to me: a massive frontage with two-storey-high shutters and a crenulated edging to the rooftop, like a castle. Bought for 24,000 pesos, she hopes to sell it for 60,000 when the interior is completed.

Carlos is a naval architect, meaning he designs boats and yachts, domestic craft mostly. Yes, he gets a fair amount of work; Uruguay has such a great coastline, for those who can afford to play.

Such a strange evening. We talk politics mostly, but also about traveling and living abroad. It's only when I check the tape that I find it has run out, and in a state of stupefied despair, completely forget that I always carry a spare. I think I kind of give up; decide too many things are working in collaboration against me. It's only when Kareen's face began to change shape that I consider I might be pissed. But Carlos said no: She

363

does that, he says calmly; She has many faces, one moment a Madonna, the next a witch. See, see how it's changing again? Look.

And he's absolutely right. It is.

## NOVEMBER 25, 1999

I am squatting on the beach under the bay wall over a scooped-out hole in the sand. My guts are in turmoil; I have the runs and no tissues. Fortunately there are few people about, because it is drizzling (just as I am!)

Informed that the British Embassy was on Rambla, I had decided to walk to save money. But the address turns out to be an unrelated business and I am completely at a loss. The guard on the door waves his arm up the coast road but the instruction is meaningless. I am tired out – not through lack of sleep; I slept fine with (oddly) no remembered dreams – but dispirited and drained of energy. Well, I decide, this is an emergency, and an emergency requires a cab. Hang the money. I guess I can always get another loan – this time from the Embassy. That's what embassies are for, right? Helping out nationals in distress? Well, I am about as distressed as I want to be ever again.

By the time I reach the correct address – a sedately pleasant large white house a little way inland – my guts have calmed down. Required to leave my camera at the gatehouse, which seems a bit unnecessary, I find myself entering another official lobby made cosy, this time with a poster for The Montevideo Players' production of *Sherlock in the Pub*, as adapted (it hastens to add) from *The Speckled band* by Sir Arthur Conan Doyle. This, together with ads for regional dishes such as Lancashire Hotpot, Welsh Lamb, Soda Bread, Stilton Cheese, Cox's Orange Pippins, Singin' Hinnies, Colchester Oysters, Cromer Crab, Cornish Pasty and Dundee Marmalade and Cake. Talk about a culture warp!

The British Pro-Consul knows that I am coming. I had faxed her from Japan, explaining that I was traveling to trace my grandfather's family. And here she is, smiling and exuding the calm confidence of one who knows she can help.

The trouble, I begin (feeling quite the fool), is that before I can even think about any research, I need a new passport. And I explain what happened.

All faith in the purported sanity, kindness and calm commonsense of British embassies is instantly restored, because the first thing Ma. Frugoni Sorace says, her face muscles twitching with genuine concern, is: Oh, you poor thing. Would you like a cup of tea?

The formalities do not take long. The only drag is that I have to get a picture taken so a new passport can be prepared. Turn left, head for the main road, walk a while and find the shopping mall on the right, I am told; I will find a photo shop somewhere inside. And so I begin to walk...

By now the weather has cheered up a little, with a few breaks in the low cloud cover, but soon I am sweating and exhausted all over again. The mall is quite a distance and once located it takes a while to find the studio. As the photographer stands me for my *fotocarne polaroid* against a suitable background, tears of humiliation begin to trickle down my face. You can't see them in the photo, thanks be, but there is a look about the eyes that suggests I have seen a ghost – or maybe that I am at my wits end? Looking at it later I am amazed at how tanned my face is, how short and blonde and bleached my hair, how much weight I have lost overall. I look like I'm turning into a different person.

Back at the embassy, after a second cup of tea and just one positive image of this most recent expedition consciously imprinted in memory – the wall of a house and its curvaceous wrought-iron stairway extravagantly swathed in layer upon layer of purple, pink and white bougainvillea – I am told to return tomorrow when, with luck, I should be able to pick up my new passport. Luck, I think bitterly. I feel distinctly out of any such commodity. Still something drives me on. Come to think of it, it always has...

I take a taxi to the British Cemetery on Avenida Rivera, which I find to be not so far distant. I can walk there next time, I realise, which is heartening. At the cemetery office, George Roper, the English official in charge is off today. (Another dose of Just my luck!) Instead an assistant – one of the many gardeners – pulls down a record book for the year 1954 and swiftly locates my grandfather's entry. There is a thrill to have come so far and yes, here he is.

Here? Where?

The gardener leads the way between the graves and monuments, looking for Sam in Sector B, set aside predominantly for British subjects. I am searching too – my eyes scanning names and inscriptions but finding nothing relevant. My helper – a man in his late thirties and very kind – scratches his head and goes back along the row, looking more carefully. He then turns down towards a path, where two beautiful conifers rise to meet the sky. I am moving in another direction altogether when I hear him gasp and call, Signora... As I walk towards him, I see a gamut of emotions racing across his features: relief, shock, sympathy, embarrassment. Because far from standing beside any kind of monument, he's looking down on to a flat piece of unkempt turf, with a small weed-covered mound, and a marker stuck in the earth alongside – a decaying stick bearing the faint, near illegible number 2957.

I look at the ground. I look at the man. He shakes his head, shrugs his shoulders, pulls a pained apologetic face.

This is it? I ask. This is Sam's burial place? The mound – slightly obscene in its uncared for state – is where his chest and heart would have lain. The trees are growing from out from near his feet.

I start crying all over again.


I hug my room the whole evening. I am not hungry. Neither do I feel like company, being caught up in a worst-case scenario where my passport is not ready and I have to accept defeat and blow off the remaining days of what is fast turning into a joke of a Grand Plan. Except, of course, I never had a plan to start with, other than to be in one certain place on one a certain day, but that was all. Instead I turn to Sam and his letters, because even when the chips were down, my grandfather was a strong role model: a brave old lion. In his final years, he was able to find comfort in my family, even though we were so far away. As I determine to find comfort in his love of this city and the country where he was born, and so tomorrow will follow in his footsteps to the place where in his correspondence at least he always seemed to be most happy.

He begins 1951 on the eve of his birthday in a reflective mood: *I have had many difficulties since 1935, and it was in 1938 that I began to find my feet, but the war lasting several years impeded my progress, and through those years I had a very lean time.* The only really good year, he admits, was 1948, *and that has been my mainstay ever since.* Cautiously provided for, he looks forward to a retirement some day, *probably in Uruguay, but perhaps within certain considerations, in England.* He is coming to England soon, not on business, but with the hope of *extending my turn on this mortal coil.* He knows little of anybody except my father, which he regrets, *but have learned by experience that one has to look after oneself, without being selfish, or mean. I am willing to help those who show some love and respect in return, and in this I regret that you are the only one to have proved loyal.*

He left for Europe on April 8 full of beans, literally: *England need not worry*, he joked; he was *bringing supplies.*

He writes in May, still in the UK but using Buenos Aires office notepaper, delighted to hear that we are now amply supplied with rice, pulses and tapioca. He notes that we must be so excited as Jo's wedding draws near, and (as if to keep his own end up when faced with the prospect of landed gentry in the family) describes a lunch at a business friend's palatial home and how they drove out to visit one of the Sassoon family.[58] There is a second letter, also dated the 7th, in which he apologises for our box of goodies getting mixed up with one sent to his sister, Mrs Stroyan; seems we missed out on some sweets and also Vascolet, which is described as being similar to Horlicks.

On June 17 he is staying at the Ladore Hotel, in Keswick, pleading with my father to send him Betty's address. At the end of the month he is in Hoylake , staying with his sister, wondering how the wedding in Coventry has gone. He will be at the Grosvenor Court Hotel in Davies Street, London from the following Friday, then leaving to see friends in Bournemouth. He says he will be very pleased to see us all and is planning to stay over two nights in mid-July. But did he come to stay? Why was he not at the wedding? Did he visit us at all? Again I have no memory.

Writing from the One Ash Hotel in Llandudno in North Wales in late July, Sam asks my father for a few days of his time in Birmingham before he heads off to await passage back to Buenos Aires in late September. *I have not heard from Betty, who could easily write to me care of your address, and if she does not do so before I leave, she will be out of luck entirely. I want to help her if I can, but if she continues to ignore me, then it will be her loss.* A short note from Hoylake dated September 15 concludes with a cryptic but telling comment with regards to his youngest son: *Sorry for Randy* (by now a chronic invalid living a restricted life in Liverpool with his wife Sally) *but as you say, got good compensation, and lives to fight another day. He all but had it, but missed the bus.*

My uncle had all but what? And which bus did he miss?

Sam's last letter before sailing is from the Cumberland Hotel at London's Marble Arch. He is upset because the train after his from Liverpool had been involved in a bad accident, with many killed and injured.[59] *My opinion is that fast trains are too long and swerve dangerously around the curves. The carriages sway when the tail is long, and I hope precautions will be taken to avoid this occurring again.*

He has been looking through his Case No. 1 (his largest piece of luggage) to see if there is anything he can gift my parents. He has already organised a present for me, something that I treasure still. *My sister Bea is sending Angela my silver cup, or tank, which was a birthday or a christening present to me from someone, and I hope she will take good care of it, as an ornament, and as a remembrance of Grandaddysammy, when he is chasing shooting stars.*

He had wanted to go to a good football match but all tickets proved sold. Instead he may go to see Jack Buchanon in an Ivor Novello play at a theatre nearby. Friday night or Saturday morning he plans to send my father his Baracuta coat; after he has sailed he can make do with his thin mackintosh.

368

*I am holding onto the fiddle,* he scribbles as an addendum; *when anyone decides to learn, they may have it.*

What fiddle? He played the fiddle? Or was it a violin? Whichever, what happened to it? Where did it end up?

Writing from on board MV *Brasil Star*, four days out of Montevideo, Sam wishes my father had made it to the railway station in Birmingham to say goodbye: *I was looking out for you until the last moment.* But he cheers himself up with good memories of a day in Lisbon, a few hours in Tenerife, and also a full day at the Brazilian port of Santos, where he took advantage of a visit to Sao Paolo, *now the growing wonder of the world.* Finally he signs off by asking my father to make sure Sal receives the enclosed message, which reads: *I send you my congratulations in remembrance of your seventieth birthday, with all my best wishes, and my unfaltering love.*

He arrives back in Buenos Aires to find three strangers moved into his room at the Hotel Hispano. Having promised to keep it for him, management had apparently been seduced by the idea of obtaining three times the rent. My grandfather is now in the Novel Hotel, a few doors down, and much put out with hurt and anxiety. Still he finds time and energy to worry about my health. I've been ill apparently. At age eleven, why don't I remember more? There's so much I don't remember… gaps that are fast driving me crazy.

By the end of the year he is thinking to make a base in Uruguay; with permits coming through, there's the hope of business. In Buenos Aires, however, *there is little I can do and Howard can look after that. He is always busy, writing letters to all and sundry, hoping that some day conditions will change and then he will have everything ready.*

Soon Sam is spending Tuesdays, Wednesdays and Thursdays on low-key business-related activities in Montevideo. The rest of the time he heads for sun, sand and sea to spend his time writing letters and enjoying mountain and ocean air. He has a very nice front room overlooking the ocean – *nice to sleep in with the windows wide open* – with terrace and bathroom. More specifically, at the Colonial Hotel, in Piriapolis.

# CHAPTER 23

# PIRIAPOLIS

**NOVEMBER 26, 1999**

The coach is comfortable and clean, and we roll out of the city on the timetabled dot. It is a miracle I am aboard; while trying to find my way to the bus station, I twice found myself off the map – my map anyway – sans direction, sans commonsense, sans everything. There is also the dis-ease[60] of this heart-stopping roller-coaster of a month with all its extremes of emotion – one minute fine, euphoric even; the next utterly miserable – being so familiar. Cavalcades of campaign trucks and cars whizz by in both directions, banners flying, hooters honking, whistles blowing. So different to Japanese electioneering, where all you hear is the name of the candidate being screamed over and over again, and the white-gloved hands of hired, pretty faces flutter out of windows to convey purity and trust.

Bowling along the coast road, northwards, there is the sense of having entered Munchkin Land. While stretching it a bit, I could be in picture-postcard England, and mostly because of the thatching. Nothing to do with She-Who-Must-Be-Obeyed, of course, but rather eccentrically thatched rooftops. Here a cottage styled like a Chinese pagoda, but with any number of little pointed and flat and curvy soft-topped roofs. Followed by a one-storey restaurant with dinky ribbon-tied curtains and a crenellated thatch as thick as that topping Japanese *minka*.[61] I wonder if reeds are used in place of wheat or rice straw; being so near the sea, maybe there is a type of die-hard reed or grass that offers a source of free roofing material.

It is a lovely ride, and I feel refreshed and almost good-humoured again. (See what I mean? Such emotional swings can hardly be normal – or healthy, for that matter.) Uruguay, I absorb from source materials: the smallest republic in South America, with 72,153 square miles of fine agricultural land, a coastline that stretches 120 miles, plus 270 miles of river bank to the east. There are no mountains above 2,000 feet, only woodland and streams and a soil so rich with potash that it is superior even to that of the Argentine *pampas*. The climate is also favourable – healthy and bracing, as Sam would say.

Then we have Montevideo: founded in 1726 on a promontory between the ocean and Horseshoe Bay, with city streets wandering out into the surrounding countryside and taking into their welcome embrace Cerro peak, the Lofty Isolated Cone, that gave Monte-vid-eo (I see a mountain!) its name. Back in 1936, when Sam was settling in across the river, the city was home to just over 666,000. Today the entire population of Uruguay stands at just under three and a half million, which is about the same as Japan's port of Yokohama. Come to think of it, Wales would fit into Uruguay about fifteen times; Israel maybe a dozen (not much larger than Wales but with seven and a half million inhabitants).

As for Piriapolis, this is the capital's nearest playground (rather as Brighton was to London in its own heyday). Sam loved this tiny resort, spending more and more time hanging out beside the ocean as he grew older. He was there towards the end of 1951, for the festive season and celebrations crossing into the new year: *We had a very nice Christmas Eve, the proprietor of the hotel putting up about two dozen bottles of champagne, nuts, figs and fruit at a table of about twenty, and we all had a very good time. Christmas day is not the gift-giving day out here, but falls on the 6th of January, the day of the King of Kings, and the Three Wise Men.*

The icing on the sadly absent Christmas cake was to receive a gift from home – my home, that is: a new photograph of my sister, which Sam says has been much admired, *And I shall surely cherish this, and it will occupy first place in my small collection of photographs. Give Bridget a kiss for being so lovely.* (I always did take second place to my sister in the looks department.)

So 1952 begins in a relatively upbeat manner. A letter from Betty has filled him with pleasure and relief; he's also happy to hear that Catherine spent the holidays in Stroud with her mother. But mostly he thinks it a very good idea that my father buys our house in Coventry (rented up to this point), and shows willing to bend over backwards to help. Having suggested that his son offer 200 pounds sterling less than the asking price of 1,450, he continues: *If I leave this earth quick enough, you would I hope have had more than the 150* (pounds) *now required to fix the deal, so I think it better to let you have this now rather than later... and I shall ask Mr Horace Alderson Smith* (described as an old friend and one of the foremost solicitors in Liverpool) *to deduct it from any sum that you might be entitled to at my decease. I don't want to call it a loan, but if I get hard up in the later days, which I do not expect, I might come to you for a pipeful of tobacco, whilst I sit on the old farm fence.*

Signing off by hand, he adds in practical fashion: *Mr A. Smith is co-executor for me, with you.*

Late February is less in balance, with first the shock of the death of King Edward in London, and then news of Princess Elizabeth's accession to the throne. *We had a mournful week... I am sure The Royal family will be tired out. I hope and trust the new Queen will be well advised by the Conservative government, and it is a blessing that Churchill is in power to help things along. I trust that all the days of <u>give</u>* (the word give heavily underlined) *are over and that we will hold fast to all the remainder of the Empire, and hit hard at any interference by terrorists or anyone else.*

Weeks later he has still not heard whether my father has gone ahead with the house purchase, and wants to know how I did in my exams. By May, he is still waiting to hear if I passed the 11+ examination (for creaming off the so-called intellectually advantaged into grammar schools) and is in sole charge of the office in Buenos Aires; Howard Pheasant and his wife, Winnie, have sailed for England. There's little to do, but still: *I am now located at the Novel Hotel... have a good room on the 5th floor, with a long balcony, separate from the others...have my carpets down, my pictures up, so it looks more comfortable. Food is good, and plentiful, but meat is missing on Fridays... Argentina boasted of its food, but cannot do so now, as things have changed so much for the worse.*

On June 16 he sends me fondest love and many kisses and is quite sure I will do better next time. Having heard of my failure to make the grade, he responds with a sensitivity and unconditional kindness that would have been more than a little welcome at the time, if I had ever seen his letter: *Extremely sorry to hear that Angela did not have any luck. I am certain she is quite capable of getting through, but she was in no doubt in such a state of excitement, and nervous, that she could not concentrate, and I would very much have liked to have seen her papers, probably quite intelligent, but very likely in a mix up, due to the causes named.* (He could have added fear as a reason for distress, but could hardly have known that his granddaughter lived in a constant state of terror of failure and familial disapproval.)

There are some complications regarding cash flow, he tells his son. So saying, he outlines plans to send Savings Certificates bought in 1949 to be cashed or deposited as my father thinks fit. If there is any left after the deposit laid down, he adds, *I might leave the balance to help out with Angela's troubles.* He then quickly follows this letter with another, explaining that he wants to help with my school fees: *In Whittakers' Guide they have a list of the principle schools, but the only one near you is Leamington High School, the fees of which appear to be from 30 to 40* (pounds) *a year. My proposal is that I pay one third of the yearly fees, but not expenses, although I might give you a start with something to help out with an outfit.* (School uniform.)

This is the first time I ever understood that Sam was in part responsible for coming to my rescue. Without his help, I would not have attended King's High and be who I am today. Having said this, I also know that in order to know where I am going, I need to know where I have been. Or as some sage wrote along similar lines: It's difficult to know where to go if you don't know where you have come from. Another solid reason for making this trip.

As we draw into Piriapolis, I collect my belongings. I am being more careful with my backpack now, wondering more and more why I never wore my usual money belt – not that this would have necessarily saved my Filofax, but it might have made the required difference. What is that saying, something about how the flutter of a butterfly's wing on one side of the world can result in a typhoon the other? Cause and effect... maybe I understand karma better than I think I do.

Near-natural parkland rolls down towards the sea; it's very quiet and near deserted. The weather is warm but there's a breeze, carrying the promise of rain, but not yet. Reaching the front, I turn instinctively to the left, gaze along the promenade and shiver: hair stands up on the back of my neck. I can place Sam exactly as he is posed for the photograph held now in my hand, taken by someone unknown to me and quite possibly a stranger to my grandfather. There is never a hint in any of his letters that he was accompanied by anyone, only the occasional mention of someone met in passing or in his hotel.

Here he is: striding along towards the camera, wearing a crumpled cream suit, and behind him, providing a near-perfect lesson in perspective, his hotel. And oh my goodness, there it is, straight-ahead, low and white-painted, exactly as it was nearly sixty years ago. There's surprisingly little development anywhere around – or that is the initial impression: Piriapolis is indeed a very small place, and so off-season it's hardly happening. Only the sound of hammering suggests preparations for busier times ahead – that, and a man up a ladder, refurbishing a sign. To my right the sea is either receding or advancing; either way it's a long way out, leaving a wide beach of pristine, nearly empty white-gold sand that stretches uninterrupted for miles. I say near, because there is a sprinkling of folks, but so distant, blown and scattered that they resemble survivors of some shipwreck, castaways.

Was Sam a castaway? Was he the survivor of a shipwreck: his marriage? Did my grandmother cast him away without a backward glance? Did my grandfather cast himself away, dramatically, hoping that someone would take note, offer pity and call him back – or did he run off more like a wounded puppy, tail between his legs? If so, this would be a good place to lick one's wounds, feeling mighty sorry for your self, or so it seems to me.

The two-storey Colonial Hotel is lovely, just as imagined, though now overlooked by an overpoweringly ugly condo with each storey decorated in attention-seeking stripes of white and blue. By contrast Sam's choice of abode looks like a small cruise liner – complete with upper deck – in genteel retirement. Art Deco in style and with the original lettering in faded sepia on flaking whitewash, there is bougainvillea around the porch and a front hedge of flowering hydrangeas. Inside it is quiet and still, as if caught in a time warp; there seems no one around. But then a young boy wanders through, followed by an attractive dark-haired woman in an advanced stage of pregnancy. With only a few words of English and a warm smile, she explains that there is only one accommodation free, and this is on the ground floor, next to the lobby and opposite her son's room. She opens the door to show me, and while small and not especially welcoming, the bed is good and the bathroom clean. I take it.

I walk along the-near deserted quay (*mole* as Sam called it, tending to spatter his letters with bits of Spanish). If the hotel is full, where are the guests? Huddled in their rooms maybe, listening to the radio, drinking cider and smoking cigars (or so I like to imagine; more likely they are simply watching TV or sleeping). To my right is the cold, fresh and lively Atlantic, to the left the ground rises gently, up to where large period villas and pensions scatter the lower reaches of Cerro San Antonia. This is one of four mountains – hills more like – along this coastal region, and it looks like an afternoon stroll. But the gradient is steeper than it looks, and soon I'm huffing and puffing. Approaching by the Rambla de los Ingles – English Road – I turn inland to explore the grid of small streets bounded by yet another Avenida de Mayo, and prowl the boundary of one especially impressive property, which appears sadly to be no longer in business: *Hotel Suizo* reads the lettering on the walls, twice, and despite being weathered to an extreme, still clearly visible. But there is a line of washing outside; as with so many of the other properties roundabout, it is clear that someone is in residence, though whether as a housekeeper, squatter or tenant who knows.

Later I sit against a windbreak on the beach and watch things liven up as late afternoon gets underway. An elderly expat, who being the colour of grilled spam has either never heard of skin cancer or believes himself immortal, is reading a novel based on RAF heroics during the Second World War. What did Sam read when he was beach-bathing, I wonder; newspapers apart, there has never been any mention of books or reading as a way of keeping the mind actively engaged or simply passing time. A fair-haired Caucasian man walks by, hand-in-hand with a beautiful black woman with braids. Children – no more than a dozen; let's be clear here – run at the vast expanse of the ocean, screaming with excitement, and then escape the gentle surf, hollering all over again. But overall there is a sense of quiet and peaceful calm. Is that what Sam found here? Peace? Or did he spend his days gazing out to sea, mostly in a state of dreamy distraction, but sometimes wondering about us all on the far, far side.

Midsummer 1952 sees him back in Buenos Aires. He has heard from my father that it had been decided I go to a school some twenty miles distant; Aunt Kathleen had sold my parents on The King's High School for Girls, Warwick, which she'd attended as a girl, believing it the perfect place for me. But Sam is worried: the school does not appear in Whittakers. So for the moment he is holding on to the 100 pounds that he plans to send us – a lot of money at the time. He suggests in theory that my father invest half in National Savings Certificates, while *the other* (half) *you can hold as two instalments towards the expenses of schooling, so that will take me to the middle of next year.* As an afterthought, he reassures my father that all is well with him. *This is winter here, of course, and sometimes very cold, but I never wear a coat, so if I disappear you will know why, poor man.* (A curiously ambiguous ending if ever there was one...)

He continues to lay plans to travel to England later in the year, intending to pass through Warwick (to pick up a school prospectus, since my father has not forwarded one as requested!), staying two weeks in Hoylake with sister Bea, visiting Scotland and spending ten days in the Lake District. *Business here is nil, so have to depend on Uruguay, which for the moment is closed.*

Piriapolis is near enough closed in itself, and I'm lucky to find a restaurant prepared to feed me: spaghetti with a simple tomato sauce (out of a can or jar, but too hungry to care). The only other people at tables are some local men playing dominoes. Outside it is drizzling slightly, or maybe spray drifting in from the sea, with street lights reflecting dim rainbows in puddles on the road. With a soap opera on TV (always riveting for the first half hour) I consider ordering another beer, remember that most probably I cannot afford one, and return to Sam, writing on October 21 with excitement about my start at school.

My school. Described by the Birmingham Post in 1952 in a series about Girls' Schools in the Midlands as offering "Progressive Education in an Ancient Setting", the expectation was that you went to university, or at the very least entered one of the caring professions like teaching or nursing. A sister school of one for boys endowed by Edward the Confessor (and that's going back a bit), KHS opened in 1879 with twenty-two pupils in buildings that even today represent the full spectrum of Warwick's history: a Queen Anne House (in which in my time the headmistress Miss Hare had her study; a row of half-timbered Tudor cottages (accommodating amongst other facilities my beloved library); and the thirteenth century clock tower (one of two gateways to east and west of the medieval castle town) that was my sixth form classroom. The school encouraged the formation of a Parent Teachers Association years before such an organisation became commonplace. Also it pioneered a School Council, with democratically elected representatives from each class, that not only encouraged changes in the curriculum but even redesigned our school uniforms. Yes, we threw out gym slips, choosing instead to wear smart grey shorts or divided skirts, yellow blouses, black hats and blazers, with a choice of five colours for summer dresses. Now, really, considering it was only a few years after the end of the war, this was cool beyond belief. (Not that I thought so at the time of course; I was too caught up in feeling miserable. Luckily I was good at Art and Literature, and proved useful in school plays; my saving grace at the time.)

Despite initial misgivings, Sam is impressed. In addition, it must be thrilling, he thinks, to travel by Omnibus each day. Also: *she* (me) *will have to grow a larger head to take in Algebra and French, as it will be a good day when she can Parley Vous in a good accent like her Pa.* (My father spoke French? Or was Sam simply referring to my father's fluency in Spanish?) Glad also to hear of our first trip to Scotland after Aunt Jo's marriage, he expresses anxiety about my father, who has been feeling out of sorts, but with no details. (The angina is diagnosed soon after; my father is never well again.) By contrast, my grandfather states firmly that he feels fit enough, and with Howard Pheasant sailed for England with his wife and not due back until December, all he can do is man the office *and knit.*

The following day he writes another letter, the only one not to my father among the one hundred and seven my mother thought to save from the bin. It is to his elder daughter, Catherine, based in Inverness, and working as a consultant in developing a centre for outdoor training for the Scottish division of The Central Council of Physical Education. *I have heard with great pleasure,* he writes, *that very shortly a book will be published, if indeed it has not already appeared, and I wish to convey to you my warmest congratulations on your advance into the ranks of authors... sailing for England on the 28th of May next, I shall obtain a copy at the first opportunity... Of course, I have not heard from you for many a long day, but with sparse news, I have followed your career with considerable interest. If you can brace yourself up to sending me a few lines, I shall be tremendously pleased... With love, and my very best wishes, Father.*

*Cairngorm Adventure at Glenmore Lodge: Scottish Centre of Outdoor Training*, written and illustrated by Catherine M. Loader, was published on the first day of 1952 by W. Brown, in Edinburgh, so it had been available for some time. No doubt Sam would have been mightily impressed with its foreword, as scribed by Lord Malcom Douglas Hamilton (OBE, DFC, MP). For myself, it is more a matter of recognition: my aunt was a writer and a photographer, as I am now. (In addition she told me that she played cricket for England, but I've yet to find her name listed or recorded anywhere in the annals of the game's history... still this is nothing new!) Her younger sister Betty too was of a literary bent; she wrote fine letters even when stretched with stress. I walk in their footsteps, not those of my father.

Catherine wrote with careful consideration, organizing factual material appropriately while allowing room for lyrical description and people to speak personally through prose and poetry. I especially like the verse she included in her book entitled "I Leave Tonight For Euston", because it celebrates the train route I have been using to visit my mother and Jo for the last thirty years or more.[62] As for my aunt's photographs, they speak for themselves, the monochrome capturing perfectly the harsh beauty of the rocky crags and snow-covered peaks of Glencoe and the mountains she loved so well. I remember how she took me there when I was twelve, provided my first and last experience on skis and pointed out across a lake from a bothy – maybe even THE bothy - and predicted (long before global warming began to manifest warning signs of climate change) that the site would one day be a winter sports wonderland. How shocked and sad she would be today to see the mess we have got ourselves into; some years there is hardly any snow at all. At other times, almost too much.

Sam's last letter of the year is scribed on November 30 to catch the RMS *Andes*, which sails a few days later. *The world has not been kind to most,* he notes, *but still it goes on.* He is filled with hope, however, that the forthcoming Coronation Year will bring *Peace and Prosperity* to the whole world, but especially *Our Commonwealth.* It has been a special year for my parents, he notes, *getting Angela started on the royal road to success, and I sincerely hope that she will have the happiness at Warwick High School to overcome nervousness, and to give her the confidence to win high honours... Please give Angela and Bridget One Pound each* (for Christmas)... *With fond love, Grandaddysammy.*

## NOVEMBER 27, 1999

It is 2a.m. and I am still reading – reading in bed, wondering which room he occupied on the floor above. My own space seems to hang in limbo, being neither pleasant nor unpleasant, simply small and cramped and lonely. With the shutters closed for security, there is a sense of isolation – of having somehow fallen off the planet; no-one knows where I am. Only I am in on this secret, and guess that if I were to die here in my sleep, as he did, a similar series of events would follow on: the hotel owners getting in touch with the embassy who would get in touch with Akii and so on. Would the remnants of my own life find their way to Japan, or the UK, to be picked up by Lee, perhaps, at Heathrow. Would he show them to anyone? Miss me? Ensure my life was not forgotten? While I have stuff in Japan and even more stuff in London, there's not a lot here to be passed on: files, recording equipment, a few clothes, my rings on the side table. That's about it, really. I know I ought try to get some rest, but sleep will not come; it eludes, hanging out there on the fringes of consciousness, taking a back seat on this part of the journey. I guess it knows that at some point, if not tonight, there is a longer deeper sleep to come; I can catch up then.

As death began to catch up with my family in 1953.

There is a letter, undated, that simply acknowledges grave tidings from England. The nature of the news is unclear, but the phrase *I expect you, Catherine and Barney will be able to do what is necessary* suggests initially that maybe my grandmother was sick. Sam has his own problems though: *I myself am not well, and might peg out at any time, and am ready without calling for help from anyone. I might just as well be found a hole in Uruguay as anywhere. When I go, don't make any fuss, or be sorry, as I wouldn't believe it from anyone excepting yourself, and family.* Suddenly he has plunged from optimism into a mood of dark self-pity.

To make things worse, a letter from England in Spring hits hard. He writes *to relieve deep feelings of grief over the report you send regarding the death of our beloved Betty… In these enlightened times it is surprising that such cases should occur, even in a countryside hospital one would think that science and experience would have been able to deal with such emergencies in a satisfactory manner… Betty was a hefty girl, and could have withstood heavy treatment in an operation after birth, but I suppose special causes prevented anything from being done.* He will make a point, he says, of seeing John Elwell (his son-in-law) in the summer, and visiting the last resting place of his daughter's remains. *I do not like cremation, but no doubt many prefer this method of the return of dust to dust.*

Betty and John already had one daughter, my cousin Genevieve. Now there was a second, named Elizabeth after her mother, who has died in childbirth, with my grandmother riding to the rescue to help look after two babies. Sam is pleased to hear that Catherine has also been helpful, taking me up North, away from tragedy I was hardly aware of, not because I was uncaring but because so little was communicated at home. In fact, I'm not even sure we were told our aunt had died, just that I was going on holiday.

*Tell Catherine I want to see her, either in Edinburgh or I would run up to Inverness,* Sam continues, wanting more than ever to mend remaining fences. He is biting at the bit to get aboard the MV *Brasil Star, because there is no business here at all. When I get back I shall probably remain at Montevideo, as I had intended, but frustrated by the Argentine Government not allowing anyone to cross over, by denying traveling certificates which are necessary.*

Did he go to England? I don't remember and neither does my mother now. There is no one else. Genevieve, whom I found and reconnected with in 1996, has no memory of him whatsoever. Her sister, she said, was not interested in meeting anyone from her mother's side of the family. I remember thinking how interesting that was: another generation angry at the world, refusing to even try to understand what had gone before and make amends. How did Genevieve become lost to me when, in my dwindling family, first cousins could be counted on one hand? Because – as she explained – after her father remarried, his second wife had insisted on cutting all links. But as Gen first wrote to me (in swift reply to my letter of enquiry via Michael Hall, where her father had taught for many years): My father always kept the memory of our birth mother alive for us and consequently she has always remained very important to me.

For years, her mother's elder sister was her only contact with the Loader family: We used to visit Granny Primrose (at the New Nursing home in Stroud) and meet up with Aunty Catherine, but after Granny died we lost touch. Did she move abroad? She came to my first wedding but I didn't hear from her after I got divorced. Gen has a son, William, from that marriage, and is now with Richard, by whom she has a second son, Jonny. Elizabeth was also married with two children, but the sisters did not appear to be close. Their father had died in 1989; their stepmother in 1994.

I try to see Gen whenever I am visiting the UK. She has multiple sclerosis and is now confined to a wheel chair that she drives at full tilt about Hilly Fields in Brockley. Synchronistically (that word again) her sister experienced a different form of the same disease, affecting her arm as a music student and therefore sabotaging her career as a concert violinist. No long-term physical consequences, but another reason for being mad at the world. Gen has another form of this abominable condition; the kind that creeps up unawares, and then continues relentlessly to do its neurological worst. Though her life is far from easy, she – like my sister – is amazingly strong and unbowed. I think of Gen, Liz, Bridget and myself, all ageing women now, all sharing the same DNA, all beset with medical problems that seek to wreck the body and weaken spirit. My sister has suffered rheumatoid arthritis since age sixteen, triggered, she claims (angrily), by the first of many defections in her life: me going away to college and leaving her with my parents. (My life has been ruled by rejection, she says, counting off the names and experiences on brave but crooked fingers.) Could it be, I wonder, that stress factors, now built into the conditioned frame and fabric of our family history, continue to take their ongoing rolling toll?

By the end of 1953, Sam is feeling increasingly under the weather: *I understand that anyone aged seventy cannot jump, and skip about, and I have had a rather hectic life, but am now feeling extremely tired, not being able to get about as previously... Insomnia is one of the worst complaints there is, and if I don't get better rest I will see a doctor and ask him to give me something useful... am not sure whether my heart is also not in good trim, but when I drop, someone will know. I won't see a doctor, excepting to get a sleeping pill, or some other.*

Yet still he can talk business. It seems that Josie (as he refers to my godmother) has been visiting my parents, and there has been talk of getting good prices in Argentina for Aberdeen Angus from my uncle's herd: *As to Bulls. The Argentine peso is down to 60 to the pound, and 13,000 pounds is a long way out of the actuality. Breeders are fools to sell their animals in auction; they should all club together, form a Limited Company, and send their animals to Adolfo Bullrich and Co, for auction in Buenos Aires. Then they might make some money. Love to all...*

Sam begins 1954 in a more upbeat mood, though struggling – happy to hear that Primrose and Catherine were with John and the babes over Christmas and New Year, but observing that the *sad loss of Betty could not but bring about sad remembrances.* He's in Piriapolis again, where he intends to stay several months getting fitted up with a nice tan: *when I next come to England you will find me almost black.* He hopes my parents

383

have a good time at The Ball (in Scotland – a rather grand event at a local castle that had my mother machining yards of black and white tulle and my father working on his waltz for weeks on end). Sam notes also that he hears regularly from his two sisters and Alex (who is both his brother-in-law and his estranged wife's brother).

February, he receives what he fears to be a mighty blow: news that The Associated Cycle Manufacturers of Coventry have been taken over by Raleigh Industries Ltd in Nottingham. Bicycles have been the benchmark of his success over the years, and he wonders whether Raleigh will want him to continue acting as agent for two TAMC models. He is also owed money – around a thousand pounds. *You cannot do anything,* he writes to my father, *but you might just quiz anyone who might know something about the state of affairs at Canley, and write me as quickly as you can.* He worries that this valuable source of income cannot be replaced, adding plaintively: *It has taken me years to build up the trade.*

Within weeks, however, he is back to his old self, having heard from Westminster Bank in Liverpool that the commission he was owed would be remitted in a week or so; also that Associated had been taken over lock, stock and barrel, with no fear of being broken up, with other payments due. On top of this far better news, there is a firm order for 600 bikes, with demands for another 600 if the UK can churn them out fast enough. Raleigh has offered him sole agency (but on their terms). *Also I am doing fairly well with accessories, and bicycle prospects are good, but...*

It is the word *but* that hangs in the air. Business is looking up but with the implication that it may be too much work for a man who regards himself as semi-retired. Even traveling between Montevideo and Piriapolis is exhausting, he admits. *Yesterday was hot, and got soaked through twice with perspiration, and so at the end of the day was all out. Feel better now after a good night's sleep, and just had a lovely bathe in the sea. Got lots of letters to write, and will have my siesta after lunch, but must catch the post before 5 p.m. FOND LOVE TO ALL, Cheerio, FATHER*

Dated March 25, 1954, there are two additional notes One (typed along the top edge as an obvious afterthought) reads: *SOLD JAPAN TEA to a very good firm here, and have great hopes of starting WHISKY also.* The second is in my father's handwriting: *Rec'd 4/5/54* it reads (just weeks before my thirteenth birthday).

This is the last letter Sam ever wrote. On the night of May 11, he died, allegedly in his sleep, of a massive heart attack. Lying here, knowing this, fills me with a kind of awe-inspired dread. How often did somewhere above me, Sam lie in the grip of sleeplessness, staring into the darkness, turning over the past and trying to visualise a future. And exactly what happened on that night of passing… did he fall asleep quickly, only to slide into a deeper sleep, quietly without pain? Or did he awake in agony, and feel a great and sudden terror? Overcome, I turn into my pillow. I am not likely to die tonight (although you never know…) Dreams however are another matter. Should Sam appear, would he be in a state of beauteous grace or grave disillusion? Or might my own father come to take me to task for being such a troublesome daughter – casting blame for ten years of heartfelt pain and his own shocking death.

For the first time, I give serious attention to the following thought: is the way we die predestined? Or are we all simply in the hands of the gods?

# CHAPTER 24

# IN THE HANDS
# OF THE GODS

**NOVEMBER 27, 1999 CONTINUED**

It is morning and, considering the shortage of sleep, I feel good. No ghost had appeared at the foot of my bed. The bedclothes have not been plucked from my body and repeatedly cast upon the floor by invisible forces, as once happened to a friend in England.[63] While the room may not have felt especially clear, it was clear of Sam. But am I clear of him? Not quite, and with the end of the month closing in fast, I have to get my skates on. Or maybe simply gather my wits about me.

Over breakfast, the man on duty explains that a family has just bought the hotel and this will be their first season. Will they change it very much, I ask. To which he shrugs and smiles. They have already changed the name, to the Colonial Riviera. As to the history of the place, he knows next to nothing and is not sure if old records still exist. It doesn't matter, I say, which comes as a surprise; I thought it would, but no. As I leave, there are people up on the balcony – maybe the balcony Sam once enjoyed. When they wave, I return the favour but at the same time feel relieved that I cannot see their faces; someone is wearing a Panama hat.

As I return along the seafront to where I must catch the bus, I pass a modestly positioned bronze bust: *Don Francisco Piria*, it reads. Well, well, I hear myself murmur: Now what did you do to have a town named after you? The immediate answer rears up in the form of a building at the far end of the promenade – a construction of such gigantic proportions (compared to the rest of the town) that I cannot believe it has not come into focus before. It's because I've been looking in the opposite direction the whole time I have been here: towards where Sam met his maker. What else I have been missing in my headlong dash towards phantoms? Life itself, perhaps? The thought is so momentous, that it can only go onto hold. So I push it away – but only into cold storage; I'll take it out, thaw it, and put it under the microscope later when there are less pressing matters to hand.

Assuming the pile ahead to be a hotel, I make a quick sortie into the lobby and some adjoining rooms and am stunned: it's beautiful – spacious, elegant, masses of period features. Now I know where the Colonial's guests – many apologies, the Colonial Riviera's guests – hang out, because this is the town's playground. The Argentino Hotel Casino Resort, as it is now called, is one of Uruguay's oldest hotels, built to replicate the Cote d'Azur in its Belle Epoch heyday. Developed in 1930 by our good doctor Piria[64] after an eye-opening trip to France, it was regarded as the most sophisticated beach resort, called a *balneario*, in all of South America when it first opened; currently it offers 300 rooms, 56 suites, a fully-equipped spa with seawater pools, masses of sports facilities (including a synthetic ice rink), a Kids Club and, of course, the hotel's raison d'être, the casino. *Fifty metres from the beach, 100 metres from the town centre* (Piriapolis has a town centre?) *and 200 metres from the bus station, it could not be more convenient and more prestigious*, reads a brochure. Yet I had missed it: for reasons beyond conscious control I had made it a blind spot.[65]

Now I can see the layout of the town as designed. The grandiose hotel-casino at one end (the infinitely more modest Colonial at the other) of a classic waterfront promenade, the Rambla de los Argentinos, named for the elite clientele for whom the resort was created. What else had I missed? Most certainly the home that the visionary doctor – selfless philanthropist, Neo-Renaissance Man, erstwhile egomaniac; there are many opinions – built for his family inland along Bulevar Artigas (which turns into Route 37) and just across what is now Route 73: Castillo de Piria, Piria's Castle. But with no time to spare, I have to rush.

As the bus draws out, two mini cavalcades of trucks and cars and bikes with flags flying and hooters honking head in opposite directions along the promenade: Tabare Ramon Vasquez Rosas, the current President of Uruguay and a member of the centrist-leftist Broad Front Coalition (*Frente Amplio* in Spanish) versus Jorge Batlle Ibanez, a member of the one of the founding political bodies of the country, the Colorado Party. Suddenly Piriapolis appears both lively and interesting. But too late for me. Close to running on empty, I have an appointment to keep, a promise to honour and – somehow – a river to cross.

A few miles out of town, I realise my hands are naked; I have left my rings on the table beside my bed. Disaster upon disaster, I tell myself, followed by, You imbecile, put yourself back to sleep! So this I do, waking only as the bus enters Montevideo and passes a totalitarian concrete block dark with water stains which claims to be Uruguay's main University Hospital of the Nation. There are so many flags flying roundabout, so many election postings... Tabare's campaign in general appears far more extensive and active compared to his competitor; is Batlle cruising on over-confidence, or does he have something up his sleeve?

So it's back to Hotel Los Angeles to say Hello, Goodbye, followed by a quick visit to the Tourist Office nearby, where I make an official complaint about having been sent into a dangerous part of town without warning. Please do better next time, I plead; I would hate what happened to me to happen to any other unsuspecting sucker. When the woman behind the desk spreads her hands as if saying, Senora, what can I do... I put on my journalist's hat, slam down my name card (English one side, Japanese the other) and pull rank. She promises to make a full report. Promises...

I have several items to buy, two of which are proving to be far from simple purchases; I have to walk a good half-mile up and down Avenida 18 de Julio before being forced to strike a compromise. I find a small glass bottle of *sidra* (cider) , but trying to locate a Brazilian cigar in the capital of Uruguay appears to be rather like trying to buy a Havana cigar in the United States: a matter of national pride and political strife.[66] In the end, I buy just any old cigar. What the hell! Who will know the difference except me and Sam, and maybe after all my struggles he'll be willing to forgive me. (The question as to whether I will be able to forgive myself is quite another matter – another consideration to tuck away for future analysis.)

My only remaining task is to find a rose bush. But this is an unlikely acquisition on any busy city street. Sounds of drumming approaching along the sidewalk signals me not to waste time but to move on – but not before tape recording a boy with a flag of the Colorado Party, dancing around two lean, poorly-clothed men beating persistent and emotive rhythms on empty, rusted oil drums hung around their necks: *Vote! Vote! Vote!* You're on the wrong side, I think, but none of my business when all is said and done.

So it is back to the Embassy by bus (I know the way now), with good news for a change: my passport is ready and waiting. Tokyo came through overnight and all I have to do is sign for its receipt. I thank my chic and efficient tea-lady from the bottom of my heart; Senora Frugoni has been an absolute angel. Then collecting my camera and tape recorder from the front entrance as before, I walk to the cemetery while cursing the money wasted on taxis over the past forty-eight hours. I should have asked yesterday, checked out its location in relation to the Embassy. Should, should, should... But did I think to do what now seems so obvious? No.

I'm trying to decide what to buy, and precious minutes are passing... There are three flower stalls across the road from the cemetery entrance, and business is so slow that the aged women flower sellers, with long aprons and headscarves, are anxious for my custom. But they sell only cut flowers, and I want something long lasting. I have this idea, you see, to plant a rose on Sam's grave – bush, standard, rambler, it doesn't really matter – which drives me back to a small shop spotted earlier from the bus. Here I find just one rose bush for sale, almost as if waiting for me, but it costs 850 pesos. Expensive. Expensive for me at least, as it would leave me little to get me back across the Plata, and I have no idea what the bus will cost to Colonia, added to which there will be the ferry fare. I pace to and fro between the shop and the flower sellers, and each time their calls to buy become more desperate and I grow more tired and depressed. My heart says buy the plant; my head says no, buy a couple of stems; take the more careful road, for a change! For once, I am pragmatic; I err on the side of caution and end up with two cut roses, one white, one red. But even as I hand over the cash, I'm at war with myself again, unable to explain how I have come so far and ended up in such a pathetic muddle.

At the graveside, I consider what to do first. In Japan, the rituals associated with death are clearly defined and continue over many years to keep the memory of deceased individuals alive within the family. When a tomb is visited, not only flowers are set in vases; it is common to find cans of beer or sake, cigarettes, offerings of a favourite food and even a newspaper to keep the dear departed up-to-date with current events. In the UK, mourners tend to lay flowers, put their hands together and weep a lot or make sympathetic noises, but little else. We English do not handle death well. Which in part is why I am here today – because of what a Buddhist priest told me in Japan long ago: that the spirit or soul is reluctant to leave this world, and so can be summoned back easily every *O-Bon* – the festival of the dead in mid-August. But after so many years – fifty I thought he said, and this is what stuck, though I could be wrong – a spirit finally passes over for good, having found peace or not. Well it is the end of the millennium and forty-five years since Sam died, and it would, I think, give my father and his family some comfort to be able to offer my grandfather – symbolically at least – the attention and respect he so craved and yet failed to receive. Yes, he had many faults, but so do we all.

I pull the weeds from the site of Sam's broken heart, then with a rake left propped against a tree, try to clear the site, creating what I hope are Zen-like tracings in the dirt all around. Realising the cider requires a bottle opener, I am forced to smash off the cap against a neighbouring grave stone. (Sorry whoever...) The neck of the bottle disintegrates and golden foam spurts into the air in every direction but the one intended. With only a few centimetres left at the bottom, I sprinkle these over the grave marker, saying Cheers! then unwrap the cigar, bite off the end and light it as best I can (having never smoked a cigar in my life and stopped smoking cigarettes in 1988!) This I stick into the soil at the head of the grave. It is easy to fill the cider bottle from a tap and insert the roses, one for love, one for peace, so symbolising an end to the bitterness that kept the two sides apart; even easier to place it beside the cigar. This is when I realise it has both *Made in America*, and the brand name *Wise Owl* printed on the wrapper.

Now, a speech of some kind, but I am shaking with effort and emotion; words do not come easy, sounding more like those of a child than an adult. But what I try to say goes something like this: Grandaddysammy, this is Angela. I'm sorry it's taken so long for me to come and find you. I'm here today because this is the anniversary of your son's death – my father, who died on November 27, 1962, just a few weeks after I left home. I never saw him again, but had to go back and help organise his funeral while knowing I was pregnant. The doctor had confirmed I was three month's gone (gone? such a strange expression this when a baby has in fact come) just a day or so before Eric rang me with the news: a massive heart attack. So many broken hearts, grandfather. So many. Unable to tell anyone about Lee for months, I had to harden my heart all over again, which did not go down well with my relatives. They thought me cold and unloving, when in fact I was simply withdrawn in shock: horror, guilt and blind terror. I was so furiously in denial that I have never really properly mourned my father. I guess I was angry with him for leaving us all like that, and especially angry that he chose to equate my leaving home with not loving him and not caring, to such an extent that he allowed it to kill him; how stupid was that. Does this make sense, Sam? I hope so. Anyway, this trip is for him as much as for you. I am saying hello to you both and sending love from everyone else. And here we all are... Primrose – your wife Sarah, Sal – Catherine, my father, Barney and his own wife Sally, Betty... also my mother, Bridget, my children, Akii, Gen and Richard and their children...

And so I continue putting names to the faces in the pictures that I have carried with me throughout my journey. (That of Gen and her family had arrived just in the nick of time, sent by e-mail and printed out in Santiago.) Having told Sam who and how everyone is, and where they are to the best of my knowledge, I slip the family photos back into their plastic envelope and bury the package as best I can beneath the surface of his grave. At the same time I go on talking, doing the best I can with words among tears, explaining the Buddhist thing, wanting him to know that people did care, that he was and still is missed and loved, and that he can rest in peace. For what I had discovered of course was that Betty and Catherine in particular had been writing to their elder brother for years, asking why their father had abandoned them, while at the same time Sam was asking the same thing of his children. Yet my father, for whatever reason, never put them together. I suppose this is what I am doing now, on his behalf: putting us all properly together.

Leaving is hard. The grave looks a soggy mess, worse than when I started. And there is a bird that, whenever I turn to go, makes a piercing call that sounds like Don't go! Not yet! But the day is glorious. The conifers arising out of Sam's feet are magnificent in their dark green and gently waving branches. There are flowers everywhere, including two on his grave. The War of the Roses is over. The family is re-united, sort of.

It is mid-afternoon when I reach the bus terminus. A ticket to Colonia is 79 pesos, which is less than feared, so I am still in credit. But how much to get back to Buenos Aires? This is the big question I am pondering as

392

the coach draws away from the city and we follow the river inland. The road is straight and smooth and I think again about there being half a million people in Montevideo and only three million in the whole country. That's staggering. No wonder the countryside is so clean and untouched and natural. As if to disconcert, two palms trees pop up from nowhere. Then two young guys run into the middle of the road, also appearing as if from nowhere, waving flags and giving V signs; Batlle again. Tracks head straight as a die across crops and pasture, converging into a pinpoint on the horizon. It really is the most lovely day – fresh breeze, near cloudless sky, very blue – with the feeling that this is a country as nature intended: streams run free and clear edged by reeds and waterfowl; no litter; little to no development and what there is, simple and subtle. I don't think I have been anywhere that looks and feels so unspoiled. Or is this a delusion also. Is idealism (laced with miserable disappointment in myself) clouding the real issue?

I think back to talking with Kareen and Carlos the night before last. They had been explaining how everyone in Uruguay has to be 100 per cent independent and not be reliant on anyone else. Professionally, she said, you have to oversee everything yourself, paying close attention to the smallest detail, then if something goes wrong, you have no-one to blame but yourself. You are responsible, only you. No-one else is at fault.

Japan is completely the opposite, I replied. There the system is organised in such a hierarchical fashion that people are enabled to pass on blame to others so as to appear blameless; they avoid responsibility wherever possible.

Extraordinary, Kareen replied: If I order windows and they are not right, then of course it is my fault. I have to explain to my draftsmen what I want down to the last detail, precisely, precisely, precisely. It forces you to be careful in everything you do.

Here the idea of everyone working together is an alien concept. Explaining to her and Carlos how in certain villages in Japan, a whole community will come together to thatch a house over three of four days, they marveled. It could never happen here in Uruguay, they said; People are totally locked into doing their own thing. And yet the left wing appears to winning people's hearts and minds, which in an ideal world means socialism and sharing and looking after the interests of community ahead of the individual. Something does not add up; something is unclear, someone deluded, but what and who? Me for one for sure.

The soil around here is nearly black. There are flowers growing in the rivers. When an avenue of eucalyptus gives way to another of palm trees, the charming young man sitting beside me – a student going to Colonia del Sacramento to meet friends – announces we are nearly there. As we draw into the town, I can see that it is lovely, full of colour and gaiety, with interesting shops and boutiques and restaurants. I can hear music too. In different circumstances I would adore to explore the cobbled streets of what I know to be the oldest town in the country, and the only Portuguese settlement along the Rio de la Plata. Founded by Manuel de Lobo in 1680, it was a long-time focus of political struggle between Portugal and Spain, and later Brazil. For years, the Spanish on the other side of the river disputed ownership of what became a contraband port, and Colonia changed hands many times. In 1742, the native Guarani fought to drive out the Portuguese. In 1816, the Banda Orientale (as Uruguay was by then generally known) was seized in the name of Rio de Janeiro. Yes, it would be fun to explore the Portuguese area, reminiscent – I am informed by my guide book – of Old Lisbon. Especially the most ancient part, built on a small peninsula jutting out into the river: Barrio Historico, named a UNESCO Heritage site in 1995. But I have a boat to catch, and anyway, look where the exploration of early settlement got me last time.

As I walk in the general direction of the port, I am told that the last boat of the day is due to leave very soon. The *cambio* is already closed, and a few Argentine notes apart I have less than a couple of hundred pesos. Already restaurants are beginning to fill up and I find myself in an interesting position. I am looking through a fence into a garden full of pretty tables and the smell of food and wine. Normally I would be on the inside, but now I am outside, with no hope of gaining entry even if I had the time: I cannot afford to eat here. Hurrying on, I am hot and dizzy and frightened. My back aches, my feet hurt, and I keep being sick. The boat seems such a distance away, with a long drawn out walk across gravel. After an eternity, or so it seems, I join the queue for tickets and find I have more than enough (but not enough to have risked that rose bush). The relief is tremendous. But as I pass through immigration, an official turns over the pages of my new blank passport and queries my status in loud aggressive tones. Unable to say more than *Robado, robado* (hopefully, robbed, robbed!) he demands to see what money I have. As a 100-peso bill plus my remaining Argentine currency and a handful of local coins spill across the desk, he scoops up the lot, stamps a page and signals impatiently that I move on.

Down in the main cabin, feeling as if I have been mugged all over again, I join the queue at the self-service counter and pick out a bun and a coffee. It is only when I get to the till and find I cannot pay that it sinks in: I have no money. And yet, as I reflect on my ring less fingers, my light backpack and even lighter purse, there is the strangest sense of liberation. This has happened before, this sense of having been stripped of all security and familiarity; and I remember those first weeks in Japan, when I could neither read nor write nor understand a single word I heard, and was failing even to walk in a straight line or negotiate a step without falling over. Now that was disorientation. So is this, but tempered somehow by a sense of distracted relief to have done what I set out to do. Also I am nearly home. For as Buenos Aires hoves into view, that is what it feels like: home.

Rallying, I unpack my backpack, shaking out every item and searching into the corners of each and every pocket. Just as I am about to give up and prepare myself for a very long walk, a miracle: I find one peso.

Which is what enables me to get the train back to Caseros. Never have I been so happy to reach the station, smell the cheese shop, respond to the wave of the man in the newspaper kiosk, and see the Tower of Pisa, in all its rusted fading glory, lurching drunkenly into view. Maria-Elena looks up from her accounts when I walk in and her mouth drops open. I guess I must look a fright. I tell her that I was robbed and place the few tiny coins of change from the train on the dining table. This is all I have left, I say.

Maria-Elena cannot believe my misfortune. She mutters a lot in Spanish, shaking her head in disbelief, and then says something so unexpected in relation to the normal level of her English ability, and yet so perceptive, that I shall never ever forget her words – an idiom learned long ago in school that until now she had thought long forgotten): You are more dangerous than a monkey with a razor.


Upstairs, unpacking the little I have left to unpack under the decidedly un-protective eye of dead Ana's rosary, I hear Maria-Elena call for me to come down quickly; Fernanda is here from Madrid for her brother's wedding, and having arrived while I was in Uruguay, has called around to say hello. She looks well – as tall and slim and lovely as ever – and we laugh at the incongruity of the situation: being here when the last time we met was in Walthamstow, with me living in Japan and her thinking to make a new life in Spain. How odd it feels, she murmurs, to be Home.

I'm not the same person, she confides; Nor do I see the people here or life in Buenos Aires in the same way. I feel profoundly changed.

I think of Luis, now a stranger to his hometown and friends. Of Karen, ten years on the move. Yes, I tell Fer, That is how it is, and you're never going to be the same again.

She pulls a face: Is this a good thing or bad?

It is what it is, I reply, and give her a comradely hug.


With everyone in a party mood, I go to bed. It's only 8 p.m. but sleep seems the best way to get out of everyone's way, and I include myself in this equation. I want to get out of my way, distance myself from myself, take a rest from yours truly. Angela is a whinging pain, and I've had enough of her.

**NOVEMBER 28, 1999**

Although waking to pee a couple of times during the night, I do not fully regain consciousness until mid-morning. It is voting day in Uruguay, Vazquez and Batlle battling it out. I have slept god knows how many hours, and having dreamed myself into a different kind of exhaustion, feel wobbly and vaguely unwell. Yet the plan is that we are all going to another party – a lunch party at Fer's parents' house.

Her father, Eduardo, proves to be a large and friendly taxi driver. Mother, Nelida, is stick-thin with a faded careworn face, but pretty and elegant: a dressmaker, who normally uses the room we are sitting down to lunch in as a workshop. As befits a family of Italian extraction, there are lots of people, including younger brother Martin (a bit of a rebel, I gather) and the newlywed happy couple. Fer's elder brother, named after his father, is lovely, a much meatier version of his slender sister but with the same kindly brown eyes and sweet smile. His tiny blonde wife Eugenia brings herself sharply into focus; she is a plastic surgeon, she tells me. Does this mean she has worked on herself, I wonder? We are ten or more around the table, demolishing Napoli-style ravioli drenched in thick cheese sauce, and I am starving. Yet no sooner have I filled my stomach than I realise it may not have been the most sensible course of action: my stomach's been feeling out-of-sorts since yesterday, and my kidneys are hurting. I go to the toilet, apologise to the cook, and make myself sick. Immediately I feel better.

At least one language behind everyone else, I learn that the lunch party is to say goodbye to Fer, who has an early evening flight. Piling into cars and heading for the airport, I am struck by the difference in the way I slip in and out of my home country with occasionally someone to meet me but never anyone to say goodbye, and the warm and emotional style in which Fer is being seen off. Everyone – a dozen or more family members and friends – is crying. At checkout – already in emotional chaos because the Argentine women's handball team is off to Oslo to compete – there is a frantic whip round to gather together 200 pesos to pay for excess baggage: Maria-Elena has stuffed Fer's suitcase full of gifts for Pablo. Only one person has gone missing from the excitement, her brother, and he returns from Duty Free with a gift for me: five volumes of *Mafalda* by the cartoonist Quino (Joaquin Salvador Lavado). To help you with your Spanish for when you come back again, he says, giving me a hug. The cover of Volume 8 has the word *Snif* written three times, which is so pertinent and to the point that soon everyone is wailing, let alone sniffing. There is music too; someone has brought along a guitar to sing Fer off into the night sky. It takes less than fifty seconds after she disappears into Departures, also weeping fit to bust, for high drama to give way to calm, and suddenly we are all back to normal and life goes on. There are lessons here to be learned, I think (without being at all sure what they are). Most definitely lessons to be learned.

On the way back, the happy couple point off the motorway to the barrio where they work at a major hospital. It is one of the most violent in the city, they explain; not a place they would want to take a visitor. All my unkind prejudices about Eugenia are blown to shreds when I learn she is a reconstructive plastic surgeon, one of those miraculous people who put people's burned, smashed and cancer-ridden bodies together when all has been thought to be lost. I am so ashamed.

## NOVEMBER 29, 1999

I sleep, again beset with dreams. The longer I sleep, the more frantic the dreams become, until finally I drag myself to the bathroom and shower into wakefulness. I wait, weak and depressed, for Maria-Elena to wake, writing a list of *Things To Do*. As a matter of urgency I need to ring Akii, ask him to send money, check with Japanese immigration that they will allow me back in without a re-entry visa and with only one aggressively smudged proof of travel in my passport. I like the fact it was issued in Montevideo; a proven link with Sam's birthplace. I also quite like my photo, which shows blonde cropped hair nearly bleached white by the sun and my skin surprisingly tanned; I might almost be smiling, except for the tightness of my lips and a moist quality to the eyes, but then only I know that I was trying my utmost not to cry, cry pathetically for Angela in Uruguay.

I go into the city early, having arranged to meet Maria-Elena later. I post one note to Kareen, to say thankyou and wish her well; another to the Colonial Riviera, enquiring about my rings. Next stop, the Chamber of Commerce, where the Relic is dusted down and stiffly on duty in the lobby, but the rest of the place in turmoil.

I'm so sorry, says formerly dapper David, now red-faced, flapping and on the run: We have a huge trade delegation coming in. Can you come back in a few days?

I can't, I explain; I'm leaving the day after tomorrow.

Well, we'll communicate by e-mail then, shall we? Thank you so much for coming. Thank you so much you so much for calling by...

To be so casually dismissed does not sit easy. Especially when I am clearly – in my own mind at least – running out of time and still with so many loose ends.

CHAPTER 25

# LOOSE ENDS

**NOVEMBER 29, 1999 CONTINUED**

With time to spare I walk to Plaza de Mayo and the Cathedral, where someone is rehearsing an organ recital for Friday. By this time, I realise with a short, sharp shock, I will have gone, be back in Japan.

Scanning the morning paper in the privacy of a pew, I learn that having sold himself to middle-class Uruguayans as a safe bet, Batlle had not only beaten off the Socialist challenge, but I had escaped the resulting brawl of a fiesta in Montevideo.

It is while wondering if this makes me lucky, unlucky or just plain out of it, that I hear a quietly distinguished melodic voice and turn to find a woman of around my age explaining architectural features to a younger woman of around Buffy's age. Their arms are linked and the girl has her head on what I assume to be her mother's shoulder. For some reason I find the sight immeasurably moving, and then realise why: when I get too close to my own daughter, she tends to stiffen and pull away, which – I realise with a shock of recognition – is how I react to my own mother when she tries to be affectionate. Does this mean, I wonder, that Buffy learned this reflex action from me? Just thinking about it makes me spin into emotion; everything makes me emotional... it seems I spend half my life in tears, the remainder in angry struggle. Why is this? What turns a soulful all-knowing baby into a frightened child into a wilful teenager into an angry adult? Why can't I be like everyone else: relaxed, confident, a happy bunny. At which ridiculous point I remember Gaby, a psychotherapist consulted in London before deciding to sell up and go travelling (only Japan was my first proper stop after a night in Hong Kong and I never moved on). I was sitting in West Hampstead in cold midwinter in a state of utter desolation, tears rolling down my face, when she asked (with some irritation it should be said, because I was surely testing her patience) what it was that I wanted. When I replied between sobs that all I wanted was to be happy, her eyebrows shot into her hairline and she shrieked with laughter: Join the human race, Angela.

She was right, of course. Except here I sit, well over a decade later, once again feeling lonely and alienated and so, so sorry for myself, believing that on some deep level no-one understands me... That I'm different and special and just do not fit. That I must have been switched at birth because my parents were surely from a different planet, or I was. That no one listens, that no-one cares. That I am utterly useless and hopeless.

On this note of deep despair – acknowledged on some deep, elusive level as pure melodrama while the same time wonderfully reassuring in its addictive familiarity – I lurch out into brilliant sunshine to find a changing-of-the-guard in progress. With sabres held at shoulder height, and spurs a-jangling, the grenadiers emerge from behind Casa Rosada's renovatory trompe l'oeil curtain to goose-step across the plaza and enter the Cathedral to relieve their comrades at the tomb of General San Martin. I prefer the photographic drape, which has perspective and depth, because the part of the building repainted and now revealed to the public is just too new; with no shading or grime, architectural detail is lost: the façade simply looks very flat and very pink. (Pink, I have to explain, has been ruined for me by Japanese marketing to all women under the age of fifty, and then not always.)

But back to this plaza, founded in 1580 as a symbol of justice, and the main gathering place for celebrations, commemorations and general gatherings ever since. There are birds singing. Clocks chiming – supposedly striking the hour but all at different times. I try to count them and acknowledge once again how beautiful are the buildings –

401

erected in Argentina's Golden Age at the end of the nineteenth century – all around. Sadly, though the grass looks green enough to sit on and sink into a romantic reverie, it stinks of dog pee.

And so back to Argentine-British Community Council on Reconquista to report on my progress – or rather lack of it – where I find Rosemary assisting a gentleman trying to buy his wife Diana-something-double-barrelled, a Christmas pudding. When he asks for some crackers, she queries what age-group they are for. Oh, he replies; they range from three to ninety.

Well then, Rosemary suggests wisely, Why don't you buy six children's crackers and six adults' crackers.

So this is what he does. As he reaches the door, though, he turns to address no-one in particular: I've had five professions you know: lawyer, humorist, magician, and I'm on two television channels – far too busy to go to a Christmas carol service. I'm seventy-four, and today's my birthday.

Rosemary shakes her head after him. It's amazing, she considers, how many people who come here feel that they have to validate their identity, because once they step back out into the street they are lost again in the city.

Everyone tells me their woes, she adds. What are yours?

Me? Oh I was dipped in Santiago and lost my money and credit card, then mugged in Montevideo and lost everything else.

Oh, you poor thing. But there again you don't look very lost to me, she adds with an enigmatic smile; In fact I think you look rather more found than the time we first met.

Pondering upon what on earth she could have meant by such an observation, I set off to find Maria-Elena, and miraculously meet up as arranged in La Recoleta. Ah the irony! Just as I am really beginning to find my way around the city that my grandfather so comfortably made his own, it's time to leave.

This time I allow Maria-Elena to choose where to eat, and she – in deference to my imminent departure I am sure – enters an open-air restaurant flanked by the most generously shade-providing trees ever seen – vast-spreading evergreen umbrellas with multiple brown barkless elephantine trunks.

What are they, I enquire later, over dessert.

*Ombue*, she replies; Maria-Elena says so.

Pardon?

*Ombue*. From *pampa*. Cows and *gauchos* like Ombue, very cool.

Cool indeed, I think, watching as my Chilean-Argentine cousin however-many-times-removed orders coffee. What would I have done without this woman, I wonder. It would have been a very different trip for sure. Really, she is the most accepting and kindly of souls, and all I have done from day one is to give her an ungrateful, impatient time. I don't much like who I've been here; it's as if a mirror has been held up and the ugly reflection being thrown back into my face found wanting. Maybe this is what I have found; that I am lacking. In the meantime, Maria-Elena peers at me over her glasses, tips back the last of her coffee in combination with the dregs of her wine and, with a mischievous *Salut!* suggests we take a taxi there, but maybe (twinkle, twinkle) a bus back?

The destination "There" turns out to be the British Hospital, where Sam was laid up after his traffic accident. Since I have no ambition beyond wanting to tick it off my list as done, we find a coffee shop in a tiny cobbled alley opposite the hospital at Perdriel 74, Ciudad Autonome de Buenos Aires, funnel down more caffeine and bask in the sun.

In 2004, the British Hospital will be one hundred and sixty years old. Funny to think of four years on, when here we are in 1999 still, wondering whether the planet will survive Y2K. The media is busy propagating all kinds of fears about some kind of technological global meltdown, and even the most rational and optimistic are beginning to feel twitchy. According to the *Buenos Aires Herald* of November 20, none of Argentina's five air traffic control radar systems had been certified as fully Year 2000 compliant. Just a little bit worrying...

My father saw no reason to worry when his father's letter written on March 25 arrived in early May. It was true that Sam talked of a tired feeling, how *running into Montevideo,* all but *wiped him out,* and how the heat often left him *drenched in perspiration.* But then there was the counterbalance of so much positivity: business on the upturn, the arrival of Spring in the UK, the joy of bathing in the sea, and so many letters to write after an après-lunch siesta.

The announcement of his death that followed on just a few days later, on May 15, from Messrs Ayrton and Alderson Smith on Dale Street in Liverpool, must have come as quite a shock. My father was told simply that a cable had arrived from Mr Pheasant, advising the family that Sam had died suddenly in Uruguay on May 11. That he (Mr Pheasant) would be arranging burial in the British Cemetery in Montevideo. And that Sam had left an English will, with my father and Alderson Smith appointed Executors.

The news travelled fast.

From Inverness, Catherine noted how extraordinary, that she had been thinking about her father the previous week and now she has my own father's letter:

*What a frightful thing family pride can be. My loyalties have been so divided & yet balanced so much over on mother's side on account of how she coped with life & us as kids. So few knew what she went through trying to keep our home & us together throughout our schooldays & teenage life & we have a great debt of gratitude towards her. There were faults on both sides & I'm not blind to mother's. I had always longed to get in touch with father but felt again – stupidly perhaps – that mother would feel it, if she ever came to know.*

*But I am very glad that he had a contact with us through you – he wasn't completely cut off & got news of us. Did he ever mention mother in his letters or in conversation with you? Being an elder daughter has been no picnic I can assure you. A daughter naturally gravitates towards her father – that's the nature of things. However, there it is.*

Catherine then goes on to say that John – Betty's widowed husband – was trying to find somewhere in Forest Row, south London, where my grandmother could live to be near Genevieve and Elizabeth: *He doesn't know what he is going to do & cannot undertake* (that additional) *responsibility – after all he is only a son-in-law, not even a daughter-in-law! The three of us must do our best to help mother enjoy her last years. When she goes I shall feel anchorless.*

Sam's sister Bea in Hoylake was also devastated: *I had a letter on Saturday from him & he seems to be well & very bright & talking about coming home soon.*


Sam was considering returning to England? Forever? Had I missed something in the letters he wrote to my father? I don't think so. But if Beatrice had received one of those last letters he wrote, maybe he was feeling unwell and insecure enough to think it might be the time to throw in the towel and return to the bosom of his family for his remaining years.

Several years earlier, when he was knocked down in the street and broke his arm, he was still feisty enough to bounce back. It was here, at the British Hospital, that the bones were set and his arm plastered, and where he visited over a period of some eighteen years at least one sick friend. Founded by the Reverend Barton Lodge in 1844, the institution was created specifically for the English-speaking citizens of Argentina, and has always been known for being on the cutting edge of modern medicine. Sam would have been in the original building on the corner. Wandering around, a nursing school looks like it was added in the 1930s. Further on, a foundation stone laid as part of a controversial visit to Argentina by HRH prince Charles earlier in the year, commemorates a spanking new wing. There are also lots of roses in the grounds roundabout – always testament to a British presence.

It is now that Maria-Elena tells me that having checked at her bank, nothing as yet has arrived from Japan. I believe this is the moment my personal humiliation is complete.

## NOVEMBER 30, 1999

Whatever does or does not happen, I leave tomorrow. In the meantime, with an appointment to keep at the British Embassy, I do my professional best to be on time. But I need not have hurried, because the Vice-Consul is late... tied up in matters of some urgency, I am informed – something to do with a bus hijack. So I wait. And wait. And wait...

Eventually I am urged forwards and Emma Nichols appears in the entrance of her office to apologise. She iş tall, fresh-faced and nice, if ever-so-slightly frazzled. From Troon, in Scotland's South Ayrshire, she has been in Argentina by appointment for two years, with another couple to go.

You're quite young for such a position, I hedge; So how does your career profile work? I presume you speak Spanish.

I do, she replies; But to be honest I read it better than I speak it. Luckily I have wonderful staff who can interpret for me.

Is it not requisite to speak the language of the country, then?

Not everywhere. One of my last posts was in Helsinki, and try Finnish! It's impossible. Of course it's necessary for key members of staff to reach a certain level...

Asked how a girl from Troon entered the diplomatic service, she explains that she did her Highers but wanted to see a bit of the world rather than going direct into university. So she joined the service at the most junior level, what is called Grade 10.

I was nineteen, she elaborated; Spent two and a half years in London, the same length of time in Helsinki, then another six months in the UK. Then I was what we call "Floated" around five countries for six months at a time.

Which were?

Spain, Russia, Armenia, Mauritius, Switzerland, she counts, ticking them off on her fingers. Floating means covering periods of leave, such as sick leave, for one to several months at a time.

A bit like a trouble-shooter?

Exactly.

Was this posting (to Buenos Aires) a promotion?

No, I was promoted while in Helsinki and managed to rise several grades while Floating.

Can you explain the hierarchy? In Japan we have an embassy in Tokyo and a consulate in Kobe. How come you have both an ambassador and a consul here?

The ambassador is the ambassador. A consul is more a historical role. In Brazil, we have an embassy in the political capital, Brasilia, but consulates in both Rio and Sao Paulo, which are much busier. But we don't have any other missions in Argentina.

So every country where there is an embassy and an ambassador also has a consul?

Pretty much.

What do you do here? What is the role of the Vice-Consul?

Emma (sighing): Well, there's a lot of tea and sympathy. Telling people what they can expect, and what they can't expect.

Was it true she had been busy earlier handling the aftermath of a bus hijack?

Yes. You may have heard about it yesterday.

Tea and sympathy?

Exactly.

How many people were involved? Was the whole bus hijacked?

Yes. Three armed men apparently got onto the bus and ten minutes out of the airport took out their weapons. One man stood up with a machine gun. Another held a pistol at the driver's head.

It was the third man who drew the curtains on the back window and then proceeded to rob everyone. Thankfully the gunmen were only interested in hard cash. If they had taken passports too it would have all been a lot more complicated.

Tell me about it, I think, remembering with gratitude the tea and sympathy doled out in Montevideo.

Why that bus, I query. Or was it just the luck of the draw?

She thought so. Taking place at 9 a.m. it was too common an occurrence to be reported on the radio or TV. The embassy only knew about it when British passport holders started turning up – like the guy who had taken up Emma's time that morning.

Was he angry?

Well he travels a lot so was more philosophical than emotional. Mostly people just want to see a friendly face, have a chat, but in this instance he wanted to claim compensation for the loss of his belongings. Initially the bus company agreed, but changed its mind because the incident was not their fault. So he wanted me to tag along while he argued his case. It's not my job to interfere, just be there to offer moral support.

She is answerable to her boss, the Consul. He is answerable to the Ambassador. There are also two consular assistants, like Miss Milani.

I explain how I had faxed this member of staff, explaining my trip and why I was coming: that my great-grandfather was listed as both the Vice-Consul of Argentina, and Consul to the Oriental Republic of Uruguay; that I had been unable to find any confirmation, or indeed records. And how I was beginning to think his postings were in Liverpool, not South America at all.

Emma believes a lot of records were lost during the Falklands conflict. Also the present embassy dates from the 1960s, and she's unsure of the location of the original site. She was sure however that the Foreign Office in London would have such information on file.

I relate how in Montevideo I was told that there are books in which all British citizens are listed, but with no apparent trace of the name Loader. It does not help that I can't give specific dates for when family members arrived and left; I know only that my grandfather was born in Uruguay and had dual nationality.

Argentina, however, does not allow two passports. As Emma explains: Here the government is of the opinion that if you are born in Argentina, you an Argentine: End of story. Having said that, there are a lot of Anglo-Argentines here, because the British government recognises dual nationality.

Are you really only tea and sympathy?

Well, we have five Brits in prison right now, all on drug-related charges, so I make sure they are being well treated, have what they need. Even that is a form of T&S I suppose.

Emma's position is unusual in that she is on a joint posting with her husband, who is the embassy's technical management officer.

What happens when you are posted to different places?

It doesn't happen like that. The service is very understanding.

Are you unusual? I'm sure my grandfather would turn in his grave if he knew there was a young woman in his position. Personally I think it's great, but you know, a man of those times...

Emma laughs: No, there are quite a few of us now, and we have at least four female ambassadors in various parts of the world.

Does Argentina have any special characteristic that sets it apart from somewhere like Finland, for example.

Well, the people are completely different of course, but I would have to say bureaucracy.

Ah! That's what the opera I saw was about – desperate people banging on official doors for weeks and weeks, to no effect. It's not like that still, is it?

Not at all. But still there is a lot of red tape in trying to deal with the Argentine authorities. Everything has to be stamped six million times.

Is that historical?

We have good relationships with the ministries. If you were talking to a political section, you might get a different answer.

Were you T&C in Finland?

No, I had a different job there. I was in charge of the Registry.

Where is your registry here?

Tucked away upstairs, in our secure zone, along with all the political files. Under wraps.

Realising I can get no further, I ask if Emma is having a good time in Argentina.

Definitely, she replies, grinning: It's a very good city, apart from the pollution, the traffic and the muggings.

Great quote, I note; I'll use it. And so I do.


I drop into the Ideal, but Karen is not there. From there I wander aimlessly, feeling foolish and puzzled. Why do I feel as if I have made such a goddamn awful mess of my time here? Who was Sam? Who am I? And where do I go – where do we all go – from here?


It is a sad evening. When Julito and Paula bring Santiago over to say goodbye, despite another lovely meal and a glass or two of good wine, none of us seem to know quite what to say. Even Kaiser is subdued. For my own part, I am mortified to find that money has still not arrived from Japan, that I must leave in debt to my cousin and her husband.


Back in 1954, there was equally tough news to swallow, for while Sam was not in debt, he was pretty close to being broke. This is what my family learned over the weeks and months that followed his death.

It was Alderson Smith who reported that the funeral service at the British Cemetery was conducted by the Reverend Tudor Isaacs of the Anglican Church, with Second Secretary Mr W. C. Butler and himself in attendance: An obituary notice has been put into the bi-weekly newspaper. The Embassy staff Press attaché will be writing to you.

Around the same time Catherine received a letter from Frederick Jones, who ran the Hotel Suizo in Piriapolis – the faded deserted building I had found so interesting for some reason and now I know why: apparently Sam used to go there often for his own required form of tea and sympathy. Her letter to my father concerning the matter, offered details of their father's demise: Mr Jones says my grandfather was supposed to go to Montevideo, but instead he (Mr Jones) received a call from the Colonial asking him to come and identify Sam, who had died two hours before. He had evidently felt ill, cancelled his trip and asked for mail to be sent up to his room.

It seems that my aunt's address – rather An Address: The Scottish Education Department, Edinburgh – together with that of Mr Loader's sister near Liverpool, was the only other found. In the main Catherine is concerned that her mother be told as little as possible, with all details kept under wraps: *Have you written to Barney? I'll drop a line tonight. I'm so heartbroken for Primrose. Another strand however slim separated from her & the family. My natural hopes are that he may have left her something in his will. No doubt copies will be available later.*

My grandmother may have been heartbroken, but she remained pragmatic, advising my father to be very careful with regards Sam's estate: *I don't know about personal items, but the cash may be a ticklish problem. He once told me he had taken Argentine citizenship – he was born in Uruguay you know. The law is funny. There's a lot of wisdom in the saying let sleeping dogs lie! Do be careful with A. Smith*, she advises, with an even more suspicious addendum: *this* (letter) *should not go to Hoylake.*

My father, it would appear, did not take her too seriously, because by May 24 he had seen his brother and visited his aunt and uncle on Merseyside. He relates as much in a letter to Alderson Smith, adding that he hopes all his father's possessions and business papers will be in the hands of the Consul before long. He asks whether commission standing to Sam's credit with Associated Cycles was ever received. Also if the family will be able to collect commission on business booked but not actually executed; it seems a company in Glasgow has told his aunt (Florence) in the city that they had commissions due to Sam's estate. Finally he reminds the family solicitor that his father has a business arrangement with Howard Pheasant as regards trade between Japan and the Argentine.

By the end of the month, Pheasant had drawn up Sam's estate, a copy of which he sent to Alderson Smith. He says that since he had heard nothing from Liverpool, he had gone ahead and settled all of my grandfather's outstanding debts, and having been assured by the British Embassy that there would be no more bills, all further charges relating to the business would be borne by him and him alone. It seems that he and Sam had a fifty-fifty arrangement so far as office expenses were concerned, my grandfather paying the rent, cleaning and telephone, while Pheasant paid the employee (employee?), stationery, postage and so on. They each paid for their own cables. Pheasant notes also that his partner had been largely absent from the office for over a year – a year! – and how he is owed 275 pounds and 49 pence exactly. What had Sam been thinking, doing, to leave his affairs so?

Catherine writes to my father soon after Pheasant's carefully detailed list of expenses arrives in the UK. Having checked on her mother in Forest Row, and found Elizabeth to be a *Super child*, and Genevieve *Far more peaceful[67]* she thinks it time for Primrose to enter the New Nursing Home in Stroud on a permanent basis, and has set up a Deed of Covenant to more than cover the cost: *I think she'd be far happier in her own room with her own things about her.*

*Now*, she continues, racking up the ante: *About this man Pheasant. Is the whole of father's business going to be handed to him on a platter, without any goodwill payment? I suggest you tell the solicitor that a certain amount of goodwill is payable & you feel his bill of 275 pounds should be waived in lieu of goodwill. It's quite absurd he should get away with the lot.*

There is another matter with which she would not have been familiar, but then no one thought to check: who was to be responsible for ensuring a stone be erected on Sam's grave.

By the end of October, the amount left by Sam was found to total just under 2,000 pounds. Not a lot these days – and not a lot for a man who had spent a lifetime in business – but back then still considered worth squabbling about. Alderson Smith suggests to my father that while everything is being sorted out between Liverpool and South America, he pays three legacies in accordance with the wishes of the will, to Miss G. M. Loader (Catherine), Mrs F. Rothwell (this mysterious great-aunt Florence that I never met or even – in my remembrance – heard of), and Mrs B. L. Stroyan (Beatrice): *If you agree to this then I will draw cheques and send them to you for signature.*

In a subsequent letter he suggests that my father and his mother both be paid a sum of 450 pounds; somewhat cautious he admits, but best to wait until he can get further information from across the Atlantic. Subsequently he thinks it only fair to pay Howard Pheasant and so discharge all indebtedness, especially since it might be some considerable time before his office could deal with any money in Uruguay.

Hopefully it will not be too long before I can deal with the money I owe Maria-Elena. How I hate being in debt, indebted in any way. The humiliation of having to ask my father for bus fare at age eighteen (there was never any allowance) still rankles, and goes a long way to explaining my passionate need – deep-lodged to the point of obstinacy – to make, own and spend my own money. My cousin will see me off at the airport tomorrow – a departure I am not looking forward to in any way at all.

Leaving Maria-Elena and her family to take their leave of one another, I go upstairs to empty the wardrobe. File tapes (one of which is nowhere to be found), pack bags, return books. Gather toiletries from the bathroom. Mooch around checking that I've not left anything behind but finding it hard to be even remotely perfectionist through a mist of emotional confusion. I say thank you to Ana for lending me her bed, give the rosary a perfunctory dust, turn down the sheets. I don't want to go to bed for fear of dreams. Or maybe I simply don't want to go, leaving so much behind. So much undone. But go I must. It's time to say *adios* and *muchos gracias.*

# CHAPTER 26

# MUCHOS GRACIAS

**DECEMBER 1, 1999**

Tarzan kisses me, pats my cheek. Marta cries, kisses my hands. As the taxi draws away, they are both waving against a backdrop of pink and magenta bougainvillea so dazzling that the swathes of colour across the front of the house make me blink. Goodbye Lisandre de la Torres, and Rosita, still sweeping... Goodbye eccentrically leaning and gently rusting Tower of Pisa. Goodbye Caseros. Goodbye Pablo No. 2. Goodbye dear Maria-Elena. Goodbye enigmatic Buenos Aires. Goodbye mysterious, unexplored, blood-drenched Argentina. My eyes are full of tears again for all that I have done and seen, and not done and not seen. But at least I am leaving in one piece, and that most certainly is something.

Handed a morning edition of the *Buenos Aires Herald* once boarded, I blow my nose and in noting the headline – "Over 20 tourists mugged" – feel on familiar if equally dramatic ground. Is Emma still offering her own brand of tea and sympathy? The unhappy Brit who two days before lost over 1,500 dollars has probably emptied both the teapot and the sugar bowl thrice over! It's not the first time tourists have been mugged on arrival at the airport either. In October, 1997, a British woman was robbed in a taxi on her way into the city, then later attacked a second time by the very man who offered her assistance. What a coincidence then that the city's ombudsman is scheduled this very day to present a new plan to protect tourists from abuse – a programme that promises to

414

include a hotline specially designed for newcomers who get into trouble due to their unfamiliarity with the place, language and currency. Too late for me, for sure – the perfect candidate – but not for all those known or unknown, who follow in my own bumbling idiotic footsteps.

It is also World AIDS Day, and really quite shocking to learn that since the first three cases were reported in 1982, Argentina now has 17,000 cases of AIDS and some 120,000 who carry the virus. What are the true numbers in Japan, I wonder, where the population is nearly five times larger and no-one talks about the ramifications of the country's rampant sex industry, nor those of lying husbands and hypocritical single men who leave their golf clubs at the airport to join sex tours to Southeast Asia. Really, for someone who dislikes large groups of people, abhors secrecy and strives for clarity of intent, I'm in the wrong place, aren't I? I remember Gaby in London, the morning I announced I was going to sell up and start a world tour with a holiday in Japan, reacting with typical frankness: Japan, the toughest language, most homogenous society and restricted culture for women on the planet? Do you not see the connection? Do you not see this as yet another example of you being really hard on yourself?

Is this why, having got a handle on Japan – made my futon and resolved to lie on it – I threw myself at South America and even more specifically a country in the grip of an ever-worsening nervous breakdown. Was I once again choosing to be hard on myself? If so, why? Too weary to retrieve my tape recorder, and remembering that I am out of clean tapes anyway, I scribble a few notes on the back of an old receipt – something to do with Argentina's disintegration matching my own? – but which (unlike all Sam's precious letters) disappears without a trace the minute I tuck it somewhere "safe". Luckily, I remember…

I'm on the last stretch of correspondence now – a mix of official letters, my father's briefly neat typing, Catherine's character-full notes and increasingly illegible scrawls from Primrose.

Remember that leather attaché case at the start of this story? The one that came by ship all the way from Buenos Aires, spent years gathering dust in a loft or wardrobe, but now sits on my desk in Zushi, in need of some tender loving care for sure (it's older than me, and that's saying something) but otherwise perfectly at home? It began its journey sometime after November 4, 1954, when H.H. Consul G. M. Warr wrote to Liverpool from the British Embassy in Montevideo, *Gentlemen: The articles listed have been placed in one suitcase with the exception of No. 8 a pair of binoculars. No binoculars were handed over either to the Vice-Consul at Maldonado or to this embassy, though there is a case of spectacles which may have converted in translation from the Spanish into binoculars.*

Later in November, Alderson Smith writes to my father concerning his query about Sam's optimism with regards to trade between Japan and Argentina. While it appears that in 1952 he did quite well, receiving approximately 2,000 pounds, half of which went to his partner, Howard Pheasant gave no intimation of any further dealings. He had his own respectful agenda towards his own country and indeed the USA, but with regards Japan, was not enthusiastic: *Unfortunately Japanese business did not come up to expectations, in fact the only worthwhile business was that I clinched in New York in 1950. The Japanese are extremely tricky people to deal with and I have learned they are not worth wasting much time on.*

Ha!

I wonder what Howard Pheasant would have made of my grandmother's belief that Japanese were a special people, possibly from another planet. Or the relatively recent discovery that many people native to the Americas have Japanese DNA. Not a lot, I should imagine. But otherwise he seems a decent enough chap; Sam trusted him, and that's enough for me. Right now though I'm sitting alongside a handsome, young dark-skinned South American with his hair in a neat pony tail. His profile, turned away from me with what I feel is a steely determination, fascinates; it's both so familiar and yet so exotically foreign. On the far side of the aisle, the other side of the genetic coin: a large, blonde, fair-skinned, big-faced Christian family– mother, father and four innocents – from a Born Again community in the Chaco region. Missionaries, of course.

It is only when we begin our descent into Sao Paulo that my companion – Alec Taylor, as he introduces himself – opens up. Born in Guatemala, he's returning to the University of Calgary in Canada after spending five months in Argentina researching Latin-American history in relation to terrorist activities.

Why do so many countries in South America have such dark sides, he wonders. Argentina and Chile are not the only nations to have plunged into the brutality of military dictatorships and the political excesses of Right and Left. Guatemala's history is also a nightmare.

Alec: I'm going back to spend the next two or three years writing my dissertation. Then who knows. Maybe I'll go and work for an NGO. But a lot can happen in that time.

A lot has happened in the last month. For one thing, I have begun to question on a truly deep level why I react and behave as I do.

Was it to do with the mixed messages I received as a child? The pressure was always to work hard and not to disappoint. As a girl, I was lucky in some respects, because there was never any assumption or mention even of marriage or children. But I was always held on a tight rein – or rather was allowed to stray so far but then jerked back under control – and as a result struggled even harder to escape, but strangling myself in the process. The encouragement to join activities was contradicted with criticism, my desire for further education restricted to college rather than university, though there was no reason at all why not. How I had to battle my father to take a job as a waitress that first summer I refused to go with the family on holiday, and escape to France the summer I came down from college. No doubt my parents were projecting their own dreams and fears onto me, and if that was their intention, they most certainly did a good job. I remember asking my mother why she and my father had refused to allow to me to even try for drama school, and her reply offering up the most convoluted twist: if I had wanted to go hard enough I would have made it happen somehow. True? Maybe. The problem was that by that time the damage had been done: my confidence was eroded beyond measure; there was some shattered part of me that no longer was sure I was good enough.

When and how had this begun? With my mother firmly convinced that I should recognise and accept my limitations, for one. Yes, I was bright, but maybe not quite bright enough? Yes, I was creative and talented, but maybe not as creative and talented as others? My limitations... To some extent I still hear these words whispering down the years: Know your limitations, Angela, know your limitations. The result? Every time I try to prove her wrong, or simply go my own way, I crash, so deeply engrained is my heartfelt anxiety that Oh God, what if she's right! And then, of course, there was her reply when I asked why my father had been so upset about my leaving home in 1962, just six weeks before his death. Well, she replied, with her sweetly manipulative little old lavender lady smile, Well we wanted you to be ambitious and succeed, but we wanted you to stay home.

There is another conundrum: how can I be happy and sad, emotional and pragmatic at the same time? It is a duality that has confused me as far back as I can remember. It is surely no coincidence that I wrote my college thesis back in 1960 on this very subject, choosing to contrast what I termed a poet of emotion with a poet of intellect – Louis MacNeice as opposed to Stephen Spender.[68] Suddenly – years since I even thought about the project – words float up from the past and form a snatch of memory – two lines from MacNeice's poem, *August*: "We jump from picture to picture and cannot follow/The living curve that is breathlessly the same."

No sooner I am airborne again, than I begin to dream of jumping from picture to picture. But where a month ago there were imagined witches and demons, now there are hundreds of fragmented memories – each shard as bright and clear as those pieces of pottery I found scattered on pathways on my very first day in El Cento – yet now they are no more than additional pieces of puzzlement that fail to fit together with the rest.

When was it I had finally taken pity on poor overheated Krieger? And after finding brushes and combs in the garage, I'd combed him out one early morning – which took some courage on my part because he is big and strong and I was not sure how mentally stable he was. As it turned out, he rolled over on his back and slobbered gratitude. When Maria-Elena came down and saw the enormous pile of winter fur, she simply laughed: Oh, another dog!

Would there be another Angela, I wonder now, if someone combed me out, relieved me of all the tangles that are driving me crazy? The coat I wear is far too heavy. It has grown heavier and heavier over the years until now I feel dragged down. How wonderful it would be to be relieved of so much excess weight and baggage. To feel light, and free and renewed.

There was that other morning, when I came down early – the house cool and quiet and at peace, yet the yard outside drenched with sunlight and vibrant with life. Even the songbirds were shrill inside their nightly shrouded cages, awakened by wild birds which dove in out of trees and shrubs, calling to their imprisoned compatriots. While Krieger – now even more of a pussy cat than Jalil (Arabic for friend), who sits on the top of the wall between the house and the dojo and cares not a jot about anything or anyone – simply opened one eye and then went back to sleep. I washed some clothes slowly, sensually, in the sink in the garage, hung out my clothes with the enormous enjoyment of independence and privacy, made a cup of tea and sat. Sat quiet and still, peacefully waiting for Marta to arrive, the house to wake up.

But maybe it is me who needs to wake up. So I do (physically at least), to find it scheduled time for another plastic meal, which I eat in a plastic shell (in part at least) flying across a plastic continent near 100 per cent dependent on oil. But is this what being awake is really about? I'm beginning to wonder...

More episodic memories. Flashes of landscape... faces... people met and unmet but passed by all the same, and now of little to no consequence for I will surely never meet them again.

Or will I? May I, please? I promise to do better next time, to pay more attention, be kinder, friendlier, less stand-offish, less fearful.

Sounds... a language not understood, misunderstood, familiar in its unfamiliarity. Music that stretches limbs and senses, stirs passions that uncoil in the gut. I hear snatches of street music, and then a whole track from Astor Piazzolla's album: *Tango: Zero Hour*. Piazzolla said this was absolutely the greatest record he had made in his entire life, that he and his fellow musicians had, Given their soul to it.

What have I given my soul to? My soul? What am I talking about? Who am I talking to? Am I really awake or this simply another dream?

A clear memory: Pablo No. 2 driving us to the municipal cemetery, for Maria-Elena to pay her respects to her mother, and he to his own. Which day was that? Yesterday? The day before? Does it matter? It happened. It did? How can I be sure? Maybe that was also a dream. All I know with any certainty is that this aircraft is following the living curve of the earth, though I doubt this is what MacNeice had in mind.

Anyway, the memory – the dream that may also have been real – played out as follows: standing before Ana's niche, Maria-Elena was overwhelmed with emotion. We have both brought flowers and arrange them just so... her own tearfully to the fore, mine hovering respectfully in the background. While she works her way through a bag stuffed with tissues, a large family party arrives alongside to pay their own respects to a deceased member. Party is the wrong word. Can one say, a wake of ten or more? Seems I am back to wakefulness even while asleep. We wait in the car for Pablo, whose own mother is buried under open skies beneath a grassy plot. I can see that he is weeping, and when he finally returns to the car, his own eyes are red and swollen.

Now here I am weeping, weeping over America. But for why? Because I touched something on my travels, and I have no idea what it was. All

I know is I don't want to leave it behind, but take it with me – carry it with me carefully, like an cracked eggshell or a wounded bird – and take a good, hard, long look.

Easier to look at others than myself, of course. I don't know how to look at my self. In fact, if I am honest, it frightens me. There was a woman I interviewed a few years ago, a kind of nomadic psychotherapist. Intriguing though she was, I felt as if Azzah could see right through me, and it scared me half to death.

There was another woman, many years ago now, when one of my children was having a rough time and I sought professional help. She told me yes, she could help, but she also thought she could help me. And in one second flat my back was to the wall: No. My life was functioning and I had all the balls in the air. In no way was I going to risk my family's sole supporting structure, thank you very much. I knew then that I was built on sand; I think I have always known.

"They fuck you up, your mum and dad," wrote Philip Larkin, a far more fucked up Englishman and poet I suspect than either MacNeice or Spender; "They may not mean to, but they do./They fill you with the faults they had/And add some extra, just for you."[69]

Yet in a book on writing, when discussing whether a difficult childhood benefits or impedes a writer's work, Ernest Hemingway (in a letter to F. Scott Fitzgerald) makes his own feelings on the subject ragingly clear: "Forget your personal tragedy. We are all bitched from the start and you especially have to be hurt like hell before you can write seriously."[70]

Thus stands his egotistical claim: I have been hurt more than anyone else and that is why I am allowed to bitch, because I am a writer to be taken very seriously indeed.

Where do I stand in this? What were my parents' thoughts about their own childhoods? Did they seek answers and cast blame, as I appear to be doing now? And what about my grandparents, great-grandparents and great-great grandparents, all the way back to Harriet

421

and whoever went before. Have we all in sleeping ignorance been passing on destructive thought patterns – like emotional immaturity, lack of confidence and fear of failure – down the ages, and if so, how can we stop the negative drift?

Sam, who sought out people and places to help boost his ego.

As so do I. (Help, I whimper again.)

Sam, who was not interested in – indeed appeared to flatly reject – all matters metaphysical: the beauty of a waterfall, the flight of a bird, the mystery of the spiral as a universal symbol – shells, cobwebs, labyrinths... At least, mention never crept into his letters; often they were 80 per cent business-orientated, with a few personal lines beginning and end. There is no hint that he ever attended church, read the bible – or read very much of anything else for that matter.

In this we are very different. In fact, I am now acknowledging with more than a little surprise, for I have never thought about it before, I am far more like my grandmother, who read voraciously – philosophy, theosophy and anthroposophy (of course) and even higher mathematics, because what are numbers but the music of the spheres. This intellectual and spiritual hunger continued well into old age, and I remember being both fascinated by and afraid of the titles of her books in her room at the nursing home in Stroud. Each and every one was beyond all understanding, and did nothing to encourage any belief in my own intellectual abilities. I knew I was bright, but... I knew I could do anything I wanted, but... I knew the world was my oyster, but... My own interests were eclectic but undemanding, or so I thought: adventure stories that began with Winnie the Pooh and Alice in Wonderland and swiftly moved through Enid Blyton to Malcom Saville's Lone Pine series (set in Shropshire, I now remember) and Arthur Ransome's Swallows and Amazons; then came (mostly with male heroes) the Hornblower series, Biggles, followed by Rider Haggard, myths and legends, poetry and novels. Oh how I loved the worlds into which they transported me... from my bedroom in Ranulf

Croft... from the lovely ancient creaking school library in Warwick... from my room in Stourbridge whenever staying with Eric and Kathleen... from the Cherry Room at Forneth, so-named because the wallpaper was covered with connected pairs of red and dark crimson cherries, such as you might wear as earrings, and where I lay reading for on my bed for hours to the accompaniment of croo-croo-cooing woodpigeons in the huge, ancient Cedar of Lebanon outside my window. Indeed to this day my idea of heaven is to escape into a book, with no interruption, far from the madding – maddening – crowd.

By the end of 1954, Sam's beneficiaries have all been paid, including Howard Pheasant, leaving a total cash balance remaining in the bank of just over 500 pounds. Alderson Smith suggests four hundred is deposited to accrue some interest, the remainder available for any expenses, *That may have to be incurred between now and the closing of the estate.*

The attaché case arrived at the beginning of the new year. By January 7, my father was typing his usual official to-the-letter missives on what I can only presume to be his father's typewriter. Sadly I never get any sense of who lay behind the words. Indeed, I have often wondered what on earth my father and mother ever found to talk about – she so creative and dreamy, forever floating somewhere between Heaven and Earth – and he so cerebral and emotionally locked in - a lot of anger, I suspect; Bridget insists she can remember hiding under tables and under the stairs to escape his fury but, for my part, I'm not sure. Kathleen always described him as the perfect gentle man. Jo says his shyness and lack of confidence was painful. He played chess, admired Winston Churchill, feared his mother, tried hard to be of comfort during my emotionally wracked teenage years, but was desperately fearful that I would go to the bad, meaning become sexually active and – the worst sin of all – pregnant. I suspect that my mother, whom I had long ago cast in the role of the Wicked Witch of the North, was in fact our Guardian Angel. But it was all a hell of a muddle, and would be for years to come.

In one letter to the solicitor (who had been seeking my grandparents' marriage certificate amongst other official papers) my father confirmed that his parents had married at the Church of St James in West Derby. St James, Santiago, another connection...

In another communication, he tells his mother that he has high hopes of getting at least half any monies remaining in Uruguay for the family. In the next paragraph, having had his knuckles wrapped for not thanking her for Christmas gifts, he stands his ground (always easier to do at long distance): *I'm sorry I did not thank you for my socks nor for Gwen's tea pot stand which is really very good. You for your part do not mention the small parcel which we sent you.*

Only in a throwaway PS does he casually mention that he had received, *A few personal things of Pa's, including this typewriter: I will let you see them later.*

The last letter in my possession regarding my grandfather's life and death is dated August 2, 1956. Addressed to my father, Alderson Smith reports that he has heard from the Estate Duty Office, and that it appears that: *as the rate of Sterling exchange for Uruguayan dollars at the date of* (Sam's) *death was exceedingly different from the rate in force in June when the estate was finally settled, the estate is therefore increased by over $2,000 and will be liable to death duties of 1%.*

What this meant in terms of how much extra was added to the pot, and what this meant to any members of my family I have no idea. Did they benefit by much, hardly anything at all or – worst case scenario – did they in fact have to give monies back to cover the death duties?

I wonder only what Sam had in mind in thinking to return Home. For despite Uruguay being the country of his birth, and there being a strong attachment, Home (as the old saying goes) is where the heart is, and for a man of seventy-four in a weakening state of health that surely meant his sisters, his wife and children, and four rapidly growing granddaughters. What did he think he was going to live on? Where and with whom? Did he think to keep the business going, perhaps drawing in my father? Maybe it was such anxieties and thoughts that aggravated his heart problem. Or was it simpler than that: after years in exile, with business just too tough to deal with anymore, and failure written large on all attempts to mend his marriage and repair damage caused to his offspring, his heart finally caved in.

How interesting that my own father should also die of a heart attack, brought on over a period of some ten years by his own internal stresses concerning work, family and relationships. Hating his job – working as a buyer of the nuts and bolts of machine parts – but doing it all the same for reasons of love and commitment, he paid a price. Trying to maintain a balance of loyalty between his parents kept him on an emotionally stressed tightrope for years; for this too he paid a heavy toll. Continuing this role of peacemaker between his father and his siblings, why did he withhold information rather than pass it on, so that they could forge the relationships they obviously so craved. I write here of Catherine and Betty, for Barney was never on the map, except in Liverpool's Menlove Avenue (the street on which John Lennon lived on as a boy.) Was my father so blinkered that he could not make connections, was unable to read between the lines? Or was his reticence deliberate – did he choose not to see what was going on? If so, why? He was most certainly an angry man, a sad man, a disappointed man. Compounded, such ingredients for an unhappy, deeply frustrated life simply served to break his own heart.

For the first time – with any genuine consciousness at least – I wonder if what Sam passed to my father has been passed on to me. If so, how can I call a halt to such an ancestral inheritance, avoid my own downward spiral into the heartbreak of disappointment?

It took many years for me to cry for my father. I was angry with him, befuddled with guilt about his death and leaving my mother alone. It is clear from letters Primrose wrote to my mother, a widow at age fifty-one, that the family expected me to fall into line and perform the role of dutiful daughter. But I couldn't. For one thing I was pregnant – so fulfilling my father's worst fears. So one by one, the family cast me off, leaving Bridget to handle our mother, and yours truly to set about forging a career and raising my own family. When Charles died of cancer in 1974, my mother moved up to Scotland to be near her sister, leaving Bridget – now married – in the family home. Catherine retired after her mother's death and went to live in Hawaii, where she lived a life not dissimilar to that of her father, returning only after a triple bypass to die of gangrene in a hospital in Stroud. After Barney died, his wife lived alone for many years, becoming more and more reclusive and odd.

An epic tale in itself, and one in which I failed to figure with any grace, other than to try and pick up the pieces when all - on one level - was far too late. Now there is my mother coming up for ninety and Jo, then lost cousin Alison and me, both in our late fifties, followed by our children, the next generation, two boys, two girls, all in their thirties. Gen and her family. Joyce and Alison, Neil and the girls on Merseyside. Plus one hundred and forty-four Loaders in Chile... Claudio, Jose, Silvia, Pepe, Daniel, Betty, Ricardo, Carole, Nelson, Alejandra... how are they all doing I wonder. And how are things in Buenos Aires? Is Maria-Elena wrestling with property accounts? Marta scrubbing out the bird cages? Tarzan swinging through his surgery doing good and waving away apologies for lack of cash from desperate parents? Do they remember me fondly or they are breathing a sigh of relief? Kindly people. Decent well-meaning people. Extra-ordinary people. I owe them everything.

I have no memory of passing through Toronto on that long trip back to Japan, other than a feeling of immeasurable sadness to be so near Buffy and yet have no time for contact. On the next leg, to Vancouver, there was a young South African woman who seemed eager to talk. Amber told me her life story – another ship passed in the night – but which I have now long forgotten. For one thing, I gave up on the tape recorder days ago. As for note-taking, what would be the point? I would surely only lose them, or have them stolen, or mess up in some other way. Sorry Amber.

426

I do remember her asking if I thought living in Japan had changed me. And my response: How could it have not? When I go to London to see friends, they all say the same thing: that I am so Japanese these days. But when I ask what this means exactly, they seem perplexed. Just as I am perplexed now.

I have so much to think about that my head hurts. It is worse than this, however, because my entire body is unhappy with me: shoulders, chest, stomach, knees, ankles, and feet in particular. You could say I'm in Extreme Pain: from head to toe, so to speak.

**DECEMBER 2, 1999**

And so to Tokyo's Narita International Airport – an eight hour flight in itself. I remember being pulled out of line (as pre-arranged by Akii) and escorted into a side office, where immigration officials make me fill-in and sign certain incomprehensible forms to explain my lack of re-entry visa and empty passport. By this time I am beyond exhaustion.

Emerging into Arrivals, I hardly recognise the long-haired, heavily bearded man who opens his arms. In choosing not to cut his hair or shave since I had left, Akii looks more like a Mexican bandit than the be-suited company man who had waved me off five weeks before. Never have I been so happy to see anyone in my life. On Buffy's birthday too.

Yet on the way back to Hayama with paddy fields and drifts of bamboo giving way to the concrete jungle that is Tokyo, and then out the other side, the landscape greening once more towards the open sea, I have a perverse but lingering thought: I wish I could go back, do the whole thing again. And this time – somehow – do it right.

# POSTSCRIPT

*We should not be ashamed to acknowledge truth and to assimilate it from whatever source it comes to us, even if it is brought to us by former generations and foreign peoples. For him who seeks the truth there is nothing of higher value than truth itself; it never cheapens or debases him who reaches for it but ennobles and honours him.*

YAQUIB IBN ISHAQ AL-KINDI

(Muslim philosopher, died c. 870)


*The only journey worth taking is the journey within.*

W.B. YEATS

(Irish poet and dramatist 1865–1939)


*Without the story in which everyone living, unborn and dead participates – we are no more than bits of paper blown on the cold wind.*

GEORGE MACKAY BROWN

(from an Emerson College catalogue detailing storytelling courses in 2003)

# FAST FORWARD
# (1999-2010)

"It is a matter of great regret to me," wrote W.H. Hudson about his Argentine-Uruguay-based novel *The Purple Land,* first published in 1885, "That this task has taken so much longer a time than I expected in its completion."

My own sentiments exactly. But then it is impossible to do anything of importance, with life-changing consequences, until the time is right. I know that now. Still sticking with this book has been far from easy. As on the trip itself, so many times I have thrown up my hands and thought, That's it, I can't go on... It took a year, for example, to move on from the mysterious record of two Fridays, encouraged by words from the crime writer Agatha Christie: "To write is to live twice". I remember thinking, aha! she may be on to something here.

It is autumn here in Zushi, to where we moved just along the coast from Hayama in 2002. And the signs have been piling up thick and fast of late, making it resoundingly clear that it's high time I draw this particular stage of my journey to a close. And it's not only because a decade on, the stores are filling with witches' hats and plastic pumpkins, readying for Halloween.

430

No, a few months ago, a pack of adhesive shooting stars arrived to decorate my window; Wakiko – one of the earliest friends made in Japan – was right in thinking I needed encouragement to cover the final lap.

One week after, a children's quiz on TV was won by the team Shooting Stars. Then in late August, the finale of Zushi's summer fireworks off the beach brought thousands of people to their feet screaming in ecstasy: the entire night sky of Sagami Bay lit to white brilliance with thousands of whirling, dashing, orgasmically flashing shooting stars, all reflected in the sea below, and as close to the Big Bang and the Act of Creation as I am ever likely to see.

And there is more, because here comes Akii with a cup of tea, and just look at the long-sleeved tee-shirt he's wearing for the first time in years – so long ago he has forgotten where it came from or even the design (he has no interest in fashion): a mountain, under which is the word *ACONCAGUA*, and beneath this, *Mendoza, Argentina*. Yes, these days I believe in signs, omens, the synchronicity of connections, call them what you will. Their purpose and integrity have become as clear as sunlight, moonlight, daylight, starlight; they flag me forward, carry me on.

Nothing was clear when I returned to Japan in late 1999. Initially it felt good to be back, and soon enough Maria-Elena mailed to say the money had arrived and all was well. My feet remained sore and unreliable, my stomach continued to churn in acidic turmoil, but still Christmas came and went, as did all fears of the world coming to an end with Y2K. I rested, counted my blessings, transcribed my tapes (one of which proved missing and remains so to this day), sorted my slides, and with an initial enthusiasm, mounted an Argentine evening for friends. Yet despite being told I had done something remarkable, extraordinary even, I was left with a disquiet that over the weeks that followed that transmogrified into an ever-deepening depression rooted in a sense of failure. Yes, I had travelled and lived to tell the tale, but what had I actually achieved, and at what cost?

I began to cry. Soon I could not stop. By March I was finding it hard to function; I could not sit on the train or talk over a table or desk without tears welling up. The recognition that once again I was unravelling down into a very dark place – that the patterning of the cycle was as old as me, myself and I – was frightening beyond measure. Was this how I was to live out the rest of my life, veering between euphoria and the depths of despair? It was at this point that I called the therapist I had so liked and feared, but who by wondrous accident or design just happened to be in town. I was in trouble, I told her. Could she help?

Walking from Tokyo's Mejiro Station to where she was staying was an effort; I could scarcely drag along the road. But such a terror was over-ridden by a determination that I now recognise as a courage born out of sheer desperation. I was heading for sixty. My last chance perhaps for rescue, to get to the root of my conflict for once and for all and set myself on a healthier more balanced path. Socrates was wiser than he knew to leave us the axiom, "An unexamined life is not worth living".

I did not want to die in the ignorance of unconsciousness. I wanted to wake up.

Well, said Azzah (looking through me once again and throwing out the challenge), We can do one-to-one sessions ('til the cows come home) or you can come with me this weekend. I have an intensive workshop organised, and if you choose to work with total commitment, I promise you'll move mountains.

That was the beginning for me: a genuine rebooting. Not the last for sure, but without doubt the most significant to date.

Throughout the year 2000, Argentina and I teetered on the brink. In 2001 we both went into meltdown, a tragedy for its people and, in one small respect, a bitter disappointment for myself. It was the year my book – *Insider's Tokyo*, as commissioned by Times Editions in Singapore – was published after four years hard graft. Sadly I did not have the energy or confidence to do the promotion required these days of most authors and, and after an initial flurry of interest it sank without trace.

The year that followed was hard and full of struggle.

With Argentina top news as its economy spiralled out of control, my pile of newspaper cuttings grew in direct proportion to the country's misfortune. Trapped by 132 billion dollars worth of public debt, its problems began to spill over into Chile and Uruguay. Soon currencies were sliding, stock tumbling just about everywhere. In fear and trembling, middle class Argentines rushed to withdraw their savings; on presidential instruction, banks shut up shop to prevent withdrawals. It was too late anyway: deposits had largely gone, Disappeared: transferred to offshore accounts or trucked over the borders by the dead of night. Did those in government – with a rapid turnover of those seeking solutions and/or power (five cabinet crises, two presidential resignations, one Senate crisis, and five different economic ministers between October 2000 and August 2002) – have any idea what was happening to Argentina's population at large, with 14 million (nearly 40 per cent of the population unemployed)? Did they care? *Portenos* are an anxious and melancholy breed on the best of days, but psychologists were describing them as, "Paralysed with fear and a sense of impotence". Across the rest of the country, people seethed, erupted into anarchic fury and then – with a resolve born out of anguish – slowly got a grip: began taking matters into their own hands with soup kitchens and the reintroduction of the barter system.

All this very much matched my own emotional rollercoaster.

As if to mirror Argentina's pain, my body (no doubt abetted by the hormonal rebalancing of menopause) went into shock. Arthritis was diagnosed in knees and hips, aggravated by unhappy feet. For fifteen months – an extreme reflection of that country's trauma – my shoulders froze. I could not lift my arms above chin level; sleeping was agony. Bridget's solution? A course in pain management. My preferred course of action: a regime of self-healing.

Keeping my grandfather's words in mind, that understanding, acceptance and forgiveness would require *Going all the way to make a cure*, I hung on (as he had done) through the grimmest of days, weeks and months and gradually gained ground. Longing for an awakening,

433

just as Sam did (though of course he was not interested in his own; it was everyone else he wanted to wake up) I began to gain the necessary tools: understanding that I had to unlearn everything I had become in order to remember who I was. Many people believe that we are born knowing everything there is to know, each one of us bringing into the world that mystical library known as the Akashic Records, a theosophical term that describes the entire knowledge of human existence and the history of the cosmos. But as we grow from baby to child to teenager – as the reality of the existence we have created in order to survive closes in – we slowly lose this information; the reason perhaps that as adults we appear to use so few of our brain cells. In other words, we devolve, not evolve.

It was a former governor of Patagonia, Nestor Kirchner, who pulled Argentina back from the brink of its own devolution. Despite what one writer called "A culture of impunity", Kirchner faced off the army, so putting to flight fear of another junta. Even more boldly, he stood up to the International Monetary Fund. In 2003 he ordered that the peso be cut free from the US dollar and allowed to float, find its own level of modus operandi. With agricultural exports soaring, the ensuing Chinese-style annual growth of 9 per cent meant that by 2006 the country had paid back its entire IMF debt of nearly 9 million US dollars. In December 2007, President Kirchner handed his sash of office to his wife, the country's first democratically elected woman – thus confirming nepotism as A-OK while poking machismo heavily in the ribs. Cristine Fernandez da Kirchner describes herself as a Social Democrat (in Peronist tradition, naturally) believing in no definite triumphs while there is poverty (hear, hear), and the sovereignty of *Las Malvinos* (oh dear).

But let us be optimistic, because before the globally reverberating economic crash of 2009, there was much better news – in El Centro at least. Real estate in the capital was booming, with Puerto Madero *the* place to invest and hang out, and a new five-star hotel designed for gay

434

tourists. The Argentine soccer team won the Gold Medal at the Beijing Olympics, an injection of confidence that went straight to the heart. And – stop press - the tango has been designated part of the world's cultural heritage by the United Nations.

The main problem is that the country's basic insecurity remains unaddressed. Until Argentina sheds its burden of guilt, anger and frustration, rooted as much in a sense of inferiority and isolation as injustice – until this healing takes place – it will continue to suffer the extremes of euphoria and despair that I too have been prone to. I can't say I'm better of course, only better than I used to be. Working my way towards that perfect state of balance called enlightenment may take rather longer than this lifetime, but at least I'm working on it.

As with any addictive habit – my own, spinning into aloofness or emotional drama worthy of an Oscar – I am prone to relapse under stress. But in the main I'm doing well. I can be proud. Especially to have full-grown finger nails for the first time in my life. It seems I no longer feel the desperate need to gnaw away, eat myself alive, in a desperate attempt to reach the calm centre of myself. I am there. I am here. I am now.

I can read back through the record of my travels and laugh. Was I asleep or what! And bless my mother – my dear mother – for she was both right and wrong. Sam and I – and she! – do have much in common, and it's not all bad. Pride, vanity, sentimentality and a certain snobbishness for sure. But also independence, bravery, generosity and optimism. Courage especially, for how many women aged eighty, having never flown before, would make the twelve hour trip to Tokyo and then spend three weeks being marched around all the major sightseeing spots in a country that is 78 per cent mountainous. On hearing of this, a friend remarked perceptively that my mother must have had something important to impart to me, to make such an effort. At the time I thought it was simply to clear the air about my father. Now I believe she was trying to make up for the fact that she was able to express her love to Bridget so much more easily than to me. (Bridget was hungry for it; I was not, fearful that it would sap me of my energy and health, as it had done my sister's own.)

I mull over the fact that so many in my family have faced death in isolation. Like both her parents, my aunt Catherine died alone. As did my own father (one hour after my mother left him in hospital in Coventry), my mother (one hour after Jo visited the retirement home in which her sister passed the last two years of her life), and Bridget, who gave up the ghost just one hour before I was able to reach her hospital bedside in Coventry. It is true that her partner George was in the room, but he was sleeping. And yes, I have resorted to beating myself up over the last year about my lack of support, availability and even basic human kindness, though I do know better. All my family members have been on their own individual journeys, just as I am on my own.

Nor am I the only one in this particular line of Loaders to leave debts in their wake. From what she told me when we met in the UK just a month or so before her death in the mid-1990s, it's likely that Catherine fled Hawaii because she was unable to pay hospital bills. As for Sam, I have learned through the British Cemetery in Montevideo that no rent has been paid on his grave since he was interred, and that if something is not done soon his bones will be cast out and the plot re-cycled. How far back does it go, I wonder, this admirable but irresponsible wanderlust? This leaving of messes for other people to clear up...

I ponder a lot on the subject of failure. What was really in Sam's mind when he submitted that quaintly appalling poem for publication? Was it of no real consequence or a genuine projection of lack in handling his own fear of failing? My father carried it into his own life, and I believe quite unwittingly passed it on to me. Did it go back further than Sam? Both John Loader and Samuel Turner would appear to have done rather well for themselves. But what emotional baggage did John carry with regards to his mother? And what negative emotions did he pass on to his own son?

Well, I can surmise. Because there is news of Harriet.

For the moment, though – since I am nearly done with the dead, and they with me – let us concentrate on the living... in London, where Lee is happily married to Su and growing the healthiest fruit and veg in E17, and Scotland, where Jo continues to stitch and garden into her ninety-eighth year. The only sadness is that with the loss of her sister and her niece – my mother who died aged ninety-six, and Bridget – my aunt no longer has anyone of her generation with whom to share memories.

Toronto, where Buffy works as a graphic designer and I now have a grandson, Maxford. (*The* surprise of 2006.) My immediate family may have shrunk on this side of the world, with only Jo, myself, Lee and Buffy, Elizabeth's two children (sadly she died of breast cancer in 2003) and Genevieve and her boys continuing the line. But Max ensures a new generation. Things were rocky for a while when my therapy began to impact other members of my family, and it was tough to hold steady-maintain a proactive stance when strong reactions were racketing back and forth – but I am hopeful now that everyone is in agreement: in the power of now – not yesterday nor tomorrow, but right now – all our lives are growing from strength to strength.

Even Liverpool is enjoying a resurgence after celebrating its designated status as European City of Culture 2008. Andy is thrilled to bits, as you can imagine. (Our ancestors are pretty pleased too.) Also, having checked with The National Archives in Kew, Richmond, the city can lay proud claim to Samuel Turner's consular duties. All the flying hither and thither to find confirmation, when all the time he was in service to King and Country on his own doorstep, so to speak. I mean, really...

And while there have been losses – my sister, my mother, friends – other people are back in my life: Alan, who it turned out had not gone to Washington with anyone's brother, but rather a black Labrador named Bodger... and – after sojourns in England and Wales – is now back in Canada, but this time with Barry. Also my cousin Alison, who was angry with me, but no longer, in part relating to ambivalent feelings about being adopted enjoying resolution through the discovery of an extended birth family. She came to Bridget's funeral because, as she said, how could she not: The Christmas holidays we spent together... all those times you came to stay... do you remember that holiday in Cornwall, and how you fell in love with our cottage's stable door?

Well, I have a stable door of my own now, at my mother's cottage in Scotland, where I am spending the money she left me to bring it up-to-date while keeping it in period. She died on July 3, 2007; Bridget two months later on September 11.

Kareen and Carlos are still in Montevideo. Not sure about Ana and her family, in Piriapolis. (After she so kindly returned those rings to me, as promised, they quickly went AWOL again. Jewellery and I never stay together for long.) I know only that her baby, born at the end of the twentieth century, was a Lovely healthy boy.

In Chile, Jose – still teaching at the University of Santiago – is the one who mostly keeps in touch. It was he who let me know after my return that the strike at the municipal theatre was over and everyone back to work. He was delighted that Lagos had won the election, though other Loaders were less pleased. The only thing the whole family agreed on was a bemused pleasure that contact had been re-established with relatives from the Old Country, albeit via Japan. More recently I heard of Chile's joy in the long-overdue recognition of divorce, and the election of someone to presidential office as different to Pinochet as it possible to imagine: Michelle Bachelet, a moderate Socialist who juggles roles as a single mother of three and being a surgeon, paediatrician and epidemiologist with studies in military strategy. I hear from Claudio now and then – he's something pretty high up in tourism these days. News of everyone else filters through on occasion via Maria-Elena or Pablo.

Pablo and Fer returned home in late 2003. Over in Spain, the Italian government had granted Fer citizenship; this meant that as a member of the EU she could stay. It had proved far tougher for Pablo, who was to some degree snubbed for his Argentine ancestry and accent. The couple, having married the previous year, tried hard to remain positive, starting an online business, creating a comfortable home. (Akii and I visited from the UK, and later I went alone; the most special time.) But eventually they became homesick, and with signs of some kind of stabilisation in Argentina, blazed a trail home that many émigrés who had fled the country began to follow in 2004. After a long struggle, they found employment, Fer working as a lawyer for a company related to the Provincia de Buenos Aires Bank, but preferring to think of herself a painter; Pablo employed at the Colombian Consulate as a social and political advisor, while running an online business in – surprise, surprise – military antiques. Sadly they are no longer together.

Julito – ever the pragmatist and now the father of three boys – remained solidly employed by his bank through thick and thin. He had some health problems (due to stress I read between the lines) but still, during the very worst of times, his mother described him as, The only person in the country that the sun was shining on. Quite how he achieved this position when all around were drowning is a mystery. He had obviously learned a vital survival strategy from his parents: how to keep his head down. But all is not perfect: he and Paula are also apart.

Pablo No. 2 disappeared off the Caseros map; so too did Marta. (As far as I can ascertain, she was "Let Go", meaning fired.) Also the Tower of Pisa has been demolished. But Tarzan survives, and so does Maria-Elena. I heard from her just the other day, asking how I was in the shadow of recent losses. And while it was hard – especially losing Bridget to a hospital bug after yet another operation, this time trying to replace an elbow joint – I have to respect that a part of her chose not to live without her mother. Their relationship, I now accept, was based on mutual need: my mother needed to be needed; my sister needed the kind of unconditional love and acceptance that only her mother could provide. Also I have to remember that Bridget's last words to me. After decades of operations, ongoing relentless pain, and a regime of fifty pills a day, her poor body was in multiple organ break down.

I've had enough Ange, she kept repeating; I just want to go home.

As I said at her funeral – at St James Parish Church, half a mile from where she was born – attended by two hundred and fifty people from all over Coventry and the Midlands – she is home.

Attempts to learn of any connections Sam may have had with the British Club and Camara de Commercio Argentino–Britanica in Buenos Aires, came to nothing. Andrew (Graham-Yool) at the *Herald* proved far more of a stalwart in keeping in touch: For one thing, he noted, You are my only journalistic contact now in Japan.

I heard from Horacio Maria Cook. Her son Lucas (to whom I had spoken to by phone because he was home from university in Illinois) had not passed on my message, so my follow-up letter from Japan had come as a great surprise. It was her great-grandfather, Frederick Charles Cook, who had offices at St Martin 132 from 1925 on. Sam's colleague would have been her grandfather, Horacio Charles, who died in 1958. She confirmed that many of the family names mentioned in letters – Newboulds, Cadmans, Carricks – were through my great-grandmother Martha's line. Maria said that today all the Cooks are farmers, with land in the southwest of Buenos Aires Province, and that I'm welcome anytime.

There were further discoveries, via Laurel and Hardy of Buenos Aires's British Cemetery: Winifred Pheasant Lee's daughters by her first marriage, Manon Peard (born 1922) and Doreen Pierre (1926), with whom Maria-Elena talked on my behalf. Though somewhat shocked, they were sad that I had come and gone without making contact. Doreen worked in the office with my grandfather and his partner (her step-father) Howard Pheasant until her marriage, after which Sam went down to the harbour to wave her off on her European honeymoon. She knew where he stayed in Belgrano, and about visits to Paysandu, upriver in Uruguay. Apparently he told the Lee-Pierre family that he was single!

I heard also from Mary Anne Lee Contaduria, Manon's cousin, who in 2002 was working at the Sheraton Hotel in Buenos Aires and about to get married. Winifred Daisy Lee, born 1900, was her aunt, and elder sister to Mary Ann's elder brother Boy Lee. Winnie had her girls, then after her divorce, married Howard Pheasant.

It gets better (if ever more complicated). Mary Ann's grandmother, Daisy Lee (nee Carrick) was born in Paysandu, and her mother was a Newbold (same family, different spelling). Robert Carrick had emigrated to Uruguay in 1852 and married a Newbold. They had two children, one of whom was named after his father. Mary Ann wrote: Most of the people mentioned are now dead. But Doreen and my mother remember your grandfather well. Everyone used to call him Uncle Sam and he was at all the parties.

In addition (now married and living in Uruguay) she sent me a copy of a long, detailed and wonderfully evocative letter – shades of the log I found in Liverpool – that Robert Carrick Sr. wrote: *To all whom it may concern, from Somewhere about the bay of Biscayne, Wednesday 12 September 1860 Fore noon.*

Adventuring it would appear is in this family's blood. As is writing – and also editing! – for I am beginning to understand that Sam was not as lonely and isolated as he often made out, having a large and extended family in Uruguay and Argentina on his mother's side. Did my father ever know, I wonder? He most certainly never appeared to try and find out. Sad that.

But there are other happy things to relate. Though Karen disappeared, so proving not to be the Ideal future daughter-in-law imagined (but no matter because now I have Su instead), I suspect she is still around. Was it coincidental that the two young women with whom I had the longest conversations on my travels had such similar names: Karen (from the Greek and Danish for pure) and Kareen (from Kore, Greek for maiden or hummingbird). I believe not.

I hear on occasion from Molly Hampton, who sent a Christmas card in 2004 (which would have made her eighty-five) announcing that she had got married, and enclosing a photo of her walking down the aisle all smiles with a charming Argentine landowner in his early nineties, so proving that it is never too late to turn life around in the most unexpected fashion.

Which – in relation to a late and unexpected marriage – leads me back to Harriet Loder , who has been alternately teasing and snapping at my heels all these years. Windsor Ancestry Research suspected that she must have given up on her son – the only way a woman fallen on hard times in those days had any chance of so-called redemption. Which makes it all the more astonishing that John survived as well as he appears to have done. I guess we Loaders are tougher than we think.

I found Harriet's descendants – my great-great grandfather and his family – on a second trip to Liverpool in 2003, which is when things began to look up. Wondering why Samuel, Martha and their daughter Gertrude were sited in Anfield Cemetery just so, a search of the surrounding graves revealed an ancient crumbling tombstone with familiar names inscribed in order. Firstly John and Susan's daughter Harriet, who had died in 1881, aged twenty-three. Then Susan, 1887, aged seventy-two, and John Loader himself (1892, seventy-five). Only two of their surviving children lie buried with their parents: Charles Whitefoot Loader, who died in 1904 aged fifty-two, and Sarah Hope, at seventy-one in 1926. Whitefoot and Hope: two names mentioned by Sam, two names from the graveyard at Ministerly. The whereabouts of Hannah and Gertrude are unknown.

There is a third grave, which will arouse interest in Chile and maybe even encourage a return pilgrimage, because it is where Charles' siblings are laid to rest: Frederick J (died 1918) aged twenty-eight; Herbert William (Bert, 1931), fifty-four; Anne Leticia (1945), sixty-nine; and Walter Henry (1947). Told that Arthur and Alice were there also, Joyce Loader's eyebrows shot into her hair: Heaven knows how or why, she commented with witty aplomb; They couldn't agree on anything in life!

WAR had noted that whenever they searched the name Loder in Shrewsbury, the names Loader and Lowther also came up. Keeping this and the possibility of other misspellings in mind, researchers found that in 1794, a child Elizabeth Lowther, of St Alkmund, Shrewsbury was put out to nurse. Her mother (of the same name) appears to have had a sister, Cath Lowther. A child Sarah Lowther was put out with the same nurse, and her mother's name was Cath, also from St Alkmund. So it's quite possible that Elizabeth and Sarah were first cousins.

In 1802, Sarah Lowther aged six was accepted into the workhouse. No mother's name was given but she was recorded as being the grand-daughter of *[blank] Lowther, Sergeant Major, Sma*. This abbreviation could mean St Mary's but more likely the Shropshire Military, which might begin to tie in with Sam's belief in being from Good yeoman stock.

Jno Peplow is named as the father of S Lowden in records dated 1795. Three years later, J Gronna was named as the father of E Lowder.

A Harriet Peplow appears in records dated 1795, associated with the child called S Lowden. Could this have been Sarah? It appears likely, since Harriet also went by the name Lowther. Confused? Who wouldn't be? But here is the miracle: on May 13, 1822, Harriet Lowther married Thomas Peplow, followed by the baptism of a child named Emma, and an earlier daughter Harriet at St Mary's. This could explain why John's mother was no longer with her son. He was in the workhouse in 1825; she had married three years earlier. Was he with his mother in the early years? Had she disowned him in order to wed? Again we will never know.

In the Shrewsbury census returns of 1851, Harriet Peplow (nee Lowther-Loder) was a 56 year-old laundress and widowed. Daughters Harriet and Mary, aged twenty and eighteen respectively, were thread spinners. A third daughter, Caroline, was a Scholar, meaning that at age twelve she was still at school. Other possible relatives named Peplow, with Christian names that resonate – fishermen, net makers and flax spinners – have been identified. According to a local phone directory of today, there are still Peplows in the city and we may well be related.

Another piece of the puzzle was put into place with the discovery of

Harriet Gronno Lowther's baptism at St Mary's in 1810, when she would have been fourteen. Remember that entry about J Gronna being named as the father of a child of E.Lowder? I believe – choose to believe – that this child was Harriet. We may be able to go even further back, because in 1794, an Elizabeth Loader (Genevieve will surely enjoy hearing about this) married Joseph Smith at St Alkmunds. This may have been Harriet's mother. As to her father, there are two possibilities: John Gronna, or James Gronna, two brothers born in the 1770s to James and Mary Gronna.

The plot thickens you might think. But no, I think this is enough. Others may choose to make family history their life work, but for me this journey that has taken nearly three decades has been a means to an end: revelation, understanding, stability. Exploring my ancestry has led me into the past so that I can move joyfully and knowingly into the future.

I no longer cast blame. My father often benignly comes to rest beside me on the train to Tokyo; I find his presence very comforting. My mother came to me a few hours after her death, and now I am astonished at the gap she has left in my life. Both she and my father were damaged goods, immensely hurt by losses and insensitive treatment in their young lives. But my father never abandoned us, as his own father abandoned his family when things got tough; no, Bob stuck with us through thick and thin and tried his very best. He has my greatest love and respect for that. Likewise my mother, who sacrificed so much in order to try and provide a stable and loving home. Yes, mistakes were made, and there is much I do not understand. But I know for sure why I chose my parents: to learn clear lessons towards the evolution of my soul. From my mother I learned to acknowledge intellect as well as creativity. She also – I am astonished to hear myself say – helped teach me how to be a good mother. From my father I learned the importance of standing up for myself, and that it is better to risk disappointment than to die disappointed. As the actor Dustin Hoffman once said "There is nothing wrong with failure. The sin is not trying... not being true to yourself".[71]

Hear, hear, I say again. And while I do not believe in sin, and by association evil, only the deep sleep of unconsciousness, I do wish my father had tried to find his bliss, instead of settling for what he obviously believed were the secure and proper values of *The Daily Telegraph*, his local Conservative Club, Winston Churchill (in three volumes), and the *Reader's Digest*.

My mother is more complicated, simply because I knew her longer and more intimately. Most certainly I recognise the cost of abusing and wasting intellectual talents. I also know to build my own energy rather than playing emotionally leeching games that leave everyone in the immediate vicinity exhausted. When asked once for any memory he had of my mother at Sunfield, David Clement – into whose duck pond at Broome Farm my father once backed his first and only car – was able to look back down seventy years with startling clarity. Quite apart from her many other talents, he wrote in 2002, She was an actress, not on the stage but in life. She was the damsel in distress! A poor girl who could not possibly manage on her own. She loved to tell stories of her innocent helplessness – all of which were quite untrue – but it led to much laughter.

My amusing, stubborn, play-acting mother and dear David died just a week apart. He went ahead, she followed on behind, most probably dramatizing the whole experience to attention-seeking effect as only she knew how.

While hard, there was a certain self-serving pleasure in dealing with my parents' role in my life, and then that of my children – though in this case it led us all into deep waters for several years. When it came to my turn – having to acknowledge my own dark side, the shadow of my pain body – the work is proving infinitely harder and more painful. One thing at least is clearer now. The only person standing in the way of my success and happiness is yours truly. Whenever I fall back into old bad habits, I return to shooting myself in the foot, sabotaging myself every step of the way. So I am watchful. Or try to be, for to stay one step ahead of ego or to put it aside – let alone letting ego go – is no easy matter.

I am reminded of a Zen story, recounted by Chilean psychologist Claudio Naranjo in *The One Quest*.[72] This was one of three books he kindly sent to me after an interview in Tokyo in 1996, and at the time I did not understand a word; they seemed incomprehensible, just as my grandmother's books had appeared incomprehensible years before. Now I accept that it was not that I was stupid (as feared), only that I was not prepared. I did not know the language; was not ready to consider the issues Claudio's book raised: Salvation, deliverance, enlightenment, healing, authenticity, self-actualisation and full-humanness as sought in both ancient and modern systems of meditation, mysticism, sensory awareness and the raising of consciousness.

At the beginning of any journey – The Journey, so Claudio's Zen story goes – the trees look like trees, the mountain looks like a mountain and the lake looks like a lake. In the middle of a journey, the trees do not look like trees anymore, the mountain does not look like a mountain, and the lake is no longer a lake. But at the end of the journey, the trees look like trees, the mountain looks like a mountain and the lake looks like a lake.

As I look out of my window now down the valley towards the Pacific Ocean, so many years since my own journeying began, at trees that are beginning to look like trees, hills that are beginning to look like hills, and (since my lake is rather large) an ocean that is beginning to look like the ocean, I thank my father, my grandfather, my great- grandfather, John Loader and his mother Harriet, and every one of my ancestors on both sides of my family that are lined up behind me into pre-history and beyond. I thank all the lucky shooting stars of my family constellation, because if any of them had lived their lives one iota differently, I would not be here now, writing in peace, flowing with forgiveness and love.

# PPS

Three days ago I received an e-mail from a previously unheard of nephew of Jose's in Santiago. It seems that Diego and others have established an online Facebook site for the descendants and relatives of Charles Loader, By Invitation Only. Wonderful to open it up, find so many familiar faces a decade older and moved on – Pablo, Maria-Elena, Claudio, Betty, Camila and Javiera, Carole and her younger brother Cristobal (the beautiful boy with the pony tail) now aged twenty-one and a Satanist. (Not really, he explained in a mail of his own: I'm not into any religion. I just believe in the soul and the mental power of all human beings.

And so the world turns. Ever more synchronistically and – because the only sure thing in life it is that we all die – ever more urgently.

Diego says everyone knows who I am in the family. And guess what? Something that makes me almost unbearably happy: They want me back.

There are only three problems: The first is simple: I need to renew my passport, and finally say *sayonara* to the pitiful weepy blonde in the photo. The second less so, because there is the problem of flying any distance these days: the responsibility for individual carbon footprints. In 1999 we were relatively ignorant of such matters – or chose to be. Nowadays, no-one has any excuse.

Oh yes, and I still have to learn Spanish. I did start to study with Zedy (also from the Yokosuka Naval Base) but then she went home to Panama and never came back. Well, that's my story, and I'm sticking to it. Maybe.

# ENDNOTES

1   Far Away and Long Ago is the title of Hudson's famed autobiography, first published in 1918. An affectionate and lyrical work, it describes a childhood spent on his father's *estancias* (sheep or cattle farms) on the grassy plains of the South American pampa.

2   According to a member of the Ocean Liner Society, based in London, the vessels Andy remembered from his childhood were most likely to have belonged to the Empress fleet – Empress of Canada, Empress of England, Empress of France, and so on.

3   Spending August 2001 in Mallorca, Andy made deeper enquiries into the name Meila and came up with quite a surprise. It is Catalan, and most probably from Mallorca itself. Josef Melia is a famous local author; the Melia Hotel chain started on the island.

    More recently he learned the name is more Mediterranean than Mallorcan, stemming from ancient Greece and a mythological tribe of nymphs called the Melia (after the ash tree). It is also the present day name for an ash tree in Spain.

4   The singer and musician Al Jolson – born Asa Yoelson in Lithuania – emigrated late to America via Liverpool in 1894. Aged eight, he made the crossing on the steamship SS Umbria. Immigrants like the

Yoelsons were at the mercy of unscrupulous landlords of squalid typhus and cholera-stricken lodging houses close by the docks. From 1870, runners would await vessels arriving from the Continent and migrants travelling overland to direct exhausted the passengers to where they could stay for a few pence a night (and to corrupt brokers for tickets to the New World). Another bad business all around.

5   On a trip to the Family Records Office in London in 2001, I came across a section of Consular Records, tucked away in a corner. In the bound edition covering the years 1886–1880, I found Florence Susan Loader (Volume 6, ref. 736), registered in Montevideo. In the volume dated 1881-1885, Samuel Charles Edward Loader (7. 2451), ditto. Sam's younger sister Bea was nowhere to be found, implying that she was born elsewhere, most probably back home in Liverpool.

   Checking out the other indexes, I found previously unknown Loaders in Vol. 1880–1865: two (let us assume) brothers, Charles Edward (3-333) and Thomas Henry (2. 301), both registered in Rio de Janerio, Brazil. Whether these individuals have any connection with my family line I have no idea. One day it might be fun to find out. But not now; it is all too easy to become distracted in detective work like this.)

6   Indigo.ca describes itself in advertorial website speak as, The world's first virtual cultural department store and a 100 per cent Canadian online book retailer. The first store opened in Burlington September 4, 1997; by autumn 2000 Indigo had 20 more outlets across Canada. In 2001 Riesman made business headlines after Indigo bought out Chapters. She and her husband (described in the Toronto Star on May 20 as Canada's Toniest Couple) live in Rosedale, one of Toronto's most venerated districts. Here they are reported to be buying up historic properties and demolishing them to further extend their empire.

7     My own generation finds this hard to understand. But here we are, over a century later, with young Japanese (women in particular) placing the purchasing power of their salaries ahead of marriage and children. Estimated to number around ten million, they regard staying at home – with Mum doing all the dirty work and Dad a security blanket on the sidelines – a steal. Japan even has a name for them: Parasite Singles. It is a growing phenomena, I understand, and not only in Japan.

8     A web site appeal in early 2001 produced a page from a directory, the A-Z of Ocean Liners. It was the author himself who made contact, delighted to be of help.

The two vessels were sisters, designed by Dr Haruki Watsuji (Osaka Shosen Kaisha's leading marine architect), built by Mitsubishi in Nagasaki, and launched just before the outbreak of war in Europe. They were built as state-subsidised emigrant ships in the wake of a quarter-of-a-century-old company policy of operating a run from Japan to South America, around the Cape of Good Hope, and returning to base via Panama and Los Angeles. Outward-bound they carried emigrants to Brazil (this country having the largest Japanese community outside Japan and the USA), and returning with commodities picked up en route.

The Argentine Maru made only four trips before the attack on Pearl Harbour in late 1941, after which she was switched first to making the crossing between Japan and Dalien in China, and then enlisted to carry troops. After being converted into the aircraft carrier Kaiyo in 1942–43, she was damaged by US aircraft in March 1945 off Japan's southern island of Kyushu. A few months after being repaired, she was hit by a mine, and had to be towed into shallow water, where she lay beached until being scrapped the following year.

To celebrate her maiden voyage, OSK had commissioned two large models of the vessel to be used in window displays. The one gifted to Cape Town is now in South Africa's Maritime Museum. The other, made for either Rio de Janerio or Buenos Aires, was recently returned to Japan, final resting place unknown.

And the chipped plate, now hanging on the wall alongside my desk? That was one of a commemorative edition given to passengers on her maiden voyage. Peter knows of two in Cape Town, one hanging on the wall of a friend's loo. Personally he owns a green glass pen tray, produced by OSK to mark the sailing of the Brasil Maru.

One of these days, I really must find out which of my Japanese neighbours is a part of ocean liner history.

9    The Auracana, otherwise known as the Chilean Pine or Monkey Puzzle is one of the few non-native species that have proved hardy in the UK, hence its popularity in Victorian England. It was introduced from Chile and Argentina in 1795, and first sold commercially by William Lobb in 1844. I remember seeing Monkey Puzzles in the front gardens of suburban homes while traveling between Coventry and Birmingham as a child. Now they are quite a rarity. Gone out of fashion, I supposed, but Mark, who identified my specimens on his last visit from London, has another theory: gardeners cut them down when they awoke to the fact that small plots were being taken over by larger-than-life aliens.

10   Even before the death of the nation's First Lady on July 27, 1952, the Chamber of Deputies was debating the erection of a monument in her name. According to A History of Argentina, 1873-1999, published by the Buenos Aires Herald in 2000 and described as The First Argentine Historical Chronicle in English, the Eva Peron Monument Committee decided to entrust its design to the sculptor Leon Tommasi. That was in September 1952. Whether this is the same project, I have no idea. If so, it has taken an awful long time to reach completion.

11 I had become familiar with the thick syrupy caramelised reduction Dulche de Leche just weeks before leaving for Canada. In launching an ice-cream of the same name in September 1999, Haagen-Dazs Japan unwittingly prepared me in the nick of time for Argentina's sweet-toothed weakness. Peron himself is said to have been so partial to the spread, that when he began to fail mentally, he was enticed into signing documents with spoons full of the stuff.

12 There are more psychologists in Argentina per capita – 110 for every 10,000 inhabitants – than any other country in the world, excepting Uruguay. It runs neck and neck with New York in claiming the most psychotherapists (including psychologists and psychiatrists) overall.

The country became a centre of psychotherapy in the 1940s, following an influx of European immigrants from Austria and Germany that included several prominent Jewish psychoanalysts. The reason for so much insecurity? As Felipe Nouera, a political analyst and pollster speculated in the *New York Times* in May 1998: Argentina is a very frustrated society because it has long suffered a crisis of expectations... rooted in a long period of economic expansion between 1880 and 1930, followed by a 60 year slump, characterised by political instability, recession and hyperinflation.

13 In 1999, Argentina's economy was sliding fast. Military dictatorships interspersed with weak, short-lived democratic governments had left the country severely in debt. After democracy was restored once again in 1983, President Raul Alfonsin attempted to stablise the economy with a new form of currency, the Austral. Since this move required new loans and new interest payments, inflation began to rise. By 1989, this had reached 200 per cent a month, or 3,000 per cent annually. After Alfonsin resigned, Carlos Saul Menem took over the reins. He immediately reneged on all promises and set economic course by a US model of trade liberalization, labour deregulation

and privatization of all state owned companies and services. Some Argentines grew ever more wealthy, the vast majority slumped ever deeper into poverty.

The government kept spending. Corruption was rampant. But despite the country's public debt growing ever larger, and no signs of how this would ever be paid off, still the IMF kept lending money to Argentina and postponing schedules for repayment. Money laundering and tax evasion are quoted as the main reasons for the disappearance – hiving off – of funds into offshore banks.

By the time I arrived just before the end of 1999, newly elected President Fernando de la Rua was facing such a frightening situation that it was little wonder he was taking his time to take up office. With unemployment at a critical high, and the country's GDP dropped four per cent, Argentina was entering what everyone feared would be a severe recession.

14  Andy reports that as of September 2001, redevelopment of Liverpool continues in much the same way. He thinks some bright entrepreneurial spirit should take a chance and open a dive named Sam's Bar on Dale Street, maybe even at the Temple address.

15  Another mystery concerns the lost cities of Northern Argentina and Paraguay. A British colonel, James Churchward, wrote a number of popular travel books back in the 1930s, speculating on the existence of ancient civilisations. He had even seen, he claimed, a map of ancient South America in a remote monastery in Tibet.

He also made this cryptic remark: Some prehistoric ruins are to be found on the banks of the River Platte (sic). A tablet found in these ruins had an inscription, discovered to be an exact duplication of one found in Asia, Mongolia.

Since the Rio de la Plata was a major transportation artery, it would not be surprising to find the remnants of ancient civilisations along its banks. The Spanish built cities along the river edge, so why should not other cultures have done so, many thousands of years before, if Churchward is to be believed.

Certainly there are remains that cannot be explained. As the magazine *Science* reported in 1897, in the Province of Tucaman, near the small town of Rioha, in the wide valley of Tafi, are some 2000 monoliths, some nearly three metres high above the soil, arranged in rows of three and five. No-one knows who put them there or why. While in San Juan Province, close to the Chilean border, petrographs of bears, machines that closely resemble aircraft, and people wearing halo-like helmets (or helmet-like halos), can be seen on cliffs in the Valle de la Luna.

Contemporary British author and prehistoric speculator Graham Hancock would no doubt have his own fascinating theories about all this.

16  The Phidias was part of Lamport and Holt's extensive fleet trading between Liverpool and South America. Launched on April 3, 1913, she made her maiden voyage to South America on May 31 the same year. She was torpedoed and sunk by a German submarine near the Azores on June 8, 1941, just nine days after I was born.

17  Each time I saw my mother between 1989 and 2000, I asked her what had happened between my grandparents. Each time she swore blind she had no idea. When I asked her yet again in February 2001, she looked at me in surprise: Well, he went bankrupt, of course! (In such matters my mother remains an enigma and indeed next year may well be back to claiming complete ignorance. Therefore I pass on this information while I can.).

18  The Theosophical Society of today is located at 60 Gloucester Place, London W1. It's a rum kind of place – steeped in the past and staffed

by predominantly middle-aged to elderly women of seriously cranky disposition – but the library is excellent.

19  ASGB is based in Rudolf Steiner House at 35 Park Road, London NW1, just around the corner from Baker Street. It is as light and bright and full of life as the Theosophical Society exists in an atmosphere of conservative gloom. (I cannot help but feel that Madam B. would be horrified to find her lifework languishing in such a fashion.)

Last refurbished in the 1980s, ASGB's decor remains true to Steiner's vision of architecture based on organic forms in harmony with the earth and a spiritual appreciation and application of colour. It houses a theatre, workshops, lecture rooms, a library and is home to the Biodynamic Agricultural Association, as promoted by my mother's dear friend, David Clement.

20  As published in *New Internationalist* 334, May 2001, the following poem was written by a young *desaparecido* (disappeared person) under the dictatorship of Jorge Rafael Videla Redonda (Argentine president from 1976–1981). Alcira Graciela Fidalgo, a 27 year-old law student , was abducted on February 4, 1977 and never seen again:

*TILCARA*
*Today I dreamed again of mountains*
*and a landscape drawn by the wind.*
*It was the afternoon, here in your sky*
*the hot bird of summer.*
*There were willows, perfumed air*
*and the silence singing a baguala.*

*A corner in the night and in life...*
A dream of colour and poetry.

*Hard-working bees*
*daily,*
*you hum through the mornings*
*and the hot coffee*
*and the shared mate.*

*Such was my home:*
*peaceful and silent*
*in the hot summer siestas.*
*Water for the mate,*
*shared evenings*
*(a clean glance*
*sliding from the faucets)*

*Dad reading a book.*
*Mom watering the grass.*
*Estela with her shadow*
*gliding across the patio.*

*Such, such was my home*
*a warm smile*
*open to the morning.*

21 According to Andrew, the Old Calvet was demolished in the 1970s to make way for car parking for the post office and also a small park.

22 The buildings pointed out to me on Avenida Libertador (yes, the same road that I walked in El Centro but far distant) were army-operated, not the Naval Mechanics School (ESMA) as assumed. But it still bore grave responsibility; up to four hundred concentration camps/torture centres operated throughout Argentina during the dictatorship. ESMA still stands on a busy street in El Centro, but is

now a museum. In 2006, President Nestor Kirchner inaugurated a new military training academy at the Puerto Belgrano Naval base, some 600 kilometres from Buenos Aires. "You must now look ahead to the future and not to the past," he told officers.

23 Even more fun in Japan, where the fireworks season is high summer, with spectacular displays over water in seaside towns like Zushi and hundreds of thousands, many dressed in cotton kimono and keeping cool with fans, sitting on beaches, drinking beer and snacking from bento lunch boxes.

24 Back in my grandfather's day, European travellers upriver were being advised that A folding mosquito net is essential. Also, gloves, high shoes, and a gauze canopy for the face and shoulders. The conditions of long distance river steamers also make it desirable to carry changes of bed-linen and an air pillow. (The South American handbook, 1937)

25 According to World Bank statistics, the number of South to South migrants – that is people living in the southern hemisphere who move ever further southwards to find work and security – numbers 74 million.

26 The Warwick Pageant has been devoted to celebrating both the history of the city and its famed castle and immediate environs, and English history in general, for near on a century. First staged in Warwick Castle Park in 1906, it commemorated the Conquest of Mercia by Queen Ethelfleda one thousand years earlier.

The 1930 pageant, to which my mother contributed, was a miscellany of events that had taken place throughout the county, entitled, *A Great Historical Pageant – The Spirit of Warwickshire*.

The pageant of 1953 celebrated the coronation of Queen Elizabeth

II, linking her ascendancy and the hope this brought for the future with Elizabeth I, who had often visited Warwick and stayed in the castle. Remembering this pageant (at age eleven) as being staged in a field opposite the castle across the river, I queried this anomaly with Warwickshire County Record Office in October, 2002. As the Archives Assistant very sweetly replied: The Coronation Pageant had to be held in the field opposite the Castle because the trees lining the route of earlier pageants had grown so much that passage and vision would have been severely restricted – so your memory is not playing tricks on you!

The last pageant was staged in 1996 as part of Warwick's 450th anniversary celebrations of being granted its charter in 1545.

27  In the 1870s, the Quaker businessman George Cadbury had a dream of creating a model community. Subsequently he moved his workers at the Cadbury chocolate factory in Birmingham's Bridge Street, out into the countryside and built a factory in a garden.

In 1906, George and his wife Elizabeth began building a school, which was opened the following year by the Bishop of Birmingham. Class sizes were smaller than usual, with 40-50 pupils instead of the more regular 60. The school hymn (as was my own at Warwick High, fifty years on): Jerusalem. After graduating, many of the children went to work, not in the dark satanic mills of Victorian Britain's Industrial Revolution, but in green and pleasant conditions that everyone regarded as a relative paradise. They were known as the Cadbury Angels.

28  Mohander Karamachand Ghandi (1869-1948) visited England to talk with trade unionists and workers in the mills, to gain their understanding for the Indian boycott of British-made textiles, which in causing the bottom to fall out of the weaving industry in India, was causing widespread unemployment and suffering. He was

promoting Khadi, which he described as cloth woven by Indians from Indian cotton to be worn by Indians.

Haile Selassie (1891-1975) was Emperor of Ethiopia from 1930. He lived in exile in England until 1941, returning home to reclaim his throne only to die in captivity one year after an army coup in 1974.

Chad Varah (born 1911 ) founded the Samaritans, a free toll phoneline that operates in the UK to help people with suicidal tendencies. My mother says he was the same age as Michael Wilson, and much drawn to Sunfield. She recalls how she, Michael, Chad and others roamed the Clent Hills together; how he longed to stay but there were pressures from his father's congregation, who had helped fund his studies in Oxford. In 1974 Varah founded Befrienders International, the worldwide body of the Samaritans.

29 As Professor J. Mayore Stycos of Cornell University wrote in his book, *Sex and the Argentine Male*, translated for Primera Plana, B. A. Atlas, March 1964: "My inquiries indicate that the typical Latin American (man) lacks confidence in his potency, but is eager to prove it on every possible occasion."

I rest my case.

30 The internationally renowned Kodo Drummers live in a community founded in 1988 close by the tiny fishing port of Ogi on Sado, a small island off the west coast of Niigata on mainland Honshu. Here, every August, a three-day festival, Earth Celebration, brings musicians together from all over the world. In 1992, together with Lee, we stayed in a *ryokan* (traditional inn) in Ogi. The percussionist group Suar Agung from Indonesia was playing that year; also The Doudou N'Diaye Rose Percussion Orchestra from Senegal. It was a sight never to be forgotten: the leader of this troupe and his twenty sons, all tall and skinnily carved from polished ebony, wearing long brightly coloured robes, walking down the high street and towering

over tiny Japanese *obaachan* (elderly women), with everyone much amused by such unlikely meetings so far from West Africa, laughing fit to bust.

31    Coincidences, coincidences: Lady Godiva (Anglo-Saxon spelling, Godgifu) is mentioned in the Domesday Book of 1086 as holding large estates in the county of Warwickshire which she inherited from her husband, Leofric, Earl of Mercian. Having made a fortune in mutton, the couple had moved – believe it or not – from Shrewsbury to Coventry where, desperate to gain acceptance among the local hoi polloi, they founded an abbey in the name of Saint Eunice of Saxmundem who had been flayed alive by the Romans for her Christian faith.

As Leofric began taxing everything he could lay his hands on, including manure, to fund an increasing number of high-flying godly projects, Godiva felt guilty about the increasing impoverishment of the peasants. Having told her husband she would do anything if only he would end the crippling taxation system, he challenged her to ride naked through the streets of the town. This she did, accompanied by two fully-clothed female attendants. But her hair did not cover all, as suggested by the statue of the lady standing in the centre of the city, and the logo of Coventry City Council to this day; this was a prudish embellishment added later by the Church in a more puritan phase. Instead her hair was plaited into two braids and coiled at the nape of her neck so her husband could not accuse her of cheating. The taxes were duly cancelled – except on horses!

32    *Alive: The Miracle of the Andes*, was based on the book by Piers Paul Read. Directed by Frank Marshall, it was released in 1993.

33    In 1998, while travelling abroad, Pinochet was arrested in London on a warrant from Spain requesting his extradition on murder charges –

news that caused equal measures of delight and fury back in Chile. There followed a legal tug-of-war, with Straw ruling in April 1999 that despite ill-health, Pinochet had to face the music in Spain. Chile continued to fight this decision, demanding he be extradited to face trial in his own country. Eventually Chile had its way and Pinochet was returned, with courts continuing to battle over his future.

At the time of his death, he was facing some 300 criminal charges of human rights abuses and embezzlement of state funds. He remained a polarizing figure until the very end, with people either hating him for his methods, or respecting him for putting Chile on the international map.

34   The report on the Belgrano born Diligenti quins was a Herald scoop. The news filled the papers for the next few days, with Leila, the Woman's Page editor, who broke the news, very much enjoying her own brief moment of fame.

35   The name Bridget can be traced back to the Celtic Feast of Brigid, which celebrated the halfway point between the winter solstice and spring solstice. The Romans then adapted it to become a Christian festival, with St Brigit's Day celebrated on February 1.

36   The term Old Packers was derogatory indeed. Peddlers were a common feature of daily life well into the twentieth century – itinerant salesmen travelling from village to village, door to door. A peddler of the Old Packer variety would be peddling small items – such as draper's goods – from a bundle or pack. Packer (in common usage from 1800 onwards) also described a person who packed cards, or juries, or was a confederate in a fraudulent design; the term Packing therefore meant a private or underhand arrangement, a fraudulent dealing, contrivance or plot. Peddler's French was the jargon used between thieves and vagabonds.

37 The site of Uriconium (Viriconium), lies under and around the small village of Wroxeter, on the road between Shewsbury and Ironbridge. Discovered in the 1700s, the various artefacts recovered were not put on display until the 1930s, when the Shrewsbury Museum (called the Uriconium Museum) was established. Built as the fifth largest Roman city in Britain, Uriconium remains largely unexcavated to this day.

38 Estimates vary as to the numbers of Chileans either executed or disappeared after the coup of 1973 – anywhere between 7,000 and 30,000, depending on who is supplying the statistics: Moderate Left or Extreme Left. Many were taken first to the Naval Mechanics School and later imprisoned and tortured aboard the cargo vessel *Andalien*, which shipped them from Valparaiso to concentration camps in the north.

39 The Greater London Council was disbanded by former Prime Minister Margaret Thatcher's conservative government at midnight on March 31, 1986 – a response to her vitriolic hatred of left-wing GLC leader Ken Livingstone. Overnight 22,000 civil servants lost their jobs. After devolving responsibility to local boroughs (and so creating chaos and increased inequality all round), the Greater London Authority was re-established in 2000. Red Ken (as dubbed by Maggie's media) was subsequently elected Mayor of London.

40 To learn more about Pablo Neruda, go to:
<http://dir.yahoo.com/arts/humanities/literature/authors/poets/ pablo_neruda_1904_1973_>

This provides a mass of information, including excerpts from *100 Sonnets* , a profile, selected links, the text of his Nobel lecture, and the entry, *Poems of Pablo Neruda*. This includes *The Me Bird*, that begins, *I am the Pablo bird/* and concludes: *That's why I come and go/ fly and dare fly but sing:/I am the furious bird/of the calm storm.*

There are also a number of odes – to salt, to sadness, wine, a lemon, and (with particular meaning for one who has visited his home) *House of Odes*, written in 1955, that concludes as follows: *I am from the South, a Chilean/a sailor/returned/from the seas./I did not stay in the islands/a king./I did not stay ensconced/in the land of dreams./ I returned to labour simply/besides others,/for everyone./So that everyone may live./I build my house here with transparent odes.*

41   At 3776 metres, Mt Fuji is Japan's most sacred peak, presided over by a female kami, or goddess. It last erupted in 1703, with great loss of life, and – to the consternation of volcanologists, geologists and local residents alike – is showing signs of activity once again.

42   A group of islands named after the H.S. Beagle that sailed in 1831 with a contemporary of Harriet, also born in Shrewsbury; aboard: the naturalist and theorist of organic evolution Charles Darwin (1809–82), all set to explore Patagonia and Tierra del Fuego, and survey the coastline of Chile and Peru.

The Beagles were in contention from 1800 on, with both Chile and Argentina arguing over 30,000 square miles of fishing and – later – mineral rights, especially oil, possibly extending into Antarctica.

In 2004, a monument was unveiled on the Argentine-Chile border at a height of 4,200 metres (13,800 feet) to commemorate the agreements made in 1902 that finally led to peace between the two countries. The presidents of the two nations were in attendance – Ricardo Lagos for Chile, and Nestor Kirchner for Argentina.

43   Peter Brown, Journal Editor, Railway and Canal Historical Society, and Heritage and Planning Officer, Shrewsbury and North Wales Branch, Inland Waterways Association, replied to my enquiry of 2005: Unfortunately I am unable to turn up anything. Actually the description 'Bridgewater Canal Co, Salop' is rather odd, as the

Bridgewater Canal was based in Manchester and, as far as I am aware, had no particular connection with 'Salop' (meaning Shropshire or Shrewsbury).

44  I could only find a Wilfred Whiteley (1882-1879) listed as an MP for Liverpool <www.nra.nationalarchives.gov.uk/nra/searches>

45  Samuel Smiles (1812–1904) was a Scot who originally trained as a doctor before turning to journalism. He wrote for a popular audience to show people how best to take advantage of the changes being brought about by the industrial revolution which was sweeping Britain and other parts of the world in the first half of the nineteenth century. In his best known work, *Self-Help* (published in 1859, the same year as Charles Darwin's *On the Origin of Species*, and John Stuart Mill's *On Liberty*) he combined Victorian morality with sound free market ideas for moral tales showing the benefits of thrift, hard work, education, perseverance, and a sound moral character. He drew upon the personal success stories of emerging self-made millionaires in the pottery industry (Josiah Wedgwood), the railway industry (Watt and Stephenson), and the weaving industry (Jacquard) to make his point that the benefits of the market were open to anyone.

Now I see what my grandfather was trying to emulate and live up to.

46  Cordoba is a major city (population around one million) in the centre of Argentina on the Rio Primero. First settled in 1573, it became a cultural centre, with a university established in 1611 and many fine Colonial buildings that still remain today. In the 1920s, it would have been almost as long a journey to Cordoba from Mendoza as to Buenos Aires, but maybe not quite.

47  The Guardian's Pass Notes, No 1052 of July 15, 1997, describes Offa's Dyke as, "A 70 mile Giant Toblerone (after the Swiss-made chocolate) rampart, with a 25 feet-high turf wall, surrounded by V-shaped ditches... Somewhat battered by marauding Welsh and hikers. Especially popular with Dutch tourists."

48  I have to thank Bjorn Envall, who became Saab's Chief of Design, for this marvellous vehicle. It was my first-ever buy, and we all loved it. Built like a tank and driving like an aircraft, never has a car felt so safe. In the end I sold it to friends – the upkeep becoming just too expensive – and not long after, Barry and Debbie wrapped it around a tree.

49  The vividly coloured and detailed glass, described as a triumph of the glazier's art, depicts the earthly genealogy of Christ – a common subject of the fourteenth century. The lowest tier contains the kneeling figures of the donors, Sir John Charlton and his wife, Dame Hawis and their two sons. Above lies the sleeping figure of Jesse, from whose loins springs a vine in oval loops, with Kings in the centre and Prophets in the side lights, terminating in Joseph and Mary and with the Crucifixion at the top.

It is believed that the window was originally made for the Old Friars Church, but removed to Old St Chad's Church at the Dissolution, and later given to St Mary's in 1791.

50  SRRC is part of Shropshire County Council's Information and Community Services Department and comprises the former Shropshire Record Office and the Local Studies Library. These services were brought together in 1995 to preserve and make available to the general public a wealth of material, including maps, parish registers, census returns, newspapers dating from 1772 and some 25,000 photographs taken since 1842, relating to Shropshire past and present. It is typical of the

resource centres that have sprung up all over the UK in response to technical advancement and a growing interest in genealogy.

51   Old Salopians, as alumni are called, include many familiar names, including Sir Philip Sydney and Charles Darwin, but more recently, novelist Nevil Shute, Literary Prize-inspiring Christopher Booker, Leftist Paul (Left) Foot, Conservatively Groomed Michael Heseltine, Private Eye Richard Ingrams, TV Presenter Nic Owens, Palaeontologist Michael Palin , DJ/Music Buff, died 2003 John Peel, Hairy/Funny Willie Rushton, and Astronomer Royal/Black Holes Sir Martin Rees.

52   In 1887 William Hesketh Lever, a successful soap manufacturer, bought a site for a new factory. Large enough for future expansion, with a river nearby for importing raw materials, and a rail track for transporting finished products, Lever employed 30 architects to designed a model village to house his soap factory workers. Subsidised and maintained with a portion of the profits from Lever Bros, in line with his ideas on prosperity-sharing, Lever personally financed Port Sunlight's church and technical institute, and the Lady Lever Art Gallery.

He introduced many schemes for welfare, education and the entertainment of his workers. A cottage hospital was built in 1907 which continued until the introduction of the National Health Service in 1948. Lever also encouraged games, recreations and any organisations which promoted art, literature, science or music.

Today, Port Sunlight is a Conservation Area, with the village and the Heritage Centre managed by The Port Sunlight Village Trust. Although houses can be bought on the open market, the Trust remains responsible for keeping the environment , landscape and community feeling true to Lever's original vision.

53   The troubles that Wilfred Price referred to most probably concerned the "Bogatozo 1948", in which the Conference of American States

was interrupted by Communist guerrillas, including the Castro brothers and Che Guevara. The ensuing riots resulted in over a thousand murders and the burning of most of the Columbian capital of Bogotá.

These conferences were held irregularly, kicking off in Washington DC (where the idea of South America cow-towing to the North was propagated) at the end of the nineteenth century. Subsequently: Mexico City, Mexico (1901–1902), Rio de Janeiro, Brazil (1906), Buenos Aires, Argentina (1910), Santiago, Chile (1923), Havana, Cuba (1928), Buenos Aires, Argentina (1933), Lima, Peru (1938), Bogotá, Colombia (1948) and Caracas, Venezuela (1954).

La Violencia – civil wars rampaging in and around Bogotá from the late 1940s into the early 1950s – were, as Sam suspected, caused by tensions between partisan groups. They claimed over 180,000 Colombian lives.

54   Joe Brown is the American actor Joe E. Brown (1892–1973). His biggest role was in *Some Like It Hot*, a 1959 comedy film by Billy Wilder with Marilyn Monroe, in which he played an aging millionaire, Osgood Fielding III. In it, Brown's character falls for Daphne (Jerry) played by Jack Lemmon. My favourite quote:

Jack Lemmon (as Jerry [as Daphne]): "You don't understand, Osgood! Aaah... I'm a man!"

Joe E. Brown (as Osgood, and perfectly straight-faced): "Well, nobody's perfect."

55   The Chinese Lunar New Year is one of the oldest chronological record in history, dating from 2600 BC, when the Emperor Huang Ti introduced the first cycle of the zodiac. Like the Western calendar, The Chinese Lunar Calendar is a yearly one, with the start of the lunar year being based on the cycles of the moon. A complete cycle takes 60 years and is made up of five cycles of 12 years each.

The Chinese Lunar Calendar names each of the 12 years after a creature. Buddhist legend has it that the Lord Buddha summoned all living creatures to come to him before he departed from earth. Only 12 came to bid him farewell and as a reward he named a year after each one in the order they arrived. The Chinese believe the creature ruling the year in which a person is born has a profound influence on personality, saying: "This is the animal that hides in your heart." PS I am a snake.

56    The Boca Juniors grew out of the BA Football Club. BJ was supposed to play its first match in May 1867, to celebrate Argentina's National Day, but the Boca Junction railway was under water, so the game was played instead on a cricket field in Palermo on the next public holiday, June 20. It was an eight-a-side match, as no more than 16 players familiar with the rules and in reasonable good physical shape could be mustered.

57    It was General Julio A. Roca who in 1879 at age thirty-five proclaimed the opening of the *pampa* or outback. Victorious in his genocidal conquest of tribal people and cultures, so freeing the land for colonisation by his cronies, he became President the following year. As recorded in the Buenos Aires Herald's *History of Argentina*, "By surrounding himself with brilliant and ambitious men – Generation 1880 – Roca began charting the policies that would guide the country for the next seventy years. Despite – or maybe because of – bloodthirsty Imperialistic tendencies and tactics, he is still referred to with respect."

58    One of the Sassoon family? So many possibilities…But mainstream opinion seems to be that all the Sassoons of Europe are descended from David (1792–1864), born in Iraq and a leader of the Jewish community in Baghdad. Hair stylist Vidal Sassoon (born 1928) who distinguished me with one of his early geometric cuts in the

1960s had a father with Iraqi roots, but was from Greece. George Thorneycroft Sassoon (1936–2006) described his father Siegfried as a man who never felt entirely comfortable in his skin. Interestingly I would say this of many residents of Argentina

59   This is quite the mystery. The Harrow and Wealdstone rail crash fits the bill, being a major disaster, involving three trains. A waiting local passenger train from Tring to Euston was hit from the rear, by all things, the express sleeper train from Perth to Euston. Seconds later an express from London to Manchester hit scattered wreckage on the main down line. One hundred and twelve passengers were killed, 340 injured.

I say this is mysterious because this accident happened on October 8, 1952. I can find no record of any accident taking place between Liverpool and London in 1951. Another time slip?

60   Here I'm using the original but now near obsolete form of the word, disease, meaning a lack of ease, or a sense of trouble.

61   *Minka* is the Japanese word for a large traditional thatched farmhouse. They are made of jointed timbers without nails, covered with an Asian form of wattle and daub: walls are made of woven bamboo, filled-in with mud and rice chaff and straw, then covered with wood or plastered white. The most famed surviving *minka* are to be found in Shirakawa, in Gifu Prefecture, where they stand up to five stories high with steep, pitched roofs and are known as *gassho zukuri* (praying hands). When a roof requires re-thatching the whole community gets to work. Together with Gokayama in Nanto, Toyama, Shirakawa is a UNESCO World Heritage site.

62   The anonymous poem, found written on the door of Ryvoan Bothy in Glencoe, was fortunately copied before the door was destroyed.

### I LEAVE TONIGHT FROM EUSTON

*I shall leave tonight from Euston*
*By the seven-thirty-train,*
*And from Perth in the early morning*
*I shall see the hills again.*
*From the top of Ben Macdhui*
*I shall watch the gathering storm,*
*And see the crisp snow lying*
*At the back of the Cairngorm.*
*I shall feel the mist from Bhrotain*
*And pass by Lairig Ghru,*
*To look on dark Loch Einich*
*From the heights of Sgoran Dubh*
*From the broken Barns of Bynack*
*I shall see the sunrise gleam*
*On the forehead of Ben Rinnes*
*And Strathspey awake from dream.*
*And again in the dusk of evening*
*I shall find once more alone*
*The dark water of the Green Loch,*
*And the pass beyond Ryvoan.*
*For tonight I leave from Euston*
*And leave the world behind;*
*Who has the hills as a lover,*
*Will find them wondrous kind.*

It is interesting to note also that the train now leaves Euston at a later hour. Presumably because it is faster these days. (But not necessarily.)

63 The British actor Tom Conti once told me that this happened to him while working on location, staying in a very old hotel.

470

64 Fernando Juan Santiago Francisco Maria Piria (1847–1933) is best remembered by his compatriots as a utopian socialist and a visionary philanthropist. He was also a science fiction writer, with a lifelong interest in alchemy.

Born in Montevideo to Italian immigrant parents from Genoa, he was sent to Italy as a child where he was tutored by a Jesuit uncle and picked up an interest in mysticism. Equally influenced by his entrepreneurial mother, who sold clocks, he became a successful businessman in Montevideo; he pioneered the mining of granite (hence the interest in turning base rocks and metals into gold), and the greening of valleys with vineyards for his Utopian dream of the good life.

In 1890, he bought 2,700 blocks of salt-strafed desert stretching from Cerro Pan de Azucar to the sea. A visit to Europe then inspired dreams of turning Maldonado County, along the Atlantic coast, into a mecca for tourists. In 1897, he built his castle home, soon after which a swarm of locusts stripped not only the entire region but his newly planted botanical garden.

Undaunted, he built his first hotel in Piriapolis as a holiday centre for children. Within five years, the *rambla* was under construction; in 1912 he auctioned off local lots and the town began to develop. Soon a steam train linked Piriapolis to Pan de Azucar; and a port enabled ships to bring tourists from Montevideo.

The poet Lorely Lazo is said to have commented: "One can find Mr Piria is everything that his iron will has created, he was a man who had a dream, it came true, and he lives it."

65 In his fine and thought-provoking book, *Theatre of the Mind – Raising the Curtain on Consciousness*, Canadian author Jay Ingram devotes a chapter to The Grand Illusion. Within this is a four-page-long spotlit section on The Blind Spot, the last sentence of which reads: Of course we say with confidence that *we* are seeing, but we simply

don't realise how little of the visual information that is available actually enters our awareness.

66  Asking for a Havana cigar from a street kiosk in New York in 1977 nearly caused a riot. I shall never forget the look on the vendor's face, or the fury of a bystander. Momentarily I had forgotten the Bay of Pigs incident of 1962 and America's own blind spot: its blind hatred of Communism and the so-called Castro regime. In 2006, my one-year-old grandson Max took his parents from Toronto to Cuba. Though too young to smoke a cigar, he has only good reports.

67  After letting my sister read the letters written between the family concerning Betty's death, I passed many of them on to Genevieve. Especially I wanted her to have those written earlier by her mother, and those from my grandmother during the time she helped John with a toddler and a newborn. Gen noted that according to our grandmother, she had become more peaceful. This harks back to a much earlier letter to my father, in which Primrose had complained about Gen's endless crying and how really, She could not imagine what was the matter with the child! The matter, Gen said, was that she had been a little girl whose mother had gone missing. She thought it quite astonishing that such an obvious connection had never been made, especially by someone who had worked as a therapist and a school matron. Reading the letters helped a lot, Gen told me. They helped fill in gaps, explain better who her mother was.

68  Frederick Louis MacNeice (1907–1963) was a British and Irish poet and playwright, Sir Stephen Harold Spender CBE (1909–1995) was an English poet, novelist and essayist. Contemporary survivors of two world wars, the two men concentrated their literary talents on themes such as social injustice. MacNeice was more the humanist; Spender very much a political animal.

69  With a synchronicity that no longer astonishes, Philip Arthur Larkin (1922–1985) was born in Coventry. He attended King Henry VIII school and, after graduating from Oxford University, took the position of municipal librarian in Wellington, Shropshire, became assistant librarian at University College Leicester and then librarian at the University of Hull, a position he retained until his death. Selected in 2003 as the Nation's best Loved Poet (by the Poetry Book Society), he had been offered the Poet Laureateship following the death of John Betjeman, but declined the post.

70  Ernest Miller Hemingway (1899–1961) was an American novelist, short-story-writer and journalist. Part of the 1920s expatriate community in Paris, and later living in Cuba, he led a turbulent social life, married four times and allegedly had multiple extra-marital relationships over many years. Hemingway received the Pulitzer Prize in 1953 for *The Old man and the Sea*. He received the Nobel Prize for Literature in 1954. Unlike my own, Hemingway's distinctive style is characterised by economy and understatement. Each to their own.

71  Hoffman was speaking with great insight on the art of acting and his career in a TV interview with James Lipton (*Inside the Actor's Studio*), first aired in 2006.

72  Pioneering transpersonal psychologist Claudio Naranjo was born in Valparaiso, Chile in 1932. After studying medicine, music, and philosophy in his home country, he became one of the founders of the Esalen Institute in California. He is also a world authority on the Enneagram, an ancient system of achieving spiritual balance attributed to Sufi wisdom but today used for understanding and rebalancing human personality.

# SOURCES

**FALSE STARTS**

*Coventry at War*, Alton Douglas, Clive Hardy, Gordon Stretch, Jo Hardy;
   Brewin Books (first published 1983; 5th impression 1996).

*Coventry – in old photographs*, David McGrory; Alan Sutton Publishing
   Limited, 1994.

Additional Information supplied by Glyn Edwards and W. R Cooper
   (Coventry, 2000).


**READY, STEADY, LET'S GO**

*The Growing Pains of Adrian Mole*, Sue Townsend; Methuen London Ltd,
   1984.

*Far Way and Long Ago*, W.H. Hudson; J. M. Dent & Sons (first published
   1918; revised edition with wood engravings by Eric Fitch Daglish
   and an introduction by R.B. Cunninghame Graham 1931).

*The South American Handbook 1937*, Trade and Travel Publications Ltd.


**THE GOSPEL ACCORDING TO ST ANDREW**

*The Guardian Weekly*, May 24, 2001, "Questions Over Census Answers".

*International Herald Tribune & Asahi Evening News* (another ill-fated
   merger) May 10, 2001, "As Air Canada Grows, Travellers Complain".

*Liverpool – A People's History*, Peter Aughton; Carnegie Publishing, 1993.

*On Course*, page 1, "What Onex is Proposing To Do" (online
   October1999 at www.cdnair.ca).

*On Course,* page 2, "You asked...Who is Onex" (ibid)

*Roget's Thesaurus;* Penguin Books Ltd (first published in 1852; first paperback edition 1972).

*The Japan Times,* November 3, 1999, "People (Who's in Charge of Your Life? You Are)", November 3, 1999

*The New International Dictionary of Quotations,* selected by Hugh Rawson and Margaret Miner; Signet 1986: page 104. "I want to seize fate by the throat – Ludvig von Beethoven, letter to Dr Franz Wegler, November 16, 1801".

ibid. "I claim not to have controlled events, but confess plainly that events have controlled me – Abraham Lincoln, letter to A.C.Hodges, April 4, 1864".

*The Oxford Dictionary of Current English;* Oxford University Press (first paperback edition 1985).

*The Toronto Star,* May 20, 2001, "Neighbourhood Watch".

*The Toronto Star,* November 9, 1999, "Airline Monopoly Needs Clear Rules".

*Welcome to the Census Website,* <http://census.pro.gov.uk/index.htm>


**MARIA-ELENA**

*A-Z of Ocean Liners,* Peter Newall.

*Guardian Weekly,* December, 1991, "The One Who Got Away".

*Los Angeles Times,* July 20, 1991, "Moving Into the First World on the Buddy System (World Report)".

*The Japan Times,* December 15, 1991, "Graham in Argentina for Crusades" *(AP).*

*The Japan Times,* December 14, 1991, "Brazil, Argentina Ink Pact To Prohibit Non-Peaceful Use Of Nuclear Technology" *(Reuter-Kyodo).*


**EL CENTRO**

*Bad Times in Buenos Aires,* Miranda France; Weidenfeld & Nicolson, Phoenix, 1999.

*Fodor's 92 South America*, edited by Andrew E. Beresky; Fodor's Travel
  Publications Inc., New York and London, 1992.
*The Penguin History of Latin America*, Edwin Williamson; Penguin Books,
  1992.
*The South American Handbook 1937*, Trade and Travel Publications Ltd.

**HELP!**

*The Japan Times*, 7 September, 1997, "Chile's Culture Fest Full of Beans"
  Angela Jeffs.
*Lost Cities and Ancient Mysteries of South America*, David Hatcher
  Childress, Childress Adventures Unlimited Press, 1986.

**X MARKS THE SPOT**

*Fodor's 92 South America*, edited by Andrew E. Beresky; Fodor's Travel
  Publications Inc., New York and London, 1992.
*Goodbye Buenos Aires*, Andrew Graham Yool; Shoestring Press, 1999 (first
  published in Spanish by Ediciones de la Flor, 1997).
*Lost Cities and Ancient Mysteries of South America*, David Hatcher
  Childress, Childress Adventures Unlimited Press, 1986.
*New Internationalist*, No. 334, May 2001. Militant Madres, written by
  Chris Moss. The poem was translated by Monique and Carlos
  Altschul for Fundacion Mujeres en Igualdad
  (malt@satlink.com or www.mei.com.ar)
*South Atlantic Seaway*, N.R.P. Bonsor; Brookside Publications 1983.

**IT'S THE WEEKEND**

*International Herald Tribune*, 2007, "South to South".
*Onassis – An Extravagant Life*, Frank Brady, Circus Books in collaboration
  with Futura Publications, 1978.

**DEFINITELY THURSDAY**

*Daily Yomiuri*, March 23, 1992, "Newly Released Nazi Documents Too

476

Late for Justice" (*AP*).

*Daily Yomiuri,* January 1, 1992, "Argentina Most Optimistic About '92" (*AFP-Jiji*).

*Daily Yomiuri,* January 8, 1992, "Argentine Rains Kill 52" (*AFP-Jiji*).

*Guardian Weekly,* April 12, 1992, "Battles Not So Very Long Ago" (*The Guardian*).

*Guardian Weekly,* February 21, 1992, "Argentina Keeps Lid on Nazi Files".

*Guardian Weekly,* January 19, 1992, "Menem Seeks Talks with Britain on Falklands" (*The Guardian*).

*Guardian Weekly,* May 17, 1992, "Menem Sees Argentina's Role as a Canada of the South" (*Le Monde*).

*The Daily Yomiuri,* March 19, 1992, "Bomb Destroys Israeli Embassy in Argentina" (*The Washington Post*).

*The Times,* April 2, 1992, "Junta Troika Keeps Its Peace on Falklands War".

*The Times,* April 4, 1992, "Embassy Bombing Ignites Political Debate".

*The Times,* April 4, 1992, "Islands Spurn Hand of Peace".

*The Times,* April 4, 1992, "A Very British Cover-up".

*The Times,* February 2, 1992, "Argentine Asks for Europe's Overflow".

*The Times,* March 23, 1992, "Argentine Veterans Would Fight Again for Falklands".

*The Times,* March 30, 1992, "Anglo–Argentines Bat on in Defence of Tea and Scones".

*Times International,* July 17, 1992, "Menem's Miracle".

*Washington Post National Weekly Edition,* January 6–12, 1992, "Why Doesn't Argentina Work?" (*Washington Post Foreign Service*).

## INTO THE HEART OF THE UNKNOWN

*A History of Argentina (1876–1999),* published by the *Buenos Aires Herald* in December 1999, page 47.

**VALPARAISO**

*Asahi Evening News International*, December 15, 1993, "Man in hospital
for pigging out" (*New York Times News Service*)

**ACROSS THE ANDES**

*Fodor's 92 South America*, edited by Andrew E. Beresky; Fodor's Travel
Publications Inc., New York and London, 1992.

**ON THE ROAD**

*The History of Minsterley*, written and published by D. T. Merry, 1976.

**PIRIAPOLIS**

*Birmingham Post*, November 29, 1952, "Progressive Education in an
Ancient Setting" Rosemary Meynell.

**IN THE HANDS OF THE GODS**

*Theatre of the Mind*, Jay Ingram; Harper Perennial, 2005.

**POSTSCRIPT**

*The One Quest*, by Claudio Naranjo; an Esalen Book, Published
by Viking, New York, 1972.
*The Power of Myth*, by Joseph Campbell. Anchor Books
(Random House) 1991.
*The Power of Now*, by Eckhart Tolle. A Namaste Publishing Book, Plume.
Penguin Group, 2005.

# ACKNOWLEDGEMENTS

In memory of those who were alive when this story began to take to the page, but sadly no longer: Noreen Melia, David Clement, Gwen Loader, Bridget Bateman, Rhona Everett, Elena (Toto) Careaga, Joyce Loader, Nellie and Alice, Krieger & Jalil.

With deepest gratitude and love to Maria-Elena Bustamante Loader who, having welcomed me into her family with such hospitable kindness and understanding, has surely ensured a place among the angels and the ranked spiritual legions of our ancestors. Also "Tarzan", Julio Jr and (the ever loyal and supportive) Pablo for their own magnanimous part in my survival.

Appreciation especially to Pepe and Olga, and Luis and Silvia, for opening their own homes with such warmth and generosity. Claudio for riding the bus, both ways. Alejandra, Carole, Daniel and Jose for coming to my rescue as interpreters. Andrew Graham-Yool and Colin Sharp for keeping the faith long after I returned to Japan.

Plus all those many others who knowingly or unwittingly helped create the richly textured fabric of this "mad romp". Including (in alphabetical order): Roberto Baretto, Barry and Debbie Bliss, John Bowstead, British Embassies & Consulates everywhere, Jerry Brosnan, George Bussey, Susan Crown, Richard Darbourne, Adriana de los Santos, Ian de Staines, Nikolas Dixon, Louise Egerton, Genevieve Elwell-Darbourne, Noemi Escudero, Kevin Finlayson, Melanie Galvin, Sandra Godoy, Anna Griffiths, Kareen Hertzfeld, Isabel Hortal, Sarah Hosking, Gordon and Anne Howe,

Jerry-Lee Jeffs, Roger Jeffs, James Keating, Rick Kendall, Frances Kennett, Alison Loader, Mike Lucas, Azzah Manukova, Gaby Marks, Brian Martin, Joan Melia, John Mortimer, Rosemary Morton, Wakiko Noguchi, Richard Oliver, Emma Parker, Pedro Pazos, Alison Phillips, Carlos Placitelli, Ximena Poblete, Chloe Riess, George Roper, Mark Silver, Gloria Waddell, Ross Waddell, David Wilson, Jenny White, and Shirley Yegliss.

All credit to Robert Kidd (http://editfast.com/) for professional support and ongoing patience.

Alan White (alanwhitecreative.ca) who laid out the content of this book for publication via Create Space.

Buffy Jeffs for her lovely cover design.

Andy Melia (http://www.merseyworld.com/andymelia/) for encapsulating in 100 well-chosen words (see back cover) the story he helped kick off near three decades before.

Kathryn Matsumura for reading every word.

Yasuyuki (Akii) Ueda for always being there, and here.

Finally, apologies to anyone forgotten, un-named, mis-named or only partially named, misrepresented, misquoted or misunderstood. (The theft of my Filofax in Montevideo meant the loss of many valuable namecards and notes. If you happen to recognize yourself within these pages, let me know and I will amend.) As to any other errors – together with all personal opinions expressed – they are mine and mine alone.

Made in the USA
Lexington, KY
23 January 2013